Vital Records

of

WARREN

New Hampshire

1887-2005

Richard P. Roberts

HERITAGE BOOKS
2006

HERITAGE BOOKS

AN IMPRINT OF HERITAGE BOOKS, INC.

Books, CDs, and more—Worldwide

For our listing of thousands of titles see our website
at
www.HeritageBooks.com

Published 2006 by
HERITAGE BOOKS, INC.
Publishing Division
65 East Main Street
Westminster, Maryland 21157-5026

International Standard Book Number: 978-0-7884-4305-4

TABLE OF CONTENTS

INTRODUCTION

Early vital records of many New Hampshire towns can be located either through the State's Vital Records Department or on microfilms made available through LDS Family History Centers. Some, however, have been lost or are inaccessible for various reasons. A valuable, but labor intensive, source of information for events occurring in 1887 and thereafter is the vital statistics which are provided in a section of the Annual Town Reports of many New Hampshire towns. Many of these town reports have been collected at the New Hampshire State Library in Concord, as well as more local repositories.

The amount of information published in these Annual Town Reports varies tremendously over time. Early records are far more detailed and comprehensive. Recent records are rather cursory, but issues of confidentiality and sensitivity to the privacy of those residents still living offsets the lack of information of genealogical value.

While the information provided is often very helpful, one must remember that it is not fool-proof or universally accurate, nor is it the primary source or the actual vital record itself. The fact that much of the data is self-reported suggests that it is reliable. However, errors in transcription, spelling (particularly with respect to French-Canadian and European families), and printing often are obvious. In addition, there may be, for example, two children listed as the third child of a particular couple, or the mother's maiden name, age or place of birth may differ or may be inconsistent from one entry to another. It is also important to note that a birth, marriage or death may have been reported in another town although the subject resided in Warren, or the entry may not have been made in the first place.

Despite these shortcomings, the information contained in the Annual Town Reports can be a valuable tool for the genealogist. Marriage and death records from the late 1800's often identify parents who were married nearly a century before. Finally, those families that have remained in Warren or adjacent towns for several generations can be traced and connected to the present.

Births - To the extent the information is available, the entries in the list of births are given as follows: child's name; date of birth; place of birth (where provided); the number of children in the family; father's name, place of birth, age and occupation; and the mother's maiden name, age and place of birth. As noted above, the amount of information in earlier records is substantially greater than in more recent years.

At times, the given names of many children are missing from the early reports. In this case, the sex of the child is given and they are listed chronologically at the beginning of the surname heading. On occasion, the child's name can be determined from marriage or death records, as well as secondary sources. These names are shown in brackets where available.

Marriages - To the extent the information is available, the entries in the list of marriages follow this format: groom's name; groom's residence; bride's name; bride's residence; date of marriage; place of marriage (where provided); H, signifying husband's information, and W, signifying wife's information, each in the following order - age, occupation, number of the marriage (if other than first), father's name, father's place of birth, father's occupation, mother's name, mother's place of birth, and mother's occupation. The name of the official conducting the marriage has been omitted but is generally provided in the original document. A separate listing of brides in alphabetical order follows this section in order to allow for cross-referencing.

2

Deaths - To the extent available, the entries in the list of deaths contain the following information: name of decedent; place of death; date of death; age at death; cause of death; marital status; birthplace; father's name; father's place of birth; mother's name; and mother's place of birth. Most of the entries listing a cause of death are self-explanatory.

WARREN
BIRTHS

ACQUISTAPACE,
Laura Jeanne, b. 3/23/1988 in Plymouth; Mark Leonard
Acquistapace (30) and Sharyn Washburn (24)

ADAMS,
Wanda Lee, b. 7/1/1957; second; Martin Blake Adams (carpenter,
Hebron) and Blanche Ida Hildreth (Warren)

ALESSANDRINI,
Barbara, b. 2/3/1933; first; Samuel Alessandrini (merchant, Rome,
Italy) and Katherine M. Hill (Sugar Hill)
Bernardino L., Jr., b. 9/17/1949 in Plymouth; first; Bernardino L.
Alessandrini (laborer, Barnet, VT) and Marion Elizabeth Oliver
(Woodsville)
Marcia Marie, b. 11/25/1950 in Plymouth; second; Bernardino L.
Alessandrini (carpenter, VT) and Marion Elizabeth Oliver (NH)

ALLEN,
Chelsea Elexia, b. 11/26/1992 in Plymouth; Mark Douglas Allen (29)
and Caron Elizabeth Heselton (25)
Jordon Elizabeth, b. 2/15/1991 in Lebanon; Mark Douglas Allen (28)
and Caron Elizabeth Heselton (24)

AMES,
son, b. 3/28/1904 in Warren; third; William M. Ames (laborer, 31,
ME) and Sadie McCormick (23, NB)
son, b. 1/20/1906 in Warren; fourth; William M. Ames (laborer, 33,
Bancroft, ME) and Sadie McCormick (25, NB)
son, b. 12/2/1906 in Warren; fifth; William M. Ames (lumberman, 26,
NB) and Sadie McCormack (24, NB)
son, b. 4/28/1926; first; Ted Ames (laborer) and Bertha Chase
(Bath)
son, b. 6/19/1926; second; Theodore Ames (laborer, Warren) and
Helen Chandler (Plymouth)
son, b. 2/22/1934; second; Spurgeon Ames (woodsman, Warren)
and Lillian Graham (Fernandina, FL)
Audrey Evelyn, b. 3/23/1943; fifth; Spurgeon M. Ames (truckman,
Warren) and Adella E. Tilley (Wentworth)
Betsy Ann, b. 2/3/1973 in Haverhill; Wesley Theodore Ames (VT)
and Elaine Marie Wood (NH)

Elizabeth C., b. 3/4/1940; fourth; Spurgeon Ames (truck driver, Warren) and Adella Tilley (Wentworth)

Ina Christine, b. 2/8/1944 in Warren; sixth; Spurgeon M. Ames (trucking, Warren) and Adella E. Tilley (Wentworth)

Jodi Lynnette, b. 8/21/1988 in Laconia; Steven Roy Ames (29) and Janet Eileen Crislip (27)

Lowell T., b. 1/10/1936; sixth; Theodore M. Ames (Warren) and Helen Chandler (Plymouth)

Madeline Ida, b. 12/24/1927; second; Theodore Ames (millman) and Bertha Chase (Bath)

Shirley L., b. 9/10/1936; second; Spurgeon Ames (Warren) and Adella Tilley (Wentworth)

William Spurgeon, b. 3/3/1945 in Warren; seventh; Spurgeon M. Ames (trucking, Warren) and Adella E. Tilley (Wentworth)

ANDERSON,

Alberta A., b. 4/13/1928; first; Fayne E. Anderson (laborer, Drew, ME) and Marcia E. Batchelder (Warren)

Esther J., b. 10/31/1930; second; Fayne E. Anderson (laborer, Drew, ME) and Marcia E. Batchelder (Warren)

ANDREWS,

daughter, b. 2/27/1925; third; Harry V. Andrews (laborer) and Etta Heath (Warren)

Donald A., b. 9/23/1916 in Warren; second; Harold V. Andrews (laborer, Woodsville) and Etta M. Heath (Piermont)

ANNIS,

daughter, b. 1/20/1889 in Warren; Perley Annis (laborer, 40) and Flovilla Swain (39, Warren)

ARGUINN,

daughter, b. 3/14/1889 in Warren; Charles Arguinn (laborer, 24, Canada) and Lida Marchans (25, Canada)

ASALINE,

son, b. 5/4/1909 in Warren; second; John B. Asaline (farmer, Canada) and Ruth Whitcher (Warren)

ASH,
son, b. 12/18/1895 in Warren; James P. Ash (farmer, 40,
Bethlehem) and Georgia Swazey (30, Bethlehem)

ASSELIN,
Claire E., b. 7/24/1934; third; Henry D. Asselin (laborer, Warren) and
Ernestine E. Perry (Medford, MA)
Harry T., b. 9/20/1931; first; Henry D. Asselin (truck driver, Warren)
and Ernestine Perry (Medford, MA)
John E., b. 6/20/1936; fourth; Henry B. Asselin (Warren) and
Ernestine E. Perry (Medford, MA)
Judith R., b. 10/27/1937; fifth; Henry D. Asselin (Warren) and
Ernestine Perry (Medford, MA)
Patricia Ann, b. 3/20/1933; second; Henry D. Asselin (laborer,
Warren) and Ernestine E. Perry (Medford, MA)

AUBREY,
Adalida B., b. 4/14/1997; Mark J. Aubrey (34) and Leonetta H.
Anderson (27)

AVERY,
daughter, b. 7/29/1893 in Warren; Hasting H. Avery (farmer, 32,
Ellsworth) and Delia D. Batchelder (27, Warren)
child, b. 2/7/1908; third; Hasting H. Avery (farmer, 48, Ellsworth) and
Della Batchelder (41, Warren)
Andrew Scott, b. 10/2/1998 in Lebanon; Frederick Alan Avery (28)
and Gloria L. Coleman (26)
Donald R., b. 11/21/1934; second; Raymond A. Avery (farmer,
Warren) and Doris Wheeler (Newport)
George D., b. 10/23/1936; first; Raymond A. Avery (Warren) and
Una French (Warren)
Paul Lewis, b. 12/4/1937; second; Raymond A. Avery (Warren) and
Una V. French (Warren)
Tyler James, b. 8/25/1996 in Lebanon; Frederick Alan Avery (26)
and Glorialynn Marie Coleman (24)

BACON,
son, b. 9/21/1896 in Warren; Fred S. Bacon (mason, 44) and Ida J.
Perry (38, Chichester)

BADGER,
son, b. 12/24/1888 in Warren; Frank L. Badger (molder, 31, Benton) and ----- L. Aldrich (27, Burke, VT)

BAGLEY,
Daniel Burt, b. 7/27/1983 in Plymouth; Donald Bixby Bagley, Sr. (34) and Donna Marie Heath (32)
Donald Bixby, Jr., b. 9/21/1976 in Plymouth; Donald Bixby Bagley, Sr. (28) and Donna Marie Heath (25)

BAILEY,
daughter, b. 10/25/1893 in Warren; R. W. Bailey (painter, 35, Warren) and Mary B. Wright (30, Benton)

BAKER,
stillborn daughter, b. 7/12/1905 in Warren; second; Earl L. Baker (wood worker, 27, St. Albans, VT) and Blanche E. Merrill (Warren)

BALDWIN,
Gabriel Lee, b. 7/20/1964; seventh; Charles H. Baldwin (truck driver, Gilford) and Evelyn M. Dunn (Morgantown, WV)
Gloria M., b. 5/19/1962; sixth; Charles H. Baldwin (truckman, Gilford) and Evelyn May Dunn (Tyrone, WV)
John Evan, b. 10/4/1960; fifth; Charles Baldwin (truck driver, Gilford) and Evelyn May Dunn (Morgantown)
Sharon Ann, b. 7/11/1958; fourth; Charles Henry Baldwin (laborer - grain mill) and Evelyn May Dunn

BALL,
son, b. 4/23/1941; second; Reginald H. Ball (mill hand, Landaff) and Charlotte M. Griffin (Tilton)
Albert L., b. 12/15/1964; first; Albert L. Ball (truck driver, Warren) and Jeanette P. Woodward (Lebanon)
Albert Leslie, b. 10/17/1941; second; Leslie A. Ball (laborer, Landaff) and Doris M. Ledger (Westminster, MA)
Alice Mary, b. 10/17/1941; third; Leslie A. Ball (laborer, Landaff) and Doris M. Ledger (Westminster, MA)
Allan Max, b. 9/12/1938; first; Reginald H. Ball (bobbin mill, Landaff) and Charlotte M. Griffin (Tilton)

Anthony Herbert, b. 10/19/1955; fifth; Reginald H. Ball (truck driver, Landaff) and Charlotte M. Griffin (Tilton)

Brian Bert, b. 2/5/1952; second; Clifford Edwin Ball (Landaff) and Ardeth Mae Stimson (Woodsville)

Burt Peter, b. 7/5/1950 in Plymouth; sixth; Leslie Albert Ball (sawmill laborer, Landaff) and Doris Mary Leger (Gardner, MA)

Christopher Scott, b. 11/14/1972 in Hanover; Bert Peter Ball (NH) and Judy Ann Thompson (NH)

Daniel Joseph, b. 11/24/1952; seventh; Leslie Albert Ball (Landaff) and Doris Mary Leger (Gardner, MA)

Darleen Ann, b. 12/9/1955; third; Clifford Edwin Ball (janitor, Landaff) and Ardeth May Stimson (Woodsville)

David Harry, b. 12/8/1947 in Haverhill; first; Reginald Herbert Ball (lumber opr., Landaff) and Charlotte Hay Griffin (Tilton)

Debbie Ann, b. 4/6/1958; third; Vincent Bruce Ball (Air Force) and Lois M. Babineaux

Diane Marie, b. 1/6/1968 in Haverhill; Albert Leslie Ball (NH) and Jeanette P. Woodward (NH)

Donald Clifford, b. 9/26/1948 in Haverhill; second; Herman G. Ball (store clerk, Glencliff) and Celia Mae Jones (Haverhill)

Edna Maxine, b. 1/9/1929; ninth; Bert Leslie Ball (bob. mill split., Landaff) and Eva Irene Moulton (Landaff)

Janice Marie, b. 3/27/1940; first; Leslie A. Ball (mail carrier, Landaff) and Doris M. Ledger (Westminster)

Kevin Ronald, b. 5/22/1959; third; Herman George Ball (maintenance man st., Landaff) and Celia Mae Jones (Piermont)

Loren Ricky, b. 11/9/1960; fourth; Herman George Ball (electrician, Landaff) and Celia Mae Jones (Piermont)

Lorraine Ann, b. 11/5/1944 in Haverhill; fourth; Leslie Albert Ball (farmer, Landaff) and Doris Mary Ledger (Gardner, MA)

Lucille Eva, b. 4/29/1947 in Haverhill; first; Herman George Ball (electrician, Landaff) and Celia May Jones (Piermont)

Meredith Leslie, b. 9/30/1973 in Haverhill; Edward James Ball (MA) and Norma Lee Clark (Canada)

Michael Loren, b. 12/22/1985 in Plymouth; Loren R. Ball (25) and Susan Simmons (20)

Nathan E., b. 8/25/1972 in Haverhill; Brian Burt Ball (NH) and Lolita May Macomber (ME)

Pamela Jane, b. 6/7/1975 in Haverhill; Bert Peter Ball (24) and Judy Ann Thompson (21)

Reginald A., b. 6/2/1997; Marc G. Ray (34) and Sheir-Lyn Ball (33)
Ronald Clifford, b. 2/1/1947 in Plymouth; first; Edna Maxine Ball
(Glencliff)
Scott Allan, b. 5/15/1965; second; Allan M. Ball (truck driver,
Woodsville) and Carol A. Pierson (Rochester)
Shane Ryan, b. 4/23/1984 in Haverhill; Anthony Herbert Ball (28)
and Pamela Gail Stimson (24)
Shauna May, b. 9/9/1982 in Haverhill; Anthony Herbert Ball (26) and
Pamela Gail Stimson (22)
Tiffany Marie, b. 6/1/1991 in Woodsville; Scott Allen Ball (26) and
Christine Nancy Hudson (24)
Weston James, b. 3/7/1991 in Plymouth; Loren Ricky Ball (31) and
Susan Simmons (25)
Zabrina Marie, b. 12/23/2000 in Plymouth; James Ball and Elaine
Ball
Zoey Marie, b. 7/27/1999 in New London; James Ball and Elaine
Spencer

BANCROFT,
Andrew Steven, b. 12/19/1985 in Homestead, FL; Steven A.
Bancroft (31) and Anita T. Stein (30)
Christopher Allison, b. 2/3/1980 in Tampa, FL; Steven A. Bancroft
(25) and Anita Thersa Stein (23)
Debora Lynn, b. 3/7/1958; fifth; Kenneth A. Bancroft (oiler
construction) and Elizabeth A. Brown
Donna Lee, b. 6/28/1947 in Haverhill; third; Kenneth A. Bancroft
(road agent, Nashua) and Elizabeth Arwin Brown (Shelburne)
Kenneth Albert, b. 2/20/1956; fourth; Kenneth A. Bancroft (oiler
const. co., Nashua) and Elizabeth A. Brown (Shelburne)
Robert Allison, b. 10/3/1924; fifth; Fred Bancroft (laborer, Nashua)
and Ida Fitzgerald (Nashua)
Shirley Ada, b. 2/18/1946 in Haverhill; second; Kenneth Albert
Bancroft (carpenter, Nashua) and Elizabeth Arwin Brown
(Warren)

BARDSLEY,
Diana E., b. 2/16/1935; third; James H. Bardsley (New Bedford, MA)
and Thelma Bancroft (Londonderry)
Norma L., b. 7/9/1933; second; James H. Bardsley (machinist, New
Bedford, MA) and Thelma Bancroft (Londonderry)

BARR,
Jacob Ezekiel, b. 11/2/1998 in Lebanon; Thomas Michael Barr (42) and Kathleen L. Forsberg (37)

BARROWS,
Christine M., b. 4/14/1962; second; Jon Ira Barrows (machinist, Stafford, CT) and Gallia Louise Rutan (Leominster, MA)

BARRY,
Charles E., b. 2/25/1937; second; Everett F. Barry (Orford) and Sadie G. Griffin (Whitefield)
Laura Beth, b. 8/16/1932; first; Everett F. Barry (laborer, Orford) and Sadie Julina Griffin (Whitefield)

BARTLETT,
Charrissa Lee, b. 6/9/1973 in Haverhill; Robert William Bartlett (CT) and Brenda Lee Vincelette (NH)

BATCHELDER,
stillborn daughter, b. 10/13/1890 in Warren; Joel I. Batchelder (teamster, 37, Warren) and Estella Clifford (25, Warren)
son, b. 7/6/1895 in Warren; second; Ed. L. Batchelder (conductor, Warren) and Cora A. Willey
daughter, b. 5/2/1897 in Warren; first; Joel Batchelder (laborer, 33, Warren) and Estella Clifford (31, Warren)
daughter, b. 7/28/1898; second; C. W. Batchelder (farmer, 37, Warren) and Cora A. Merrill (24, Warren)
stillborn daughter, b. 8/16/1901 in Warren; second; Joel I. Batchelder (laborer, 37, Warren) and Stella A. Clifford (36, Warren)
Arthur M., b. 4/6/1895 in Warren; first; C. W. Batchelder (farmer, 34, Warren) and Cora A. Merrill (21, Warren)
Avis J., b. 1/1/1919 in Warren; third; Albert N. Batchelder (lumber dealer, Warren) and Nettie M. Merrill (Warren)
Bonnie L., b. 10/18/1942; first; L. A. Batchelder (laborer, Warren) and Bernice Ada Libby (Ashland)
Laurence A., b. 7/25/1917 in Warren; first; Arthur M. Batchelder (laborer, Warren) and Leona M. Pike (Warren)
Marcia Elise, b. 5/5/1905 in Warren; second; Albert N. Bachelder (farmer, 35, Warren) and Nettie M. Merrill (Warren)

11

Marcia N., b. 1/25/1903 in Warren; first; Albert N. Batchelder (farmer, 33, Warren) and Nettie M. Merrill (23, Warren)

BEAMIS,
Herbert Glen, b. 1/6/1952; second; Harold Glen Beamis (NH) and Priscilla Doane Cutting (NH)

BEAN,
Wilfred Ai, b. 9/11/1929; fourth; Theodore G. Bean (laborer) and Edith B. Fisher (Lowell, VT)

BEANBIER,
son, b. 4/21/1890 in Warren; first; A. Beanbier (laborer, Landaff) and Lucy ----- (Holland, VT)

BEATTIE,
Isabelle May, b. 9/2/1931; fourth; Hugh B. Beattie (laborer, Londonderry, VT) and Bessie J. Elliott (Portland, IA)
Lillian Irene, b. 3/10/1927; third; Hugh Beattie (farmer, Londonderry, VT) and Bessie I. Elliott (Cour Delane, IA)

BEAULIEU,
stillborn daughter, b. 6/1/1919 in Warren; first; Alex. Beaulieu (laborer, Canada) and Lucy G. Copp (Warren)
Clyde J., b. 11/9/1907 in Warren; first; Alex. J. Beaulieu (laborer, 22, Canada) and Mabel A. Copp (19, Warren)

BELAVANCE,
daughter, b. 3/3/1906 in Warren; fourth; Archie Belavance (laborer, 37, Canada) and Delina Bushway (42, E. Canaan)

BELEVANCE,
stillborn son, b. 10/8/1903 in Warren; third; Archie P. Belevance (laborer, 37, Canada) and Delina Bushea (40, Canaan)

BELYEA,
son, b. 10/12/1896 in Warren; James Belyea (farmer, 32, Olensville, NB) and Mary M. Fifield (28, Warren)
daughter, b. 11/24/1898 in Warren; second; James I. Belyea (farmer, 35, Olinville, NB) and Mary M. Fifield (30, Warren)

daughter, b. 9/25/1900 in Warren; third; James I. Belyea (farmer, 38, Olanville, NB) and Mary M. Fifield (32, Warren)

son, b. 5/5/1902 in Warren; fourth; James I. Belyea (farmer, 39, NB) and Mary M. Fifield (34, Warren)

stillborn son, b. 1/10/1930; first; George Alfred Belyea (laborer, Benton) and Marguerite Wallace (Meredith); residence - Benton

daughter, b. 7/27/1931; first; Charles M. Belyea (lineman, Benton) and Alberta Harriman (Tilton)

Anne Marie, b. 7/6/1971 in Haverhill; Charles Neal Belyea (NH) and Carol Ann Wright (NH)

Chad Michael, b. 6/4/1974 in Haverhill; Robert Michael Belyea (22) and Jean Alice Bigelow (19)

Charles Neal, b. 1/10/1941; third; Charles M. Belyea (postmaster, Benton) and Alberta Harriman (Tilton)

Clayton Ronald, b. 11/27/1982 in Haverhill; Jay Lynn Belyea (NH) and Marcia Lynne Spencer (NH)

Delbert W., b. 9/15/1933; second; Charles M. Belyea (laborer, Benton) and Alberta Harriman (Tilton)

Donald Elmer, b. 3/1/1947 in Woodsville; fourth; George Arthur Belyea (mgr. ser. sta., Benton) and Marguerite Anita Wallace (Woodsville)

Elaine Celia, b. 2/6/1945 in Haverhill; fifth; Charles Moses Belyea (postmaster, Benton) and Alberta Harriman (Tilton)

Jared Llewellyn, b. 3/19/1974 in Plymouth; Roy Robert Belyea (26) and Eileen Louise Robie (26)

Jason Jeffrey, b. 4/20/1973 in Plymouth; Jeffrey Scott Belyea (NH) and Betty Irma Streeter (MA)

Jay Lynn, b. 4/14/1960; third; Ronald Roy Belyea (road grader, Glencliff) and Esther J. Anderson (Warren)

Jeffrey Scott, b. 8/26/1948 in Plymouth; second; Ronald Roy Belyea (state highway, Warren) and Esther Jane Anderson (Warren)

Kathryn Florence, b. 7/17/1944 in Haverhill; third; George Alfred Belyea (farmer, Benton) and Marguerite A. Wallace (Woodsville)

Keith Everett, d. 2/19/1944 in Haverhill; fourth; Charles Moses Belyea (postmaster, Benton) and Alberta L. Harriman (Tilton)

Kenneth W., b. 3/1/1939; second; George A. Belyea (carpenter, Benton) and Marguerite Wallace (Woodsville)

Michelle Andrea, b. 6/3/1971 in Plymouth; Jeffrey Scott Belyea (NH) and Betty Irma Streeter (MA)

Norman Bruce, b. 5/18/1950 in Haverhill; fifth; George Alfred Belyea (fish & game, Benton) and Marguerite Anita Wallace (Woodsville)

Paul Roland, b. 6/7/1953; second; Roland Mearl Belyea (Warren) and Lydia Ellen Derosia (Warren)

Ray Robert, b. 5/5/1947 in Plymouth; first; Ronald Ray Belyea (laborer, Glencliff) and Esther Jane Anderson (Warren)

Robert Leo, b. 9/25/1926; first; Llewellyn Belyea (bobbin turner, Warren) and Blanch Lavoia (Manchester)

Ronald Roy, b. 6/12/1928; second; Llewellyn Belyea (laborer, Glencliff) and Blanche M. Lavoie (Manchester)

Susan, b. 3/12/1973 in Plymouth; Roy Robert Belyea (NH) and Eileen Louise Robie (NH)

Wilma Jeanne, b. 11/11/1927; first; William Henry Belyea (truck driver, Benton) and Helen Inez Perry (Haverhill)

BEMIS,

daughter, b. 2/5/1896 in Warren; William H. Bemis (laborer, 23, Haverhill) and Bertha M. Crane (22, Wentworth)

Laura Elizabeth, b. 1/19/1954; third; Edmund S. Bemis (station att. garage, Cambridge, MA) and Hazel Dorothy Wall (MA)

Paul Edmund, b. 11/26/1956; fourth; Edmund S. Bemis, Jr. (self employed, Cambridge, MA) and Hazel D. Wall (Somerville, MA)

Shirley Anne, b. 1/11/1951; second; Edmund S. Bemis, Jr. (MA) and Hazel Dorothy Wall (MA)

Shirley Elizabeth, b. 8/22/1946 in Glencliff; second; Harold G. Bemis (laborer, Haverhill) and Sheila A. French (E. Haverhill)

Victoria Ione, b. 3/10/1943; first; Harold G. Bemis (laborer, Haverhill) and Sheila A. French (E. Haverhill)

BENEDICT,

Jacob Royce, b. 5/24/1982 in Haverhill; Royce Benedict (NH) and Melanie Ann Carr (NH)

BENNETT,

daughter, b. 9/15/1895 in Warren; first; Adell Bennett (21, Ellsworth)

son, b. 5/15/1898 in Warren; second; Della E. Bennett (26, Ellsworth)

Marilyn A., b. 8/13/1937; fifth; Lewis Bennett (Grantham) and Geneva Pike (Warren)

Richard W., b. 4/8/1941; eighth; Lewis H. Bennett (truck driver, Gayesville, VT) and Geneva Maude Pike (Warren)

Shirley, b. 4/2/1936; fourth; Lewis H. Bennett (Grantham) and Geneva Maud Pike (Warren); residence - W. Rumney

BENT,
Aron Hannd, b. 12/18/1969 in Haverhill; Norman Lamont Bent (NH) and Claire Jeanne Hurlbutt (NH)

BERRY,
child, b. 7/28/1908; first; Charles F. Berry (46, Rumney) and Ora May Smith (19, Sanbornton)

BETANCOURT,
Jose M., Jr., b. 4/14/1961; first; Jose M. Betancourt, Sr. (US Army, San Juan, PR) and Ida May Weeks (Warren)

BICKFORD,
James R., b. 1/17/1960; fourth; James R. Bickford (railroad engineer, Naugatuck, CT) and Aurelia M. Kingsley (Sawyerville, CT)

BILADEAU,
Mary Antonette, b. 3/28/1912 in Warren; fourth; Darisse Biladeau (laborer, Canada) and Mary Gagne (Canada)

BISHOP,
Ernest Newell, b. 9/22/1933; second; Harold L. Bishop (laborer, Medford, MA) and Marion E. Weeks (Warren)

Glendon, b. 5/12/1936; third; Harold L. Bishop (Medford, MA) and Marion E. Weeks (Warren)

Harold L., Jr., b. 5/12/1932; first; Harold Leslie Bishop (laborer, Medford, MA) and Marion Elsie Weeks (Warren)

BIXBY,
son, b. 3/23/1899 in Warren; second; Willard M. Bixby (farmer, 24, Warren) and Hattie L. Currie (21, Canada)

son, b. 12/12/1900 in Warren; third; William M. Bixby (laborer, 26, Warren) and Hattie L. Currie (23, Canada)

son, b. 8/23/1902 in Warren; fourth; Willard M. Bixby (farmer, 28, Warren) and Hattie L. Curry (24, Canada)

Alicia Me, b. 7/3/1987 in Haverhill; Lloyd Wayne Bixby (25) and Laurie Ann Borger (24)

Annette Marie, b. 12/31/1942; sixth; Leroy C. Bixby (labor def. plant, Warren) and Eva Monroe (Marshfield, MO)

Bridget Michelle, b. 11/28/1983 in Hanover; Jerry Wayne Bixby (29) and Jayne Linda Brown (24)

Debra Lynn, b. 12/1/1960; first; Reginald W. Bixby (carpenter, Wentworth) and Jeanette M. Haines (Warren)

Justin Tyler, b. 8/12/1993 in Lebanon; Jerry Wayne Bixby (39) and Jayne Linda Brown (34)

Lloyd Wayne, b. 6/23/1962; second; Reginald W. Bixby (truck driver, Wentworth) and Jeanette M. Haines (Warren)

Richard, b. 1/4/1937; fourth; Roy Bixby (Warren) and Eva Monroe (Marshfield, MO)

Robert Willard, b. 4/1/1929; second; Maurice H. Bixby (manufacturer, Warren) and Mildred Hunkins (Groton)

Roland M., b. 11/2/1931; third; Maurice H. Bixby (manufacturer, Warren) and Mildred Hunkins (Groton)

Sarah Brittany, b. 8/19/1986; Jerry Wayne Bixby (32) and Jayne Linda Brown (27)

Shirley Loraine, b. 1/24/1957; second; Robert W. Bixby (truck driver, Warren) and Margaret E. Kramer (Cook, NE)

Susanne M., b. 2/1/1967l; third; Reginald W. Bixby (truck driver, Wentworth) and Jeanette M. Haines (Warren)

Todd Wayne, b. 11/25/1984 in Haverhill; Lloyd Wayne Bixby (21) and Laurie Ann Borger (22)

Verona Louise, b. 4/14/1927; first; Maurice Bixby (manufacturer, Warren) and Mildred Hunkins (Groton)

Virginia M., b. 6/19/1934; fourth; Maurice H. Bixby (manufacturer, Warren) and Mildred Hunkins (Groton)

Willard M., b. 4/30/1937; fourth; Vernon Bixby (Alberta, Canada) and Gertrude Walls (Woburn, MA)

BLACK,
son, b. 5/25/1919 in N. Adams, MA; Louis J. Black (farmer, Greenfield) and Bertha Warner (Bernardston)

BLAKE,
son, b. 4/21/1890 in Warren; first; Oscar A. Blake (laborer, 29, Warren) and Rose E. French (18, Laconia)

daughter, b. 12/13/1894 in Warren; A. C. Blake (sect. hand, 27, Rumney) and L. M. Foster (23, Wentworth)
stillborn daughter, b. 9/12/1896 in Warren; Osco A. Blake (carpenter, 35, Wentworth) and Rose French (25, Laconia)
son, b. 4/10/1897 in Warren; fourth; Alvah C. Blake (section man, 30, Rumney) and Lulu M. Foster (25, Wentworth)
son, b. 9/25/1897 in Warren; third; Oscar Blake (carpenter, 36, Warren) and Rose French (26, Laconia)
stillborn daughter, b. 4/12/1901 in Warren; first; Harry I. Blake (laborer, 24, Warren) and Martha A. Simpson (24, Haverhill)
Earl Henry, b. 9/25/1924; second; Eugene Blake (laborer, W. Thornton) and Della Heath (Orford)
Francis C., b. 6/27/1914 in Warren; first; Robert L. Blake (laborer, Haverhill) and Lillian L. Gale (Warren)
Isaac, b. 1/19/1894 in Warren; Oscar A. Blake (laborer, 32, Warren) and Rose E. French (22, Laconia)
Lyris A., b. 2/19/1939; second; Wyman Blake (patrolman, Haverhill) and Bernice A. Wright (Warren); residence - E. Barnet, VT
Narene Ruby, b. 12/7/1937; first; Wyman W. Blake (Haverhill) and Bernice M. Wright (Warren); residence - E. Barnet, VT
Roland Eugene, b. 5/11/1922; first; Eugene Blake (laborer, W. Thornton) and Della Heath (Orford)

BLODGETT,
Amanda Renne, b. 1/26/1991 in Lebanon; Scott Milton Blodgett (28) and Joyce Elizabeth Hudson (24)
Raymond Harris, b. 9/16/1905 in Warren; first; Charles N. Blodgett (farmer, 25, Hebron) and Maud E. Harris (Bath)

BOULANGER,
Ephram, b. 12/28/1909 in Warren; sixth; Ephriam Boulanger (carpenter, Canada) and Rose Belevance (Canada)

BOUTIN,
Katherine Ann, b. 10/15/1991 in Concord; Robert James Boutin (28) and Paula Jean Marsh (29)
Samantha Jo, b. 10/17/1989 in Concord; Robert James Boutin (26) and Paula Marsh (27)

BOWLES,
son, b. 12/29/1902 in Warren; second; Herbert J. Bowles (farmer, 28, Lisbon) and Catharine M. Short (24, Newfoundland)
son, b. 4/18/1905 in Warren; third; Herbert J. Bowles (laborer, 30, Lisbon) and Katherine Short (Newfoundland)
son, b. 2/14/1926; second; Clarence Bowles (poultryman, Franconia) and Adelina Adams (Milton)
Albert W., b. 7/15/1899 in Warren; first; Herbert Bowles (laborer, 25, Milton) and Katie M. Short (19, Newfoundland)
Alice May, b. 1/9/1935; third; Kenneth Bowles (Warren) and Eva Lovette (Plymouth)
Dorothy H., b. 7/4/1930; fourth; Clarence H. Bowles (caretaker, Franconia) and ----- Adams (Milton, MA)
Harriet Alice, b. 3/2/1927; third; Clarence Bowles (poultryman, Franconia) and Adaline A. Adams (Milton, MA)
Walter Allen, b. 7/25/1932; fifth; Clarence H. Bowles (laborer, fish hatchery, Franconia) and Adeline A. Adams (Milton, MA)

BOYCE,
David Arnold, b. 6/4/1964; eighth; Arthur S. Boyce (laborer, Thornton) and Arline R. Glines (Brentwood)
Lyman Fred, b. 9/28/1955; fourth; Arthur Steven Boyce (mill work, Thornton) and Arlene Ruth Glines (Brentwood)
Robin Lee, b. 2/28/1957; fifth; Arthur S. Boyce (laborer, Thornton) and Arlene Ruth Glines (Brentwood)
Rosabell A., b. 3/28/1962; seventh; Arthur S. Boyce (laborer, Thornton) and Arlene Ruth Glines (Brentwood)

BREADON,
daughter, b. 3/17/1887 in Benton; William E. Breadon (farmer, NB) and Kate A. Cutting (Benton); residence - Benton

BRILEY,
son, b. 6/11/1887 in Warren; Royal E. Briley (laborer, 24, Barnet, VT) and Florence B. Whitcher (21, Warren)
daughter, b. 2/6/1892 in Warren; R. E. Briley (day laborer, 30) and F. D. Whitcher (25, Warren)

BROCHU,
John Philip, b. 6/26/1985 in St. Johnsbury, VT; Guy Charles Brochu (30) and Debra Suzanne Buttrick (27)

BROWN,
daughter, b. 10/8/1909 in Warren; second; Mabel Brown (White River Jct., VT)

Alicia Jean, b. 11/30/1983 in Haverhill; James Robert Brown (30) and Barbara Evelyn Martin (24)

Amanda Lynn, b. 2/28/1989 in Woodsville; James Robert Brown (36) and Barbara Evelyn Martin (30)

Andrew A., b. 6/23/1989 in Lebanon; Kevin Scott Brown (28) and Carol Irene Hudson (27)

Gary Leon, b. 1/3/1942; first; Earland V. Brown (truck driver, New Bedford, MA) and Hildegarde C. Gould (Piermont); residence - New Brunswick, NJ

Gregory Alan, b. 8/28/1954; first; Clyde Francis Brown (laborer, NH) and Viola Fay Ames (NH)

Kevin Scott, II, b. 11/2/1981 in Haverhill; Kevin Scott Brown (19) and Carol Irene Hudson (19)

Luann Lyn, b. 3/1/1957; second; Clyde Francis Brown (laborer, Wentworth) and Viola Fay Ames (W. Rumney)

Mollie Rebekah, b. 1/30/1999 in Littleton; Duane Brown and Jennifer Brown

Toby Victor, b. 5/4/1952; third; Earland V. Brown (MA) and Hildegarde Clara Gould (NH)

Travis Ryan, b. 2/22/1989 in Lebanon; Gregory Alan Brown (35) and Rosanne Marie Delorenzo (28)

Wyatt William, b. 2/5/1947 in Woodsville; second; Earland Victor Brown (truck driver, New Bedford, MA) and Hildegarde Clara Gould (Piermont)

BUCK,
Margaret G., b. 3/7/1930; fourth; Archie Buck (laborer, Newport, VT) and Flora A. Russell (Grantham)

BUCKLEY,
daughter, b. 4/19/1904 in Warren; fourth; John H. Buckley (barber, 27, Concord) and Nellie Fifield (25, Thetford, VT)

BUCKLIN,
H. Henrietta, b. 3/17/1893 in Warren; William A. Bucklin (physician, 57, Royalton, VT) and Olive H. Whitcomb (36, Hyde Park, VT)

19

BUMFORD,
Brian Craig, b. 10/27/1969 in Plymouth; Bruce Hill Bumford (NH) and Nancy Elaine Linscott (NH)

BURNELL,
stillborn son, b. 1/23/1915 in Warren; first; Chester A. Burnell (station agent, PQ) and Sadie Marie Ellis (Brentwood)
Mary Ellis, b. 5/7/1916 in Warren; second; Chester A. Burnell (station agent, PQ) and Sadie M. Ellis (Brentwood)

BURT,
Claudette Rita, b. 9/25/1947 in Plymouth; first; Alden Leroy Burt (store clerk, W. Rumney) and Charlotte Rita Wistner (Pike)
Norma Leiler, b. 9/25/1933; third; Harold J. Burt (laborer, Lyman) and Pearl E. Veazey (Warren)

BUSHAW,
Jesse Edward, b. 8/29/1949 in Plymouth; second; Jesse Edward Bushaw (garage mech., Bradford, VT) and Tssabelle Blanche Shortt (Warren)
Julie Ann, b. 7/17/1974 in Laconia; Jesse E. Bushaw, Jr. (24) and Kathleen L. Cheney (25)

BUSKEY,
Allen Argustus, b. 12/22/1927; second; Albert James Buskey (millman, Canada) and Winnifred B. Tuttle (Lisbon)
Audrey J., b. 5/19/1936; fifth; Albert J. Buskey (Sutton Flats, PQ) and Winifred B. Tuttle (Lisbon)
Donald K., b. 2/2/41930; third; Albert J. Buskey (laborer, Sutton Flats, PQ) and Winnifred B. Tuttle (Lisbon)
Harold Neil, b. 12/12/1931; fourth; Albert J. Buskey (laborer, Sutton Flats, PQ) and Winnifred V. Tuttle (Lisbon)

BUTSON,
Angela Lynn, b. 1/1/1972 in Haverhill; Donald Arthur Butson (NH) and Darlene Ann Ball (NH)

BYTHROW,
daughter, b. 1/18/1922; fourth; Herbert J. Bythrow (mechanic, Cornish) and Ida E. Chadwick (Manchester)

CAMARA,
Kali Ann, b. 7/26/1999 in Lebanon; Todd Camara and Theresa Veillette

CANFIELD,
Helen L., b. 10/17/1930; second; George Canfield, Jr. (cook, Lebanon) and Mary M. Canfield (W. Charleston); residence - Hanover

CANTERBURY,
Shawn Patrick, b. 6/30/1999 in Plymouth; David Canterbury and Crystal Ewens

CARBEE,
Dorothy E., b. 9/1/1911 in Warren; second; Edgar S. Carbee (electrician, Hooksett) and Alice M. Head (Warren)

CAREY,
son, b. 1/16/1924; third; George W. Carey (laborer, Keene) and Nina B. Swinger (Northfield, VT)

CARPENTER,
son, b. 6/1/1900 in Warren; first; Frank A. Carpenter (blacksmith, 24, Vershire, VT) and Nettie A. Merrill (20, Warren)
Clarice Annetta, b. 11/2/1906 in Warren; second; Frank Carpenter (blacksmith, 31, Vershire, VT) and Nettie Merrill (27, Dorchester)
Orra E., b. 6/13/1915 in Warren; stillborn; third; Frank A. Carpenter (farmer, Warren) and Nettie A. Merrill (Dorchester)

CARR,
Jem Linda, b. 1/16/1987 in Hanover; Donald Ray Carr (31) and Linda Fay Hawes (44)

CARROLL,
Gloria May, b. 7/13/1944 in Glencliff; third; Walter D. Carroll (fireman, Richford, VT) and Agnes M. Lombard (Barre, VT)

CARSON,
Frank, b. 1/21/1904 in Warren; stillborn; first; Frank Carson (laborer, 26, Bangor, NY) and Julia M. Lontine (16, Westmore, VT)

CARTER,
Adam Derrick, b. 7/28/1989 in Lebanon; Derrick Noel Carter (31)
and Fawn Marie Pushee (29)
Harry William, b. 2/17/1923; stillborn; first; William J. Carter (laborer,
Lunenburg, VT) and Evelyn B. Hildreth (Warren)
Lindsey Jane, b. 1/3/1992 in Lebanon; Derrick Noel Carter (34) and
Fawn Marie Pushee (32)

CARTWRIGHT,
Byron Kenneth, b. 2/27/1958; second; David N. Cartwright (odd
jobs) and Thelma M. Ramsdell
Darlene Florence, b. 6/5/1956; first; David N. Cartwright (laborer,
Bridgewater, MA) and Thelma M. Ramsdell (Windsor, VT)

CASS,
Davin James, b. 1123/2001 in Lebanon; Bobby Cass and Stacey
Cass

CATE,
Ashley Rose, b. 10/17/1993 in Lebanon; Nicholas Lloyd Cate (28)
and Paula Marie Rocchi (27)
Joshua Michael, b. 6/17/1989 in Lebanon; Nicholas Lloyd Cate (24)
and Paula Marie Rocchi (23)
Peter Jason, b. 10/5/1977; Lloyd Dennis Cate (42) and Anita Sarah
Butson (42)

CAVERHILL,
Angela Jean, b. 7/23/1975; Wayne Phillip Caverhill (24) and Vicki
Lynn Moody (20)
Charlene M., b. 11/11/1960; fourth; David W. Caverhill (maintenance
mech., Ashland) and Helen E. Hildreth (Warren)
Shaun Philip, b. 4/8/1978 in Haverhill; Wayne Philip Caverhill (26)
and Vicki Lynn Moody (22)
Wayne Philip, b. 5/30/1951; third; David Wayne Caverhill (NH) and
Helen Elizabeth Hildreth (NH)

CHAMPOU,
John B., b. 3/8/1875 in Warren; second; Napolian Champou
(laborer, 30, Kingsey, PQ) and Emily Micleon (20, Richmond,
PQ); residence - Warren Summit (1907)

CHARLES,
Seth Green, b. 12/3/1976; Ralph Stillman Charles, III (27) and
Nancy Elizabeth Seymour (27)

CHARLONE,
Jason Patrick, b. 5/18/1977 in Plymouth; Louis Joseph Charlone
(31) and Joan Missel (30)

CHASE,
Anna Mae, b. 9/5/1938; first; George S. Chase (bobbin mill, Bath)
and Maud Leighton (Bradford, VT)
Annalee Katharyn, b. 1/13/2005 in Lebanon; Timothy Chase and
Heather Nystrom
Eldon Meral, b. 11/14/1919 in Warren; seventh; Frank E. Chase
(laborer, Bath) and Phebe M. Chase (SD)
Judy Lee, b. 6/6/1965; fifth; Leon E. Chase (truck driver, Wentworth)
and Edna L. Dimond (Orange)
June Rose, b. 6/26/1950 in Haverhill; second; Leon Edward Chase
(farmer, Wentworth) and Lena Belle White (Piermont)
Lucy Ina, b. 6/5/1922; eighth; Frank E. Chase (farmer, Glencliff) and
Avis M. Gray (Center Harbor)
Robert Dean, b. 9/6/1950 in Haverhill; first; Robert Cecil Chase (gen.
laborer, Woodsville) and Noreen Ellen Stimson (Woodsville)

CHASSON,
Helen Rebecca D., b. 9/1/1905 in Warren; first; Fred J. H. Chasson
(teamster, 23, Portland, ME) and Ella A. Houghton (Warren)

CLARK,
daughter, b. 7/5/1889 in Warren; Horace W. Clark (farmer, 34,
Burlington, VT) and Lucy Moses (28, Chichester)
daughter, b. 12/14/1891 in Warren; first; George L. Clark (laborer,
31, Groton) and Cora J. Sanborn (29, Warren)
stillborn daughter, b. 6/3/1926; fourth; Enos I. Clark (farmer,
Warren) and Avis Gray (Center Harbor)
Abigail Theresa, b. 3/23/1998 in Lebanon; Daniel Jay Clark (28) and
Angela Ruth Boutin (29)
Audrey Beryl, b. 5/2/1930; third; Wilbur A. Clark (truck driver,
Meredith) and Dorothy Sweet (Sheldon, VT)
Bernard A., b. 6/14/1935; fourth; Wilbur Albah Clark (Meredith Ctr.)
and Dorothy Mae Sweet (Sheldon, VT)

Brian Douglas, b. 7/22/1987 in Hanover; Brian William Clark (34) and Eileen Marita Joyce (21)

Elizabeth Z., b. 3/24/1928; second; Wilbur A. Clark (truck driver, Meredith) and Dorothy May Sweet (Sheldon, VT)

Eric Michael, b. 1/6/1976 in Haverhill; Thomas Joseph Clark (26) and Emily Jane Wright (25)

Holly Christine, b. 3/26/1975 in Haverhill; Richard Duane Clark (28) and Marilyn Jean Wright (20)

Jean Marie, b. 4/28/1972 in Haverhill; Richard Duane Clark (Canada) and Marilyn Jean Wright (NH)

Jordan Michael, b. 5/6/1998 in Haverhill; Michael Joseph Clark (26) and Lori Ann Craveiro (32)

Julie Dawn, b. 6/1/1971 in Haverhill; Richard Duane Clark (Canada) and Marilyn Jean Wright (NH)

Katie Lynn, b. 2/23/1989 in Plymouth; Chester Lee Clark (30) and Lori An Bowen (25)

Keith Allen, b. 6/24/1972 in Haverhill; Thomas Joseph Clark (Canada) and Emily Jane Wright (NH)

Leona May, b. 5/15/1922; third; Enos I. Clark (laborer, Bath) and Phoebe M. Wright (SD)

Marita Louise, b. 5/26/1991 in Lebanon; Brian William Clark (38) and Eileen Marcia Joyce (25)

Mark Ryan, b. 3/13/1988 in Plymouth; Chester Lee Clark (29) and Lori Ann Bowen (24)

Matthew Richard, b. 7/20/2001 in Lebanon; Daniel Clark and Angela Clark

Michael Joseph, b. 6/18/1972 in Haverhill; Douglas Allen Clark (MA) and Janice Sharyn Urbaniak (MA)

Phyllis Louise, b. 7/10/1929; sixth; Enos I. Clark (farmer, Warren) and Avis M. Gray (Center Harbor)

Roger Owen, b. 4/4/1921 in Warren; second; Enos I. Clark (farmer, Warren) and Avis May Gray (Center Harbor)

Stanley R., b. 1/23/1928; fifth; Enos Isbel Clark (farmer, Glencliff) and Avis May Grey (Centre Harbor)

Thomas Joseph, Jr., b. 9/10/1970 in Haverhill; Thomas Joseph Clark (Canada) and Emily Jane Wright (NH)

Timothy Ryan, b. 5/16/1981 in Haverhill; Thomas Joseph Clark (31) and Emily Jane Wright (30)

Walter M., b. 3/18/1919 in Warren; first; Enos I. Clark (farmer, Warren) and Avis M. Gray (Center Harbor)

Wilbur Oscar, b. 8/5/1926; first; Wilbur A. Clark (chauffeur, Meredith) and Dorothy M. Sweet (Sheldon, VT)

CLEMENT,
daughter, b. 2/20/1887 in Warren; Frank C. Clement (farmer, Warren) and Hannah K. Bixby (Warren)
daughter, b. 3/12/1887 in Warren; Daniel I. Clement (postmaster, 60, Warren) and Grace Woodworth (42, Dorchester)
daughter, b. 11/3/1888 in Warren; fourth; Frank Clement (produce dealer, 35, Warren) and Anna K. Bixby (30, Warren)
daughter, b. 7/8/1891 in Warren; fifth; Frank C. Clement (prod. dlr., 38, Warren) and Anna K. Bixby (33, Warren)
son, b. 8/29/1898 in Warren; sixth; Frank C. Clement (prod. dealer, 45, Warren) and Anna K. Bixby (40, Warren)

CLIFFORD,
Fred Grant, b. 4/23/1887 in Warren; Frank P. Clifford (farmer, 31, Warren) and Katie ----- (21, Bancurrig, Ireland)
Iolas W., b. 12/2/1900 in Warren; third; Iolas C. Clifford (harnessmaker, 36, Warren) and Anna Cameron (30, Winchester, MA)

COBB,
Harry H., b. 4/13/1935; first; Russell B. Cobb (Wrentham, MA) and Pollyanna Henderson (Dover)
Roger M., b. 11/25/1939; third; Russell B. Cobb (laborer, Wrentham, MA) and Pollyanna Henderson (Dover)
Russell B., Jr., b. 4/9/1938; second; Russell Bonsall Cobb (laborer, Wrentham, MA) and Pollyanna Henderson (Dover)

COE,
Tesha Rae, b. 12/11/1997; Katrina A. Coy (21)

COLLETTE,
Donna Frances, b. 12/3/2001 in Lebanon; Donald Collette and Christina Collette

COLLIER,
Dawn M., b. 12/9/1937; first; Freeman Collier (Drew, ME) and Shirley M. Keysar (Warren)

COLLINS,
son, b. 5/28/1917 in Warren; sixth; David Collins (laborer, NB) and
Lena Wallace (NB)

COMETT,
Charlotte E., b. 5/9/1914 in Warren; second; Warren L. Comett
(farmer, Littleton) and Florence B. Jewell (Warren)
Geraldine, b. 11/22/1915 in Warren; third; Warren Comett (laborer,
Littleton) and Flossie B. Jewell (Warren)

CONKEY,
Jeremiah Seth, b. 11/22/1987 in Laconia; Jeffrey Seth Conkey (19)
and Jody Sue Plant (22)

CONRAD,
Allison Lyn, b. 7/26/1974 in Hanover; Franklin R. Conrad (25) and
Rebecca Ruth Emerson (20)
Philip Rodney, b. 2/13/1953; fourth; John M. Conrad, Jr.
(Woodsville) and Betty Mae Thompson (Woodsville)

COOKE,
Stanley Neil, b. 8/8/1931; first; Alfred Cooke (insurance agt., New
Britain, CT) and Mary Brandaburg (Elizabeth, NJ)

COPP,
son, b. 11/21/1888 in Warren; Byron Copp (farming, 38, Haverhill)
and A. Geralds (29, Warren)
daughter, b. 3/28/1892 in Warren; Byron Copp (laborer, 43,
Haverhill) and Alma Jerrolds (30, Warren)

CORTHELL,
Edgar Henry, b. 5/2/1924; second; Edgar Corthel (laborer, Tatis
Center, KS) and Agnes Hudson (Oklahoma City, OK)

COTTING,
daughter, b. 11/24/1926; first; Charles E. Cotting (laborer, Piermont)
and Margaret Dyer (Hartford, CT)

COTTON,
son, b. 4/21/1889 in Warren; Edward D. Cotton (farmer, 32, Warren)
and Flora A. Pillsbury (24, Warren)

daughter, b. 11/30/1897 in Warren; third; Edward Cotton (farmer, 41, Warren) and Flora A. Pillsbury (33, Warren)
son, b. 5/11/1900 in Warren; first; Henry L. Cotton (farmer, 39, Warren) and Lizzie M. Moses (18, Warren)
son, b. 8/15/1913 in Warren; second; Henry L. Cotton (carpenter, Warren) and Elizabeth Moses (Warren)
Edward Dean, b. 6/26/1918 in Warren; second; Ralph P. Cotton (farmer, Warren) and Mary E. Moran (Philadelphia)
Marion, b. 12/22/1913 in Warren; first; Ralph Cotton (farmer, Warren) and Mary Moran (Philadelphia, PA)

CRANE,
daughter, b. 8/21/1902 in Warren; second; Charles L. Crane (laborer, 30, Wentworth) and Jennie R. Dowse (19, Haverhill)

CRAWFORD,
son, b. 4/12/1901 in Warren; fourth; Charles L. Crawford (carpenter, 53, Colebrook) and Nellie L. Haynes (28, Stewartstown)

CRONYN,
Sarah Kathleen, b. 3/2/1979 in Plymouth; Kenneth William Cronyn, III (27) and Evelyn Virginia Farrell (27)

CROSS,
daughter, b. 12/11/1898 in Warren; second; Horace H. Cross (farmer, 23, Benton) and Ada E. Libbey (20, Warren)
daughter, b. 1/19/1901 in Warren; third; Horace H. Cross (laborer, 26, Benton) and Ada E. Libbey (23, Warren)
son, b. 6/8/1902 in Warren; fourth; Horace H. Cross (laborer, 27, Benton) and Ada M. Libbey (24, Warren)

CRUTCHER,
Kasey Sue, b. 9/22/1988 in Concord; Thelbert Odell Crutcher (31) and Lana Lee Johnson (26)

CUMMINGS,
daughter, b. 9/26/1904 in Warren; first; Maynard Cummings (farmer, 27, Warren) and Lillian L. Gale (24, Warren)

CURRAN,
Christopher Paul, b. 12/21/1987 in Plymouth; Paul Douglas Curran (30) and Linda Frances Brantz (28)
Matthew Kenneth, b. 11/23/1985 in Plymouth; Paul D. Curran (28) and Linda F. Brantz (26)

CURRIER,
daughter, b. 3/13/1944 in Haverhill; stillborn; eighth; Ralph Francis Currier (laborer, Lock Mills, ME) and Harriet Loretta Williams (Burlington, VT)
Ann Frances, b. 10/21/1950 in Plymouth; second; John Downing Currier (dental tech., NH) and Mary Frances Kasheta (MA)

CUSHING,
Donna Lorraine, b. 5/9/1956; second; Irving B. Cushing (clerk, Warren) and Avis M. Huckins (Wentworth)
Estella, b. 10/3/1926; first; Irving Cushing (pullman conductor, Freeport, ME) and Pearl Batchelder (Warren); residence - Freeport, ME
Irving B., Jr., b. 6/6/1928; second; Irving B. Cushing (pullman con., Freeport, ME) and Pearl E. Batchelder (Warren); residence - Cambridge, MA
Rhonda Colleen, b. 11/10/1952; first; Irving Beecher Cushing (NH) and Avis Marjorie Huckins (NH)

CUTTING,
Charles G., b. 2/22/1928; second; Charles E. Cutting (laborer, Piermont) and Margaret Dyer (Hartford, CT)
Janice L., b. 5/27/1937; fourth; Charles Cutting (Piermont) and Margaret Dyer (Hartford, CT)
Priscilla D., b. 8/25/1930; third; Charles E. Cutting (farmer, Warren) and Margaret Dyer (Hartford, CT)

DASHNER,
Lucille M., b. 4/24/1918 in Warren; third; Oliver Dashner (shoemaker, Harwick, PQ) and Florence Lampman (Bangor, NY)

DAVIS,
son, b. 9/20/1895 in Warren; first; John E. Davis (farmer, 34, E. Haverhill) and Effie L. Annis (23, Warren)

son, b. 9/24/1896 in Warren; John E. Davis (farmer, 35, E. Haverhill) and Effie Annis (25, Warren)
son, b. 12/10/1898 in Warren; fourth; John E. Davis (farmer, 38, E. Haverhill) and Effie E. Annis (27, Warren)
daughter, b. 12/22/1900 in Warren; fifth; John E. Davis (laborer, 40, E. Haverhill) and Effie Annis (29, Warren)
son, b. 4/23/1909 in Warren; fifth; John E. Davis (RR section man, E. Haverhill) and Effie L. Annis (Warren)

DAVISON,
Doris A., b. 8/20/1914 in Warren; first; Harry C. Davison (grocer, Woodsville) and Mildred E. Washburn (Haverhill)

DAVOY,
son, b. 2/3/1890 in Warren; first; Cleffos Davoy (lumberman, 30, Canada) and ----- (29, Canada)

DEBLOIS,
Lorraine Day, b. 5/27/1951; seventh; Melvin Guy Deblois (Lowell, VT) and Beatrice Lillian Irwin (St. Johnsbury, VT)

DEOLIVERIRA,
Michael, b. 2/22/1992 in Lebanon; Dennis DeOliverira (45) and Christine Cretinon (32)

DEROSIA,
daughter, b. 8/1/1925; first; Louis Derosia (lineman, Benton) and Flossie Rollins (Piermont)
Adelphane B., b. 9/18/1932; fifth; Lewis J. Derosia (tel. lineman, Benton) and Flossie M. Rollins (Warren)
Coral Ann, b. 5/21/1942; second; Louis B. Derosia (forest guard, Haverhill) and Earline M. Ramsay (Warren)
Flossie, b. 2/11/1907 in Warren; first; Peter Derosia (farmer, 21, Canada) and Hattie Derosia (17, Canada)
Harold E., b. 9/25/1939; first; Louie B. Derosia (forest ranger, Benton) and Earline M. Ramsay (Glencliff)
Leo Fred, b. 12/16/1908; Fred Derosia (Ste. Rose, PQ) and Bessie Davis (Warren) (1962)
Phyllis Harriett, b. 1/10/1925; first; Philip Derosia (laborer, St. Rose, PQ) and Maude Brooks (Wildwood)

Ruth Marilyn, b. 9/27/1927; third; Louis Derosia (t. lineman, Benton) and Flossie Rollins (Piermont)

William Z., b. 1/13/1930; fourth; Lewis J. Derosia (tel. foreman, Benton) and Flossie M. Rollins (Wentworth)

DERRICK,

Cheryl Ann, b. 2/19/1959; seventh; Raymond W. Derrick (laborer, Wentworth) and Louise M. A. Turcotte (Laconia)

Gerald George, b. 4/24/1952; fourth; Raymond William Derrick (Wentworth) and Louise Mary Alice Turcotte (Laconia)

Regina Alberta, b. 2/17/1957; sixth; Raymond W. Derrick (lumberman, Wentworth) and Louise M. A. Turcotte (Laconia)

Sharon Marie, b. 3/15/1956; fifth; Raymond W. Derrick (woodsman, Wentworth) and Louise Turcotte (Laconia)

William Edward Grover, b. 7/29/1950 in Laconia; second; Raymond William Derrick (woodsman, NH) and Louise Mary Alice Turcotte (NH)

DEVOID,

Arthur Francis, b. 10/24/1923; second; George E. Devoid (mill hand, N. Frensburgh, VT) and Christine E. Sprague (Framingham, MA)

DICEY,

Garfield Wendell, b. 8/9/1921 in Warren; first; Verner Dicey (laborer, Alexandria) and Ella Rollins (Wentworth)

Olive Virginia, b. 10/31/1928; second; Verner A. Dicey (woodsman lr., Alexandria) and Ella Maud Rollins (Wentworth)

DIMOND,

Erin Lee, b. 8/14/1976 in Hanover; Alan Fred Dimond (21) and Cheri Ann Buttrick (19)

DIXON,

Ethel Irene, b. 3/18/1931; first; Harold F. Dixon (laborer, Lawrence, MA) and Marion E. McKinley (Warren)

DOHERTY,

Michael Patrick, b. 1/22/1959; first; William G. Doherty (cook, Boston, MA) and Pauline M. Bancroft (Haverhill)

DONNELLY,
Joseph, Jr., b. 9/10/1939; first; Joseph B. Donnelly (Army officer, Pittsfield, MA) and Marguerite Smith (Morrisville, VT)

DONSIER,
son, b. 5/28/1903 in Warren; fourth; Joseph Donsier (laborer, 31, Canada) and Lena Deneno (20, Canada)

DRAPEAU,
stillborn daughter, b. 1/9/1904 in Warren; fifth; Amos Drapeau (laborer, 28, Stratford) and Maggie Glode (22, Canaan)

DRAPER,
son, b. 8/23/1896 in Warren; Alvah E. Draper (minister, 32, Plymouth) and Mary A. Dustin (34, Salisbury)

DREGHORN,
Douglas N., b. 1/19/1941; first; Samuel H. Dreghorn (tele. operator, Malden, MA) and Victoria Elizabeth Nicol (Warren)

DUBE,
Stacey Evelyn, b. 2/17/1975 in Plymouth; Kenneth B. Dube (33) and Donna F. Crosby (27)

DUNKLEE,
Rebecca A., b. 6/3/1954; second; Harold F. Dunklee (laborer, NH) and Eleanor Marie Brown (MA)

DUNN,
son, b. 10/22/1896 in Warren; Charles H. Dunn (salesman, 31, New London, CT) and Phebe E. Martin (32, New Park, NS)

DURLING,
son, b. 3/16/1902 in Warren; second; John P. Durling (laborer, 32, NS) and Amy A. Brown (20, Hodgdon, ME)

DUSSAULT,
Justin Richard, b. 7/5/1980 in Hanover; Thomas Michael Dussault (28) and Cynthia Marie Hamel (24)

EASTMAN,
daughter, b. 9/23/1897 in Warren; first; George C. Eastman (farmer, 38, Warren) and M. McCutcheon (25, St. John, NB)
son, b. 9/23/1897 in Warren; second; George C. Eastman (farmer, 38, Warren) and M. McCutcheon (25, St. John, NB)
son, b. 2/26/1900 in Warren; third; George C. Eastman (farmer, 40, Warren) and Margaret McCutcheon (28, St. Johns, NB)
son, b. 9/6/1903 in Warren; fourth; George C. Eastman (farmer, 42, Warren) and Maggie McCutcheon (31, St. John, NB)
daughter, b. 6/24/1922; second; Edwin T. Eastman (motorman, Providence, RI) and Lydia Bailey (Warren)
S. Christine, b. 10/23/1893 in Warren; Arthur E. Eastman (RR cond., 32, Littleton) and Nellie D. Eastman (29, Warren)

EATON,
son, b. 7/26/1887 in Wentworth; Clarence A. Eaton (farmer, 27, Wentworth) and Emma L. Hobbs (23, Dorchester); residence - Wentworth

ELLIOTT,
daughter, b. 5/8/1903 in Warren; second; Edward A. Elliott (laborer, 45, Canada) and Winona Bishop (23, Brighton, VT)
Laura Arlene, b. 9/8/1930; eighth; John G. Elliott (laborer, Benton) and Mildred A. Ball (Landaff)

EVANS,
Deborah Lynne, b. 9/18/1957; first; Wayne Lloyd Evans (student, Warren) and Shirley Mae Bennett (Bradford, VT)
Diane Marie, b. 11/28/1958; second; Wayne Lloyd Evans (teacher) and Shirley Mae Bennett
Donna Lee, b. 7/31/1960; third; Wayne Lloyd Evans (teacher, Warren) and Shirley May Bennett (Bradford, VT)
Gerald W., b. 1/9/1932; first; Reginald S. Evans (dep. warden, Madbury) and Helen Kemp (Warren)
Reba Marie, b. 7/28/1959; first; Gerald W. Evans (laborer st. hwy, Woodsville) and Emily May Olin (Concord)
Robb Stuart, b. 9/27/1972 in Plymouth; Gerald Wallace Evans (NH) and Emily May Olin (NH)
Ross Gerald, b. 2/3/1962; second; Gerald W. Evans (truck driver, Woodsville) and Emily May Olin (Concord)

Wayne L., b. 10/28/1934; second; Reginald S. Evans (fish culturist, Madbury) and Helen E. Kemp (Warren)

FAGNANT,
Kevin Lee, b. 9/30/1959; second; Fernand R. Fagnant (truck driver, Troy, VT) and Nancy May Ball (Benton)
Michele Lynn, b. 7/30/1968 in Haverhill; Fernand Roger Fagnant (truck driver, VT) and Nancy May Ball (NH)
Robert Edward, b. 3/10/1958; first; Fernand R. Fagnant (truck driver) and Nancy May Ball

FELLOWS,
Nichole-Ann, b. 8/12/1982 in Haverhill; Jeffrey Michael Fellows (NH) and Theresa-Ann Taylor (MA)

FERGUSSON,
daughter, b. 2/8/1901 in Warren; fourth; Daniel Fergusson (laborer, 28, Canada) and Edith McFarland (28, Canada)

FIFIELD,
daughter, b. 5/6/1891 in Warren; second; E. B. Fifield (laborer, 24, Warren) and May F. Morrison (28, Lawrence, MA)
stillborn child, b. 4/6/1908; sixth; Ethelbert Fifield (farmer, 41, Warren) and Marion Morrison (46, Lawrence)
Alvah E., b. 4/27/1901 in Warren; first; Melvin B. Fifield (farmer, 22, Warren) and Effie M. Heath (16, Meredith)
Clayton A., b. 5/8/1924; first; Alba Fifield (laborer, Warren) and Bella Thompson (Exbury, MA)

FILLIAN,
Arnold Albert, b. 8/25/1948 in Haverhill; David Albert Fillian (lumberman, Orford) and Hattie Nellie Shortt (Warren)

FILLIOD,
daughter, b. 3/29/1922; first; Dominac Filliod (laborer, Benton) and Millie Coates (Haverhill)

FLAGG,
Sierra Cheyenne, b. 12/23/2003 in Plymouth; Brian Flagg and Suzanne Flagg

33

FLANDERS,

stillborn son, b. 10/9/1899 in Warren; fifth; Rufus Flanders (farmer, 34, Warren) and Lulia Bancroft (25, N. Benton)

son, b. 5/14/1902 in Warren; first; Leonard M. Flanders (laborer, 24, Warren) and Ellen A. Dowes (17, Newbury, VT)

son, b. 7/28/1905 in Warren; third; Leonard Flanders (contractor, 27, Warren) and Ellen A. Dowse (Newbury, VT)

child, b. 3/12/1908; fourth; Leonard Flanders (lumberman, 30, Warren) and Ellen Douse (23, Newbury Ctr.)

son, b. 4/18/1912 in Warren; fourth; Walter Flanders (farmer, Sharon) and Clara Sargent (Warner)

Audrey Mae, b. 11/21/1926; fourth; Maurice Flanders (laborer, Warren) and Myra Evans (Madbury)

Mary, b. 2/12/1909 in Warren; stillborn; first; Ben Knighton (mill hand) and Nancy Flanders

Mauris B., b. 8/7/1895 in Warren; first; Frank S. Flanders (farmer, 38, Warren) and Jessie J. Boynton (36, Warren)

Olive Muriel, b. 10/15/1901 in Warren; second; Frank L. Flanders (farmer, 45, Benton) and Jesse J. Boynton (42, Warren)

Robert E., b. 12/6/1919 in Warren; first; Maurice B. Flanders (laborer, Warren) and Myra E. Evans (Madbury)

Roger Morton, b. 7/25/1924; third; Maurice Flanders (board sawyer, Warren) and Myra Evans (Madbury, VT)

FLEMING,

Frederick E., b. 2/6/1929; second; Robert E. Fleming (laborer, Wells River, VT) and Doris V. Rollins (Wentworth)

FONTAINE,

son, b. 6/20/1900 in Warren; first; Paul Fontaine (laborer, 21, Canada) and Elodie Denet (16, Canada)

FOOTE,

daughter, b. 3/10/1890 in Warren; seventh; Charles G. Foote (farming, 37, Warren) and Emma F. Eastman (35, Derry)

son, b. 3/16/1897 in Warren; second; Burt L. Foote (laborer, 23, Warren) and Jennie Whitcher (22, Warren)

son, b. 10/6/1902 in Warren; third; Bert L. Foote (laborer, 28, Warren) and Jennie T. Whitcher (28, Warren)

son, b. 8/4/1904 in Warren; fourth; Bert L. Foote (farmer, 29, Warren) and Jennie T. Whitcher (28, Warren)

daughter, b. 6/17/1911 in Warren; first; Harry L. Foote (farmer, Warren) and Emma Wright (Wentworth)
Andrew Bear, b. 4/7/1977 in Hanover; Charles Avery Foote (29) and Sheila Lee Robertson (28)
Anthony Buck, b. 6/7/1979 in Hanover; Charles Avery Foote (31) and Sheila Lee Robertson (30)
Emma A., b. 10/19/1895 in Warren; first; first; Burt Foote (railroad, 21, Warren) and Jennie T. Whitcher (20, Warren)
Jonathon Charles, b. 6/7/1970 in Haverhill; Charles Avery Foote (NH) and Mary Lynn Koski (VT)

FORD,
daughter, b. 1/21/1887 in Warren; Frank P. Ford (farmer, 28, Orford) and Carrie E. ----- (24, Warren); residence - Bradford, VT

FOSS,
son, b. 8/5/1904 in Warren; first; Edward A. Foss (stage driver, 20, Benton) and Cora E. Veazey (16, Bradford, VT); residence - Benton

FOSTER,
daughter, b. 2/17/1911 in Warren; fourth; George A. Foster (pharmacist, Garland, ME) and Lula E. Keysar (Clarksville)
E. Frank, b. 5/7/1898 in Warren; second; Harry C. Foster (actor, 38, NY City) and Lena King (36, Exeter)
Eileen Geneva, b. 1/22/1912 in Warren; fifth; George Foster (pharmacist, Garland, ME) and Lula Keysar (Clarksville, VT)
George Dewey, b. 5/7/1898 in Warren; first; Harry C. Foster (actor, 38, NY City) and Lena King (36, Exeter)

FOUNTAIN,
son, b. 12/14/1898 in Warren; second; Joseph Fountain (laborer, 27, St. John, NB) and Arnada Ray (20, PQ)
daughter, b. 12/29/1904 in Warren; second; Napoleon J. Fountain (laborer, 26, Canada) and Elodia Bermett (20, Canada)

FREEMON,
George G., b. 3/12/1892 in Warren; G. Freemon and Lillian ----- (22, W. Topsham, VT); residence - Hooksett

FRENCH,
son, b. 8/26/1888 in Warren; Oscar H. French (farmer, 52, Rumney)
 and E. Savage (36, Warren)
daughter, b. 3/24/1897 in Warren; first; Charles B. French (laborer,
 26, Warren) and Mabel Molway (20, Piermont)
son, b. 4/3/1897 in Warren; first; Grace French (17, Warren)
son, b. 5/18/1897 in Warren; second; Herbert H. French (farmer, 32,
 Warren) and Eva M. Whiteman (29, Johnville, PQ)
stillborn son, b. 5/16/1934; second; Alve Fry (Army man) and
 Addline L. French (Haverhill)
Edna, b. 2/16/1894 in Warren; Herbert H. French (laborer, 28,
 Warren) and Eva M. Whiteman (26, Canada)
Edna May, b. 4/5/1910; first; George French (farmer, 35, E.
 Concord, VT) and Florence Smith (26, E. Concord, VT)
Emma V., b. 4/17/1920 in Warren; fifth; George W. French (farmer,
 Warren) and Flora O. Smith (E. Concord)
George W., Jr., b. 10/21/1915 in Warren; fourth; George W. French
 (farmer, Warren) and Florence O. Smith (E. Concord)
Guy William, b. 3/16/1924; second; Reuben French (laborer, PQ)
 and Velma Ladeau (Piermont)
James Lester, b. 8/12/1922; eighth; George W. French (teamster,
 Warren) and Florence O. Smith (E. Concord, VT)
Marguerite Louise, b. 1/14/1899 in Warren; first; Asa L. French
 (merchant, 25, Northfield, VT) and Jessie M. Williams (25,
 Colebrook); residence - Colebrook
Richard J., b. 6/8/1937; fourth; Reuben French (Arford, Canada) and
 Velma Ladeau (Piermont)
Stanley E., b. 4/6/1932; first; Addline L. French (Haverhill)

FRYE,
daughter, b. 10/11/1905 in Warren; first; Simeon C. Frye
 (bookkeeper, 40, Sanbornton) and Mary T. Macrae (Upper
 Canada)

GALE,
daughter, b. 5/14/1889 in Warren; William F. Gale (farmer, 44,
 Warren) and Belle K. Simpson (25, Haverhill)
daughter, b. 4/4/1910; first; Harry Gale (laborer, 28, Warren) and
 Laura Libby (17, Warren)
Anna May, b. 12/25/1892 in Warren; William F. Gale (butcher, 47,
 Warren) and Belle K. Simpson (31, Haverhill)

Burton Nelson, b. 2/2/1920 in Warren; second; Harry B. Gale (trackman, Warren) and Laura E. Libbey (Warren)

GALLANT,
daughter, b. 3/3/1910; second; Thomas W. Gallant (filer in mill, 32, PEI) and Florence Balch (26, Goffstown)
Natalie Mary, b. 8/20/1905 in Warren; first; Thomas Gallant (mill hand, 27, Canada) and Florence J. Balch (Goffstown)
Ruth Balch, b. 2/24/1913 in Warren; third; Thomas Gallant (sawyer, PEI) and Florence Balch (Goffstown)

GARDNER,
Elizabeth, b. 11/7/1940; second; Richard T. Gardner (rec. promotion, Watertown, MA) and Ethel Moore Worth (Watertown, MA)
Stephen Allen, b. 12/31/1952; seventh; Harold Hillman Gardner (NH) and Sophronia May Emerson (Topsham, VT)

GARRETT,
Aurora Jean, b. 5/25/1960; fourth; Floyd Alfred Garrett (logger, Winchester, MA) and June Althea Marsh (Wentworth)
Barbie Lynn, b. 6/14/1963; fifth; Floyd A. Garrett (driller, Winchendon, MA) and Jane Althea Marsh (Wentworth)
Bruce Wayne, b. 2/28/1966; sixth; Floyd A. Garrett (lumberjack, Winchendon, MA) and June Althea Marsh (Wentworth)
Kathryn Althea, b. 10/16/1956; third; Floyd A. Garrett (truck driver, Wentworth) and June A. Marsh (Wentworth)
Yvonne Marie, b. 9/19/1964; sixth; Floyd A. Garrett (lumberjack, Winchendon, MA) and June A. Marsh (Wentworth)

GAUTHIER,
Alfred R., b. 12/25/1933; fifth; Lawrence L. Gauthier (laborer, Gorham) and Ruth M. Morse (Fitchburg, MA)

GILBERT,
Theresa Sybil, b. 9/20/1906 in Warren; second; Leon Gilbert (laborer, 20, Orford) and Della Agnes Fay (20, Newtonville)

GILLIS,
Warren F., b. 3/20/1914 in Warren; tenth; John J. Gillis (painter, Providence, RI) and Mary E. McGavern (Methuen, MA)

GLEASON,
Kenneth P., b. 7/19/1900 in Warren; first; Fred C. Gleason (merchant, 34, Warren) and Etta L. Prescott (31, N. Haverhill)

GODVILLE,
James, b. 1/9/1928; third; James Godville (laborer, Russia) and Edna S. Short (Warren)
Louella J., b. 6/26/1937; fourth; James Godville (laborer, Lithuania) and Edna Short (Warren)
Marie Odette, b. 11/8/1951; second; James Godville (NH) and Lorraine Ann Drewer (NY)
Sandra Mary, b. 7/9/1943; first; Oscar Roulx and Mabel Godville (Warren)

GOGUEN,
Miranda Sue, b. 3/28/1989 in Plymouth; Dennis Alfred Goguen (33) and Susan Kathleen Bryant (27)

GOODALE,
Brandon Scott, b. 9/25/1995 in Lebanon; Scott Gregory Goodale (25) and Pamela Jane Ball (20)

GOODRICH,
Eleanor G., b. 1/4/1937; second; Frank W. Goodrich (Haverhill, MA) and Eleanor Ellis (Saugus, MA)
Virginia L., b. 12/2/1935; first; Frank W. Goodrich (Haverhill, MA) and Eleanor F. Ellis (Saugus, MA)

GOODWIN,
son, b. 11/23/1887 in Warren; Walter Goodwin (25, Warren) and Georgianna Pease (20, Wentworth)
son, b. 10/25/1888 in Warren; first; Charles Goodwin (farmer, 24, Warren) and Nellie E. Morey (23, Elyria, OH)
son, b. 5/31/1890 in Warren; second; Walter H. Goodwin (farmer, 28, Warren) and Georgianna Pease (23, Wentworth)
son, b. 11/16/1891 in Warren; second; Charles B. Goodwin (farmer, 27, Warren) and Nellie E. Morey (26, OH)
daughter, b. 6/26/1895 in Warren; third; C. B. Goodwin (farmer, 30, Warren) and Nellie E. Morey (29, Elyria, OH)
daughter, b. 5/30/1897 in Warren; fourth; Charles B. Goodwin (laborer, 33, Warren) and Nellie E. Morey (32, Elyrig, OH)

stillborn son, b. 5/25/1930; second; Harry L. Goodwin (millwright, Haverhill) and Bertha G. Gale (MA)

Jean G., b. 3/3/1936; first; Everett Goodwin (Orford) and Helen V. Gale (Warren)

Lila S., b. 12/8/1915 in Warren; first; Walter J. Goodwin (farmer, Dover) and Maud W. Hill (Irasburg, VT)

Raymond Arthur, b. 7/7/1921 in Warren; first; Raymond Goodwin (chauffeur, Hanover, MA) and Flora Young (Waterford, VT); residence - Littleton

GOSLAY,

daughter, b. 6/8/1901 in Warren; second; Lewis Goslay (laborer, 30, Burke, VT) and Mary Doroza (28, Canada)

daughter, b. 12/28/1902 in Warren; third; Lewis Goslay (laborer, 31, Burke, VT) and Mary Derosia (28, Canada)

son, b. 9/18/1905 in Warren; fourth; Lewis Goslay (laborer, 34, Burke, VT) and Mary Derosier (Canada)

GOSSELIN,

Helen Lorraine, b. 10/6/1945 in Plymouth; fourth; John Edward Gosselin (laborer, Lancaster, MA) and Marie Isabelle McCarthy (Milford, MA)

John Edward, b. 5/21/1944 in Plymouth; third; John Edward Gosselin (mechanic, Lancaster, MA) and Marie Isabelle McCarthy (Milford, MA)

Robert Alfred, b. 5/5/1948 in Plymouth; fifth; John Edward Gosslin (laborer, Lancaster, MA) and Marie Isabelle McCarthy (Milford, MA)

GOULD,

stillborn daughter, b. 8/6/1912 in Warren; second; Frank Gould (farmer, Warren) and Mabel Brown (Bradford, VT)

Llewellyn L., b. 6/9/1920 in Warren; third; Leon R. Gould (laborer, Stewartstown) and Clara R. Russell (Crassbury, PQ)

GRAVES,

Debra Jean, b. 10/9/1952; first; Robert Charles Graves (NH) and Janet Winifred Hobart (NH)

Robert C., b. 3/1/1933; second; Ronald Graves (mechanic, Berlin) and Ethel Little (Warren)

GREEN,
Emily Mar'n, b. 4/3/1940; fifth; Milton L. Green (laborer, Lubec, ME)
and Lillian F. Merrill (Warren)
Lillian R., b. 9/23/1937; third; Milton L. Greene (Lubec, ME) and
Lillian F. Merrill (Warren)
Milton E., b. 5/28/1936; second; Milton Green (Lubec, ME) and
Lillian Merrill (Glencliff)
Shirley C., b. 9/5/1938; fourth; Milton Green (laborer, Lubec, ME)
and Lillian Merrill (Glencliff)

GREGORI,
Katharine Lee, b. 8/11/1982 in Warren; Peter Avery Gregori (NY)
and Jane L'Hommedieu (TX)
Lucas William, b. 11/13/1980 in Warren; Peter Avery Gregori (32)
and Jane L'Hommedieu (29)

GRIFFIN,
John Ray, b. 10/18/1921 in Warren; first; Ray Griffin (watchman,
Laconia) and Ethel Spooner (Warren)

GUENETTE,
Joseph E., b. 11/24/1940; third; Henry Guenette (farmer, Jay, VT)
and Diane Robillard (Troy, VT)

HAINES,
Jeanette M., b. 7/30/1939; second; Wilbur N. Haines (ry. mail clerk,
Newmarket) and Cora A. Morrison (Warren)
Norma C., b. 2/26/1937; first; Wilbur N. Haines (Newmarket) and
Cora Morrison (Warren)
Stanley R., b. 1/28/1941; third; Wilbur N. Haines (ry. mail clerk,
Newmarket) and Cora A. Morrison (Warren)

HAIR,
Jeremy David, b. 10/6/1974 in Haverhill; Allen Walter Hair (29) and
Sandra Whitcher (32)
Lauren Elizabeth, b. 10/24/2002 in Plymouth; Jeremy Hair and
Sandra Hair
Sarah, b. 6/14/1973 in Haverhill; Allen Walter Hair (NH) and Sandra
Whitcher (NH)
Walter Charles, b. 12/30/1969 in Haverhill; Allen Walter Hair (NH)
and Sandra Whitcher (NH)

HALEY,
Caleb Elmer, b. 3/16/2001 in Plymouth; Elmer Haley and Jill Haley
Erin Joyce, b. 2/11/1999 in Plymouth; Elmer Haley and Jill Whitcher

HANNETT,
Ty Matthew, b. 6/8/1998 in Haverhill; Ricky Alfred Hannett (38) and
Dawnette M. Hannett (21)

HANSON,
Hiram H., b. 1/24/1928; third; Bert Hanson (laborer, China, ME) and
Bertha May Wallace (Milan)

HARLOW,
Christine Lynn, b. 8/27/1974 in Plymouth; Ralph Gordon Harlow (26)
and Jeanne Irene Foote (23)

HARMON,
Charles E., b. 5/2/1916 in Warren; first; Everett B. Harmon (farmer,
Island Pond, VT) and Clara C. Shortt (Warren)
Irene M., b. 4/4/1919 in Warren; second; Everett B. Harmon (farmer,
Island Pond, VT) and Clara C. Short (Warren)

HARRIMAN,
Peter Allen, b. 9/28/1956; second; Alton M. Harriman (pastry cook,
Easton) and Ethel U. Eldred (Montgomery, VT)

HARTLY,
daughter, b. 1/27/1888 in Warren; second; Fred Hartly (teamster,
Canada) and Flora Beamus (Benton)
daughter, b. 12/4/1890 in Warren; third; Fred L. Hartly (laborer, 29,
Magog, PQ) and Flora J. Beamis (24, Benton)

HARVEY,
son, b. 8/24/1911 in Warren; first; Henry H. Harvey (engineer, NY)
and Nancy Houghton (Warren)
Bernard A., b. 1/25/1919 in Warren; fourth; Henry Harvey (laborer,
Chazy, NY) and Nancy E. Houghton (Manchester)
Joseph Herbert, b. 2/10/1913 in Warren; second; Henry Harvey
(engineer, Rouses Pt., NY) and Nancy Houghton (Manchester)
Pauline E., b. 7/11/1916 in Warren; third; Henry H. Harvey
(engineer, Chiesie, NY) and Nancy Houghton (Manchester)

HATCH,

Barbara, b. 7/11/1918 in Warren; third; Fairfax Hatch (clerk, Waltham, MA) and Claribel Clark (Warren)

Diane Lynn, b. 11/26/1979 in Haverhill; Stephen Wilder Hatch (28) and Sharon Ann Babbit (23)

Geraldine, b. 10/18/1915 in Warren; second; Fairfax Hatch (clerk, Waltham, MA) and Claribel Clark (Warren)

Malena Denise, b. 5/20/1985 in Hanover; Stephen W. Hatch (33) and Sharon A. Babbit (29)

Winston Fais, b. 4/5/1927; fifth; Fairfax Hatch (merchant, Waltham, MA) and Claribel Clark (Warren)

HAVELOCK,

Earl Lawrence, b. 5/1/1947 in Warren; ninth; James Havelock (mechanic, Howland, ME) and Marjorie A. Phinney (Millbridge, ME)

HEAD,

son, b. 4/21/1896 in Warren; Charles W. Head (laborer, 19, Boone, IA) and Alice M. Bartlett (22, Bath)

son, b. 7/27/1899 in Warren; second; Charles W. Head (laborer, 26, Iowa) and Alice M. Bartlett (24, Bath)

daughter, b. 4/19/1904 in Warren; first; Archie A. Head (clerk, 27, Hooksett) and Mabel S. Gerald (25, Hyde Park, MA)

stillborn child, b. 4/7/1908; second; Archie A. Head (liquor dealer, 30, Hooksett) and Mabel Geralds (28, Hyde Park)

Francis A., b. 7/30/1909 in Warren; second; Archie A. Head (hotel keeper, Hooksett) and Mabel Gerald (Hyde Park, MA)

John Loren, b. 4/14/1913 in Warren; fourth; Archie A. Head (farmer, Hooksett) and Mabel S. Gerald (Hyde Park, MA)

Muriel A., b. 9/7/1914 in Warren; fifth; Archie A. Head (farmer, Hooksett) and Mabel S. Gerald (Hyde Park, MA)

HEATH,

daughter, b. 1/21/1904 in Warren; fourth; Joshua M. Heath (farmer, 35, Warren) and Ada M. Chase (32, Wentworth)

son, b. 10/11/1913 in Warren; first; Etta Heath (Piermont)

Arthur George, b. 1/16/1958; fifth; Elmer Herbert Heath (laborer sawmill) and Jennie M. Raymond

Charles A., b. 5/22/1967; second; Raymond E. Heath (IPC Bristol, Woodsville) and Irma I. Angers (Laconia)

42

Crystal Rose, b. 4/19/1984 in Franklin; Arthur George Heath (26) and Robin Jill Russell (26)

Donna Marie, b. 6/6/1951; third; Elmer Herbert Heath (NH) and Jennie May Raymond (MA)

Esther G., b. 11/18/1939; first; Elmer H. Heath (laborer, Warren) and Jennie M. Raymond (Leominster, MA)

Myrtle Mae, b. 6/26/1981 in Plymouth; Raymond Elmer Heath (NH) and Irma Irene Angers (NH)

Raymond E., Jr., b. 5/12/1965; first; Raymond Heath (IPC operator, Woodsville) and Irma I. Angers (Laconia)

Raymond Elmer, b. 3/9/1942; second; Elmer Herbert Heath (fireman, Warren) and Jennie Mae Raymond (Leominster, MA)

Trudy Lee, b. 4/28/1956; fourth; Elmer H. Heath (sawyer saw mill, Warren) and Jennie M. Raymond (Leominster, MA)

HEATLEY,
Crystal Joy, b. 11/15/1979 in Haverhill; Grant Ross Heatley (25) and Sandra Mae Roulx (26)

HEITZ,
Steven Joseph, b. 4/16/1971 in Haverhill; George James Heitz (NY) and Ann Alice Marley (NY)

HIBBARD,
Elaine Marie, b. 6/21/1954; first; Lloyd C. Hibbard (truck driver, Piermont) and Eudora M. Wetherbee (Warren)

Lawrence Lloyd, b. 4/27/1956; second; Lloyd C. Hibbard (truck driver, Piermont) and Eudora M. Wetherbee (Warren)

Michael Lloyd, b. 1/2/1981 in Haverhill; Lawrence Lloyd Hibbard (NH) and Kimberly Jayne Burnham (NH)

Nicholas Royal, b. 10/5/1982 in Haverhill; Lawrence Lloyd Hibbard (NH) and Kimberly Jane Burnham (NH)

HIGGINS,
David Allen, b. 1/6/1992 in Plymouth; Michael Scott Higgins (27) and Chardell Marie Tash (23)

William H., b. 9/27/1939; first; Richard W. Higgins (common laborer, Barnet, VT) and Agnes M. Lombard (Barre, VT); residence - Barre, VT

HIGHT,
Glenna M., b. 2/12/1936; first; Arthur Hight (Laconia) and Shirley
Manion (Wentworth)
Linwood G., b. 1/31/1939; second; Arthur L. Hight (laborer in woods,
NH) and Shirley E. Manion (Wentworth)
Margaret Myrle, b. 3/21/1925; second; William R. Hight (laborer, W.
Topsham, VT) and Iva Smith (Warren)
Marilyn Ann, b. 2/16/1940; third; Arthur L. Hight (laborer) and Shirley
E. Manion (Wentworth)
Michael Clarence, b. 6/27/1995 in Heidelberg, Germany; Benjamin
Vernon Hight (20) and Melissa G. Crosby (27)
Nathan Thomas, b. 6/7/1981 in Haverhill; George Thomas Hight (39)
and Patricia Ann Pease (28)
Steven Glynn, b. 3/27/1954; first; William R. Hight, Jr. (car
salesman, Warren) and Nancy Jane Sleeper (Hanover)
Tari Lynn, b. 1/5/1958; third; William Rogers Hight, Jr. (repairman
tel.) and Nancy Jane Sleeper
Wanda Lee, b. 9/20/1956; second; William R. Hight, Jr. (NE Tel &
Tel Co., Warren) and Nancy Jane Sleeper (Hanover)
William Rogers, b. 2/15/1927; third; William R. Hight (laborer, W.
Topsham, VT) and Iva D. Smith (Warren)

HILDRETH,
daughter, b. 11/1/1898 in Warren; third; Ed. E. Hildreth (carpenter,
37, Haverhill) and Ida S. Flanders (32, Warren)
daughter, b. 8/9/1906 in Warren; third; Charles L. Hildreth
(carpenter, 28, Haverhill) and Electa Boynton (21, Warren)
child, b. 10/2/1908; fourth; Charles Hildreth (farmer, 30, Haverhill)
and Mary E. Boynton (23, Warren)
daughter, b. 5/11/1924; fourth; Edwin Hildreth (laborer, Warren) and
Marguerite Veasey (Bristol)
Blanche I., b. 6/22/1930; fifth; William E. Hildreth (chauffeur,
Warren) and Marguerite Veazey (Bristol)
David Wayne, b. 9/19/1949 in Plymouth; fourth; Harold Linwood
Hildreth (laborer, Warren) and Doris Audrey Perry (Franklin)
Ed., b. 10/26/1893 in Warren; Elroy E. Hildreth (farmer, 33,
Haverhill) and Ida Flanders (28, Warren)
Edward Leroy, b. 7/20/1917 in Warren; first; William E. Hildreth
(chauffeur, Warren) and Margaret Veasy (Bristol)
Glenna L., b. 4/17/1937; sixth; William E. Hildreth (Warren) and
Margaret G. Veazey (Bristol)

Gwendolin May, b. 7/23/1902 in Warren; stillborn; first; Charles L. Hildreth (mechanic, 24, Haverhill) and Mary E. Boynton (17, Warren)

Harold Linwood, b. 4/19/1922; second; W. E. Hildreth (chauffeur, Warren) and Margaret Veasey (Bristol)

Mary Ellen, b. 8/9/1948 in Plymouth; third; Harold L. Hildreth (state highway, Warren) and Doris Audrey Perry (Franklin)

Paula Yvonne, b. 4/22/1969 in Plymouth; David Wayne Hildreth (NH) and Patricia Ellen Smith (MA)

Priscilla Phillis, b. 9/17/1946 in Plymouth; first; Harold Linwood Hildreth (state hy. d., Warren) and Doris Audrey Perry (Franklin)

HILL,
Leslie Hervie, Jr., b. 3/25/1948 in Plymouth; fourth; Leslie Hervie Hill (logger, Castleton, VT) and Amelia Bessie Wheeler (Langdon)

Nancy Lee, b. 7/29/1957; third; Oscar Bowman Hill (mill hand, Piermont) and Eleanor D. O'Keefe (Grafton)

Oscar Ervin, b. 2/14/1955; second; Oscar Bowman Hill (laborer, Piermont) and Eleanor D. O'Keefe (Grafton)

HILLIARD,
daughter, b. 1/18/1925; second; Joseph Hilliard (laborer, Hill) and Leona Shortt (Warren)

daughter, b. 2/14/1927; third; Joseph Hilliard (laborer, Hill) and Leona Shortt (Warren)

Edward J., b. 3/1/1933; fourth; Joseph N. Hilliard (woodsman, Hill) and Leona Shortt (Warren)

Marion Helen, b. 1/10/1924; first; Joseph Hilliard (laborer, Hill) and Leona Shortt (Warren)

HODGDON,
daughter, b. 8/6/1891 in Warren; first; Charles D. Hodgdon (laborer, 21) and Maggie R. Sinclair (16)

HOLDEN,
Kara Jeanne, b. 5/20/1982 in Haverhill; Stanley Frederick Holden (NH) and Terry Agnes Chase (NH)

HOLLIDAY,

Carla Marie, b. 4/26/1973 in Haverhill; John Douglas Holliday (Canada) and Rosalie Ann Bailey (ME)

HORTON,

Emma Lee, b. 9/6/1990 in Lebanon; Michael Eugene Horton (41) and Peggy Casper (38)

HOUGHTON,

daughter, b. 6/1/1925; first; Harry Houghton (laborer, Cabot, VT) and Helen Chasson (Warren)

Edna, b. 3/20/1887 in Warren; Edwin L. Houghton (farmer, 48, Thetford, VT) and Delia A. Wolcott (36, Concord)

Herbert W., b. 8/25/1891 in Warren; first; E. L. Houghton (farming, 32, Thetford, VT) and Delia Wolcott (40, Concord)

HOWARD,

Betina Marguerite, b. 5/16/1923; second; Elroy Howard (photographer, Barrington) and Marguerite Hildreth (Warren)

Ethelyn Lowren, b. 7/19/1921 in Warren; first; Elroy C. Howard (photographer, Barrington) and Marguerite Hildreth (Lakeport)

Sarah Joan, b. 7/22/1974 in Plymouth; Earl Sampson Howard (43) and Joan S. Simonatis (32)

Theresea Inez, b. 7/15/1921 in Warren; first; Hollis A. Howard (telegraph op., Orford) and Hattie Coumor (W. Thornton)

HOWLAND,

Alice E., b. 1/26/1895 in Warren; John A. Howland (miller, 27, Woodstock, VT) and Mary M. Eastman (25, Henniker)

Arthur E., b. 10/3/1893 in Warren; John A. Howland (miller, 25, Woodstock, VT) and Mary M. Eastman (24, Henniker)

J. W. [son], b. 5/23/1896 in Warren; John Howland (miller, 28, Woodstock, VT) and Mary H. Eastman (27, Henniker)

HUNKINS,

Corinne Evelyn, b. 4/6/1926; first; Dana Hunkins (electrician, Groton) and Eva Currie (Piermont)

HURST,

Randi Jean, b. 11/25/1986; Russell Norman Hurst, Jr. (31) and Lisa Jane MacDonald (25)

IMHOFF,
Benjamin Ross, b. 12/24/1980 in Hanover; David William Imhoff (27) and Diane Lee Evenson (26)

INGALLS,
son, b. 2/26/1905 in Warren; first; Guy H. Ingalls (blacksmith, 28, Canada) and Eva B. Short (Thetford, VT)
Roy E., b. 4/6/1907 in Warren; second; Guy H. Ingalls (carpenter, 30, Canada) and Eva B. Short (19)

JACKSON,
Hamilton C., b. 11/14/1904 in Warren; first; Frank C. Jackson (laborer, 27, Belfast, ME) and Edith B. Colby (24, Whitefield)

JENKS,
son, b. 4/8/1900 in Warren; fifth; William F. Jenks (laborer, 28, Lyme) and Emma D. Smith (21, Lyme)

JESSEMAN,
son, b. 5/7/1923; second; Raymond Jesseman (trackman, Plymouth) and Marguerite Whitcher (Warren)
daughter, b. 1/8/1934; third; Elmer Jesseman (laborer, Newbury, VT) and May Barry (Warren)
Alan David, b. 11/7/1950 in Laconia; first; Elmer Whitcher Jesseman (truck driver, NH) and Hazel Emma Buskey (NH)
Brian Keith, b. 2/24/1958; third; Elmer W. Jesseman (trucking) and Hazel Emma Buskey
Clarice M., b. 4/20/1933; second; Elmer Jesseman (laborer, Newbury, VT) and Ora May Barry (Warren)
Gary Donald, b. 8/7/1954; first; Raymond Jesseman, Jr. (fish culturist, NH) and Dorothy E. Libbey (NH)
Neil E., b. 12/25/1937; fourth; Elmer C. Jesseman (Newbury, VT) and Ora May Barry (Warren)
Raymond J., b. 6/15/1919 in Warren; first; Raymond Jesseman (trackman, Bridgewater) and Margaret L. Whitcher (Warren)
Richard E., b. 8/16/1929; first; Elmer C. Jesseman (laborer, Newbury, VT) and Ora May Barry (Warren)
Stanley W., b. 8/14/1931; third; Raymond Jesseman (RR trackman, Plymouth) and Margaret L. Whitcher (Warren)
Susan Diana, b. 5/25/1955; second; Elmer W. Jesseman (trucking, NH) and Hazel Emma Buskey (NH)

JEWELL,
daughter, b. 2/5/1892 in Warren; Frank E. Jewell (sawyer, 35, Warren) and Eva Cross (19, Whitefield)
Robin Sue, b. 6/3/1953; first; Robert Leonard Jewell (NH) and Verla Jean Peoples (NH)

JOHNSON,
son, b. 10/8/1904 in Warren; fifth; Bert W. Johnson (stat. engineer, 34, Orford) and Evelyn M. Gove (29, Wentworth)
son, b. 8/25/1906 in Warren; sixth; Berton Johnson (machinist, 39, Orford) and Evelyn M. Gove (32, Wentworth)
child, b. 2/6/1908; seventh; Berton W. Johnson (machinist, 37, Orford) and Eveline Gove (33, Wentworth)
son, b. 5/4/1910; eighth; Berton Johnson (engineer, 40, Orford) and Evelyn Gove (Wentworth)
son, b. 1/2/1912 in Warren; ninth; Bert Johnson (electrician, Orford) and Evelyn Gove (Wentworth)
Alice E., b. 3/29/1901 in Warren; fourth; Bert W. Johnson (electrician, 28, Orford) and Mary E. Gove (26, Wentworth)
Helen E., b. 6/3/1899 in Warren; third; Burton Johnson (electrician, 29, Orford) and Eveline Gove (25, Wentworth)
Lawrence, b. 3/3/1897 in Warren; second; Berton Johnson (laborer, 27, Orford) and Evelyn Gove (23, Wentworth)
Lucille, b. 7/31/1943; third; Homer Cecil Johnson (state trooper, Burlington, VT) and Marjorie Daniels (Rochester)

JOLIN,
son, b. 3/29/1899 in Warren; first; Joseph Jolin (farmer, 27, Quebec) and Mary E. Gagne (17, Bath)

JONES,
Josephine Anne, b. 10/3/1951; second; Daniel Nelson Jones (Wentworth) and Dorothy Hildreth (Newport)

KANE,
son, b. 7/30/1892 in Warren; Moses Kane (22) and Cora A. ----- (19, Warren); residence - Laconia

KAZENAS,
Leila Rene, b. 6/18/2002 in Plymouth; Audrius Kazenas and Dalia Kazenas

KELLEY,
son, b. 7/14/1889 in Warren; John H. Kelley (farmer, 25, Ellsworth) and Georgia Kelly (27, Rumney)
daughter, b. 10/17/1892 in Warren; John H. Kelley (laborer, 28) and Effie L. Annis (20, Warren)
John Mudgett, b. 10/21/1895 in Warren; first; John Kelley (farmer, 31, Ellsworth) and Mary Bennett (20, Thornton)

KEMP,
son, b. 12/22/1902 in Warren; first; Clarence W. Kemp (laborer, 22, Lyme) and Annie B. Smith (17, Sanbornton)
daughter, b. 7/6/1905 in Warren; second; Clarence W. Kemp (mill hand, 25, Lyme) and Annie B. Smith (Sanbornton)

KENNEDY,
Charlene, b. 10/29/1957; first; Nelson L. Kennedy (laborer, Fairlee, VT) and Lora Lee Whitcher (Warren)
Lorie Ann, b. 8/8/1962; third; Nelson Lee Kennedy (laborer, Fairlee, VT) and Loralee Whitcher (Warren)
Nelson Leo, Jr., b. 12/11/1959; second; Nelson L. Kennedy, Sr. (laborer, Fairlee, VT) and Lora Lee Whitcher (Warren)

KEYSAR,
stillborn son, b. 10/26/1937; third; Miles H. Keysar (Colebrook) and Bertha N. Snelgrove (Wentworth)
Donald Berkley, b. 8/12/1948 in Plymouth; sixth; Miles Herman Keysar (laborer, Colebrook) and Bertha Nellie Snelgrove (Warren)
Eleanor M., b. 8/17/1915 in Warren; first; Royal E. Keysar (clerk, Colebrook) and Marion L. Averill (Lakeport)
Franklin F., b. 1/22/1939; fourth; Miles H. Keysar (laborer, farmer, Colebrook) and Bertha N. Snelgrove (Warren)
Gary Michael, b. 4/4/1957; seventh; Miles N. Keysar (retired, Colebrook) and Bertha N. Snelgrove (Warren)
Kellie Lynn, b. 3/29/1975 in Plymouth; Donald Berkley Keysar (26) and Meca Ann Williams (24)
Patti Lee, b. 2/4/1955; seventh; Miles H. Keysar (retired, NH) and Bertha N. Snelgrove (NH)
Philip E., b. 9/1/1935; second; Miles H. Keysar (Colebrook) and Bertha Snelgrove (Warren)

Shirley Marie, b. 9/20/1919 in Warren; second; Royal E. Keysar (farmer, Colebrook) and Marion L. Averill (Lakeport)

KINERSON,
Margaret, b. 6/10/1939; first; Kenneth Kinerson (salesman, Peacham, VT) and Priscilla Blodgett (Peacham, VT)

KING,
Arthur Irwin, b. 11/10/1931; second; Arthur J. King (US mail carrier, Canterbury) and Irene H. Burns (St. Anthony, Texas)
Francis Russell, b. 5/8/1933; third; Arthur J. King (laborer, Canterbury) and Irene H. Burns (St. Anthony, Texas)

KINSLEY,
Alberta Ruth, b. 5/20/1932; second; Chester Kinsley (farmer, Everett, MA) and Ethel M. Sanborn (Rumney); residence - W. Plymouth
Frederick M., b. 7/1/1930; first; Chester R. Kinsley (weaver, Everett, MA) and ----- Sanborn (Plymouth, MA)

KITTREDGE,
daughter, b. 6/14/1900 in Warren; first; Carlton S. Kittredge (merchant, 33, Waldon, VT) and Julia M. Morse (26, Chester)

KNAPP,
son, b. 1/3/1888 in Warren; Fred Knapp (farmer, 32, Piermont) and Etta S. Harris (27, Warren); residence - Piermont
Jaben Dexter, b. 9/14/1979 in Haverhill; Dexter Allen Knapp (32) and Sandra Faye Holden (31)

KOKAL,
Barbara Gail, b. 7/10/1942; first; Lewis J. Kokal (machinist, NJ) and Eva Rose M. Arruda (Fall River, MA); residence - New Brunswick, NJ

KRAMER,
William Charles, b. 8/22/1947 in Haverhill; first; William Charles Kramer (woodsman, Orwigsbury, PA) and Joyce Ruth Cutting (Warren)

KROMMES,
Taryn Lee, b. 11/27/1988 in Plymouth; David Allen Krommes (30) and Donna May Dennison (29)

KRUSE,
Kimberly Ann, b. 6/1/1961; second; Donald Ray Kruse (USAF, Duluth, MN) and Carole Anne Rogers (Medford, MA)

KYDD,
daughter, b. 3/11/1913 in Warren; third; David Kydd (farmer, Scotland) and Lena McLauchlin (Scotland)
John M., b. 6/22/1909 in Warren; second; David Kydd (barber, Scotland) and C. L. McLauchlin (Scotland)
Mary Helen R., b. 8/30/1906 in Warren; first; David Kydd (barber, 38, Scotland) and C. I. McLauchlen (30, Scotland)

LAAUWE,
Brandy Alexis, b. 4/18/1999 in Lebanon; William Laauwe and Megan Quinn
Casey Scott, b. 5/28/1999 in Lebanon; Brandt Laauwe and Denise Beam

LABELL,
Pauline Maude, b. 4/19/1921 in Warren; sixth; Feed LaBell (laborer, Bangor, ME) and Georgie Buzzell (Aubrey, PQ)

LABOUNTY,
Donna K., b. 9/9/1943; first; Guy Earl Labounty (farmer, Irasburg, VT) and Madeline R. Hood (Groton, VT)

LABRIE,
Joseph R., Jr., b. 4/5/1946 in Warren; second; Joseph R. Labrie (fireman, Canada) and Frances E. Shortt (Warren); residence - Ashland
Milton James, b. 3/11/1953; sixth; Joseph Romeo Labrie (Canada) and Frances Ellen Shortt (Warren)
Roger Shortt, b. 12/27/1947 in Warren; third; Joseph R. Labrie (mill laborer, Canada) and Frances E. Shortt (Warren); residence - Ashland

LADD,

Avis Amoetta, b. 4/22/1930; first; Oscar Ladd (laborer, Pike) and
Lindsie Mae Perry (Haverhill); residence - Orford
Ona, b. 8/24/1898 in Warren; first; Elmer E. Ladd (physician, 30,
Nashua) and H. Mabel Church (34, Braintree, VT)

LADUE,

daughter, b. 2/13/1911 in Warren; second; Levi James Ladue
(farmer, Hyde Park, VT) and Dora Smith (Orford)

LAFOE,

daughter, b. 9/6/1904 in Warren; third; Jack Lafoe (farmer, 37,
Hartford, CT) and Lovis Morrison (24)
son, b. 7/1/1913 in Warren; seventh; John E. Lafoe (laborer,
Hartford, CT) and Rose Morrison (Lexington, VT)
Beatrice L., b. 2/24/1917 in Warren; ninth; John E. LaFoe (laborer,
Hartford, CT) and Rosie Morrison (Lemington, VT)

LALLY,

Bridget Francis, b. 10/18/1992 in Lebanon; Mark Owen Lally (31)
and Joan Marie Bourgoin (22)

LAMOTHE,

Alana Ann, b. 7/28/1972 in Haverhill; Peter Edward LaMothe (NH)
and Marie Delia Thompson (NH)
Lisa Marie, b. 2/25/1965; second; Peter E. Lamothe (carpenter,
Warren) and Marie D. Thompson (Plymouth)
Peter E., b. 11/23/1936; first; Roderick Lamothe (Winchendon, MA)
and Bernice M. Lupien (Warren)
Sherri Lee, b. 2/13/1963; first; Peter Lamothe (carpenter, Warren)
and Marie D. Thompson (Plymouth)

LANE,

Floyd Albert, b. 6/27/1916 in Warren; second; Earl T. Lane
(trackman, PQ) and Gertrude Bell (Holland, VT)

LAPIERRE,

Dolores D., b. 9/22/1934; first; Albert Lapierre (mechanic, Lawrence,
MA) and Irene A. Lambert (Manchester)

LAVOY,

George, b. 7/18/1887 in Benton; Lewis Lavoy (farmer, Temisguata Lake) and Carrie -----

LEE,

Jacob Edward, b. 9/17/1995 in Lebanon; Joshua Lee (22) and Meredith Ball (22)

LESTER,

Benjamin James, b. 1/21/1979 in Hanover; John Gregory Lester (23) and Linda Lee Tapper (22)

LIBBEY,

son, b. 2/1/1888 in Warren; Nelson Libbey (farming, Warren) and Lucia A. Whiteman (Warren)

son, b. 4/20/1889 in Warren; Albin Libbey (laborer, 33, Warren) and Rachael Stewart (29, Warren)

daughter, b. 6/24/1896 in Warren; Ira H. Libbey (farmer, 44, Warren) and Lucia Whiteman (38, Warren)

daughter, b. 7/2/1899 in Warren; ninth; Ira N. Libbey (carpenter, 42, Warren) and Fanny Whiteman (41, Warren)

daughter, b. 7/1/1923; second; Natt Libbey (farmer, Goffstown) and Florence Balch (Warren)

Blanche I., b. 5/23/1930; second; Elmer M. Libbey (F & G ward., Warren) and Vera V. Ball (Granville, VT)

Donald Everett, b. 4/23/1921 in Warren; first; Natt E. Libbey (carpenter, Warren) and Florence B. Balch (Goffstown)

Grover Elmer, b. 6/2/1928; first; Elmer Morrill Libbey (laborer, Bath) and Vera Viola Ball (Granville, VT)

Harold E., b. 12/8/1933; fourth; Elmer M. Libbey (laborer, Bath) and Vera B. Ball (Grantville, VT)

Mary C., b. 3/26/1930; third; Earl B. Libbey (garage prop., Wentworth) and Elsie McCloud (Colebrook)

Robert Merrill, b. 9/3/1902 in Warren; first; Ralph Libbey (farmer, 32, Warren) and Eda R. Grammont (18, Orford)

Roger E., b. 1/25/1932; third; Elmer M. Libbey (laborer, Bath) and Vera V. Ball (Granville, VT)

LIBBY,

Grover Basil, b. 9/27/1955; first; Grover Almer Libby (truck driver, Warren) and Harriet Sadie Ames (Wentworth)

Kristal Jean, b. 3/6/1981 in Haverhill; Grover Basil Libby (25) and
Vicki Gay Brooks (24)
Ronald Edwin, b. 6/18/1960; first; Harold Edwin Libby (laborer,
Glencliff) and Rebecca Sue Corliss (Berwick, ME)
Susan Melissa, b. 11/22/1971 in Haverhill; Albert Earl Libby (NH)
and Melissa Sue Wetherbee (NH)
Travis James, b. 11/11/1982 in Haverhill; Grover Basil Libby (NH)
and Vicki Gay Brooks (NH)

LITTLE,
stillborn son, b. 1/18/1887 in Warren; first; George M. Little
(clergyman, Warren) and Polly T. ----- (Lebanon)
stillborn son, b. 3/–/1897 in Warren; second; Ernest R. Little (tel.
operat., 28, Haverhill) and Hattie Hayward (28, Pembroke)
son, b. 11/30/1899 in Warren; third; Ernest R. Little (telegrapher, 31,
Haverhill) and Hattie Hayward (30, Pembroke); residence -
Summit
Ethel M., b. 7/4/1907 in Warren; Charles F. Little (depot master, 37,
Warren) and Mary A. Howard (24, Lyme)
Frank Howard, b. 7/5/1901 in Warren; third; Charles F. Little
(telegraph operator, 30, Warren) and Mary A. Howard (28,
Lyme)
Marion G., b. 8/22/1899 in Warren; second; Charles F. Little
(telegraphing, 29, Warren) and Mary Howard (26, Lyme);
residence - Summit

LOCKMAN,
son, b. 6/18/1903 in Warren; third; William H. Lockman (carpenter,
31, Staten Island) and Caroline Crooker (24, Port Washington)

LONGCHAMPS,
Michael David, b. 12/26/1966; fifth; Leo Longchamps (VT) and Alma
M. Baggett (Warren)

LOWE,
Gavin Benjamin, b. 3/20/2004 in Plymouth; Benjamin Lowe and
Virginia Davis

LUGTON,
Shaun Michael, b. 5/17/1978 in Haverhill; Russell Earl Lugton (26)
and Judith Ann Quinlan (21)

LUND,
daughter, b. 9/9/1900 in Warren; third; Ed Lund (conductor, 39, Warren) and Cora A. Willey (38, Warren)
son, b. 7/25/1903 in Warren; fourth; Edward A. Lund (RR conductor, 44, Warren) and Cora A. Willey (40, Warren)
John E., b. 6/5/1893 in Warren; Ed Lund (RR man, 33, Warren) and Cora A. Willey (30, Warren)

LUPIEN,
stillborn son, b. 4/21/1925; third; Edward R. Lupien (mica mfg., Newbury, VT) and India Elliott (Warren)
Bernadette Meanie, b. 6/9/1926; fourth; Edward R. Lupien (mica crystal co., Newbury, VT) and India Elliott (Warren)
Edward R., Jr., b. 8/16/1928; fifth; Edward Rowe Lupien (supt. grist mill, Newbury, VT) and India Maud Elliott (Warren)
Edwin Lewis, b. 2/29/1913 (sic) in Warren; second; Edward Lupien (carpenter, Newbury, VT) and India Elliott (Warren)
Francis Mahala, b. 11/15/1910; first; Edward Lupien (carpenter, 25, Newbury, VT) and India Elliott (Warren)

MACDONALD,
Ashley Beatrice, b. 5/9/1992 in Lebanon; Barry Scot MacDonald (28) and Kathy Lynn Cass (23)
Barry Scot, b. 6/22/1964; fifth; John MacDonald (paper mill, Plymouth) and Grace H. Tewksbury (Warren)
Deborah Jean, b. 1/26/1955; fourth; John H. MacDonald (truck driver, Plymouth) and Grace H. Tewksbury (Warren)
John H., 3rd, b. 5/28/1947 in Warren; second; John H. MacDonald (truck driver, Plymouth) and Grace H. Tewksbury (Warren)
Sharon Lee, b. 8/2/1950 in Plymouth; third; John Herbert MacDonald (laborer, Plymouth) and Grace Helena Tewksbury (Warren)
Stephanie Lynn, b. 9/25/1996 in Lebanon; Barry Scot MacDonald (32) and Kathy Lynn Cass (27)
Tristan Elizabeth F., b. 5/5/1995 in Lebanon; Barry Scot MacDonald (31) and Kathy Lynn Cass (26)

MADEIROS,
Carolyn B., b. 3/10/1939; third; Ralph Madeiros (truck driver, Taunton, MA) and Barbara Whitcher (Warren)
Gloria J., b. 1/11/1937; first; Ralph Madeiros (Taunton, MA) and Barbara Whitcher (Warren)

Ralph, Jr., b. 4/8/1938; second; Ralph F. Madeiros (laborer, Taunton, MA) and Barbara Whitcher (Warren)

MAHER,
Rene Julien, b. 3/11/1995 in Concord; Thomas Mitten Maher (31) and Janine Sandra Leduc (32)
Thomas Harley, b. 12/21/1987 in Plymouth; Thomas Mitten Maher (23) and Janine Sandra Leduc (24)

MANSUR,
Gail Elizabeth, b. 4/18/1949 in Plymouth; first; Arthur John Mansur (soldier, Lawrence, MA) and Priscilla Doane Cutting (Warren)

MARGRIM,
David A., b. 1/19/1898 in Warren; second; Henry G. Margrim (lumberman, 24, Paris, France) and Annie Gagne (25, Canada)

MARQUIS,
Anne Marie, b. 4/23/1959; second; Joseph Marquis (woodsman, St. Agatha, ME) and Janice Lois Cutting (Woodsville)
Dennis C., b. 3/31/1962; fourth; Joseph Marquis (woodsman, St. Agatha, ME) and Janice Lois Cutting (Woodsville)
Joseph, b. 11/3/1960; third; Joseph Marquis (woodsman, St. Agatha, ME) and Janice Lois Cutting (Woodsville)

MARSH,
daughter, b. 8/28/1900 in Warren; sixth; George R. Marsh (carpenter, 50, Dixville, ME) and Sarah Daniels (36, Bristol, VT)
Carol Jean, b. 12/3/1946 in Plymouth; first; William Marsh (US Army, Stewartstown) and Barbara E. Morrison (Warren)
Galen Roy, b. 8/24/1960; fourth; Ernest E. Marsh (logger, Enfield) and Erma May Tarr (Marlboro)
Gerald Calvin, b. 1/18/1968 in Hanover; Gene Leonard Marsh (NH) and Jacqueline Gay Snyder (MA)

MARSTON,
daughter, b. 5/4/1888 in Warren; second; Ezra L. Marston (sawyer, 32, Warren) and Emma Batchelder (29, Warren)
Jean Margaret, b. 2/5/1952; second; Theodore Ezra Marston (NH) and Gladys Featherstone Payne (Kent, England)

Neil C., b. 11/7/1960; third; Theodore E. Marston (NH probation officer, Warren) and Gladys F. Payne (England)
Pauline Elizabeth, b. 4/24/1949 in Plymouth; first; Theodore Ezra Marston (teacher, Warren) and Gladys Featherstone Payne (Orpington, England)
Theodore E. K., b. 5/27/1914 in Warren; first; Ezra L. Marston (board sawyer, Warren) and Helen G. Kemp (Lyme)

MARTIN,
daughter, b. 4/3/1890 in Warren; first; Henry D. Martin (farming) and Ellen Martin
Barbara Evelyn, b. 8/23/1959; second; Richard A. Martin (laborer, Bloomfield, VT) and Elizabeth C. Ames (Warren)
Carol Ann, b. 11/5/1958; first; Richard A. Martin (laborer) and Elizabeth C. Ames
Gloria Jean, b. 2/4/1945 in Plymouth; first; Rosario Martin (carpenter) and Helen Elizabeth Hildreth (Warren)
Sandra Jane, b. 1/21/1948 in Warren; second; Rosario Martin (carpenter) and Helen Hildreth (Warren); residence - Pike
Sandra Lee, b. 8/13/1962; third; Richard A. Martin (dye setter, Bloomfield, VT) and Elizabeth C. Ames (Warren)

MATHEWSON,
child, b. 10/7/1908; second; Charles C. Mathewson (dentist, 47, Acworth) and G. Eastman (41, Littleton)
Avis D., b. 4/26/1920 in Warren; first; Henry G. Mathewson (laborer, Unity) and Ivie E. Reed (Wentworth)
Ila May, b. 1/23/1914 in Warren; first; Elliott Matheson (student) and Marguerite Veasey (Bristol)

MATSON,
Carol J., b. 5/22/1938; second; John Milton Matson (greens keeper, W. Newton, MA) and Viney T. Strojny (Taunton, MA)
James Louis, b. 10/27/1943; fourth; John Milton Matson (caretaker, Newton Ctr., MA) and Viney T. Strojny (Taunton, MA)
John M., Jr., b. 10/27/1943; third; John Milton Matson (caretaker, Newton Ctr., MA) and Viney T. Strojny (Taunton, MA)
Shirley A., b. 5/22/1938; first; John Milton Matson (greens keeper, W. Newton, MA) and Viney T. Strojny (Taunton, MA)

MAUNULA,

Wanda Lee, b. 7/8/1949 in Haverhill; first; Tavo John Maunula (Norwood, MA) and Ardeth May Simpson (Haverhill)

MAWSON,

Mark Joseph, b. 9/24/1959; first; Robert James Mawson (teacher, Lawrence, MA) and Elinor Joyce Perfect (Exeter)

MAYHEW,

Hazel Louise, b. 6/17/1923; first; J. J. Mayhew (laborer) and Mary Short (Warren)

McCUTCHEON,

son, b. 3/15/1889 in Warren; David McCutcheon (laborer, Canada)

McDONALD,

Christopher Boyd, b. 10/5/1969 in Warren; Boyd McDonald (NH) and Anne Marie House (NH)

McISAAC,

son, b. 6/28/1897 in Warren; first; Henry McIsaac (laborer, 25, Porthood Co.) and Mabel Eastman (22, Warren)

daughter, b. 6/19/1899 in Warren; second; Henry McIsaac (teamster, 27, Cape Britain) and Mabelle L. Eastman (25, Warren)

son, b. 1/4/1925; first; Henry E. McIsaac (laborer, Warren) and Natalie Gallant (Warren)

McKAY,

Patricia Lou, b. 3/11/1947 in Plymouth; second; Clarence Andrew McKay (hotel waiter, McKinley, ME) and Esther Almina Whitcher (Warren)

McKINLEY,

daughter, b. 9/12/1904 in Warren; first; Ralph McKinley (mechanic, 21, Windsor, NS) and Susie E. Whitney (18, Groveton)

son, b. 11/13/1906 in Warren; second; Ralph McKinley (laborer, 22, Windsor, NS) and Susie E. Whitney (19, Northumberland)

child, b. 9/18/1908; third; Ralph McKinley (laborer, 24, NS) and Susie E. Whitney (22, Groveton)

McLAUGHLIN,
daughter, b. –/–/1892 in Warren; James McLaughlin (preacher, 25, PEI) and Mary J. McLeod (24)

McVETY,
daughter, b. 7/13/1892 in Warren; John E. McVety (farming, 38, Canada) and E. M. Baker (39, Canada)

McVITTY,
Beatrice C., b. 9/18/1887 in Warren; John E. McVitty (farmer, 32, St. Sylvester, PQ) and Eliza M. ----- (29, St. Sylvester, PQ)

MELLO,
Shawn David, b. 7/3/1972 in Haverhill; Frank Roderick Mello (MA) and Marilyn Ann Hight (NH)

MERREY,
Lewis Edward, b. 10/23/1931; first; James E. Merrey (laborer, Littleton) and Gladys M. Whitney (Lincoln)

MERRILL,
stillborn son, b. 4/1/1895 in Warren; fifth; Fred Merrill (farmer, Warren) and Lizzie Cummings (Warren)
son, b. 9/10/1896 in Warren; Fred J. Merrill (farmer, 38, Rumney) and L. B. Cummings (28, Warren)
son, b. 10/27/1897 in Warren; seventh; Fred Merrill (laborer, 39, Rumney) and Eliza B. Cummings (29, Warren)
son, b. 7/15/1899 in Warren; third; Velorious Merrill (laborer, 28, Dorchester) and Velma Follansbee (21, Orford)
son, b. 12/22/1899 in Warren; seventh; Fred J. Merrill (laborer, 40, Rumney) and Lizzie B. Cummings (30, Warren)
daughter, b. 2/21/1902 in Warren; eighth; Fred J. Merrill (farmer, 43, Rumney) and Lizzie B. Cummings (34, Warren)
son, b. 12/3/1903 in Warren; first; Earl Young (clerk, 26, Laconia) and Blanche E. Merrill (18, Warren)
daughter, b. 7/10/1904 in Warren; ninth; Fred J. Merrill (farmer, 47, Rumney) and Lizzie Cummings (37, Warren)
child, b. 5/6/1908; thirteenth; Fred J. Merrill (farmer, 50, Rumney) and Lizzie Cummings (40, Warren)
daughter, b. 1/6/1909 in Warren; first; Flossie Merrill (Warren)

daughter, b. 11/10/1910; first; John Merrill (telephone opr., Warren) and Hattie Elliott (Warren)

daughter, b. 5/17/1912 in Warren; fourteenth; Fred Merrill (farmer, Rumney) and Lizzie Cummings (Warren)

daughter, b. 10/8/1913 in Warren; first; Lyman Merrill (farmer, Warren) and Fanny Fifield (Warren)

son, b. 5/3/1924; fifth; Ernest Merrill (RR fireman, Warren) and Mildred Fifield (Warren)

Ernest E., b. 11/17/1919 in Warren; second; Ernest E. Merrill (fireman, Warren) and Mildred C. Fifield (Warren); residence - Woodsville

George B., b. 8/2/1930; sixth; Ernest E. Merrill (farmer, Warren) and Mildred C. Merrill (Glencliff)

Jesse Henry, b. 8/16/1913 in Warren; second; John Merrill (fire patrolman, Warren) and Hattie Elliott (Warren)

Joyce Mae, b. 9/4/1933; first; Reginald Ball (laborer, Landaff) and Lillian F. Merrill (Warren)

Lillian F., b. 7/24/1917 in Warren; Ernest E. Merrill (laborer, Warren) and Mildred Fifield (Warren)

Miriam Elizabeth, b. 4/8/1923; fourth; Earnest E. Merrill (RR fire., Warren) and Mildred Fifield (Glencliff)

Olga Luise, b. 11/20/1917 in Warren; second; Lyman G. Merrill (laborer, Warren) and Fannie S. Fifield (Warren)

Paul F., b. 2/6/1907 in Warren; twelfth; Fred J. Merrill (farmer, 48, Rumney) and Lizzie B. Cummings (38, Warren)

MILLER,
Kolby Cassel, b. 6/15/1991 in Plymouth; Todd Jeffrey Miller (33) and Dena Lee Cassel (30)

MINAERT,
Gayle Elizabeth, b. 10/6/1947 in Plymouth; Charles Theodore Winaert (garage mech., Manchester) and Gertrude Eugenia Gilman (Rochester, NY); residence - Manchester

MITCHELL,
daughter, b. 2/9/1906 in Warren; third; Napoleon Mitchell (laborer, 32, Canada) and Alice Jarvis (26, Canada)

MOODY,
Corrine Leigh, b. 6/2/1970 in Haverhill; Stephen Ross Moody (NH)
and Marlene Stevens (NH)
Duane E., b. 9/30/1967; first; Stephen R. Moody (construction,
Plymouth) and Marlene Stevens (Woodsville)
Lyle Clayton, b. 4/22/1923; first; Kenneth Moody (laborer, Tamworth)
and Marion Whitcher (Warren)
Margurette Ethel, b. 8/23/1924; second; Kenneth Moody (laborer,
Albany) and Marion Whitcher (Warren)
Michael Lyle, b. 5/17/1953; second; Lyle Clayton Moody (Warren)
and Jean Gertrude Lumsden (New York City)
Owen K., b. 8/19/1934; fourth; Kenneth V. Moody (laborer, Albany)
and Marion F. Whitcher (Warren)
Stephen Ross, b. 6/2/1947 in Plymouth; fifth; Kenneth V. Moody
(carpenter, Albany, NY) and Marion Whitcher (Warren)
Thelma V., b. 9/23/1930; third; Kenneth V. Moody (laborer, gar.,
Albany) and Marion F. Whitcher (Warren)

MOORE,
Grace Autumn, b. 3/8/2001 in Lebanon; Christopher Moore and Ami
Moore

MORRILL,
son, b. 6/28/1900 in Warren; third; Edmond M. Morrill (chemist, 31,
Deering, ME) and Charlotte W. Safford (31, Charlestown, MA)
son, b. 5/29/1904 in Warren; fourth; Edward N. Morrill (chemist, 35,
Deering, ME) and Charlotte Safford (36, Charlestown, MA)

MORRIS,
Amanda Lee, b. 5/29/1978 in Plymouth; R. Patrick Morris (19) and
Gretchen Melded Palmer (19)

MORRISON,
son, b. 10/7/1906 in Warren; third; Rodney Morrison (fireman, 36,
Halifax, NS) and Cora Merrill (32, Warren)
son, b. 5/31/1910; fifth; Rodney Morrison (fireman, 40, NS) and Cora
Merrill (Warren)
daughter, b. 2/2/1912 in Warren; fourth; Rodney Morrison (fireman,
NS) and Cora Merrill (Warren)
stillborn son, b. 7/7/1917 in Warren; fifth; Rodney Morrison
(lumberman, NS) and Cora A. Merrill (Warren)

son, b. 7/30/1924; fourth; John Morrison (HW dept., Groton) and
Myra Evans (Meredith); residence - Concord
Annie, b. 9/21/1907 in Warren; fourth; Rodney Morrison (farmer, 37,
NS) and Cora A. Merrill (33, Warren)
Barbara E., b. 4/20/1929; first; Tina Louise Morrison (Warren)
Chester A., b. 10/12/1918 in Warren; first; John H. Morrison (road
builder, Groton, VT) and Alice E. Plaisted (Meredith)
Donald E., b. 3/3/1932; first; Everett A. Morrison (forest guard,
Warren) and Frances Benson (Portland, ME)
Ellison K., b. 11/5/1897 in Warren; second; Louis R. Morrison (tel.
operat., 27, Montfort, WI) and Reiddell Clifford (21, Colebrook)
Gladice, b. 6/1/1896 in Warren; Lewis R. Morrison (tel. operator, 26,
Montford, WI) and Lysle R. Clifford (19, Colebrook)
Sarah Lynn, b. 2/10/1980 in Plymouth; Lee Alan Morrison (21) and
Lorie Lynn Filion (21)

MORSE,
daughter, b. 11/12/1897 in Warren; second; George Morse
(carpenter, 31, Cabot, VT) and Nellie Jewett (22, Ludlow, VT)

MOSES,
son, b. 7/22/1891 in Warren; fourth; John Moses (laborer, 40,
Chichester) and Viola F. Moses (34, Warren)
daughter, b. 12/4/1901 in Warren; second; Elmer O. Moses (farmer,
30, Warren) and Winnie B. Glines (27, Franconia)
daughter, b. 2/3/1906 in Warren; third; Elmer O. Moses (farmer, 35,
Warren) and Winnie B. Glines (32, Franconia)
daughter, b. 4/14/1913 in Warren; first; Clarence Moses (farmer,
Warren) and Lucy Fisher (England)
son, b. 2/16/1919 in Warren; fourth; Clarence H. Moses (farmer,
Warren) and Lucy Fisher (Manchester, England)
daughter, b. 2/26/1926; sixth; Clarence Moses (farmer, Warren) and
Lucy Fisher (Manchester, England)
Clarence H., Jr., b. 8/24/1932; eighth; Clarence H. Moses (teamster,
Warren) and Lucy Fisher (Manchester, England)
Florence J., b. 4/2/1917 in Warren; third; Clarence Moses (laborer,
Warren) and Lucy Fisher (Manchester, England) ·
George W., b. 9/23/1893 in Warren; John B. Moses (laborer, 42,
Chichester) and Viola F. Merrill (36, Warren)
Gladys E., b. 5/14/1907 in Warren; first; Clarence H. Moses (laborer,
21, Warren) and Lena M. Foote (17, Warren)

Iran M., b. 2/11/1896 in Warren; Fred A. Moses (c'ch'keeper, 22, Warren) and Stella A. Boynton (19, Warren)

Joseph Walter, b. 10/15/1921 in Warren; fifth; Clarence Moses (farmer, Warren) and Lucy Fisher (England)

Lawrence C., b. 12/22/1914 in Warren; second; Clarence H. Moses (farmer, Warren) and Lucy Fisher (Manchester, England)

May, b. 5/7/1928; seventh; Clarence H. Moses (laborer, Warren) and Lucy Fisher (Manchester, England)

Ralph William, b. 12/4/1913 in Warren; first; Anna Gale (Warren)

MOULTON,
Geraldine, b. 4/18/1937; sixth; Rockwood Moulton (Landaff) and Bernice C. Blandin (Ely, VT)

MURDOCK,
Walter J., b. 7/11/1906 in Warren; third; Jesse Murdock (laborer, 32, Portland, ME) and Mary Merchant (35, Alexandria)

MURPHY,
Angelica Marie, b. 4/30/1992 in Lebanon; Douglas Windsor Murphy, Jr. (24) and Myrtie Mae Heath (21)

MYERS,
Jacob Robert, b. 9/22/1988 in Plymouth; Robert James Myers, Jr. (28) and Nanci-Beth Hurst (27)

NEWTON,
Christopher Michael, b. 11/7/1990 in Plymouth; Jeffrey Scott Newton (22) and Penny Shortt (22)

Elizabeth Jane, b. 12/10/1988 in Plymouth; Jeffrey Scott Newton (20) and Penny Shortt (20)

Jason Mark, b. 7/2/1975 in Haverhill; Robert Henry Newton (33) and Sylvia Ann Carlson (32)

Justin Charles, b. 9/8/1972 in Haverhill; Robert Henry Newton (NH) and Sylvia Ann Carlson (IL)

NICOL,
son, b. 11/10/1905 in Warren; second; William B. Nicol (blacksmith, 37, NB) and Alice M. Libbey (Warren)

Berkley Charles, b. 2/19/1941; fourth; John H. Nicol (store clerk, Warren) and Marjorie A. Brown (Wentworth)

Charles Laurence, b. 11/6/1963; first; John L. Nicol (pressman, Warren) and Carol Jane Matson (Woodsville)

Janet Alice, b. 5/4/1933; first; John Henry Nicol (clerk, Warren) and Marjorie A. Brown (Wentworth)

John Laurence, b. 2/20/1937; third; John H. Nicol (Warren) and Marjorie Brown (Wentworth)

Mark Allan, b. 9/16/1934; second; John Henry Nicol (clerk, Warren) and Marjorie Brown (Wentworth)

Robert S., b. 9/17/1965; second; John L. Nicol (pressman, Warren) and Carol J. Matson (Woodsville)

Victoria Elizabeth, b. 1/13/1919 in Warren; third; William B. Nicol (blacksmith, Bathurst, NB) and Alice M. Libbey (Warren)

NOLAN,
Jeffrey George, b. 1/6/1995 in Lebanon; Courtney Lee Nolan (31) and Susan Lynn Farnham (29)

NYSTROM,
Alden Craig, b. 7/7/2003 in Lebanon; Timothy Chase and Heather Nystrom

PANUS,
Cathryn Rose, b. 2/3/2004 in Plymouth; Michael Panus and Julie Panus

Jon Christopher, b. 12/13/2001 in Plymouth; Michael Panus and Julie Panus

PARADIS,
Joseph Daniel, b. 7/11/1989 in Plymouth; Edward Daniel Paradis (25) and Robin Jean Rock (25)

Richard Edward, b. 3/29/1988 in Plymouth; Edward Francis Paradis (24) and Robin Jean Rock (24)

PARKER,
Deborah M., b. 3/23/1967; fourth; Robert L. Parker (press operator, Providence, RI) and Janice E. Octeau (Providence, RI)

PARSONS,
Anna Patricia, b. 12/16/2003 in Lebanon; Mark Parsons and Patricia Parsons

Mark Benjamin, b. 7/19/2001 in Lebanon; Mark Parsons and Patricia Parsons

PEBBLES,
Marjory, b. 12/9/1911 in Warren; third; George Pebbles (telegraph opr., Plymouth) and Antonette Savorok (Chelsea, MA)

PEETERS,
son, b. 2/6/1911 in Warren; first; Freeman R. Peeters (farmer, Halifax, NS) and Bertha Heath (Benton)

PERRY,
daughter, b. 2/1/1894 in Warren; Onslow D. Perry (farmer, 33, Chichester) and Annie B. Leighton (25, Haverhill)
George H., b. 2/16/1902 in Warren; fourth; John J. Perry (laborer, 35, England) and Ellen L. Chase (32, Pittsburg)
Marjorie Inez, b. 6/22/1921 in Warren; first; George D. Perry (station agent, Jefferson) and Gladys T. Clifford (Medford, MA)

PETELLE,
Jade Mary, b. 7/30/1978 in Hanover; David Bruce Petelle (30) and Joanne Patricia Cochrane (26)

PETERSON,
Bernadette, b. 12/15/1931; fifth; Ernest S. Peterson (carpenter, Denmark) and Anna Millay (Everett, MA)
Heather Janet Eleanor, b. 3/12/1983 in Hanover; Peter Arne Peterson (31) and Diane Margaret Conklin (31)
Samuel Raymond, b. 5/23/1980 in Laconia; Peter Arne Peterson (28) and Diane Margaret Conklin (28)

PETITO,
Charlotte Rose, b. 12/8/1913 in Warren; first; Andrew Petito (laborer, NY) and Leona Pike (Warren)

PETTEE,
Morgan Grace, b. 11/10/2002 in Lebanon; Jeffrey Pettee and Kristine Pettee

PHEIR,
daughter, b. 5/15/1897 in Warren; second; Thomas Pheir (farmer, 28, Ireland) and Josephine Flanders (25, Warren)

PHILBRICK,
daughter, b. 5/7/1912 in Warren; first; Ira Philbrick (laborer, Haverhill) and Alice Bosley (Vernon, CT); residence - Bradford, VT

PHILBROOK,
daughter, b. 11/28/1923; second; William A. Philbrook (laborer, Wytopitlock, ME) and Kathlene Pike (Warren)

PHIPPS,
Owen MacGregor, b. 4/28/1979 in Laconia; Joel Duncan Phipps (39) and Carol Louise Cashin (29)

PICKARD,
Frank Edward, b. 6/26/1935; first; Milton A. Pickard (W. Newbury, MA) and Katherine Applebee (Carroll)

PIKE,
daughter, b. 10/6/1889 in Warren; Arthur Pike (laborer, 27, Warren) and Eva Judkins (19, Danville, VT)
son, b. 9/14/1892 in Warren; Arthur L. Pike (farming, 29, Benton) and Eva G. Judkins (22, Danville, VT)
son, b. 4/3/1896 in Warren; Arthur L. Pike (farmer, 33, Warren) and Eva G. Judkins (26, Warren)
daughter, b. 9/5/1898 in Warren; fourth; Arthur L. Pike (farmer, 35) and Eva G. Judkins (28)
daughter, b. 9/10/1904 in Warren; first; Joseph W. Pike (laborer, 34, Warren) and Jennie F. Tibbetts (28, Benton)
Beverly Jean, b. 9/28/1932; first; Geneva M. Pike (Warren)
Brandon James, b. 8/2/1974 in Haverhill; Richard Morey Pike (27) and Sandra Jane Caverhill (26)
Geneva M., b. 2/20/1916 in Warren; second; Leona M. Pike (Warren)
Patricia Louise, b. 10/6/1933; second; Lewis H. Bennett (bobbin maker) and Geneva M. Pike (Warren); residence - Waterbury, VT

Richard Alanson, b. 10/14/1919 in Warren; first; Alanson J. Pike
(laborer, Warren) and Dorothy Irene Morey (Orford)
Richard Morey, b. 6/23/1947 in Plymouth; first; Richard Alanson Pike
(fish culturist, Warren) and Barbara May Gove (Wentworth)
Robert Arthur, b. 3/18/1921 in Warren; second; Lanson Pike
(laborer, Warren) and Dorothy Morey (Orford)

PLANT,
son, b. 12/20/1888 in Warren; Frank Plant (farming, 30, Colebrook)
and ---- Miller (25, PA)

PRESCOTT,
daughter, b. 9/4/1923; second; Grover C. Prescott (laborer,
Bradford, VT) and Lucy May Harris (Bath)
Ernest Grover, b. 4/27/1922; first; Grover Cleveland Prescott
(lumber, Bradford, VT) and Lucy May Harris (Bath)

PREW,
son, b. 6/16/1887 in Benton; Fred Prew (laborer, 26, St. Albans, PQ)
and Mary Prew (21, St. Albans, PQ)

RAMSAY,
Eric Robinson, b. 7/11/1992 in Lebanon; Brian William Ramsay (31)
and Barbara Ann Cunningham (29)
Kimberly P., b. 3/27/1962; fourth; Dale V. Ramsay (rural mail man,
Pike) and Estella C. Cushing (Warren)
Ronald Ricky, b. 11/27/1953; second; Earl Edwin Ramsay (Glencliff)
and Eunice Marion Moses (Haverhill)

RAMSDELL,
Rachel, b. 6/19/1940; second; Carleton Ramsdell (farmer,
Claremont) and Angeline Robillard (Troy, VT)

RAMSEY,
Cheryl Estella, b. 3/23/1948 in Plymouth; first; Dale Vernon Ramsey
(lab const. co., Glencliff) and Estella Clarise Cushing (Warren)
Earl Edward, b. 2/4/1920 in Warren; second; Earl E. Ramsey
(engineer, Haverhill) and Edith M. Belyea (Warren)
Erline Mae, b. 7/7/1921 in Warren; third; Earl E. Ramsey (farmer,
Haverhill) and Edith M. Belyea (Warren)

Linda Gayle, b. 7/31/1949 in Plymouth; second; Dale Vernon Ramsey (laborer, Glencliff) and Estella Clarisse Cushing (Warren)

Lisa Marie, b. 11/1/1957; third; Dale V. Ramsey (RFD mail carrier, Pike) and Estella C. Cushing (Warren)

Virginia, b. 1/29/1918 in Warren; first; Earl E. Ramsey (engineer, Haverhill) and Edith M. Belyea (Warren)

RANDALL,

Chelsea Lynn, b. 10/23/1991 in Concord; Vincent G. Randall (27) and Susan Melissa Libby (20)

Mahala A., b. 11/4/1997; Vincent G. Randall (33) and Susan M. Randall (26)

Samantha Jo, b. 9/2/1992 in Woodsville; Vincent G. Randall (28) and Susan Melissa Libby (21)

RAY,

Alex Eastman, Jr., b. 3/29/1981 in Haverhill; Alex Eastman Ray (21) and Ellen Ann White (20)

Michelle Elizabeth, b. 3/27/1966; first; Donald G. Ray (state highway emp., Plymouth) and Donna Lee Bancroft (Woodsville)

RAYMOND,

Gary Duane, b. 8/18/1948 in Plymouth; second; Arthur Guy Raymond (laborer, Claremont) and Patricia Rose Blanchard (Berlin)

Irene, b. 4/13/1927; fourth; Fred Raymond (laborer, Woodsville) and Lydia Shortt (Warren); residence - Plymouth

Juanita Rosanne, b. 10/6/1951; third; Arthur Guy Raymond (NH) and Patricia Rose Blanchard (NH)

Keith Alan, b. 11/29/1955; fourth; Arthur G. Raymond (laborer, Claremont) and Patricia R. Blanchard (Berlin)

Nancy Lee, b. 9/17/1946 in Plymouth; first; George Edward Raymond (sawmill wk., Cornish) and Catherine Patton Wilson (Warwick, MD)

William L., b. 6/2/1920 in Warren; first; Fred A. Raymond (laborer, Woodsville) and Lydia J. Shortt (Warren)

REYNOLDS,

daughter, b. 4/6/1888 in Warren; Frank Reynolds (farming, 36, Ashburnham, MA) and Flora E. ----- (35, Fergn's, ME)

Brenda Carol, b. 8/29/1949 in Plymouth; first; Ernest Albin Reynolds
(hairdresser, ME) and Margaret Myrle Hight (Warren)
John, b. 1/23/1907 in Warren; third; Mabel L. Pest (29, Corinth, VT)
Peter Arnold, b. 4/20/1954; second; Ernest A. Reynolds, Jr. (barber,
Eagle Lake, ME) and Margaret M. Hight (Warren)

RIEL,
Evan David, b. 8/21/1991 in Lebanon; David Frank Riel (31) and
Jenette Marie Quattricci (31)

RISLEY,
Ernest Adams, Jr., b. 3/14/1952; second; Ernest Adams Risley (MA)
and Aletea Beatrice Durand (NH)

ROBERTS,
Jeanette E., b. 6/4/1940; first; Kenneth E. Roberts (mill hand,
Warren, AZ) and Ethel M. Avery (Warren)

ROBY,
son, b. 7/31/1891 in Warren; fifth; Alfred Roby (laborer, 35, Paris,
France) and Ella Roby (24, Halifax, NS)
Melia M., b. 2/–/1887 in Warren; Fred Roby (laborer, Canada) and
Mary E. ----- (Hillsboro)

ROLLINS,
son, b. 2/25/1887 in Warren; Albion L. Rollins (laborer, 35) and
Lizzie O. Ferguson (18, Warren)
son, b. 8/3/1896 in Warren; Forrest A. Rollins (farmer, 32,
Wentworth) and Emma J. Clement (26, Warren)
daughter, b. 5/24/1900 in Warren; third; Forest A. Rollins (farmer,
37, Wentworth) and Emma J. Clement (30, Warren)
Evelin Dorothy, b. 4/30/1922; first; Flossie May Rollins (Wentworth)

ROMON,
Jose A., b. 2/21/1962; first; Anthony J. Romon (laborer, Camury,
PR) and Marie M. F. Roulx (Warren)

ROOD,
Paul P., b. 9/21/1915 in Warren; fourth; Owen C. Rood (station
agent, Canton, NY) and Dorothy Duegaw (Brasher, NY)

69

ROOT,
Nancy Ellen, b. 3/17/1939; second; John C. Root (US forester, Providence, RI) and Elinor Kendall (Danbury, VT)

ROSS,
George S., III, b. 8/23/1986; George S. Ross, Jr. (25) and Debra Bixby Ross (25)

ROULX,
Germaine Norma, b. 10/18/1947 in Warren; first; Oscar Roulx (trucking, Fenswick, Canada) and Mabel Godville (Warren)
Norman Roland, b. 7/22/1946 in Warren; third; Oscar A. Roulx (trader, Canada) and Mable L. Godville (Warren)
Sandra Mae, b. 3/15/1953; fifth; Oscar A. Roulx (Canada) and Mable Louise Shortt (Warren)

ROY,
son, b. 7/4/1898 in Warren; second; George Roy (laborer, 35, PQ) and Grace French (20, Warren)
son, b. 8/31/1899 in Warren; third; George Roy (farmer, 36, Canada) and Grace French (21, Warren); residence - Summit
Elaine Alice, b. 11/4/1948 in Plymouth; second; George Stanley Roy (truck driver, E. Otis, NH) and Mamie Madeline Hilliard (Warren)
Rowell R., b. 12/19/1941; first; Floyd Randolph Roy (sales clerk, Dorchester, MA) and Doris Hoyt Rowell (Meredith)
Wilfred, b. 11/9/1907 in Warren; eighth; George Roy (lumberman, 45, Canada) and Grace E. French (29, Warren)

RUAL,
son, b. 7/20/1891 in Warren; third; Alphonsie Rual (miner, 27, PQ) and Exdira Rual (27, PQ)

RUDOLPH,
Mary Cathrine, b. 1/31/1925; fourth; Harold Rudolph (farmer, NS) and Laura Stone (St. Peters, CB)
Roy Warren, b. 5/13/1932; second; Roy Harold Rudolph (cook, l. rm., Canada) and Julia May Roghaar (Lynn, MA)

RUEL,
son, b. 7/14/1895 in Warren; fifth; Ezra Ruel (miner, 32, Canada)
and Alphonsine ----- (32, Canada)
daughter, b. 9/7/1898 in Warren; sixth; Ezra Ruel (laborer, 36,
Canada) and Alphonsin Bisse (36, Canada)
daughter, b. 9/17/1901 in Warren; sixth; Ezra Ruel (miner, 38, PQ)
and Alphonsine Bison (38, PQ)
son, b. 9/20/1903 in Warren; ninth; Ezra Ruel (laborer, 40, Canada)
and Alphonsine Bisson (41, Canada)
stillborn son, b. 10/7/1907 in Warren; first; Joseph Ruel (farmer, 28,
Canada) and Mary M. Vallier (25, Canada)

RUELL,
Lawrence Joseph, b. 11/10/1911 in Warren; third; Joseph Ruell
(farmer, Canada) and Mary Vallier (Canada)

RUFF,
Malerie Pige, b. 8/27/2005 in Lebanon; Timothy Ruff and Shane
Vincelette
Nathan Allen, b. 9/20/2004 in Lebanon; Timothy Ruff, Jr. and Shane
Vincelette

RUTHERFORD,
Mark Alan, b. 5/15/1963; first; R. A. Rutherford (student, Goffstown)
and Marjorie A. Stevens (Woodsville)

SACKETT,
Jessica Lynn, b. 2/7/1983 in Hanover; Bradley Jay Sackett (20) and
Sherly Lynn Pease (18)
Kayla, d. 2/7/1993 in Lebanon; Timothy Sackett (28) and Lorie Ann
Kennedy (31)
Megan Amy Lyn, b. 3/9/2003 in Lebanon; Michael Sackett and Traci
Sackett
Michael Charles, b. 9/2/2004 in Lebanon; Michael Sackett and Traci
Sackett
Tell Dakota, b. 12/25/1989 in Lebanon; Timothy James Sackett (24)
and Lorie Ann Kennedy (27)
Traci Lyn, b. 10/4/1981 in Haverhill; Charles Nelson Sackett (22)
and Tammy Lyn Irwin (20)
William Peter, b. 6/29/1969 in Plymouth; Charles Nelson Sackett
(PA) and Janice Marie Ball (NH)

SAMUELSON,
Darrah Elizabeth, b. 2/14/1971 in Haverhill; Peter Bogardus
Samuelson (MA) and Susan Lee Darrah (Texas)

SAYRE,
Ford Kent, Jr., b. 12/29/1935; first; Ford Kent Sayre (Glenridge, NJ)
and Margaret F. Lincoln (Westbrook, ME)

SCHIEBER,
Jean-Paul, b. 5/1/1971 in Haverhill; Larry Ralph Schieber (IN) and
Brenda Vincelette (NH)

SCHOFIELD,
Carol Jean, b. 11/10/1946 in Plymouth; second; Ernest Henry
Scofield, Jr. (woodchopper, Orford) and Jasmine Alice Weeks
(Warren)
Sandra Joyce, b. 11/6/1944 in Plymouth; first; Ernest Henry
Schofield (US Army, Orford) and Jasmine Alice Weeks
(Warren)

SCOTT-WAKEFIELD,
Adam Craig, b. 2/18/1982 in Hanover; Craig Roos Wakefield (MA)
and Marsha Scott (NY)
John, b. 9/4/1978 in Hanover; Craig Roos Wakefield (29) and
Marsha Scott (24)

SEELEY,
son, b. 4/30/1903 in Warren; sixth; Roubine Seeley (laborer, 32,
Canada) and Chailde Blais (31, Canada)

SEIDL,
Jason Robert, b. 5/3/1971 in Plymouth; Robert Leslie Seidl (MA) and
Judith Ellen Phillips (MA)

SHEEHAN,
Christopher Brian, b. 3/5/1975 in Haverhill; Christopher Paul
Sheehan (22) and Darleen Ann Ball (19)

SHELLEY,
John C., b. 2/24/1928; first; Sidney C. Shelley (foreman, Haverhill)
and Glenna Maud Hunt (Johnson, VT)

Raymond J., b. 5/5/1930; second; Sidney Calvin Shelley (millwright, Haverhill) and Glenna Maud Hunt (Johnson, VT)

SHINN,
Bill Warren, b. 12/21/1970 in Plymouth; Gerry Warren Shinn (NH) and Larraine Ann Brown (NH)

SHORES,
daughter, b. 1/2/1924; second; Pearl J. Shores (Wells River, VT)

SHORT,
daughter, b. 9/20/1896 in Warren; William J. Short (laborer, 22, Newfoundland) and Mabel N. Gould (17, Warren)
daughter, b. 7/25/1898 in Warren; second; William Short (laborer, 23, Newfoundland) and Mabel L. Gould (19, Warren)
daughter, b. 10/12/1900 in Warren; third; William J. Short (laborer, 26, Newfoundland) and Mabel M. Gould (21, Warren)
daughter, b. 3/25/1903 in Warren; fourth; William Short (laborer, 29, Newfoundland) and Mabel M. Gould (24, Warren)
son, b. 3/19/1905 in Warren; fifth; William Short (laborer, 31, Newfoundland) and Mabel M. Gould (Warren)
daughter, b. 3/19/1905 in Warren; sixth; William Short (laborer, 31, Newfoundland) and Mabel M. Gould (Warren)
daughter, b. 10/8/1910; eighth; William Short (farmer, 38, Newfoundland) and Mable Gould (Warren)
son, b. 10/8/1910; eighth; William Short (farmer, 38, Newfoundland) and Mable Gould (Warren)
Aaron William, b. 9/12/1922; second; George A. Short (RR sect., Walpole) and Nellie M. Wright (Piermont)
Eda Mae, b. 1/24/1924; third; George Short (laborer, Walpole) and Nellie Wright (Piermont)
Frances Ellen, b. 6/22/1918 in Warren; fourteenth; William J. Short (laborer, Newfoundland) and Mabel M. Gould (Warren)
Harry E., b. 10/29/1907 in Warren; seventh; William J. Short (farmer, 33, Newfoundland) and Mabel M. Gould (29, Warren)
Hattie Nellie, b. 3/31/1929; sixth; George Aaron Short (farmer, Walpole) and Nellie May Wright (Piermont)
Milton Ray, b. 5/24/1918 in Warren; first; Edna S. Short (Warren)
Myrtle Lela, b. 9/20/1934; eleventh; George A. Short (farmer, Walpole) and Nellie May Short (E. Piermont)

SHORTELL,

Sarah Carley, b. 7/20/2004 in Plymouth; James Shortell and Crystal Shortell

SHORTT,

son, b. 11/18/1912 in Warren; tenth; William Shortt (laborer, Newfoundland) and Mabel Gould (Warren)

daughter, b. 11/18/1912 in Warren; eleventh; William Shortt (laborer, Newfoundland) and Mabel Gould (Warren)

son, b. 11/9/1914; eleventh; William J. Shortt (laborer, Newfoundland) and Mabel M. Gould (Warren)

daughter, b. 1/25/1925; sixteenth; William J. Shortt (laborer, Newfoundland) and Mabel M. Gould (Warren)

Alan Phillie, b. 9/2/1947 in Plymouth; first; Leland Phillie Shortt (mechanic, Warren) and Regina Arlene Huckins (Wentworth)

Bonnie Lee, b. 4/4/1953; first; Stanley Fay Shortt (NH) and Marjorie Louise Libby (NH)

Darlene F., b. 7/16/1956; second; Stanley F. Shortt (mechanic garage, Warren) and Marjorie L. Libby (Lisbon)

Earl Eugene, b. 10/14/1927; fifth; George A. Shortt (farmer, Walpole) and Nellie May Wright (E. Piermont)

Edith Gould, b. 3/17/1916 in Warren; thirteenth; William J. Shortt (laborer, Newfoundland) and Mabel M. Gould (Warren)

Lealand Phillie, b. 12/28/1925; fourth; George A. Shortt (laborer, Walpole) and Nellie M. Wright (Piermont)

Mabel Louise, b. 5/12/1921 in Warren; second; Edna Shortt (Warren)

Mar. Labrie, b. 7/1/1942; first; Joseph Labrie and Francis E. Shortt (Warren)

Marjory E., b. 8/4/1932; tenth; George A. Shortt (farmer, Walpole) and Nellie M. Wright (Piermont)

Merle X., b. 11/17/1920 in Warren; third; George Shortt (laborer, Walpole) and Nellie Wright (Piermont)

Penny Louise, b. 1/9/1968 in Haverhill; Stanley Fay Shortt (NH) and Marjorie L. Libby (NH)

Stanley Fay, b. 1/9/1931; ninth; George A. Shortt (farmer, Walpole) and Nellie M. Wright (Piermont)

Tessirel Blanche, b. 8/2/1921 in Warren; fifteenth; William J. Shortt (RR emp., Newfoundland) and Mabel Gould (Warren)

SIMPSON,
son, b. 8/23/1903 in Warren; first; Harry C. Simpson (laborer, 24, Piermont) and Lena Brown (19, Rumney)

SIRLIN,
Edward Allen, III, b. 6/2/1983 in Hanover; Edward Allen Sirlin (35) and Joan Ann Forrest (35)
Shelby Rae, b. 11/19/1981 in Hanover; Edward Allen Sirlin (34) and Joan Ann Forrest (34)

SITES,
Saunya Dee, b. 12/2/1970 in Haverhill; Larry Lee Sites (OH) and Audrey Evelyn Ames (NH)

SMITH,
daughter, b. 7/18/1888 in Warren; first; Malcolm Smith (brakeman, 33, Canada) and Eva M. Whiteman (20, Canada)
daughter, b. 10/26/1889 in Warren; Walter P. Smith (farmer, 35, Grantham) and Nellie M. Upton (34, Burlington, VT)
daughter, b. 5/15/1895 in Warren; fifth; Zebulon Smith (blacksmith, 52, Littleton) and Eliza E. Flanders (32, Warren)
daughter, b. 4/24/1902 in Warren; first; Arthur L. Smith (farmer, 23, W. Topsham) and Lena O. Merrill (22, Warren)
daughter, b. 4/10/1903 in Warren; first; Lawson Smith (laborer, 28, NS) and Angeline Smith (20, NS)
daughter, b. 7/18/1904 in Warren; second; Arthur L. Smith (farmer, 25, W. Topsham, VT) and Lena O. Merrill (25, Warren)
son, b. 2/19/1922; first; Guy Warren Smith (farmer, N. Woodstock) and Annabelle Hildreth (Haverhill)
Angela Marie, b. 10/16/1969 in Plymouth; Paul Steven Smith (NH) and Charlene Ann Downing (NH)
Arthur, b. 5/21/1894 in Warren; Walter P. Smith (farmer, 40, Plainfield) and Nellie M. Upton (39, Burlington, VT)
Carl Louis, b. 5/24/1943; first; Carl Wilbur Smith (farmer, Gilford) and Louise Rose Abler (W. New York, NJ)
Daniel-Paul, b. 3/29/1987 in Hanover; Wendell Alfred Smith, Jr. (24) and Bonnie-Lynn Taylor (21)
E. Herald, b. 5/3/1898 in Warren; first; G. E. Smith (merchant, 28, Plymouth) and C. Maud Smith (23, Cincinnati, OH)

75

George William, b. 2/15/1948 in Wentworth; second; Charles H.
Smith, Jr. (laborer, New Canaan, CT) and Gwendolyn Brown
(Wentworth)
Jason-Scott, b. 3/29/1987 in Hanover; Wendell Alfred Smith, Jr. (24)
and Bonnie-Lynn Taylor (21)
Jessica Lynn, b. 4/22/1988 in Laconia; Brian Scott Smith (30) and
Michelle Gut (22)
John Walter, b. 12/14/1946 in Woodsville; first; Charles Henry
Smith, Jr. (farmer, Darien, CT) and Gwendolyn Isabelle Brown
(Wentworth)
Kenneth Charles, b. 9/6/1982 in Haverhill; Wendell Alfred Smith, Jr.
(NH) and Bonnie-Lynn Taylor (MA)
Milton Everett, b. 6/7/1921 in Warren; third; Harry W. Smith
(carpenter, N. Woodstock) and Catherine Whitcher (Warren)
Paige Erin, b. 9/2/2005 in Plymouth; Gary Smith and Erin Decotis
Therese Larraine, b. 3/15/1950 in Haverhill; third; Charles Henry
Smith, Jr. (landscaper, New Canaan, CT) and Gwendolyn
Isabella Brown (Wentworth)
William Elmer, b. 1/5/1924; sixth; Harry W. Smith (RR emp., N.
Woodstock) and Catherine Whitcher (Warren)
Zoe Rose, b. 3/26/2004 in Plymouth; Gary Smith and Erin DeCotis

SMOLEN,
Alexander Joseph, b. 8/21/1992 in Laconia; Gary Edward Smolen
(38) and Jean Helen Kaluziak (36)

SNELGROVE,
Bertha N., b. 1/19/1915 in Warren; first; Frank Snelgrove (laborer,
NB) and Edna M. Wright (Wentworth)

SNOGREN,
Hilarie Ruth, b. 2/25/1985 in Hanover; Eric D. Snogren (28) and
Sandra K. Olsen (26)
Krista Anne, b. 3/9/1982; Eric Dorraine Snogren (25) and Sandra
Kay Olsen (23)

SORRELL,
stillborn son, b. 1/17/1893 in Warren; Frank Sorrell (miner, 39,
Northfield, VT) and Delia Ruel (23, Canada)
son, b. 7/1/1896 in Warren; Frank Sorrell (farmer, 45, Northfield, VT)
and Delia Ruel (26, Stanstead, Canada)

son, b. 4/7/1902 in Warren; third; Frank Sorrell (farmer, 50,
    Northfield, VT) and Delia Ruel (32, Canada)
stillborn daughter, b. 2/15/1904 in Warren; fifth; Frank Sorrell
    (farmer, Northfield, VT) and Delia Ruel (Canada)
Lawrence D., b. 12/17/1894 in Warren; Frank Sorrell (miner, 43,
    Northfield, VT) and Delia Ruel (25, Canada)

SPENCER,
Johnathan Edward, b. 5/30/1999 in Lebanon; Michael Spencer and
    Pamela Spencer
Thayne M., b. 9/28/1994; Michael D. Spencer (26) and Pamela Jo
    Kinne (22)

SPOONER,
daughter, b. 4/9/1894 in Warren; Daniel Spooner (farmer, 28,
    Haverhill) and Nora Burke (20, Lewiston, ME)
daughter, b. 6/20/1896 in Warren; Dan. J. Spooner (farmer, 30,
    Benton) and Hanoso M. Burke (23, Lewiston, ME)
son, b. 11/29/1898 in Warren; fourth; Daniel Spooner (laborer, 36,
    Benton) and Nora Burke (25, Lewiston, ME)
son, b. 9/7/1902 in Warren; sixth; Daniel Spooner (carpenter, 37,
    Benton) and Nora Burke (29, Lewiston, ME)
daughter, b. 5/11/1919 in Warren; third; Harold E. Spooner (farmer,
    Benton) and Mildred M. Lyman (S. Columbia)

SPRAGUE,
Deborah Lee, b. 7/13/1960; seventh; Ronald Milo Sprague (Roxbury,
    VT) and Naomi May Garrett (Fitzwilliam)

SPRUYT,
Eric Jan, b. 8/20/1958; first; Dirk J. Spruyt (doctor - medicine) and
    June S. Spongberg

STALLINGS,
Hillary Caroline, b. 1/24/1971 in Haverhill; Erik Arthur Stallings
    (Puerto Rico) and Sandra Jane Caverhill (NH)
Marla Lynn, b. 10/24/1966; first; Eric A. Stallings (carpenter, Puerto
    Rico) and Sandra J. Caverhill (Plymouth)

STANLEY,
daughter, b. 2/27/1898 in Warren; first; Linwood Stanley (bookkeeper, 27, ME) and Alice Smith (24, Belmont)

STARK,
Amber Lynn, b. 1/15/1981 in Haverhill; Wayne Douglas Stark (NH) and Monica Lynn Valdes (NH)
Shauna Lynn, b. 12/24/1982 in Haverhill; Wayne Douglas Stark (NH) and Monica Lynn Valdes (NH)
Shirley B., b. 4/1/1962; second; Gary George Stark (truck driver, Hanover) and Audrey E. Ames (Warren)
Wayne D., b. 6/21/1960; first; Gary George Stark (mechanic, Hanover) and Audrey Evelyn Ames (Warren)

START,
Brandon Wesley, b. 5/8/1996 in Plymouth; John Steven Start (28) and Loretta Parenteau (24)
Brianna Lee, b. 4/6/1999 in Plymouth; John Start and Loretta Parenteau
Heather Lynn, b. 8/16/1983 in Plymouth; Allen Richard Start (25) and Doreen Marie Simpson (23)

STEVENS,
Bette Lee, b. 1/24/1948 in Haverhill; sixth; Charles E. Stevens (mill hand, Warren) and Avis J. Batchelder (Warren)
Brenda Lee, b. 10/2/1950 in Plymouth; stillborn; sixth; Wallace Stevens (construction, Warren) and Althea Gould (Piermont)
Charlie Eben, b. 2/3/1913 in Warren; second; Walter Stevens (laborer, Coventon, VT) and Pearl Whitcher (Warren)
Donald W., b. 12/6/1940; second; Charles E. Stevens (st. h. worker, Warren) and Avis J. Batchelder (Warren)
Dorothy P., b. 4/13/1919 in Warren; fourth; Walter P. Stevens (laborer, Coventry, VT) and Pearl L. Whitcher (Warren)
Eileen B., b. 6/6/1930; seventh; Walter P. Stevens (carpenter, Coventry, VT) and Pearl Whitcher (Warren)
Emily Jane, b. 10/27/1943; fourth; Charles Eben Stevens (lumberman, Warren) and Avis J. Batchelder (Warren)
Marjorie Ann, b. 5/5/1945 in Haverhill; fourth; Wallace A. Stevens (teamster, Warren) and Althea June Gould (Piermont)
Marlene, b. 1/17/1949 in Haverhill; fourth; Wallace Arthur Stevens (laborer, Warren) and Althea June Gould (Piermont)

Nancy Carol, b. 11/25/1942; third; Charles Eben Stevens
(lumberman, Warren) and Avis J. Batchelder (Warren)
Richard, b. 10/3/1920 in Warren; fifth; Walter P. Stevens (teamster,
Coventry, VT) and Pearl Whitcher (Warren)
Richard J., b. 8/8/1939; first; Charles E. Stevens (truck driver,
Warren) and Avis J. Batchelder (Warren)
Sandra Jean, b. 10/19/1943; second; Wallace A. Stevens (laborer,
Warren) and Althea June Gould (Piermont)
Wallace A., b. 7/27/1911 in Warren; first; Walter Stevens (RR
employee, Newport, VT) and Pearl L. Whitcher (Warren)
Wayne E., b. 5/1/1940; first; Wallace A. Stevens (common laborer,
Warren) and Althea J. Gould (Piermont)

STILES,
Benjamin Scott, b. 4/4/1995 in Lebanon; Dean Alger Stiles (38) and
Emilie Marie Roberge (35)
Eliza Rose, b. 9/28/1996 in Lebanon; Dean Alger Stiles (39) and
Emilie Marie Roberge (36)
Nathaniel Paul, b. 10/25/1993 in Lebanon; Dean Alger Stiles (36)
and Emilie Marie Roberge (33)

STIMPSON,
Ardeth May, b. 3/19/1928; fifth; Elmer G. Stimpson (tel. operator,
Haverhill) and Lilla Martin (Warren)

STIMSON,
Alan Lee, b. 12/27/1951; third; Delton Gerald Stimson (Woodsville)
and Rita Mae Chase (Woodsville)
Andrew M., b. 10/18/1994 in Lebanon; Andrew P. Stimson (29) and
Martiza G. Godfrey (24)
Delton Gerald, b. 3/24/1927; fourth; Elmer Gerald Stimson (tel.
oper., Haverhill) and Lilla Martin (Warren)
Delton Gerald, b. 7/28/1949 in Haverhill; first; Delton Gerald Stimson
(student, Woodsville) and Rita May Chase (Woodsville)
Dennis Roy, b. 11/27/1950 in Haverhill; second; Delton Gerald
Stimson (laborer, Woodsville) and Rita May Chase
(Woodsville)
Elsine Erma, b. 10/16/1921 in Warren; first; Gerald Stimson
(telegraph opr., Haverhill) and Lilla M. Martin (Warren)
Preston E., b. 11/9/1930; sixth; Elmer Gerald Stimson (tel. operator,
Woodsville) and Lilla Martin (Warren)

STRICKLAND,
Whitney Rose, b. 12/10/1990 in Plymouth; Ricky Allen Strickland (25) and Annemarie Rivers (22)

STROUT,
Sally Ann, b. 5/5/1969 in Haverhill; Leslie Jackson Strout (NH) and Mary Ellen Hildreth (NH)
William Edwin, b. 4/14/1970 in Haverhill; Leslie Jackson Strout (NH) and Mary Ellen Hildreth (NH)

STUBBARD,
daughter, b. 9/19/1900 in Warren; second; George H. Stubbard (steam fitter, 40, Sidney, CB) and Mary Short (26, Newfoundland)

SULLHAM,
Ralph M., b. 6/28/1918 in Warren; first; Ralph Sullham (soldier, Underhill, VT) and Iva E. Reed (Wentworth)

SUTTON,
Cassie Lu, b. 3/29/1987 in Hanover; Wendell Alfred Smith, Jr. (24) and Bonnie-Lynn Taylor (21)
Jacob Neil, b. 3/29/1987 in Hanover; Wendell Alfred Smith, Jr. (24) and Bonnie-Lynn Taylor (21)

SWAIN,
daughter, b. 7/19/1888 in Warren; first; Willie H. Swain (brakeman, 22, Warren) and Flora Brooke (27, Canada)
son, b. 6/6/1894 in Warren; Natt L. Swain (farmer, 23, Warren) and Mary A. Lock (18, Concord)
son, b. 12/18/1895 in Warren; first; Elmer E. Swain (farmer, 31, Warren) and Eva L. Upton (21, Warren)
son, b. 4/10/1901 in Warren; second; Harry W. Swain (laborer, 28, Warren) and Nettie L. Downing (29, Ellsworth)
daughter, b. 10/8/1901 in Warren; second; William H. Swain (carpenter, 35, Warren) and Flora W. Cotey (40, Canada)
son, b. 2/16/1911 in Warren; first; Grace Swain (Warren)
Derwin, b. 12/19/1888 in Warren; second; Darius O. Swain (pensioner, 44, Warren) and Lydia ----- (40, Hillsboro)
Floyd Burke, b. 1/17/1908; first; Derwin Otis Swain (teamster, 19, Warren) and Mary Alice Burke (29, Burke, VT)

Theodore W., b. 7/1/1909 in Warren; second; Darius O. Swain (farmer, Warren) and Mary Alice Burke (E. Burke, VT)

SWANFELDT,
Eric Scott, b. 10/24/1959; second; Eric F. Swanfeldt (minister, Cambridge, MA) and Jean M. Van Buskirk (Newton, MA)
Mark P., b. 10/5/1960; fourth; Eric Folke Swanfeldt (clergyman, Cambridge, MA) and Jean M. Van Buskirk (Newton, MA)

TANGUAY,
son, b. 6/7/1910; third; Nobet Tanguay (laborer, 25, Canada) and Leona M. Sorrell (W. Thornton)

TATHAM,
Chad Daniel, b. 2/18/1983 in Haverhill; Joel Howard Tatham (26) and Pamela Ann Green (28)
Corey Peter, b. 9/26/1980 in Haverhill; Joel Howard Tatham (23) and Pamela Ann Green (25)
Heidi Elizabeth, b. 3/4/1986; Joel Howard Tatham (29) and Pamela Ann Green (31)

TAYLOR,
Jessica Lynn, b. 12/19/1984 in Hanover; Walter Darrell Taylor (23) and Lisa Marie Lamothe (19)
Nathan Edward, b. 4/8/1988 in Hanover; Walter Darrell Taylor (27) and Lisa Marie Lamothe (23)

TEWKSBURY,
daughter, b. 8/24/1926; second; Clarence Tewksbury (bobbin turner, Bath) and Lydia Bailey (Warren)
Madeline, b. 4/9/1931; fifth; Clarence E. Tewksbury (laborer, Bath) and Lydia M. Bailey (Warren)
Roscoe Merrill, b. 4/5/1925; first; Clarence Tewksbury (bobbin mfg., Bath) and Lydia M. Bailey (Warren)
Weston L., b. 6/5/1933; sixth; Clarence E. Tewksbury (laborer, Swiftwater) and Lydia M. Bailey (Warren)

THOMPSON,
Hannah M., b. 4/14/1997; James H. Thompson (27) and Jennifer L. Lech (24)

James Harold, b. 5/6/2002 in Lebanon; James Thompson and
    Jennifer Thompson
Lindsey Ann, b. 2/11/1984 in Littleton; Stephen Edward Thompson
    (23) and Wendy Lee Piascik (16)

TIBBETTS,
daughter, b. 5/23/1888 in Warren; Leon Tebbitts (sect. man, 22,
    Haverhill) and Carry Fifield (18, Warren)
child, b. 4/9/1891 in Warren; fifth; D. H. Tibbetts (laborer, 38,
    Haverhill) and R. N. ----- (32, Canada)
daughter, b. 2/1/1893 in Warren; Leon R. Tebbets (section hand, 25,
    Haverhill) and Carrie R. Fifield (22, Warren)
daughter, b. 5/14/1898 in Warren; fifth; Leon R. Tebbetts (RR sect.,
    30, Haverhill) and Carrie R. Fifield (28, Warren)
daughter, b. 5/26/1901 in Warren; sixth; Leon R. Tibbetts (laborer,
    34, Haverhill) and Carrie R. Fifield (31, Warren)
daughter, b. 7/24/1906 in Warren; eighth; Leon R. Tibbetts (laborer,
    40, Haverhill) and Carrie R. Fifield (36, Warren)
Mary A., b. 12/10/1903 in Warren; seventh; Leon R. Tibbetts
    (section hand, 27, Haverhill) and Carrie R. Fifield (33, Warren)
Millie A., b. 10/4/1894 in Warren; Leon R. Tibbetts (laborer, 27,
    Haverhill) and Carrie R. Fifield (24, Warren)

TILLY,
daughter, b. 8/13/1900 in Warren; first; William Tilly (farmer, 33, NB)
    and Sarah J. Merrill (22, Warren)

TITUS,
Ralph Martin, b. 4/28/1951; first; Donald Albert Titus (MA) and
    Patricia Ann Asselin (NH)

TOBEY,
Gail L., b. 12/24/1936; second; Guy H. Tobey (Brookline, MA) and
    Christine Bilodeau (Laconia)
Guy H., Jr., b. 10/17/1935; first; Guy Harrison Tobey (Brookline, MA)
    and Christine Bilodeau (Laconia)

TOOMEY,
Adam John, b. 9/6/1994 in Lebanon; Thomas V. Toomey (30) and
    Sarah A. Baylis (26)

Benjamin J., b. 6/18/1997; Thomas V. Toomey (33) and Sarah A. Baylis (29)

Ryan Richard, b. 9/21/1984 in Plymouth; Rick Allan Toomey (25) and Darlene Ann Dreschel (30)

Taniya Ann, b. 6/11/1998 in Lebanon; Steven Michael Toomey (28) and Busaba Karntakosol (25)

TRESCA,
Catherine Lois, b. 10/16/1945 in Plymouth; first; John Dominic Tresca (mer. marine) and Grace H. Tewksbury (Warren); residence - Boston, MA

TRUCHON,
Priscilla Margaret, b. 7/7/1920 in Warren; sixth; Joseph V. Truchon (laborer, Canada) and Rena Beaule (Canada)

TRUELOVE,
Margurite J., d. 12/21/1904 in Warren; first; Harry J. Trulove (laundryman, 27, Patterson, NJ) and Cora M. Elliott (21, Warren)

UPTON,
son, b. 1/31/1903 in Warren; second; Fred N. Upton (blacksmith, 31, Warren) and Etta M. McConnell (29, Stoneham, MA)

child, b. 6/5/1908; third; Fred N. Upton (wheelwright, 37, Warren) and Etta McConnell (34, Stoneham)

Carl Elisha, b. 9/11/1895 in Warren; first; Fred N. Upton (wheelwright, 24, Warren) and Etta M. McConnell (22, Stoneham, MA)

VALDES,
Monica L., b. 1/1/1962; second; Jorge M. Valdes (cook, Havana, Cuba) and Dolores Ann Wood (Woodsville)

VALLEY,
Michael Espy, b. 10/12/1953; third; Clifton Herbert Valley (Landaff) and Velma Mae Litz (Akron, OH)

VARNUM,
Bernice L., b. 3/20/1930; third; Clarence L. Varnum (laborer, Gloucester, MA) and Bertha Chase (Bath)

VIEIRA,
Amy Marie, b. 10/14/1982 in Hanover; John Paul Vieira (MA) and
Elaine Marie Plummer (NH)

VINCELETTE,
Brenda Lee, b. 7/24/1953; first; Everett Lloyd Vincelette (NH) and
Blanche Irene Libby (NH)
Carol Ann, b. 4/8/1957; third; Everett L. Vincellette (road agent,
Warren) and Blanche I. Libbey (Glencliff)
Everett Lloyd, b. 2/23/1955; second; Everett L. Vincelette (laborer,
NH) and Blanche Irene Libby (NH)

VINCOLLETTA,
Everett Lloyd, b. 9/14/1926; eighth; Edmond Vincolletta (laborer,
Calcoat, PQ) and Alice Ketchin (Fairlee, VT); residence -
Claremont

WALKER,
Arthur F., b. 4/25/1916 in Warren; second; Arthur Frederick Walker
(wood chopper, Manchester) and Lillian A. Heath (Littleton)

WALLACE,
Matthew, b. 6/23/1990 in Lebanon; Bradford Malcolm Wallace (26)
and Kimberly Dawn Bryant (24)

WARBIN,
Zachariah James, b. 7/6/1981 in Haverhill; Richard Charles Warbin
(20) and Lorie Ann Kennedy (18)

WARD,
Joseph Leroy, b. 11/15/1944 in Hanover; first; William Ralph Ward
(laborer odd jobs, Sullivan) and Marjorie Grace Pero (Thetford,
VT)

WASHBURN,
Casey Cascade, b. 12/28/1989 in Lebanon; Shawn Maurice
Washburn (27) and Juli Marie Kenworthy (28)
Shawn M., b. 3/19/1962; second; Harvey H. Washburn (truck driver,
Hanover) and Marlene S. Whitcher (Laconia)

WEAVER,

Constance, b. 8/20/1905 in Warren; first; George A. Weaver (physician, 37, Manchester) and Etta E. Hoisington (Pomfret, VT)

Sherman, b. 7/16/1907 in Warren; second; George A. Weaver (physician, 38, Manchester) and Etta E. Hoisington (30, Pomfret, VT)

WEEKS,

son, b. 4/1/1889 in Warren; Henry E. Weeks (laborer, 26, Warren) and Elvira Smith (25, Barton, VT)

son, b. 4/1/1891 in Warren; first; Charles L. Weeks (teamster, 26, Warren) and Sarah W. French (20, Haverhill)

daughter, b. 4/23/1892 in Warren; Henry E. Weeks (day laborer, 29, Warren) and Elvira Smith (27, Barton, VT)

son, b. 9/1/1895 in Warren; fifth; Henry E. Weeks (painter, 33, Warren) and Elvira L. Smith (32, Barton, VT)

son, b. 11/5/1896 in Warren; Charles L. Weeks (farmer, 32, Warren) and Sarah W. French (25, Haverhill)

son, b. 5/28/1899 in Warren; seventh; Henry E. Weeks (farmer, 37, Warren) and Elvira L. Smith (36, Barton, VT)

son, b. 8/3/1900 in Warren; fifth; Charles L. Weeks (laborer, 36, Warren) and Sarah W. French (29, Haverhill)

son, b. 1/9/1903 in Warren; sixth; Charles L. Weeks (farmer, 38, Warren) and Sarah W. French (32, Haverhill)

daughter, b. 1/4/1904 in Warren; eighth; Henry E. Weeks (farmer, 41, Warren) and Elvira Smith (40, Barton, VT)

son, b. 6/27/1905 in Warren; seventh; Charles L. Weeks (painter, 40, Warren) and Sarah W. French (Haverhill)

child, b. 12/24/1908; first; Ira M. Weeks (painter, 23, Warren) and Eliza E. Pickering (18, Piermont)

daughter, b. 10/8/1910; second; Ira Weeks (painter, 24, Warren) and Eliza Pickering (Piermont)

son, b. 8/26/1912 in Warren; third; Ira Weeks (painter, Benton) and Eliza Pickering (Haverhill)

daughter, b. 12/6/1912 in Warren; third; Sidney Weeks (laborer, Warren) and Sarah Shuber (Franklin)

daughter, b. 8/28/1915 in Warren; second; Vallie J. Weeks (laborer, Warren) and Lillian M. Dennis (Boscawen)

daughter, b. 4/8/1922; eighth; Sidney C. Weeks (laborer, Warren) and Sarah E. Streeter (Franklin)

son, b. 5/20/1923; ninth; Sidney Weeks (laborer, Warren) and
Elizabeth Streeter (Franklin)
daughter, b. 9/18/1924; tenth; Sidney Weeks (laborer, Warren) ad
Elizabeth Streeter (Franklin)
daughter, b. 11/2/1925; second; James R. Weeks (painter, Warren)
and Joseph Currier (Tuftonboro)
Beatrice L., b. 1/17/1920 in Warren; seventh; Sidney C. Weeks
(laborer, Warren) and Elizabeth Streeter (Franklin)
Bertha M., b. 6/23/1928; twelfth; Sidney Clyde Weeks (farmer,
Warren) and Elizabeth Streeter (Franklin)
Cale Brian, b. 11/24/1989 in Laconia; Brian Harold Weeks (28) and
Charlene Mae Caverhill (29)
Carlyle R., b. 11/19/1937; fifth; Henry Edgar Weeks (Warren) and
Jessie M. Spencer (Watervliet, NY)
Carlyle Richard, Jr., b. 6/11/1964; second; Carlyle R. Weeks
(mechanic, Warren) and Alma E. Jacques (Fairfax, VT)
Christine H., b. 7/21/1965; third; Carlyle B. Weeks (mechanic,
Warren) and Alma E. Jacques (Fairfax, VT)
Clara Louise, b. 5/26/1928; stillborn; second; Henry Edgar Weeks
(RR, laborer, Warren) and Jessie May Spencer (Troy, NY)
Clinton S., b. 12/22/1914 in Warren; fourth; Sidney C. Weeks
(laborer, Warren) and Elizabeth Streeter (Franklin)
David Merrill, b. 5/9/1944 in Warren; sixth; H. Edgar Weeks
(farming, Warren) and Jessie M. Spencer (Watervliet, NY)
Dorothy M., b. 7/19/1916 in Warren; third; Valley J. Weeks (farmer,
Warren) and Lillian M. Dennis (Boscawen)
Ella Frances, b. 9/14/1917 in Warren; sixth; Sidney Weeks (laborer,
Warren) and Elizabeth Streeter (Franklin)
Elvira C., b. 9/30/1914 in Warren; first; Vallie J. Weeks (lumberman,
Warren) and Lillian N. Dennis (Penacook)
Esther C., b. 6/9/1929; first; Wilbur R. Weeks (laborer, Warren) and
Margaret M. Prescott (Newbury, VT)
Helen Edna, b. 11/3/1946 in Warren; seventh; H. Edgar Weeks
(laborer, Warren) and Jessie M. Spencer (Watervliet)
Helen Marie, b. 4/12/1934; first; Armand Mahaney (laborer, Canada)
and Dorothy May Weeks (Warren)
Henry E., b. 10/21/1907 in Warren; tenth; Henry E. Weeks (painter,
45, Warren) and Elvira L. Smith (44, Barton, VT)
Henry E., Jr., b. 5/26/1928; first; Henry E. Weeks (RR laborer,
Warren) and Jessie May Spencer (Troy, NY)

Ida May, b. 8/7/1932; third; Henry Edgar Weeks (laborer, Warren) and Jessie May Spencer (Watervliet, NY)

Inez, b. 8/10/1893 in Warren; Charles L. Weeks (farm. butcher, 29, Warren) and Sarah W. French (27, Haverhill)

Ira M., Jr., b. 6/1/1919 in Warren; sixth; Ira M. Weeks (farmer, Benton) and Eliza Pickering (Piermont)

James Roderick, Jr., b. 1/12/1929; stillborn; fourth; James R. Weeks (painter, Warren) and Josephine M. Currier (Moultonboro)

Jessie Elvira, b. 8/6/1927; third; James R. Weeks (painter, Warren) and Josephine M. Currier (Moultonboro)

Josephine R., b. 7/11/1939; fifth; James R. Weeks (postal clerk, Warren) and Josephine M. Currier (Moultonboro)

Joyce Currier, b. 12/22/1923; first; James R. Weeks (painter, Warren) and Josephine M. Currier (Moultonboro)

Kate C., b. 4/11/1926; eleventh; Sidney C. Weeks (laborer, Warren) and Elizabeth Streeter (Franklin)

Laura Ellen, b. 9/3/1931; second; Wilbur R. Weeks (laborer, Warren) and Margaret M. Prescott (Newbury, VT)

Newell Eaton, b. 4/2/1910; first; Sidney Weeks (laborer, 22, Warren) and Sarah Streeter (19, Franklin Falls)

Olga Louise, b. 1/3/1915 in Warren; fourth; Ira M. Weeks (farmer, Warren) and Eliza Pickering (Piermont)

Raymond R., b. 9/15/1901 in Warren; eighth; Henry E. Weeks (farmer, 39, Warren) and Alvira L. Smith (38, Barton, VT)

Robert L., b. 5/12/1935; fourth; Henry Edgar Weeks (Warren) and Jessie May Spencer (Watervliet, NY)

Sydney C., b. 10/26/1887 in Warren; Henry E. Weeks (laborer, Warren) and Elvira Smith (Barton, VT)

Walter H., b. 6/10/1916 in Warren; fifth; Sidney C. Weeks (laborer, Warren) and Elizabeth Streeter (Franklin Falls)

Wilburn R., b. 3/5/1934; third; Wilbur R. Weeks (painter, Warren) and Margaret M. Prescott (Newbury, VT)

Winifred K., b. 8/19/1916 in Warren; fifth; Ira M. Weeks (painter, Benton) and Eliza Pickering (Piermont)

WELCH,
stillborn daughter, b. 8/3/1887 in Benton; Edgar S. Welch (farmer, 26, Benton) and Flora S. Tyrell (26, Benton); residence - Benton

WEST,
Izia Eric, b. 9/7/1999 in Plymouth; Neil West and Heather Roth

WESTOVER,
daughter, b. 9/5/1899 in Warren; fourth; Abr. Westover (laborer, 43, England) and Permelia Boardman (43, Canada)

WETHERBEE,
Bernard O., b. 5/12/1943; third; Walter H. Wetherbee (construction, Haverhill) and Lois Mahala Merrill (Warren)
Cary Bernard, b. 5/7/1968 in Haverhill; Bernard O. Wetherbee (barber, NH) and Gloria Jean Caverhill (NH)
Eudora M., b. 9/8/1931; first; Walter H. Wetherbee (carpenter, N. Haverhill) and Lois M. Merrill (Warren); residence - N. Haverhill
Gabrielle Claire, b. 9/25/2005 in Lebanon; Hue Wetherbee and Hailey Wetherbee
Hue Owen, b. 4/22/1954; fifth; Walter H. Wetherbee (carpenter, Haverhill) and Lois Mahala Merrill (Warren)
Melissa Susan, b. 4/18/1950 in Haverhill; fourth; Walter Hugh Weatherbee (carpenter, Haverhill) and Lois Mahala Merrill (Warren)
Stacey Diane, b. 9/13/1970 in Haverhill; Bernard Orrin Wetherbee (NH) and Gloria Jean Caverhill (NH)
Sylvia, b. 5/31/1936; second; Walter Wetherbee (N. Haverhill) and Lois M. Merrill (Warren); residence - N. Haverhill

WHEELER,
Harold A., b. 5/8/1931; first; Clyde Boleau (laborer) and Beatrice Wheeler (Pike)

WHITCHER,
son, b. 1/21/1888 in Warren; Samuel Whitcher (farmer, Warren) and Almina Whitcher (Corinth, VT)
son, b. 2/13/1891 in Warren; first; Arthur D. Whitcher (laborer, 29, Warren) and Elanor ----- (20, Ireland)
daughter, b. 7/17/1892 in Warren; A. D. Whitcher (30, Warren) and E. Short (20, England)
son, b. 10/7/1894 in Warren; A. D. Whitcher (farmer, 33, Warren) and Eleanor S. Short (23, Grand Banks)
daughter, b. 10/19/1897 in Warren; fourth; Arthur D. Whitcher (farmer, 37, Warren) and Nellie Short (26, Newfoundland)

son, b. 5/21/1898 in Warren; second; George Whitcher (farmer, 33, Warren) and Sarah W. Stickney (34, Campton)

daughter, b. 9/27/1898 in Warren; fourth; Fred J. Whitcher (farmer, 30, Warren) and A. Jane Houghton (34, Danville, VT)

son, b. 8/6/1900 in Warren; fifth; Fred J. Whitcher (laborer, 52, Warren) and D. J. Houghton (36, Danville, VT)

daughter, b. 5/14/1906 in Warren; third; George Whitcher (farmer, 41, Warren) and Sarah Stickney (41, Campton)

child, b. 6/26/1908; second; Harry A. Whitcher (farmer, 36, Warren) and Mildred E. Libby (21, Boston)

son, b. 7/30/1909 in Warren; seventh; Frank L. Whitcher (merchant, Wentworth) and Nora Stevens (Rumney)

son, b. 11/3/1911 in Warren; second; Eugene Whitcher (farmer, Warren) and Elsie Lindsey (NS)

son, b. 8/7/1924; sixth; Eugene Whitcher (farmer, Warren) and Elsie Lindsay (NS)

Angela Marie, b. 12/15/1970 in Plymouth; Eugene Rand Whitcher (NH) and Gloria Louise Blake (NH)

Barbara A., b. 11/24/1935; first; Maurice A. Whitcher (Warren) and Helen M. Ball (Landaff)

Bruce K., b. 3/17/1937; first; William H. Whitcher (Warren) and Vera Bixby (Alberta, Canada)

Charles H., b. 10/24/1934; third; Ernest L. Whitcher (laborer, Warren) and Ruth C. Iverson (Laramie, WY)

Cheryl Lou, b. 12/11/1944 in Plymouth; fourth; William Harry Whitcher (shop worker, Warren) and Vera Leona Bixby (Alberta, Canada)

Chester Norman, b. 3/15/1948 in Hanover; third; Chester Rand Whitcher (milk plan opr., Warren) and Esther Blanch Cooper (Lincoln)

Christopher Martin, b. 7/30/1984 in St. Johnsbury, VT; Ronald M. Whitcher (30) and Mary L. Boutin (27)

Clifton L., b. 5/12/1893 in Warren; first; George W. Whitcher (farmer, Warren) and Sarah Stickney (Campton) (1918)

David Ralph, b. 8/11/1948 in Plymouth; second; Kenneth Everett Whitcher (mill laborer, Warren) and Marion Cotton (Warren)

Edward L., b. 4/3/1914 in Warren; third; Eugene R. Whitcher (farmer, Warren) and Elsie E. Lindsay (NS)

Esther Almina, b. 5/19/1921 in Warren; fifth; Eugene Whitcher (farmer, Warren) and Elsie Lindsay (NS)

Ethel B., b. 10/6/1918 in Warren; fourth; Eugene R. Whitcher
(farmer, Warren) and Elsie E. Lindsay (Belmont)

Eugene Rand, b. 8/12/1947 in Plymouth; first; Eugene Rand
Whitcher (carpenter, Warren) and Margaret Lucille Gove
(Plymouth)

Fern M., b. 12/1/1938; fourth; Clayton S. Whitcher (carpenter,
Warren) and Margaret Prescott (Newbury, VT)

Jill Christine, b. 5/27/1972 in Haverhill; David Ralph Whitcher (NH)
and Judy Lee King (NH)

Joseph Lindsey, b. 5/2/1910; first; Eugene Whitcher (farmer, 34,
Warren) and Elsie Lindsey (NS)

Kenneth E., b. 8/20/1917 in Warren; third; Harry A. Whitcher
(farmer, Warren) and Mildred Libbey (Boston)

Lawrence Clifton, b. 8/24/1921 in Warren; third; Clifton L. Whitcher
(laborer, Warren) and Bertha Tibbetts (Warren)

Leroy Edward, b. 12/19/1943; second; Edward L. Whitcher
(woodsman, Warren) and Esther Irene Ball (Landaff)

Lewis, b. 1/17/1920 in Warren; fourth; Harry A. Whitcher
(lumberman, Warren) and Mildred E. Libbey (Boston)

Loralee, b. 10/13/1939; first; Edward L. Whitcher (laborer, Warren)
and Esther I. Ball (Landaff)

Mabel A., b. 11/19/1917 in Warren; second; Clifton L. Whitcher
(laborer, Warren) and Bertha Tibbetts (Warren)

Margaret C., b. 11/30/1915 in Warren; first; Clifton L. Whitcher
(laborer, Warren) and Bertha B. Tibbetts (Warren)

Marlene S., b. 10/20/1937; second; Maurice E. Whitcher (Warren)
and Helen M. Ball (Landaff)

Maurice A., Jr., b. 9/24/1943; third; M. A. Whitcher, Sr. (lumbering,
Warren) and Helen Marian Ball (Landaff)

Neil C., b. 7/1/1939; second; William H. Whitcher (carpenter,
Warren) and Vera L. Bixby (Ver. Val., Canada)

Orrin L., b. 11/7/1880 in Warren; third; Charles Whitcher (farmer, 58,
Warren) and Mary E. Batchelder (54, Warren) (1907)

Philip Buck, b. 10/5/1974 in Haverhill; David Ralph Whitcher (26)
and Judy Lee King (23)

Ralph Hall, b. 8/12/1888 in Warren; first; Harry Whitcher (29,
Warren) and Emily B. Hall (26, Wentworth)

Ronald Martin, b. 8/25/1953; second; Eugene Rand Whitcher (NH)
and Margaret Lucille Gove (NH)

Sally P., b. 11/21/1941; third; William H. Whitcher (road agent,
Warren) and Vera Leona Bixby (Alberta, Canada)

Sandra, b. 4/18/1942; first; Ken. E. Whitcher (laborer, Warren) and
Marion Cotton (Warren)
Stacey Jane, b. 8/12/1980 in Haverhill; Ronald Martin Whitcher (26)
and Mary Louise Boutin (23)
Victoria Mae, b. 6/16/2005 in Lebanon; Christopher Whitcher and
Jaime Whitcher
William H., b. 4/20/1907 in Warren; first; Harry A. Whitcher (farmer,
35, Warren) and Mildred E. Libbey (20, Boston)

WHITE,
Aaron Charles, b. 8/26/1976 in Haverhill; James Robert White (31)
and Doreen Joyce Wiggins (28)
Alicia Marie, b. 9/15/1994 in Lebanon; Lawrence R. White, Jr. (29)
and Lisa Marie Turner (29)
Doris May, b. 7/3/1944 in Glencliff; third; Raymond A. White (farmer,
N. Haverhill) and Ella M. Elliott (Ctr. Haverhill)
Nettie Annie, b. 4/7/1942; first; Robert F. White (truck driver,
Newbury, VT) and Lottie B. Boardman (Pike)
Patrick James, b. 5/8/2005 in Lebanon; Donna White
Todd James, b. 8/7/1971 in Haverhill; James Robert White (NH) and
Doreen Joyce Wiggins (NH)

WHITEMAN,
daughter, b. 3/30/1890 in Warren; first; Willie E. Whiteman (laborer,
26, Warren) and Hattie Kelley (21, Ellsworth)
daughter, b. 2/3/1892 in Warren; Willie Whiteman (laborer, 30,
Warren) and Hattie ----- (23, Ellsworth)

WHITNEY,
daughter, b. 3/22/1924; first; Earle Whitney (laborer, Lancaster) and
Cora Flanders (Warren)
Carolyn Anne, b. 9/7/1945 in Haverhill; second; Percy Leverton
Whitney (paper mill emp., Lincoln) and Evelyn L. Hilliard
(Warren)
Sheila, b. 4/6/1925; second; Earl H. Whitney (laborer, Lancaster)
and Cora E. Flanders (Warren)
Shirley, b. 4/6/1925; third; Earl H. Whitney (laborer, Lancaster) and
Cora E. Flanders (Warren)

WILKINS,
son, b. 3/19/1905 in Warren; second; Alfred H. Wilkins (miner, 27, Canada) and Jennie A. Anthony (Canada)
stillborn son, b. 8/25/1924; third; Tracy Wilkins (milk mgr., Craftsbury, VT) and Lula Fellows (Rumney)
Eva May, b. 10/11/1906 in Warren; third; Alfred Wilkins (miner, 28, Canada) and Jennie Artbury (30, Canada)
Grace Joy, b. 8/18/1985 in Plymouth; Tyler B. Wilkins (38) and Beverly A. Holman (32)
Hope Lynn, b. 1/9/1984 in Haverhill; Tyler Bentley Wilkins (36) and Beverly Ann Holman (30)

WILLIAMS,
Davy Brian, b. 5/25/1974 in Haverhill; Dave Brian Williams (18) and Susan Marie LaRochelle (15)
Nathan Raymond, b. 2/13/1977 in Haverhill; Davy Brian Williams (21) and Susan Marie Larochelle (17)

WILLIS,
Ronald Ralph, b. 2/15/1946 in Plymouth; first; Donald Carrol White (gen. motors, Troy, VT) and Patricia Rose Blanchard (Berlin)

WILMOT,
Jacob Jonathon, b. 8/19/1996 in Haverhill; Troy Alan Wilmot (30) and Vicki Lynn Clark (27)

WILSON,
daughter, b. 5/1/1910; first; Eva May Wilson (17, Lakeport)

WISTNER,
son, b. 10/21/1909 in Warren; first; Charlie Wistner (electrician, Mt. Hope, NJ) and Catherine Short (Newfoundland)
daughter, b. 12/17/1912 in Warren; third; Charles Wistner (farmer, Mt. Hope, NJ) and Catherine Shortt (Newfoundland)
Charles A., b. 1/17/1917 in Warren; eighth; Charles A. Wistner (laborer, Mt. Hope, NJ) and Katherine Short (Newfoundland)
Marion G., b. 2/7/1915 in Warren; fourth; Charles Wistner (farmer, NJ) and Catherine Shortt (Newfoundland)

WOOD,

Dolores Ann, b. 10/20/1942; first; William Donald Mood (labor, mica mine, Warren) and Anna Mae Ball (Bath)

Elaine Marie, b. 8/2/1945 in Haverhill; second; William Donald Wood (mining, Warren) and Anna Mae Ball (Bath)

William D., b. 7/7/1919 in Warren; first; William L. Wood (laborer, St. Johnsbury, VT) and Amy E. Smith (Warren)

WRIGHT,

son, b. 8/13/1901 in Warren; second; Fred Lewis Wright (farmer, 27, Wentworth) and Lizzie Mary Kennerson (24, Concord, VT)

daughter, b. 8/9/1902 in Warren; first; Lewis A. Wright (railroad, 25, Warren) and Mamie L. Harris (29, Warren)

daughter, b. 11/17/1903 in Warren; fourth; Fred L. Wright (laborer, 28, Wentworth) and Lizzie M. Kenerson (29, Concord, VT)

daughter, b. 8/2/1909 in Warren; second; Frank N. Wright (livery, Piermont) and Sarah P. Smith (Gilford)

daughter, b. 6/10/1910; first; Arthur Wright (farmer, 27, Piermont) and Nancy Flanders (Warren)

son, b. 12/4/1925; tenth; Arthur G. Wright (laborer, Piermont) and Nancy V. Flanders (Warren)

Aimee Louise, b. 9/29/1974 in Haverhill; Lewis Arthur Wright (25) and Susan Maude Smith (23)

Bernice A., b. 5/17/1914 in Warren; third; Frank N. Wright (liveryman, Piermont) and Sarah P. Smith (Gilford)

Bertha Mamie, b. 8/21/1924; ninth; Arthur Wright (farmer, Piermont) and Nancy Flanders (Warren)

Carolyn Vicki, b. 10/11/1966; first; Glenn G. Wright (laborer, Wentworth) and Gertrude A. Johnson (Hanover)

Charyl E., b. 6/12/1961; fourth; Fay Everett Wright (press cutter, Warren) and Joan Caverhill (Cornwall, CT)

Christopher David, b. 12/20/1968 in Haverhill; Lewis Arthur Wright (NH) and Susan Maude Smith (NH)

Clarence F., b. 12/21/1900 in Warren; first; Frank N. Wright (preacher, 22, Piermont) and Sarah P. Smith (18, Gilford)

Donald Erwin, b. 9/13/1928; twelfth; Arthur G. Wright (RR laborer, Piermont) and Nancy V. Flanders (Warren)

Eleanor Frances, b. 10/18/1921 in Warren; eighth; Arthur G. Wright (laborer, Piermont) and Nancy V. Flanders (Warren)

Emily Jane, b. 10/21/1950 in Plymouth; second; Faye Everette Wright (sawmill lr., Warren) and Joan Caverhill (CT)

Glenn George, b. 8/11/1943; third; George I. Wright (farmer,
    Wentworth) and Martha M. Foote (Warren)
Harry T., b. 11/5/1940; second; George I. Wright (farmer,
    Wentworth) and Martha M. Foote (Warren)
Harry Tilden, Jr., b. 9/17/1973 in Plymouth; Harry Tilden Wright (NH)
    and Lorraine Ann Ball (NH)
Inez M., b. 1/15/1920 in Warren; seventh; Arthur G. Wright (laborer,
    Piermont) and Nancy V. Flanders (Warren)
Lawrence R., b. 7/16/1967; fifth; Fay E. Wright (disabled, Warren)
    and Joan Caverhill (Warren)
Leslie Irwin, b. 3/4/1964; first; Harry T. Wright (lumber mill, Warren)
    and Lorraine A. Ball (Woodsville)
Lloyd Albert, b. 12/31/1929; twelfth; Arthur G. Wright (laborer,
    Piermont) and Nancy B. Flanders (Warren)
Madelyn Louise, b. 5/1/1927; eleventh; Arthur G. Wright (RR man,
    Piermont) and Nancy V. Flanders (Warren)
Marilyn Jean, b. 8/7/1954; third; Fay Everett Wright (laborer,
    Warren) and Joan Caverhill (Cornwall, CT)
Michael Wallace Roy, b. 1/5/1975 in Haverhill; Michael Wallace
    Frank Wright (25) and Marlene Stevens (25)
Michelle Lee, b. 12/14/1968 in Plymouth; Harry Tilden Wright (NH)
    and Lorraine Ann Ball (NH)
Norma Louise, b. 8/18/1924; second; Clarence Wright (farmer,
    Warren) and Freda Donn (Lakeport); residence - Lakeport
Rebecca Ann, b. 11/23/1964; fourth; Donald E. Wright (fireman,
    Warren) and Geraldine L. Wright (Plymouth)
Roland M., b. 3/11/1921 in Warren; first; Alice Wright (Wentworth)
Tilden George, b. 8/25/1957; second; Richard A. Wright (truck
    driver, Pike) and Rita Louise McCoy (Walpole)
Wallace, b. 2/26/1923; first; Clarence Wright (butcher, Warren) and
    Freda Dame (Lakeport)

WURTZ,
Thomas Arnold, b. 9/12/1999 in Lebanon; John Wurtz and Sandra
    Wurtz

WYSS,
Donna Jean, b. 12/10/1948 in Plymouth; second; Carl Wyss
    (laborer, Lansdowne, PA) and Marjorie Edwina Young (New
    Bedford, MA)

WARREN
MARRIAGES

ACQUISTAPACE,

Mark L. of Goodyear, AZ m. Sharyn M. **Washburn** of Warren
8/23/1986 in Piermont; H - 29, s/o Andrew Acquistapace and
Judith Lowman; W - 22, d/o Horton Washburn and Marlene
Whitcher

ADAMS,

B. S. of Lancaster m. Grace A. **Currie** of Warren 5/17/1898 in
Warren; H - 19, farmer, b. Lancaster, s/o H. B. Adams
(Lancaster, farmer); W - 16, domestic, b. Canada, d/o James
E. Currie (Canada)

David M. of Plymouth m. Catherine **MacDonald** of Warren 7/7/1963
in Warren; H - 17, store clerk, s/o Edward D. Adams and Ruth
E. Thompson; W - 17, at home, d/o John H. MacDonald and
Grace H. Tewksbury

Donald Linwood of Warren m. Michele **Papio** of Campton 6/13/1971
in Plymouth; H - 20, s/o Martin B. Adams and Blanche I.
Hildreth; W - 18, d/o Michael E. Papio and Dorothy Carrincione

Martin B.of Hebron m. Blanche I. **Hildreth** of Warren 8/20/1955 in
Warren; H - 25, well driller, s/o Harold Adams and Gladys
Barnard; W - 25, waitress, d/o William E. Hildreth and Margaret
Veasey

ALESSANDRINI,

Bernardino L. of Warren m. Marion **Oliver** of Newbury, VT 5/8/1949
in Groton, VT; H - 20, poultry raiser, b. Barnet, VT, s/o Simeone
Alessandrini (Rome, Italy) and Mura V. Dorset (ME); W - 18, b.
Woodsville, d/o George Oliver (Battle Creek, MI) and Phyllis
Willey (NH)

Bernadino L., Jr. of Warren m. Jo-Ann **Gould** of Plymouth 12/3/1971
in Plymouth; H - 22, s/o Bernadino L. Alessandrini, Sr. and
Marion Oliver; W - 19, d/o Charles A. Gould and Meda Munn

Simeone of Warren m. Mildred E. **Manning** of Moultonboro
1/18/1958 in Woodsville; H - 60, mason, s/o Lucian
Alessandrini and Anna Ricci; W - 60, cook, d/o Edward C.
Brogan and Mabel J. Jewell

Simeone of Warren m. Eleanor **Chase** of Warren 12/21/1964 in
Wells River, VT; H - 67, mason, s/o Lucien Alessandrini and
Anna Richie; W - 21, d/o Leon Chase and Lena White

AMES,

Roy H., Jr. of Warren m. Joan L. **Morrison** of Wentworth
11/16/1957 in Warren; H - 21, paper maker, s/o Roy H. Ames,
Sr. and Helen I. Crafts; W - 19, typist, d/o William A. Morrison
and Hazel M. Whitney

Spurgeon of Warren m. Adella **Tilley** of Wentworth 3/27/1935 in
Woodsville; H - 28, trucking, b. Warren, s/o William Ames and
Sadie McCormick; W - 21, at home, b. Wentworth, d/o William
Tilley and Sarah J. Merrill

Wesley T. of Warren m. Elaine Marie **Wood** of Warren 12/30/1963
in Glencliff; H - 21, mill operator, s/o Earl F. Brown and Mabel
Ames; W - 18, at home, d/o William D. Wood and Anna M. Ball

AMSDEN,

Paul A. of Warren m. Mary Elizabeth **Hight** of Warren 9/1/1968 in
Glencliff; H - 24, b. NH, s/o Roland Amsden (NH) and Joyce
Martin (NH); W - 21, b. NH, d/o George E. Hight (VT) and
Orilene Millette (NH)

ANDERSON,

Fayne E. of Warren m. Marcia E. **Batchelder** of Warren 10/24/1926
in Warren; H - 23, laborer, b. Drew, ME, s/o Fred Anderson
(Lawrence, MA, photographer) and Pansy Collier (ME,
housewife); W - 21, at home, b. Warren, d/o Albert N.
Batchelder (Warren, lumber deal.) and Nettie Merrill (Warren,
housewife)

James W. of Warren m. Edith Chamberlin **Corliss** of Newbury, VT
8/15/1953 in Newbury, VT; H - 32, miner, s/o James A.
Anderson and Doris Wilson; W - 24, office, d/o George H.
Chamberlin and Louella Heath

ANDREWS,

Harold V. of Warren m. Etta **Heath** of Warren 9/2/1916 in
Wentworth; H - 39, laborer, 2nd, b. Woodsville, s/o Norris P.
Andrews (Danville, PQ) and Martha J. Cheney (Warner); W -
21, housemaid, b. Warren, d/o J. M. Heath (Warren) and Ada
M. Chase (Wentworth)

ARNOLD,

Walter J. of Pike Station m. Blanche **Hardy** of Warren 4/21/1900 in
Warren; H - 21, laborer, b. Pike Station, s/o Robert R. Arnold

(NY State, farmer); W - 19, domestic, b. E. Haverhill, d/o
Joseph Hardy (Haverhill, farmer)

ASSELIN,

Daniel M. of Warren m. Mary L. **Mauchly** of Warren 4/3/1982 in
Wentworth; H - 20, s/o H. T. Asselin and Sheila Moore; W - 18,
d/o James T. Mauchly and Flora J. Hand

David B. of Warren m. Karen L. **Hapsis** of Warren 10/8/1982 in
Warren; H - 22, s/o Henry T. Asselin and Sheila Moore; W - 33,
d/o Howard Helleberg and Janet Price

Henry D. of Warren m. Ernestine E. **Perry** of Warren 1/30/1930 in
Warren; H - 21, laborer, b. Warren, s/o John Asselin
(Drummondsville, PQ, deceased) and Ruth A. Whitcher
(Warren, deceased); W - 18, at home, b. Medford, MA, d/o
George S. Perry (St. Johns, NB, laborer) and Martha Wright
(Liverpool, England, housewife)

Michael Dearborn of Warren m. Audrey Lynn **Marland** of Woodsville
11/10/1973 in Woodsville; H - 17, s/o Henry T. Asselin and
Sheila E. Moore; W - 16, d/o Joseph L. Marland, Jr. and
Jeanette L. Flint

AUBREY,

Mark J. of Warren m. Leonetta H. **Anderson** of Warren 12/23/1996;
H - 33, s/o John Aubrey, Jr. and Mary Ann Howarth; W - 26, d/o
Henry G. Anderson and Margaret R. DeBow

AVERILL,

Ray R. of York Beach m. Nellie A. **Brown** of Warren 9/21/1911 in
Haverhill; H - 27, loco. fireman, b. Barton, VT, s/o Fred Averill;
W - 19, domestic, b. Wentworth, d/o William Brown

AVERY,

Clifton A. of Warren m. Helen E. **Swan** of Rumney 9/28/1935 in
Fairlee, VT; H - 27, truck driver, b. Rumney, s/o Arthur Avery
and Florence Avery; W - 25, b. Stark, d/o Charles Emery and
Gertrude H. Sawyer

Raymond A. of Warren m. Doris E. **Wheeler** of Woodsville 4/5/1930
in Berlin; H - 22, tool maker, b. Warren, s/o Hasting Avery
(Ellsworth, laborer) and Della Batchelder (Warren, deceased);
W - 21, nurse, b. Woodsville, d/o Robert Wheeler (Newport,
fireman, RR) and Annie E. Burpee (Winchester, deceased)

Raymond A. of Warren m. Una Violet **French** of Warren 7/24/1936
in Newbury, VT; H - 28, farmer, b. Warren, s/o Hasting Avery
and Della Batchelder; W - 19, b. Ashland, d/o George French
and Flora Smith

Raymond A. of Glencliff m. Mabel Merrill **Draper** of Glencliff
11/11/1947 in Warren; H - 39, chef, 3rd, b. Warren, s/o Hastings
Avery (Ellsworth, farmer) and Della Batchelder (Warren,
housewife); W - 39, top stitcher, 2nd, b. Canada, d/o Rutherford
Hussey (Hooksett, farmer) and Grace Smith (Hooksett)

BAGLEY,
Donald Bixby of Franklin m. Donna Marie **Heath** of Warren
5/11/1974 in Warren; H - 25, s/o Arthur Bagley and Ruth Bixby;
W - 22, d/o Elmer Heath and Jennie Raymond

BAKER,
Earle L. of Pike m. Blanche **Merrill** of Warren 1/1/1905 in Warren; H
- 26, carpenter, b. St. Albans, VT, s/o Lucien Baker (Canada,
carpenter); W - 20, domestic, b. Warren, d/o Fred Merrill
(Rumney, farmer)

BALCH,
William of Warren m. Angelia **Charles** of Warren –/–/2003 in
Warren

BALL,
Albert Leslie of Warren m. Janette P. **Woodward** of Orford
7/27/1973 in Warren; H - 21, scourer, s/o Leslie Albert Ball and
Doris Mary Ledger; W - 18, at home, d/o Norman C. Woodward
and Grace Elmira Lear

Allan Max of Glencliff m. Carol Ann **Pierson** of Orford 1/12/1963 in
Glencliff; H - 24, Navy, s/o Reginald H. Ball and Charlotte
Griffin; W - 20, nurse, d/o Wallace H. Pierson and Evelyn
Weeks

Anthony Herbert of Glencliff m. Pamela Gail **Stimson** of Glencliff
6/24/1978 in Woodsville; H - 23, s/o Reginald Ball and Charlotte
Griffin; W - 19, d/o Delton Stimson and Rita Chase

Bert Peter of Warren m. Judy Ann **Thompson** of Warren
10/18/1971 in Warren; H - 21, s/o Leslie Ball and Doris Ledger;
W - 18, d/o George Thompson and Delia Comeau

Brian of Glencliff m. Lolita **Macomber** of Rumney 5/6/1972 in
Rumney; H - 20, s/o Clifford E. Ball and Ardeth M. Stimson; W -
19, d/o Elwin E. Macomber and Ruth H. Marsh
Brian Bert of Glencliff m. Susan Denise **Raptis** of Glencliff
5/27/1978 in Warren; H - 26, s/o Clifford Ball and Ardeth
Stinson; W - 26, d/o Raymond Brassard and Georgette Miville
Clifford E. of Warren m. Ardeth M. **Maunula** of Warren 11/3/1951 in
Warren; H - 39, laborer, s/o Bert L. Ball and Eva I. Moulton; W -
23, housewife, d/o Elmer G. Stimson and Lilla May Marten
Daniel Joseph of Warren m. Susan Elaine **Field** of Concord
4/10/1976 in Concord; H - 23, s/o Leslie Ball and Doris Ledger;
W - 23, d/o Alfred Field, Sr. and Marion Abbott
David Harry of Hanover m. Gloria Jean **Gowen** of Hanover
10/17/1970 in Glencliff; H - 22, s/o Reginald Ball and Charlotte
Griffin; W - 17, d/o Guy Gowen and Patricia Smith
Herman George of Warren m. Celia Mae **Jones** of Haverhill
2/19/1945 in Piermont; H - 22, US Army, b. Landaff, s/o Bert
Leslie Ball (Landaff, retired) and Eva Moulton (Landaff,
housewife); W - 20, unemployed, b. Haverhill, d/o Frederick
Jones (CT, state highway worker) and Lucy Sawyer (Pike,
housewife)
James Edward of Warren m. Elaine Marie **Bean** of Warren
2/15/1996; H - 25, s/o Edward James Ball and Norma Clark; W
- 29, d/o Edward Clinton Spencer and Marie Elaine White
Kevin R. of Warren m. Angela D. **Davis** of Woodsville 2/23/1980 in
Warren; H - 21, s/o Herman G. Ball and Celia Jones; W - 19,
d/o Charles R. Davis and Maebell Paxton
Leslie Albert of Glencliff m. Doris M. **Ledger** of Glencliff 1/16/1939 in
Woodsville; H - 21, mail carrier, b. Landaff, s/o Bert Ball
(Landaff) and Eva Moulton (Landaff); W - 22, housework, b.
Gardner, MA, d/o Fred Ledger (NB) and Delina Sawyer (NB)
Loren R. of Warren m. Susan **Simmons** of Warren 7/20/1985 in
Warren; H - 24, s/o Herman Ball and Celia Jones; W - 20, d/o
John Simmons and Nancy Dimond
Reginald H. of Warren m. Charlotte M. **Griffin** of Tilton 2/12/1938 in
N. Haverhill; H - 27, mill hand, b. Landaff, s/o Bert L. Ball
(Landaff) and Eva I. Moulton (Landaff); W - 19, servant, b.
Tilton, d/o Harry C. Griffin (Tilton) and Bertha M. Belyea
(Glencliff)

Scott A. of Glencliff m. Christine N. **Hudson** of Bath 5/16/1986 in N. Haverhill; H - 21, s/o Allan M. Ball and Carol A. Pierson; W - 19, d/o Bernard G. Hudson and Christine E. Dann

BALLESTER,

Michael Dennis of Laconia m. Annette Marie **Hurlbutt** of Warren 6/23/1973 in Warren; H - 21, s/o George B. Ballester and Jeanne Beauchene; W - 17, d/o William H. Hurlbutt and Lucille Friend

BANCROFT,

Earl Robert of Warren m. Susan May **Forrest** of Wentworth 10/16/1971 in Warren; H - 22, s/o Lewis Bancroft and Dorothy Young; W - 21, d/o Wayne Forrest and Jessie Ryder

Kenneth Albert, Jr. of Warren m. Patricia Susan **Buttrick** of Warren 10/27/1979 in Warren; H - 23, s/o Kenneth A. Bancroft, Jr. and Elizabeth A. Brown; W - 19, d/o Ronald H. Buttrick and Lois J. Carbone

Robert Allison of Warren m. Elizabeth Louise **Hollinrake** of Warren 8/29/1992 in Warren; H - 67, s/o Fred L. Bancroft and Ida May Fitzgerald; W - 61, d/o Leon Elmer Meserve and Harriet Blatchford

Steven Allison of Germany m. Anita Theresia **Stein** of Germany 5/13/1977 in Kirchberg, Germany; H - 22, s/o Robert A. Bancroft and Marjorie P. Moore; W - 21, d/o Heinrich Alois Stein and Erika Sturmer

BARBER,

Frank W. of Willimantic, CT m. Vernie D. **Clement** of Warren 12/27/1910 in Warren; H - 31, supt. of schools, b. Hancock, s/o Alfred Barber (Hubbardston, MA, farmer); W - 23, office clerk, b. Warren, d/o Frank Clement (Warren, wholesale merchant)

BARKER,

Carl E. of Warren m. Helen M. **Hutchins** of Warren 5/29/1900 in Warren; H - 26, laborer, widower, b. Nashua, s/o E. Barker (Antrim, blind maker); W - 26, domestic, b. Plymouth, d/o George Hutchins (Plymouth, carpenter)

BARRY,

Everett F. of Warren m. Sadie Julina **Griffin** of Monroe 10/16/1932 in Woodsville; H - 20, truck driver, b. Orford, s/o Charles F. Barry (Rumney, mfg.) and Ora May Smith (Sanbornton, housewife); W - 22, at home, b. Whitefield, d/o Thomas H. Griffin (St. Johnsbury, VT, retired) and Laura Helena Kelly (PQ, housewife)

BARTLETT,

Charles C. of Webster m. Maud M. **Hayward** of Northfield 5/16/1908; H - 30, b. Bath, s/o Alonzo Bartlett (Dalton, sheriff); W - 18, b. Northfield, d/o Porter Hayward (Concord, engineer)

Homer E. of Warren m. Blanche I. **Keith** of Warren 6/5/1901 in Charlestown; H - 21, clerk, b. Bath, s/o Alonzo F. Bartlett (dep. sheriff); W - 21, domestic, d/o William Keith (carpenter)

Robert William of Warren m. Brenda Lee **Schieber** of Warren 1/27/1973 in Warren; H - 24, s/o Meredith L. Bartlett and Janet Botsford; W - 20, d/o Everett L. Vincelette and Blanche I. Libby

BASSLER,

Allen Eugene of Pike m. Wanda Lee **Ball** of Glencliff 7/19/1969 in Warren; H - 20, s/o Edwin Bassler and Agnes Steiner; W - 20, d/o Clifford Ball and Ardeth Stimson

BATCHELDER,

Albert N. of Warren m. Nettie M. **Merrill** of Warren 12/25/1900 in Warren; H - 31, farmer, b. Warren, s/o Charles H. Batchelder (Warren, farmer); W - 21, domestic, b. Warren, d/o Jesse O. Merrill (Warren, farmer)

Arthur M. of Warren m. Leona May **Petito** of Warren 6/6/1917 in Warren; H - 21, laborer, b. Warren, s/o Charles W. Batchelder (Warren) and Cora A. Merrill (Warren); W - 19, housekeeper, 2nd, divorced, b. Warren, d/o Arthur L. Pike (Warren) and Eva Judkins (Danville Green, VT)

C. W. of Warren m. Cora A. **Merrill** of Warren 12/5/1893 in Warren; H - 32, laborer, b. Warren, s/o C. H. Batchelder (Warren, farmer); W - 19, b. Warren, d/o Asa B. Merrill

William H. of Warren m. Rozella E. **Watts** of Rumney 11/9/1898 in Laconia; H - 38, laborer, b. Warren, s/o Reuben Batchelder (Warren, farmer); W - 34, domestic, b. Ellsworth, d/o Joseph Avery (Warren, farmer)

BATES,

Kenneth Ray of Warren m. Olive M. **Belyea** of Wentworth 7/14/1974 in W. Newbury, VT; H - 73, s/o Elmer L. Bates and Frances Raymond; W - 72, d/o Frank Flanders and Jessie Boynton

BEAMIS,

Harold G. of Haverhill m. Sheila A. **French** of Warren 4/28/1942 in Haverhill; H - 21, farming, b. Haverhill, s/o Herbert L. Beamis (Warren) and Mary Flanders (Bradford); W - 16, unemployed, b. Haverhill, d/o Reuben French (Canada) and Velma Ladeau (Haverhill)

Herbert Glen of Warren m. Penny Lee **Franusiak** of Plymouth 8/8/1970 in Bradford, VT; H - 18, s/o Harold Beamis and Priscilla Cutting; W - 19, d/o Walter Franusiak and Pauline Avery

BEAN,

Ray Charles of Warren m. Arlene Agusta A. **Hopkins** of W. Thornton 8/2/1946 in N. Haverhill; H - 30, mechanic, b. Orford, s/o Dana J. Bean (Orford) and Nellie Wright (Piermont, housewife); W - 31, housewife, 2nd, b. W. Thornton, d/o William Amer (Bancroft, ME, lumbering) and Sadie McCormick (Bancroft, ME, housewife)

Stuart K. of Warren m. Elaine M. **Spencer** of Warren 6/27/1986 in Warren; H - 30, s/o Metton Bean and Evelyn Webster; W - 20, d/o Edward Spencer and Marie White

BEEDE,

William C. of Warren m. Hattie **Burke** of Benton 3/7/1898 in Wentworth; H - 41, mechanic, 2nd, b. Dalton, s/o David Beede (Lindon, laborer); W - 19, domestic, b. Franklin, VT, d/o Napoleon Burke (Canada, farmer)

BELL,

Richard A. of Maple Shade, NJ m. Betty M. **Williams** of Maple Shade, NJ 9/22/1979 in Warren; H - 38, s/o Fillmore H. Bell and Martha G. Logan; W - 34, d/o Frederick W. Williams and Maureen M. Bryant

BELYEA,

George A. of Warren m. Marguerite A. **Wallace** of Meredith 10/14/1928 in Meredith; H - 21, farmer, b. Benton, s/o George Belyea (Canada, farmer) and Jennie N. Moses (Norton Mills, VT); W - 19, waitress, b. Haverhill, d/o Harry Wallace (Glasgow, Scotland, trainman) and Alma Aldrich (Sugar Hill, housewife)

George N. of Warren m. Jennie H. **Moses** of Warren 9/21/1895 in Haverhill; H - 28, laborer, b. NB, s/o George S. Belyea; W - 25, domestic, b. Norton, VT, d/o Jonathan Moses

Jay L. of Warren m. Marcia L. **Spencer** of Warren 6/18/1982 in Warren; H - 22, s/o Ronald Belyea and Esther Anderson; W - 20, d/o Edward Spencer and Marie White

Jay L. of Warren m. Marie L. **Taylor** of Warren 6/21/1986 in Piermont; H - 26, s/o Ronald Belyea and Esther Jane Anderson; W - 21, d/o Elmer Taylor and Phyllis Louise Roystan

Llewellyn of Glencliff m. Blanch M. **Lavoie** of Glencliff 6/26/1926 in Haverhill; H - 24, bobbin turner, b. Warren, s/o James Belyea (NB, laborer) and Mary Fifield (Warren, at home); W - 23, at home, b. Manchester, d/o Peter Lavoie (Groton, VT, lumber dealer) and Lydia Derosia (Groton, VT, housewife)

Philip Roy of Warren m. Lauren Elizabeth **Cook** of Orford 9/4/1971 in Orford; H - 22, s/o Roland N. Belyea and Lydia E. Derosia; W - 20, d/o Foster G. Cook, Jr. and Jean A. Smith

Robert Leo of Warren m. Thelma Mabel **Edwards** of Groton, VT 7/1/1950 in Groton, VT; H - 23, signal man, b. Warren, s/o Llewellyn Belyea (Warren) and Blanche Lavoie (Manchester); W - 28, bookkeeper, b. Thetford, PQ, d/o Harley W. Edwards (Barre, VT) and Orphia Amadon (Maple Gro., PQ)

Roland Mearl of Haverhill m. Lydia Ella **Derosia** of Warren 8/26/1947 in Haverhill; H - 26, mill worker, b. Warren, s/o Roy Belyea (Warren, laborer) and Alice Cora Wright (Wentworth, housewife); W - 22, telephone operator, b. Warren, d/o Louis J. Derosia (Benton, tel. lineman) and Flossie May Rollins (Wentworth, housewife)

Roland Roy of Warren m. Esther Jane **Anderson** of Warren 5/3/1947 in Warren; H - 18, laborer, b. Warren, s/o Lewis Belyea (Piermont, laborer) and Blanche Lavoie (Manchester, housewife); W - 16, at home, b. Warren, d/o Fayne E. Anderson (Drew, ME, carpenter) and Marcia Batchelder (Warren, housewife)

Ronald R. of Warren m. Judith A. **Bushor** of Lebanon 10/21/1966 in
Lebanon; H - 38, bridge super., s/o Llewellyn Belyea and
Blanche M. Lavoie; W - 24, secretary, d/o Harry B. Manfield
and Marguerite LaBombard
William H. of Warren m. Helen I. **Perry** of Haverhill 5/2/1925 in
Haverhill; H - 23, truck driver, b. Benton, s/o George Belyea
(NB, S. R. pat.) and Jennie N. Moses (Norton Mills, housewife);
W - 17, housework, b. Haverhill, d/o Charles A. Perry
(Whitefield, farmer) and Inez C. Lindsey (Benton, housewife)

BENEDICT,
Royce of Warren m. Melanie A. **Smith** of Warren 9/11/1981 in
Warren; H - 25, s/o Max Benedict and Beverly Brown; W - 24,
s/o Collins F. Carr and Roberta M. Hatch

BENT,
Anthony G. of Warren m. Norma J. **Parenteau** of Warren
10/23/1983 in Warren; H - 18, s/o Norman Bent and Claire
Hurlbutt; W - 18, d/o Wilfred A. Parenteau and Barbara Rollins

BICKFORD,
Arthur of Warren m. Lena **Gale** of Warren 4/15/1905 in Warren; H -
29, teamster, 2nd, b. Dorchester, s/o Albert Bickford
(Dorchester, farmer); W - 19, domestic, b. Warren, d/o William
F. Gale (Warren, farmer)

BILODEAU,
William of Warren m. E. Millie **Belanger** of Ashland 10/2/1906 in
Ashland; H - 44, laborer, b. Canada, s/o John Bilodeau
(Canada, farmer); W - 34, semer, b. Ashland, d/o Edward
Belanger (Canada, laborer)

BISHOP,
Harold L. of Warren m. Marion E. **Weeks** of Warren 4/15/1932 in
Warren; H - 20, laborer, b. Medford, MA, s/o Thomas R. Bishop
(Bath, ME) and Annie I. Brent (Boston, MA); W - 18, at home,
b. Warren, d/o Sidney G. Weeks (Warren, laborer) and
Elizabeth Streeter (Franklin, housewife)

BIXBY,

Lawrence P. of Warren m. Catherine M. **Hall** of Warren 10/7/2000 in Warren; H - 40, s/o Robert W. Bixby and Margaret E. Kramer; W - 38, d/o Glenn G. Hall and Edith H. Muckelberg

Steven V. of Warren m. Kathy A. **Colby** of Bradford, VT 9/12/1987 in Piermont; H - 20, s/o Arthur W. Bixby and Rita Greenwood; W - 24, d/o John E. Colby and Carilyn C. Benjamin

W. M. of Warren m. Hattie L. **Currie** of Warren 7/5/1895 in Warren; H - 21, laborer, b. Warren, s/o Solomon C. Bixby (Warren, farmer); W - 18, domestic, b. Canada, d/o James Currie (farmer)

BLAKE,

Alvah C. of Warren m. Lula M. **Foster** of Wentworth 6/28/1890 in Rumney; H - 23, laborer, b. Rumney, s/o Oscar F. Blake; W - 19, d/o Alva Foster

Ernest Raymond, Jr. of Conway m. Verona Louise **Bixby** of Warren 8/21/1949 in Salem; H - 20, student, b. Conway, s/o Ernest Raymond Blake (Brownfield, ME) and Zelpha McKinney (Conway); W - 22, teacher, b. Warren, d/o Maurice H. Bixby (Warren) and Mildred Hunkins (Groton)

Eugene of Warren m. Josephine **Sargent** of Bangor, ME 10/1/1909 in Warren; H - 40, laborer, 2nd, b. W. Thornton, s/o Oscar F. Blake (farmer); W - 36, mill worker, 2nd, b. Bangor, ME, d/o Edgar E. Ellis

Harry I. of Warren m. Martha A. **Simpson** of Warren 5/25/1898 in Warren; H - 20, farmer, b. Warren, s/o Isaac Blake (Salem, VT, farmer); W - 21, domestic, b. Warren, d/o Henry Simpson (laborer)

John W. of Warren m. Edith M. **Cotton** of Warren 6/1/1907 in Warren; H - 24, telegraph opr., b. Warren, s/o William F. Blake (Sydneham Pl, PQ, policeman); W - 23, b. Warren, d/o Edward D. Cotton (Warren, farmer)

Robert of Haverhill m. Lillian **Cummings** of Warren 3/26/1913 in Warren; H - 18, teamster, b. Haverhill, s/o Joseph Blake (Haverhill, lumbering); W - 32, housework, 2nd, b. Warren, d/o Fred Gale (Warren, watchman)

Wyman W. of Haverhill m. Bernice A. **Wright** of Warren 11/10/1934 in N. Haverhill; H - 22, laborer, b. Haverhill, s/o Charles S. Blake (Haverhill, laborer) and Maude Brooks (Franconia, homemaker); W - 20, stenographer, b. Warren, d/o Frank N. Wright (farmer) and Sarah Smith (homemaker)

BLANCHARD,

Robert Allen of Warren m. Judith Ann **Robertson** of Warren 3/8/1991 in Warren; H - 35, s/o Clarence Everett Blanchard and Mildred Edwina Stone; W - 47, d/o Nelson Valmore Lemner and Marie Irene Hannan

BLODGETT,

Charles N. of Warren m. Maud E. **Harris** of Warren 10/14/1903 in Worcester, MA; H - 23, farmer, b. Hebron, s/o John T. Blodgett (Plymouth, farmer); W - 24, domestic, b. Swiftwater, d/o Nelson L. Harris (Ashland, farmer)

Scott M. of Warren m. Yvonne M. **Garrett** of Warren 12/17/2005 in Warren

BLOOM,

Brian George of Warren m. Rhonda Marie **Heath** of Warren 8/11/1994 in Warren; H - 29, s/o George W. Bloom and Joan E. Breton; W - 19, d/o Arthur G. Heath and Robin J. Russell

BOLDUC,

Michael W. of Warren m. Barbara C. **Fitts** of Warren 9/2/2000 in Laconia; H - 39, s/o Francis E. Bolduc and Alice N. Bossey; W - 37, d/o Ralph N. Fitts and Dorothy A. Chapman

BONAZZI,

Charles of Montpelier, VT m. Jessie E. A. **Arnold** of Montpelier, VT 5/14/1955 in Warren; H - 54, banker, s/o Ferdinando Bonazzi and Aurelia Rossi; W - 39, at home, d/o Joseph T. Atchison and Euphratese Wheeler

BOND,

Francis J. of Warren m. E. Barbara **Medeiros** of Warren 2/4/1950 in Warren; H - 35, heating, b. Berlin, s/o James A. Bond (Somerville, MA) and Cassie Priscilla Cutting (Lyme); W - 31, housewife, b. Warren, d/o Eugene R. Whitcher (Warren) and Elsie Lindsey (NS)

BOULET,

William Lawrence of Warren m. Eleanor Arlene **Benson** of Littleton 7/14/1976 in Warren; H - 50, s/o William J. Boulet and Eileen Bowers; W - 55, d/o Carroll P. Howard and Lillian Hanscom

BOURASSA,

Andrew G. of Warren m. Renee L. **Chenez** of Plymouth 8/6/2004 in Plymouth

BOUTIN,

Robert James of Warren m. Paula Jean **Marsh** of Warren 7/23/1988 in Warren; H - 25, s/o Joseph Boutin and Priscilla Paradie; W - 25, d/o Martin A. Marsha and Pauline Audet

BOWLES,

Albert W. of Warren m. Florence **Coates** of E. Haverhill 10/27/1918 in Warren; H - 20, bobbin turner, b. Warren, s/o Herbert L. J. Bowles (Lisbon) and Catherine Short (Newfoundland); W - 20, domestic, b. N. Haverhill, d/o Will Coates (Cornhill, NB) and Etta Sealey (Bethlehem)

Kenneth H. of Warren m. Eva **MacDonald** of Plymouth 2/15/1930 in Plymouth; H - 25, iron worker, b. Warren, s/o Herbert L. Bowles (Lisbon, engineer) and Catherine Shortt (St. John, NF, housework); W - 23, pow. mach. op., 2nd, b. Plymouth, d/o Lyman A. Lovett (W. Campton, deceased) and Nellie M. Andrews (Woodsville, housewife)

Roy E. of Warren m. Eglantine **Bushey** of St. Albans, VT 7/7/1928 in Warren; H - 24, laborer, b. Warren, s/o Herbert Bowles (Easton, laborer) and Katherine Short (Warren, housewife); W - 28, waitress, b. St. Albans, VT, d/o Seraphin Bushey (Tursso, Canada, blacksmith) and Alphonsine Sovey (Valefield, PQ, housewife)

BOYNTON,

Carl M. of Warren m. Elmeda May **Moses** of Meredith 6/1/1920 in Warren; H - 37, board sawyer, b. New Hampton, s/o Elbridge Boynton (Center Harbor) and Nellie Haynes (New Hampton); W - 18, domestic, b. Laconia, d/o Stephen A. D. Moses (Groton) and Laura E. Campbell (Lakeport)

Elmer W. of Warren m. Grace G. **Copeland** of Everett, MA 4/11/1920 in Warren; H - 34, millman, 2nd, widower, b.

Bridgewater, s/o Elbridge Boynton (New Hampton) and Nellie Haynes (New Hampton); W - 32, housekeeper, 2nd, divorced, b. Tatanagouche, NB, d/o Joseph Goss (River John, NS) and Margaret Carr (St. John, NB)

Lester W. of Warren m. Nancy **Jewett** of Warren 10/2/1981 in Plymouth; H - 33, s/o Walter J. Boynton and Myrtle N. Ordway; W - 33, d/o Edna Dimond Chase

BRADBURY,

Lester Ray of Bridgeport, CT m. Gladys F. **Clement** of Warren 9/17/1918 in Warren; H - 24, baker mfg., b. Bridgeport, CT, s/o Frederick L. Bradbury (Kingston, CT) and Ida Myatts Tompkins (Ashland, NY); W - 26, teacher, b. Warren, d/o Frank Carrol Clement (Warren) and Anna Kezer Bixby (Warren)

BRADLEY,

Jack Louville of Warren m. Patricia J. **Duffy** of Pittsburg 7/19/2001 in Warren; H - 58, s/o Richard Lester Bradley and Dorothy Winifred Corkum; W - 43, d/o John Henry Duffy and Joan Pl. Lambert

BREER,

Charles of Hyde Park, VT m. Isadore **Hurlbutt** of Hyde Park, VT 4/4/1915 in Warren; H - 29, farmer, b. N. Troy, VT, s/o Charles Breer (Fairfield, VT) and Nancy Perry (Sheldon, VT); W - 18, housemaid, b. Hyde Park, VT, d/o Wyatt Hurlbutt (Hyde Park, VT) and Adelia Boyce (Hyde Park, VT)

BRILL,

James Allen of Haverhill m. Sylvia A. **Wetherbee** of Warren 11/20/1954 in Haverhill; H - 19, Army, b. St. Johnsbury, VT, s/o Nathan L. Brill (Stowe, VT) and Marjorie M. Smith (VT); W - 18, nurse, b. Warren, d/o Walter H. Wetherbee (Haverhill) and Lois M. Merrill (Warren)

BRINGHURST,

Arthur Wesley of Woodsville m. Elizabeth **Tibbetts** of Warren 5/24/1948 in Plymouth; H - 21, RR fireman, b. Lisbon, s/o Bertram Bringhurst (Harrisburg, PA, sec. foreman) and Clara M. Gordon (Lisbon, housewife); W - 19, sewing baseballs, b. Littleton, d/o Mary Ann Tibbetts (Glencliff, housewife)

BRITTON,

Thomas Allen of Warren m. Joanne M. **Keniston** of Warren
12/14/1991 in Warren; H - 22, s/o Gene Britton and Flora Kelly;
W - 19, d/o Fred Keniston and Ruth Mary Kimball

BROCHU,

Denis Omer of Warren m. Linda Lee **Camp** of Franklin 8/12/1972 in
Franklin; H - 25, s/o Omer Brochu and Denise LeBourdais; W -
26, d/o Rolfe Camp and Florence Bennett

Joseph Charles Guy of Warren m. Debra Suzanne **Buttrick** of
Warren 9/24/1977 in Warren; H - 19, s/o Omer Brochu and
Denise LeBourdais; W - 22, d/o Ronald Buttrick and Lois
Carbone

BROWN,

Clyde Francis of Wentworth m. Viola Fay **Ames** of Warren
6/26/1954 in Orford; H - 18, laborer, b. Wentworth, s/o
Frederick A. Brown (Canada) and Helen Griffin (USA); W - 18,
at home, b. W. Rumney, d/o Roy Henry Ames (USA) and Helen
Crafts (USA)

Earland V. of Warren m. Hildegarde C. **Gould** of Warren 8/30/1939
in Woodsville; H - 25, painter, b. New Bedford, s/o Alvin D.
Brown (New Bedford, MA) and Elmina Jones (New Bedford,
MA); W - 22, secretary, b. Piermont, d/o Leon R. Gould
(Stewartstown) and Clara Buzzell (Crossbury, PQ)

Edward William of Hampton m. Marjorie A. **Stevens** of Warren
7/10/1965 in Glencliff; H - 18, operator, s/o Norman F. Brown
and Esther L. Brown; W - 20, at home, d/o Wallace A. Stevens
and Althea J. Stevens

George C. of W. Rumney m. Althea June **Gould** of Glencliff
2/28/1931 in Rumney; H - 20, farmer, b. W. Rumney, s/o Henry
J. Brown (W. Rumney, section hand) and Viola Belle Downing
(W. Rumney, housewife); W - 19, housework, b. Piermont, d/o
Leon Gould (Colebrook, carpenter) and Clara Buzzell
(Cookshire, Canada, housewife)

George E. of Warren m. Grace M. **Dearborn** of Bristol 10/21/1903 in
Wentworth; H - 28, clerk, b. Lowell, MA, s/o George H. Brown
(Lowell, MA, farmer); W - 27, stenographer, b. Bristol, d/o K. E.
Dearborn (Wolfeboro, lawyer)

Gregory Alan of Warren m. Rosanne M. **DeLorenzo** of Warren
12/23/1988 in Plymouth; H - 34, s/o Clyde F. Brown and Viola

109

Fay Ames; W - 27, d/o Francis P. DeLorenzo and Patricia M. Powdly

James R. of Warren m. Barbara E. **Martin** of Warren 10/24/1981 in Warren; H - 28, s/o Robert Brown and Patricia Brown; W - 22, d/o Richard A. Martin and Elizabeth Ames

Kevin S. of Wentworth m. Carol I. **Hudson** of Warren 5/23/1981 in Wentworth; H - 19, s/o Alfred Brown and Velma Gendreau; W - 19, d/o Reginald Hudson and Diane DeForest

Theodore, Jr. of Glencliff m. Patricia **Bryant** of Glencliff 7/11/1992 in Glencliff; H - 35, s/o Theodore Brown, Sr. and Alma Jackson; W - 29, d/o George Bryant and Kathaleen Campbell

Walter Henry of Wentworth m. Edna Maxine **Ball** of Glencliff 4/10/1953 in Wentworth; H - 37, farmer, s/o Henry J. Brown and Viola B. Downing; W - 24, nurse attendant, d/o Bert L. Ball and Eva I. Moulton

BURGESS,

Hollis A., Jr. of Littleton m. Sandra M. **Ramsay** of Glencliff 11/18/1961 in Littleton; H - 21, engineer, s/o Hollis A. Burgess, Sr. and Marguerite Carpenter; W - 19, X-ray tech., d/o Earl E. Ramsay and Eunice M. Moses

BURNHAM,

Royal S. of Warren m. Nancy D. **Keniston** of Rumney 2/14/1958 in W. Rumney; H - 18, lumbering, s/o Richard A. Burnham and Dorothy E. McKee; W - 17, student, d/o Raymond S. Keniston and Ila V. Bixby

BURT,

Alden L. of Rumney m. Charlotte P. **Wistner** of Warren 2/26/1947 in Rumney; H - 26, laborer, b. W. Rumney, s/o Alden S. Burt (Long Island, NY, mill operator) and Flora B. Hall (Groton, housewife); W - 26, stenographer, 2nd, b. Pike, d/o Charles A. Wistner (Rockaway, NJ, bobbin mill) and Catherine Shortt (Grand Banks, NF, housewife)

BUSHAW,

Jesse Edward of Warren m. Kathleen Lea **Cheney** of Plymouth 10/8/1971 in Plymouth; H - 22, s/o Jesse E. Bushaw, Sr. and Tessebell Shortt; W - 22, d/o Walter A. Cheney and Anita G. Longchamp

BUSHNELL,
Horace Lewellyn of Warren m. Marie Margaret **Seifert** of Warren 10/23/1949 in Warren; H - 30, waiter, b. Wallingford, CT, s/o Howard Bushnell (Canterbury, CT) and Alice Lotis (Sprague, CT); W - 19, at home, b. Brooklyn, NY, d/o Emil Seifert (Germany) and Margaret Zigmann (Germany)

BUTSON,
Donald Arthur of Woodsville m. Dany Marie **LaRochelle** of Warren 3/9/1974 in Woodsville; H - 21, s/o Charles L. Butson and Doris J. Martin; W - 16, d/o Raymond LaRochelle and Patricia Douillard

CAIL,
Harry Arthur of Laconia m. Alberta Alice **Anderson** of Warren 7/3/1948 in Warren; H - 20, knitting mach. tester, b. Malden, MA, s/o Harry A. Cail (NB, retired) and Bernice Pickers (Franklin, housewife); W - 20, bookkeeper, b. Warren, d/o Fayne E. Anderson (Drew, ME, carpenter) and Marcia E. Batchelder (Warren, housewife)

CAMPBELL,
Carl A. of Brookfield, VT m. Natasha M. **Anderson** of Glencliff 10/10/1987 in Glencliff; H - 23, s/o Laurence F. Campbell and Theresa M. Boivin; W - 18, d/o Henry Anderson and Margaret Ruth Debow

CANO,
Jose of Barre, VT m. Edith **McGuire** of Graniteville, VT 5/29/1958 in Warren; H - 42, sawyer, s/o Jose Cano, Sr. and Lorenza Cano; W - 26, nurse

CANTERBURY,
David S. of Warren m. Andrea V. **Chase** of Rochester 4/10/2004 in Orford

CARBEE,
Edward S. of Hooksett m. Alice M. **Head** of Warren 4/30/1902 in Warren; H - 23, farmer, b. Hooksett, s/o Henry Carbee (Ryegate, VT, farmer); W - 20, lady, b. Warren, d/o George H. L. Head (Hooksett, landlord)

CARPENTER,

Frank A. of Warren m. Nettie A. **Merrill** of Warren 4/10/1900 in Warren; H - 23, laborer, b. Vershire, VT, s/o William C. Carpenter (Benton, farmer); W - 20, domestic, b. Dorchester, d/o John Merrill (Andover, laborer)

Frank A. of Warren m. Lettie A. **Palmeter** of Warren 10/17/1918 in Warren; H - 42, farmer, 2nd, widower, b. Vershire, VT, s/o William E. Carpenter (Haverhill) and Ora E. Clough (Warren); W - 42, housekeeper, 2nd, widow, b. Westford, VT, d/o John Morgan (Georgia, VT)

CARTER,

Derrick Noel of Warren m. Fawn Marie **Pushee** of Warren 8/9/1988 in Bradford, VT; H - 30, s/o Derrol E. Carter and Dona E. Sweet; W - 28, d/o Clarence L. Pushee, Jr. and Hazel B. Davis

Michael J. of Warren m. Jessica A. **Plant** of Warren 6/5/2005 in Warren

William M. of Warren m. Evelyn B. **Hildreth** of Warren 11/11/1922 in Warren; H - 22, farmer, b. Lunenburg, VT, s/o Alex Carter (Concord, VT, farmer) and Elizabeth Hubbard (Concord, VT, housewife); W - 15, at home, b. Warren, d/o Charles Hildreth (Haverhill, carpenter) and Electa Boynton (Warren, housewife)

CARTWRIGHT,

David N. of Warren m. Thelma M. **Ramsdell** of Warren 11/27/1955 in Rumney; H - 31, laborer, s/o Byron E. Spooner and Laura Cartwright; W - 22, at home, d/o Kenneth S. Ramsdell and Florence Chase

CASS,

Bobby James of Warren m. Stacey D. **Wetherbee** of Warren 5/20/2000 in Warren; H - 32, s/o Robert P. Cass and Barbara J. Hutchins; W - 29, d/o Bernard O. Wetherbee and Gloria J. Caverhill

CASWELL,

Charles E. of Warren m. Edna M. **Colby** of Whitefield 10/24/1894 in Warren; H - 23, printer, b. Warren, s/o Edward T. Caswell (Haverhill, merchant); W - 20, milliner, b. Whitefield, d/o Ira M. Colby (Whitefield, carpenter)

Charles H. of Warren m. Jennie H. **Sanborn** of Lakeport 4/16/1892
in Laconia; H - 49, 2nd, b. Haverhill, s/o Newell Caswell; W - 36,
2nd, d/o Follsm Hunt

George H. of Warren m. Myrtie M. **Turner** of Sutton, VT 4/9/1892 in
Warren; H - 42, hostler, 3rd, b. Haverhill, s/o Newell Caswell; W
- 20, b. Craftsbury, VT, d/o Henry W. Turner (Bolton, PQ,
farmer)

CATE,

Nicholas L. of Warren m. Paula M. **Rocchi** of Warren 9/12/1987 in
Warren; H - 22, s/o Lloyd Cate and Anita Butson; W - 21, d/o
Michael Rocchi and Elizabeth Tomlinson

CATES,

William H. of Brunswick, ME m. Grace H. **Kerr** of Warren 6/2/1903
in Warren; H - 37, carpenter, 3rd, b. Freeport, ME, s/o Levi A.
Cates (Strong, ME); W - 37, domestic, 2nd, b. Warren, d/o
Albert M. Barber (Manchester, England, carpenter)

CAVERHILL,

David Wayne of Warren m. Helen Elizabeth **Hildreth** of Warren
8/24/1950 in Wentworth; H - 22, farmer, b. Rumney, s/o
Ulysses N. Caverhill (NB) and Mary Beeman (Laconia); W - 26,
at home, b. Ashland, d/o William E. Hildreth (Warren) and
Margaret Veasey (Warren)

CHAMBERLAIN,

Wilbur of Rumney m. Martha Lee **Sears** of Glencliff 8/15/1964 in W.
Rumney; H - 20, press operator, s/o Shirley Chamberlain and
Olive E. Tuttle; W - 18, tel. co. traf. op., d/o George F. Sears
and Rita May Hutchins

CHANDLER,

Allen L. of Warren m. Martha C. **Gale** of Warren 1/15/1916 in
Wentworth; H - 31, trackman, b. Wentworth, s/o Leroy E.
Chandler (Wentworth) and Carrie Thayer (Wentworth); W - 25,
housemaid, b. Warren, d/o William F. Gale (Warren) and Belle
K. Simpson (Haverhill)

CHAPMAN,

Allan H. of Keene m. Florence A. **Highland** of Warren 11/23/1937 in Warren; H - 46, night clerk, b. Lynn, MA, s/o Edwin Chapman and Alice Ladd; W - 41, at home, b. Warren, d/o Daniel Spooner and Nora Burke

CHARIST,

Louis of Warren m. Albina **Trudou** of Warren 2/5/1906 in Woodsville; H - 34, millwright, b. Hardwick, VT, s/o Jerry Charist (Canada, farmer); W - 22, domestic, 2nd, b. Canada, d/o Oliver Charist (Canada, carpenter)

CHASE,

David of Warren m. Jennifer **Govoni** of Warren –/–/2003 in Warren

Leon E. of Warren m. Edna L. **Diamond** of Rumney 8/16/1959 in Rumney; H - 59, woodworking, s/o Amos L. Chase and Jennie L. Cutting; W - 28, housework, d/o Walter H. Dimond and Alice M. Eastman

Robert Cecil of Haverhill m. Noreen Ellen **Stimson** of Warren 7/24/1950 in Woodsville; H - 25, taxi driver, b. NH, s/o Forrest Chase (NH) and Georgy Arlene LaFrance (NH); W - 18, unemployed, b. NH, d/o Elmer Gerald Stimson (NH) and Lilla May Martin (NH)

Ronald Arthur of Warren m. Linda Pauline **Thornhill** of Warren 8/13/1988 in Woodstock; H - 41, s/o Arthur N. Chase and Alice M. Parrott; W - 35, d/o Pauline Loizenbauer

Timothy of Warren m. Heather L. **Nystrom** of Warren 6/21/2002; H - 29, s/o Mariellun J. Hughes; W - 29, d/o Robert Nystrom and Joanne L. Thomas

Warren of Warren m. Edith **Simpson** of Orford 1/11/1902 in Wentworth; H - 22, engineer, b. Orford, s/o John B. Chase (blacksmith); W - 18, domestic, b. Orford, d/o Eugene Simpson (Orford, carpenter)

CHASSON,

Frederick J. H. of Warren m. Ella A. **Houghton** of Warren 11/28/1904 in Warren; H - 22, teamster, b. Portland, ME, s/o H. H. Chasson (St. John, NB, carpenter); W - 17, teacher, b. Warren, d/o Edward L. Houghton (Thetford, VT, justice)

CLANCEY,
Daniel J. of Warren m. Sandra K. **Langston** of New York, NY
11/11/1994 in Warren; H - 51, s/o Daniel J. Clancey and
Margaret O'Donnell; W - 48, d/o Clayton E. Langston and
Monah Son

CLARK,
Chester L. of Warren m. Lori A. **Davis** of Warren 10/10/1987 in
Piermont; H - 28, s/o Erwin Clark and Shirley Buttler; W - 23,
d/o Gordon Bowen and Leona Reynolds
Daniel Jay of Warren m. Angela Ruth **Boutin** of Warren 9/21/1996;
H - 25, s/o Douglas A. Clark and Janice S. Urbaniak; W - 26,
d/o Joseph N. Boutin and Priscilla T. Paradise
Douglas A. of Warren m. Luane C. **Cole** of Lyme 2/26/2005 in Lyme
Center
Enos I. of Warren m. Avis **Gray** of Danbury 9/27/1917 in Warren; H -
39, lumberman, b. Warren, s/o Horace W. Clark (Montpelier,
VT) and Lucy M. Moses (Chichester); W - 17, sch. teacher, b.
Center Harbor, d/o Frank Gray (Alexandria) and Mary Bonner
(Montreal, Canada)
Frank W. of Warren m. Lillian **Graham** of Warren 8/12/1939 in
Bradford, VT; H - 57, farmer, b. Warren, s/o Walter Clark
(Montpelier, VT) and Lucy Moses (Chichester); W - 26, b.
Fernandina, FL, d/o Frank Graham (CA) and Julia Manning
(Sutton Flats, Canada)
Michael John of Warren m. Diana Alvern Grace **Loehr** of Warren
9/5/1999 in Warren; H - 40, s/o Daniel Henry Clark, II and
Winifred Beal; W - 35, d/o Duane Eben Barnes and Sharon
Jean McGee
Stephen K. of Warren m. Sally M. **Heath** of Piermont 12/20/1893 in
Warren; H - 38, carpenter, 3rd, s/o John Clark (Piermont); W -
31, housekeeper, 2nd
Wilbur A. of Warren m. Dorothy M. **Sweet** of Warren 10/22/1925 in
Warren; H - 19, laborer, b. Meredith, s/o Frank W. Clark
(Warren, laborer) and Zella Reed (Tilton, housewife); W - 19, at
home, b. Sheldon, VT, d/o Charles B. Smith (laborer) and
Melissa M. Breer (housewife)

CLEMENT,
Edward E. of Warren m. Mary A. **Davis** of Warren 9/26/1894 in
Warren; H - 27, merchant, b. Dorchester, s/o Samuel W.

Clement (Weare, farmer); W - 22, music teacher, b. Warren, d/o John E. Davis (Bath, station agent)

COBB,
Russell B. of Warren m. Pollyanna **Henderson** of Warren 6/30/1934 in Woodsville; H - 22, laborer, b. Wrentham, MA, s/o Jeremiah A. Cobb (Wrentham, MA, laborer) and Mary A. Bonsall (Sheffield, England, deceased); W - 19, at home, b. Dover, d/o Harry T. Henderson (Dover, farmer) and Lettie Goodwin (Dover, housewife)

COLLETTE,
Donald Davis of Warren m. Christina A. **Simard** of Warren –/–/1997; H - s/o Paul P. Collette and Donna J. Taylor; W - d/o H. Joseph Simard and Frances Kay Rescowski

COLLIER,
Freeman W. of Warren m. Shirley Marie **Keysar** of Warren 8/1/1937 in N. Haverhill; H - 20, laborer, b. Drew, ME, s/o Otis F. Collier and Ethel Gibbs; W - 17, stenographer, b. Warren, d/o Royal E. Keysar and Marion Averill

Otis Floyd of Warren m. Pearl Batchelder **Cushing** of Warren 11/6/1949 in Wentworth; H - 56, barber, 2nd, b. Wytopitlock, ME, s/o Lorenzo William Collier (Orient, ME) and May Belle Pierce (Houlton, ME); W - 52, merchant, 2nd, b. Warren, d/o Joel Ingalls Batchelder (Warren) and Estella Amelia Clifford (Colebrook)

COMETTE,
Warren L. of Warren m. Flossie B. **Jewell** of Warren 11/5/1910 in Warren; H - 19, farmer, b. Littleton, s/o Edward Comette (Canada, farmer); W - 18, domestic, b. Warren, d/o Frank Jewell (Warren, board sawyer)

CONNAUGHTON,
F. E. of Springfield, MA m. Mabel E. **Wiggett** of Warren 6/18/1941 in Warren; H - 27, clerk, b. S. Hadley, MA, s/o W. Connaughton (Albany, NY) and Ella M. Steeves (Canada); W - 16, student, b. Blair, d/o E. A. Wiggett (W. Milan) and Mary E. Driscoll (Plymouth)

CONRAD,
Peter L. of Warren m. Cynthia M. **Bancroft** of Warren 8/6/1983 in
Haverhill; H - 31, s/o Adrian R. Conrad and Diana L. Tyler; W -
26, d/o Robert A. Bancroft and Marjorie P. Moore
Philip R. of Pike m. Kimberly P. **Ramsay** of Warren 2/7/1981 in
Warren; H - 28, s/o John Conrad and Betty M. Thompson; W -
19, d/o Dale V. Ramsay and Estella Cushing

COOK,
Wesley Norman of Concord m. Bonnie Lee **Shortt** of Warren
5/3/1975 in Warren; H - 26, s/o Norman Cook and Barbara
Jones; W - 22, d/o Stanley Shortt and Marjorie Libby

COSINE,
Michael J. of Warren m. Carol S. **Day** of Warren 8/31/1985 in
Center Harbor; H - 30, s/o Garrett E. Cosine and Leonna
LaPlante; W - 41, d/o James W. McCall and Hazel Zicafoose

COTTON,
Henry L. of Warren m. Lizzie M. **Moses** of Warren 6/6/1899 in
Haverhill; H - 35, carpenter, 2nd, b. Warren, s/o Dudley B.
Cotton and Martha Abbott; W - 18, domestic, b. Warren, d/o
John B. Moses and Viola B. Merrill
Norris H. of Warren m. Ruth **Isaacs** of U. City, TN 5/11/1927 in
Wentworth; H - 26, law student, b. Warren, s/o Henry L. Cotton
(Warren, turnkey) and Elizabeth M. Moses (Warren,
housewife); W - 34, secretary, b. Lynville, TN, d/o Caspar
Isaacs (TN, merchant) and Mattie Curlin (KY, retired)
Ralph P. of Warren m. Mary E. **Moran** of Providence, RI 6/1/1910 in
Warren; H - 21, farmer, b. Warren, s/o Edward Cotton (Warren,
farmer); W - 19, domestic, b. Philadelphia, d/o James Moran

CRAWFORD,
Sumner J., III of Torrington, CT m. Brandy Lee **French** of
Torrington, CT 5/20/1995; H - 21, s/o Sumner J. Crawford, Jr.
and Susan Gadje; W - 21, d/o David Lee French and Venus
Christine Anderson

CROSBY,
Arthur of Warren m. Annie F. **Prescott** of Warren 1/25/1890 in
Warren; H - 21, laborer, b. Harvour, France, s/o Jesse Crosby;
W - 19

CROSS,
Horace H. of Warren m. Ada E. **Libbey** of Warren 9/26/1895 in
Warren; H - 21, farmer, b. Benton, s/o E. H. Cross (farmer); W
- 18, domestic, b. Warren, d/o Nelson Libbey (Warren,
carpenter)

CUMMINGS,
George Charles of Warren m. Pamela Jean **Pease** of Wentworth
7/3/1976 in Wentworth; H - 37, s/o George W. Cummings, Jr.
and Mazie Wistner; W - 24, d/o Vernon Pease and Jane Hay
George W. of Plymouth m. Mazie P. **Wistner** of Warren 6/1/1936 in
Plymouth; H - 25, laborer, b. Keene, s/o George W. Cummings
and Ada B. Davis; W - 23, b. Glencliff, d/o Charles Wistner and
Catherine Wistner
Maynard of Warren m. Lillian L. **Gale** of Warren 2/19/1899 in
Warren; H - 22, farmer, b. Warren, s/o Francis Cummings and
Ellen Cummings; W - 18, student, b. Warren, d/o Fred Gale
and Hattie Gale
Maynard E. of Warren m. Florence L. **Heath** of Manchester
10/3/1914 in Nashua; H - 37, laborer, 2nd, divorced, b. Warren,
s/o Francis G. Cummings (Chester, VT) and Ellen H. Wright
(Benton); W - 38, mill operative, 2nd, divorced, b. Marlboro, d/o
John C. Strickland (Washington) and Anna M. Woods (Nashua)
Vance of Warren m. Gloria **Landon** of Dorchester 9/28/1968 in
Bradford, VT; H - 51, b. MA, s/o George William Cummings
(NH) and Ada Beatrice Davies (VT); W - 41, b. NH, d/o Lucien
Marcel Parris (France) and Violet Goldie Parris (NH)
Walker F. of Springfield, MA m. Gracia **Prescott** of Warren 9/3/1919
in E. Piermont; H - 44, insurance, b. Jonesport, ME, s/o
Thomas Cummings (Jonesport, ME) and Ellen M. Barker
(Jonesport, ME); W - 45, teaching, b. Rumney, d/o Lucien W.
Prescott (Bridgewater) and Julia P. French (Stratford)

CURLEY,
Roger Damien of MI m. Sarah Elizabeth **Sharer** of FL 6/10/1972 in
Warren; H - 22, s/o John Curley and Leonor Cortes; W - 22, d/o
Robert Sharer and Marian White

CUSHING,
Irvin Beecher of Warren m. Avis Marjorie **Huckins** of Warren
11/12/1948 in Warren; H - 20, filling sta. operator, b. Warren,
s/o Irving B. Cushing (Freeport, ME, merchant) and Pearl E.
Batchelder (Warren, merchant); W - 16, at home, b.
Wentworth, d/o Harvey Huckins (New Hampton, mechanic) and
Marjorie Smith (Orford, factory worker)

CUTTING,
Charles F. of Warren m. Pauline E. **Greenwood** of Lincoln
4/20/1957 in N. Woodstock; H - 29, lumber, s/o Charles E.
Cutting and Mary Theurer; W - 30, waitress, d/o Victor Cloutier
and Eva B. Major
F. D. of Piermont m. Sadie D. **Flanders** of Warren 6/24/1899 in
Warren; H - 25, farmer, b. Benton, s/o C. W. Cutting and Ella
Cutting; W - 20, domestic, b. Warren, d/o Emery Flanders and
Martha Moody

DARLING,
Clifford Calvin of Groton, VT m. Sheila Agnes **Beamis** of Warren
10/18/1949 in Plymouth; H - 30, trucking, b. Groton, VT, s/o
Calvin Darling (Groton, VT) and Zoa Page (Groton, VT); W -
23, at home, 2nd, b. Haverhill, d/o Reuben French (Canada) and
Velma Ladeau (Wentworth)

DAVIDSON,
David Allen of Saxtons River, VT m. Marie Elaine **Blanchard** of
Warren 7/13/1974 in Warren; H - 29, s/o Lyman E. Davidson
and Marjorie Hamilton; W - 30, d/o Fred White and Irene
Eldridge

DAVIS,
Jeffrey Lyle of Warren m. Sarah Renee **Ball** of Warren 6/3/2000 in
Rumney; H - 21, s/o Warren G. Davis and Wendy M. Phillips;
W - 19, d/o Brian B. Ball and Susan D. Brassard

John E. of Warren m. Mary **Heath** of Warren 3/17/1917 in Warren;
H - 53, section man, 3rd, widower, b. E. Haverhill, s/o Benjamin
Davis (Haverhill) and Orilla Carr (E. Haverhill); W - 54,
housekeeper, 2nd, widow, b. Easton, d/o Samuel Howland
(Lisbon) and Lucinda Bowles (Lisbon)
John R. of Orford m. Barbara M. **Bushaw** of Warren 10/3/1965 in
Orford; H - 20, electrician, s/o Robert C. Davis and Frances L.
Hunt; W - 21, beautician, d/o Jesse E. Bushaw and Tessabell
B. Short
Scott Stephen of Warren m. Ramandeep Kaur **Brar** of Warren
8/7/1999 in Waterville Valley; H - 28, s/o Stephen George Davis
and Paula May King; W - 27, d/o Dr. Gurdarshau Singh Brar
and Kuldeep Kaur

DEFOREST,

Frank Croxford of Warren m. Barbara Ann **DeRoehn** of Warren
9/24/1988 in Warren; H - 41, s/o George DeForest and Marie
Croxford; W - 38, d/o John J. Shortt and Mary H. Molloy
William Edward, Jr. of Webster, MA m. Virginia C. **Allen** of
Worcester, MA 11/18/1961 in Warren; H - 34, crane oper., s/o
William Edward DeForest, Sr. and Victoria K. Vednat; W - 40,
IBM clerk, d/o Frederick H. Paige and Loda Louise LeBeau

DEMERITT,

Lester C. of Warren m. Jessie **Wilkins** of Warren 2/9/1925 in
Warren; H - 43, laborer, 2nd, b. Eden, VT, s/o William Demeritt
(Eden, VT, farmer) and Abbie Hill (Eden, VT, housewife); W -
57, housework, 2nd, b. Portland, ME, d/o Henry Portlaw
(Holland, VT, carpenter) and Martha Dean (Wells River,
housewife)

DEMOREST,

Cornelius G. of Angola, IN m. Jean G. **Goodwin** of Warren 7/9/1955
in Plymouth; H - 21, Air Force, s/o Glenwood F. Demorest and
Virginia May Lowe; W - 19, Air Force, d/o Everett W. Goodwin
and Helen V. Gale

DENNIS,

Craig M. of Piermont m. Annemarie **Strickland** of Warren 3/12/2005
in Wentworth

DEOLIVEIRA,
Dennis of Warren m. Christie **Wheeler** of Warren 7/7/1991 in
Warren; H - 43, s/o Aguinol DeOliveira and Saccorra Correia;
W - 30, d/o Richard A. Cretinon and Viola Braz

DERES,
Richard Bernard of Worcester, MA m. Pamela Ethel **Ordway** of
Worcester, MA 9/20/1975 in Warren; H - 29, s/o Bernard
Joseph Deres and Alice Skibauskas; W - 21, d/o Dale Vernon
Ordway and Rita Rowe

DEROSIA,
Dominac of Warren m. Celina **Leblance** of Salem, MA 10/10/1907
in Salem, MA; H - 62, farmer, 3rd, b. Canada, s/o Dominic
Derosia (Canada, farmer); W - 58, 2nd, b. Canada, d/o Francis
Lavoie (Canada)
Fred of Warren m. Bessie **Annis** of Warren 8/31/1907 in Warren; H
- 20, laborer, b. Canada, s/o Dominac Derosia (Canada,
farmer); W - 15, b. Warren, d/o John Kelly (farmer)
Leo F. of Warren m. Ruth **Merrill** of Tilton 7/12/1932 in Ashland; H -
23, chauffeur, b. Warren, s/o Fred Derosia (Canada, laborer)
and Bessie A. Davis (housewife); W - 18, waitress, b. Tilton, d/o
Laurie Merrill (Dorchester, laborer) and Maude Goodwin
Leo F. of Warren m. Lynneth O. **Claro** of Philippines 11/19/2002; H -
37, s/o Leo F. Derosia and Marianne True; W - 32, d/o Joseph
M. Claro and Nelly Ouana
Louis B. of Warren m. Earline M. **Ramsay** of Warren 3/4/1939 in N.
Haverhill; H - 23, US For. serv.; b. E. Haverhill, s/o Louis
Derosia (Benton) and Josie Bemis (Barre, VT); W - 17, at
home, b. Haverhill, d/o Earl Ramsay (Pike) and Edith Belyea
(Warren)
Louis J. of Warren m. Flossie M. **Rollins** of Warren 5/23/1925 in
Claremont; H - 32, lineman, 2nd, b. Benton, s/o Joseph Derosia
(Canada) and Josephine Lavoy (Canada); W - 23, waitress, b.
Wentworth, d/o Benjamin Rollins (Piermont) and May Smith
(Piermont)
Phillip of Warren m. Lucy Hardy **Blake** of E. Haverhill 5/12/1917 in
E. Haverhill; H - 27, laborer, b. Canada, s/o Joseph Derosia
(Canada) and Josephine Lavoie (Canada); W - 31,
housekeeper, 2nd, widow, b. E. Haverhill, d/o Fred Hardy
(Haverhill) and Cora Blake (Benton)

Phillip of Warren m. Maude E. B. **Blake** of Plymouth 3/5/1921 in
Plymouth; H - 32, teamster, 2nd - divorced, b. St. Rose, PQ, s/o
Joseph Derosia (St. Rose, Canada) and Josephine Lavoie (St.
Rose, Canada); W - 32, housekeeper, 2nd - divorced, b.
Wildwood, d/o Willard Brooks (Easton) and Mertie E. Annis
William Joseph of Warren m. Millie Ann **Tibbetts** of Warren
12/10/1914 in Warren; H - 19, laborer, b. Manchester, s/o
Joseph Derosia (Canada) and Josephine Lavoie (Canada); W -
19, housemaid, b. Warren, d/o Leon R. Tibbetts (Haverhill) and
Carrie Fifield (Warren)
Zebulon of Warren m. Nellie M. **Tibbetts** of Warren 7/15/1912 in
Warren; H - 25, section man, b. Canada, s/o Joe Derosia; W -
19, housework, b. Warren, d/o Leon Tibbetts (Haverhill, farmer)

DERWAY,
Joseph of Warren m. Susan **Fowler** of Warren 10/14/1905 in
Warren; H - 49, laborer, b. Canada, s/o Richard Derway
(Canada, farmer); W - 46, housekeeper, 3rd, b. Warren, d/o
Nich. Whiteman (Canada, carpenter)

DIAMOND,
Allen Fred of Warren m. Sheryl Ann **Buttrick** of Warren 5/8/1976 in
Warren; H - 21, s/o Leon Chase and Edna Diamond; W - 19,
d/o Ronald Buttrick and Lois Carbone

DICEY,
Arthur Ralph of Warren m. Muriel Barbara **Shortt** of Warren
4/4/1947 in Warren; H - 25, mill worker, b. Ashland, s/o Arthur
Ralph Dicey (Ashland, B&M RR) and Ellen Cross (Warren); W -
22, clerk, b. Warren, d/o William J. Shortt (Newfoundland) and
Mabel Gould (Warren, housewife)

DILLON,
Robert Erwin of Warren m. Ramona Leigh **Jasper** of Campton
9/10/1988 in Plymouth; H - 27, s/o Earl R. Dillon and Elizabeth
Enderle; W - 24, d/o Vernon L. Jasmer and Dorothy M.
Anderson

DOBSON,
Walter E. of Warren m. Annie Mae **MacCutcheon** of Plymouth
12/25/1903 in Plymouth; H - 24, laborer, b. ME, s/o Samuel

Dobson (NB, lumberman); W - 19, domestic, b. Warren, d/o David McCutcheon (farmer)

DONAHUE,
Sean T. of Warren m. Sandra M. **Newell** of Warren 9/17/2005 in Warren

DOOLEY,
David P. of Warren m. June **Motta** of Plymouth, MA 6/27/1986 in Wentworth; H - 19, s/o Stanley Jesseman and Mildred Stanley; W - 19, d/o Lionil Motta and Charlotta A. Perry

DOW,
Levi of Warren m. Nettie **Annis** of Warren 10/17/1891 in Rumney; H - 35, lumberman, b. Hodgdon, ME, s/o Enoch Dow (Canterbury, NB, farmer); W - 35, 2nd, b. Whitefield

DOWNS,
Jean P. of Warren m. Marsha L. **Meuse** of Warren 8/1/1998 in Warren; H - 27, s/o Kenneth A. Downs and Brenda L. Vincelette; W - 51, d/o Stanley E. Flagg and Claire E. Barthelmess

DREGHORN,
Samuel of Warren m. Victoria E. **Nicol** of Warren 6/17/1939 in Warren; H - 29, bookkeeper, b. Malden, MA, s/o William Dreghorn (Millbury, MA) and Janet Copeland (Glasgow, Scotland); W - 20, housework, b. Warren, d/o William B. Nicol (Bathurst, NB) and Alice Libbey (Warren)

DUKE,
Horace of E. Calais, VT m. Clorinda **Calcagny** of Hardwick, VT 10/30/1937 in Warren; H - 32, granite sawer, b. Marshfield, VT, s/o Forrest L. Duke and Susan Hollister; W - 23, teacher, b. Hardwick, VT, d/o Carlo Calcagny and Maria Rossi

DUNKLEE,
Kenneth C. of Wentworth m. Audrey Jean **Libbey** of Warren 9/15/1961 in Warren; H - 26, mill worker, s/o Osceola L. Dunklee and Florence M. Goodwin; W - 24, domestic, d/o Elmer Libbey and Vera Ball

DUSSAULT,

Thomas Michael of Warren m. Cynthia Marie **Hamel** of New Boston 2/2/1980 in New Boston; H - 28, s/o Robert Thomas Dussault and Gloria May Hale; W - 25, d/o Alphonse J. Hamel and Marian E. Bose

DYKE,

Horace Henry of Woodsville m. Pearl **Couture** of Warren 8/10/1942 in Lyndonville, VT; H - 24, US Army, b. Woodsville, s/o Horace Dyke (Colebrook) and Margaret -----; W - 34, chambermaid, b. Victory, VT, d/o Milo Shores (Victory) and Cora Smith (Conticook, PQ)

DYSON,

William James of Warren m. Valerie Jean **Burnham** of Warren 4/29/1979 in Warren; H - 44, s/o Dave Dyson and Carrie Miller; W - 30, d/o Richard Burnham and Dorothy McKee

EASTMAN,

Edmund of Warren m. Myra E. **McCrillis** of Warren 5/1/1899 in Warren; H - 53, merchant, 2nd, b. Orange, VT, s/o L. M. Eastman and Polly Patch; W - 41, domestic, 2nd, b. Nashua

Edward V. of E. Haverhill m. Lydia M. **Bailey** of Warren 3/25/1914 in Warren; H - 26, farmer, b. Providence, RI, s/o Moses H. Eastman (Lowell, MA) and Mary L. Newton (Newton, MA); W - 20, b. Warren, d/o Russell W. Bailey (Warren) and M. Blanche Wright (Benton)

George C. of Warren m. M. **McCutcheon** of St. John 11/4/1896 in Somerville; H - 37, farmer, b. Warren, s/o B. F. Eastman (Warren, farmer); W - 24, domestic, b. St. John, d/o – McCutcheon (St. John, farmer)

EATON,

Edgar F. of Warren m. Beulah F. **Chase** of Warren 4/6/1930 in Wentworth; H - 21, machinist, b. Malden, MA, s/o William T. Eaton (S. Carver, MA, machinist) and Laura A. Fraser (NS, housewife); W - 16, at home, b. Bath, d/o Frank Chase (Bath, deceased) and Phoebe Wright (SD, housekeeper)

Ezra B. of Warren m. Alice L. **Eastman** of Warren 12/17/1903 in Warren; H - 74, retired merchant, 2nd, b. Plymouth, s/o Ezra B.

Eaton (Wentworth); W - 52, housekeeper, b. Corinth, VT, d/o
Lyman Eastman (Orange, VT)
William F. of Warren m. Hannah B. **French** of Warren 8/25/1889 in
Warren; H - 55, farming, b. Warren; W - 50, b. Warren

ELLINGSON,
William Roger of WI m. Beverly B. **Nelson** of Warren 12/15/1956 in
Warren; H - 23, US Navy, s/o William Ellingson and Melva
Johns; W - 22, tel. operator, d/o William B. Nelson and Bernice
B. Nelson

EMERY,
Charles A. of Warren m. Ida W. **Lord** of Newport 1/4/1935 in
Newport; H - 20, laborer, b. Percy, s/o Bert Emery and Gertrude
E. Sawyer; W - 18, at home, b. Ellenburg, NY, d/o Fred W. Lord
and Mabel Hedden

EVANS,
Gerald W. of Warren m. Emily May **Olin** of Sutton 5/5/1957 in
Warner; H - 25, truck driver, s/o Reginald S. Evans and Helen
Eva Kemp; W - 21, nurse, d/o John Lawrence Olin and Mura
Blanche Fifield
Reginald S. of Wentworth m. Helen Eva **Kemp** of Warren 11/2/1929
in Warren; H - 28, fish & game wdn., b. Madbury, s/o Harry H.
Evans (Madbury, carpenter) and Bertha L. Swain (Barrington,
housewife); W - 24, teacher, b. Warren, d/o Clarence W. Kemp
(Lyme, millwright) and Annie B. Smith (Sanbornton, housewife)
Wayne Lloyd of Warren m. Shirley Mae **Bennett** of Warren
2/17/1957 in Glencliff; H - 22, student, s/o Reginald S. Evans
and Helen E. Kemp; W - 20, nurse, d/o Lewis Bennett and
Geneva M. Pike

EVERETT,
Joseph Alexander of Warren m. Alice May **Bowles** of Warren
6/1/1953 in Plymouth; H - 25, student, s/o Levi Everett and
Agnes McKinnon; W - 18, at home, d/o Kenneth N. Bowles and
Eva Lovett

FAGNANT,
Fernand R. of Piermont m. Nancy May **Ball** of Warren 11/16/1957 in
Woodsville; H - 22, truck driver, s/o Alcide Fagnant and

Laurette Paquette; W - 17, unemployed, d/o Reginald H. Ball and Charlotte Griffin

FALETRA,
Peter Paul of Warren m. Elaine Marie **Balsamo** of Warren 6/4/1988 in Warren; H - 36, s/o Ben Faletra and Mary Campo; W - 32, d/o Joseph Balsamo and Ann Petralia

FALEY,
John of Warren m. Mary **Balch** of Warren 6/27/1903 in Warren; H - 35, millman, b. PQ, s/o James Faley (Ireland); W - 37, housekeeper, 2nd, b. Goffstown, d/o Harrison Moses (Epsom)

FASSNACHT,
Eugene T. of Warren m. Leslie Martha **Thompson** of Warren 9/10/2001 in Bow; H - 43, s/o Philip Fassnacht and Barbara Kane; W - 39, d/o Royce E. Johnson and Jean Bradbury

FELLOWS,
Jeffrey M. of Milton, VT m. Teresa-Ann **Taylor** of Glencliff 9/1/1979 in Warren; H - 16, s/o Theodore H. Fellows and Florence Hall; W - 16, d/o Walter Taylor and Charlotte-Ann Dumas

FIFIELD,
Alva E. of Glencliff m. Belle **Sampson** of Glencliff 1/9/1924 in Warren; H - 22, woodsman, b. Warren, s/o Melvin Fifield (Warren, woodsman); W - 24, housekeeper, b. Portsmouth, d/o Albaner Sampson (E. Boston, MA, shoemaker)
Harry A. of Warren m. Mabel L. **McIsaac** of Warren 12/9/1903 in Warren; H - 29, laborer, b. Warren, s/o Lorenzo D. Fifield (Warren, farmer); W - 29, domestic, 2nd, b. Warren, d/o Benjamin F. Eastman (Warren, farmer)
Melvin B. of Warren m. Effie May **Heath** of Warren 8/1/1898 in Warren; H - 19, laborer, b. Warren, s/o E. L. Fifield (Warren, farmer); W - 14, domestic, b. Meredith, d/o Albee Heath (S. Reading, VT, laborer)

FINERTY,
Frank of Warren m. Ruby Lee **Tetley** of Peterboro 7/9/1917 in Keene; H - 26, US Cavalry, b. Woburn, MA, s/o Rufus S.

Finerty (Boston) and Ella L. Ralston; W - 22, clerk, b. Camden, ME, d/o William E. Tetley and Aldeva E. Buzzell

FLAGG,

Brian of Warren m. Suzanne **Bixby** of Warren –/–/2003 in Warren

FLANDERS,

Carl L. of Warren m. Shirley **Nadeau** of Lebanon 2/7/1927 in Warren; H - 24, laborer, b. Warren, s/o Leonard Flanders (Warren, lumberman) and Ellen Dowse (Newbury, VT, housewife); W - 20, waitress, 2nd, b. Derby, VT, d/o Roscoe Lowell (Canaan, teamster) and Idella Gardner (Canada, housekeeper)

Fred L. of Warren m. Susie Belle **Merrill** 8/7/1889 in Warren; H - 22, farming, b. Orford; W - 17, b. Warren

Leonard M. of Warren m. Ellen A. **Dowse** of Warren 8/16/1900 in Warren; H - 22, laborer, b. Warren, s/o Jason E. Flanders (Warren, farmer); W - 15, domestic, b. Newbury, VT, d/o Asa Dowse (Newbury, VT, laborer)

Leonard M. of Warren m. Eva B. **Ingalls** of Warren 1/4/1919 in Wentworth; H - 40, lumberman, 2nd, widower, b. Warren, s/o Jason E. Flanders (Warren) and Sarah J. Muchmore (Orford); W - 31, housekeeper, d/o Ed B. Short (England) and Laura Warner

Leonard M. of Warren m. Nora B. **Spoonor** of Warren 11/12/1921 in Woodsville; H - 43, lumberman, 3rd, divorced, b. Warren, s/o Jason E. Flanders (Warren) and Sarah J. Muchmore (Orford); W - 47, at home, 2nd, divorced, b. Lewiston, ME, d/o Napoleon Burke (Montreal, PQ) and Laura Ganette (Plattsburg, NY)

FOLEY,

Edward W. of Sterling, VA m. Laurie-Anne M. **Spencer** of Warren 10/5/1985 in Warren; H - 36, s/o Raymond R. Foley and Hattie Eldred; W - 23, d/o Edward Spencer and Marie E. White

FOOTE,

Bert L. of Warren m. Jennie T. **Whitcher** of Warren 11/16/1893 in Piermont; H - 19, laborer, b. Warren, s/o Charles G. Foote (Warren, farmer); W - 17, b. Warren, d/o Henry D. Whitcher (Warren, farmer)

Charles A. of Warren m. Nancy L. **Taggart** of Warren 10/12/1991 in Glencliff; H - 43, s/o Claude Foote and Leona Paige; W - 39, d/o James Najarian and Avis Hill

Charles Avery of Warren m. Mary Lynn **Koski** of Keene 11/8/1969 in Keene; H - 21, s/o Claude Foote and Leona Paige; W - 19, d/o Toivo Koski and Mary Preedom

Charles Avery of Warren m. Sheila Lee **Robertson** of Warren 6/21/1975 in Warren; H - 27, s/o Claude Foote and Leona Paige; W - 26, d/o Edward Robertson and Roberta Emerson

Charles G. of Warren m. Annie L. **Swain** of Warren 8/27/1898 in Warren; H - 21, farmer, b. Warren, s/o C. G. Foote (Warren, farmer); W - 19, domestic, b. Warren, d/o William Swain (Warren, farmer)

Harry Lee of Warren m. Emma Cora **Wright** of Piermont 10/19/1902 in Wentworth; H - 21, farmer, b. Warren, s/o Charles G. Foote (Warren, farmer); W - 22, domestic, b. Piermont, d/o Ximenius Wright (farmer)

Leslie M. of Warren m. Effie May **Lee** of Piermont 4/29/1903 in Piermont; H - 24, farmer, b. Warren, s/o Charles G. Foote (Warren, farmer); W - 22, domestic, b. Orford, d/o John Lee (Warren, farmer)

FOSTER,

Fred L. of Warren m. Eva D. **Fales** of Warren 8/15/1900 in Warren; H - 24, laborer, b. Wentworth, s/o William A. Foster (Rumney, farmer); W - 21, school teacher, b. Rumney, d/o W. W. Fales (Warren, miller)

FOUNTAIN,

Paul of Warren m. Lougee **Ruell** of Warren 4/5/1899 in Haverhill; H - 20, laborer, b. PQ, s/o Joe Fountain and Bridget Fountain; W - 15, student, b. PQ, d/o Ezra Ruell and Alflorence Ruell

FRANKS,

Robert D. of Manchester m. Mary Helen **Kydd** of Warren 10/1/1927 in Warren; H - 28, electrician, b. Manchester, s/o Arthur Franks (Manchester, el. contrac.) and Mary Davis (Nashua, housewife); W - 21, at home, b. Warren, d/o David Kydd (Scotland, farmer) and Lena McLauchlan (Scotland, housewife)

128

FRAZER,

George of Warren m. Sibbell **Clifford** of Warren 3/15/1905 in Warren; H - 43, laborer, b. NS, s/o Charles Frazer (NS, butcher); W - 52, housekeeper, 2nd, b. Warren, d/o Joseph Whitcher (farmer)

FREI,

Steven Allen of Parsippany, NJ m. Nancy Jean **Gohde** of Parsippany, NJ 4/15/1988 in Warren; H - 33, s/o William S. Frei and Cordis A. Replogle; W - 29, d/o Fred W. Gohde and Norma F. Larson

FRENCH,

A. V. of Warren m. Bell **Gould** of Warren 2/21/1895 in Warren; H - 27, laborer, b. Warren, s/o O. H. French; W - 25, housekeeper, 2nd, b. Groton

Benjamin H. of Warren m. Ina Florence **Martin** of Warren 10/25/1928 in Wentworth; H - 40, laborer, b. Warren, s/o Oscar H. French (Warren) and Emma E. Page (Warren); W - 40, housekeeper, 3rd, b. Hanover, d/o J. Franklin Brown (Bradford, VT) and Georgianna Hutton (Lunenburg, VT)

Charles B. of Warren m. Mabel E. **Molway** of Haverhill 3/10/1896 in Warren; H - 25, laborer, b. Warren, s/o C. O. French (Warren, laborer); W - 19, b. Bradford, VT, d/o L. E. Molway (Standards, laborer)

Glenn Robert of Warren m. Shirley Elizabeth **Geraw** of Enosburg Falls, VT 11/7/1945 in Enosburg Falls, VT; H - 23, laborer, b. Benton, s/o Reuben French (NH) and Velma Ladue (Piermont); W - 19, counter bobbin, b. Montgomery, VT, d/o Francis Geraw (Enosburg Falls, VT)

Lewis E. of Warren m. Anna G. **Little** of Warren 12/31/1887 in Warren Summit; H - 23, laborer, s/o Alonzo French (Warren, shoemaker) and Ruhannah Fifield (Warren, deceased); W - 21

Richard J. of Warren m. Wyllian E. **Prue** of Haverhill 9/3/1955 in Rumney; H - 18, kitchen helper, s/o Reuben French and Velma Ladeau; W - 18, housework, d/o William H. Prue and Leora Greenwood

FRYE,

Lewis A. of Gorham m. Lillian B. **Kittredge** of Warren 10/12/1898 in Warren; H - 25, fireman, b. Ossipee, s/o Joseph P. Frye

(Portsmouth, clergyman); W - 20, teacher, b. Walden, d/o John
W. Kittredge (Walden, VT, merchant)

Simeon Cheney of Warren m. Mary T. **Nickerson** of Chelsea, MA
1/2/1904 in Chelsea, MA; H - 38, bookkeeper, 2nd, b.
Sanbornton, s/o Jonathan J. Frye (Medford, MA, teacher); W -
33, stenographer, 2nd, b. NS, d/o James MacKea (Pictou, NS,
farmer)

GAGE,

Charles E. of Montpelier, VT m. Ilene C. **Mansfield** of Montpelier,
VT 12/6/1956 in Warren; H - 45, truckman, s/o Nathaniel Gage
and Lena M. Elliott; W - 40, prac. nurse, d/o Walter Woodard
and Eva Gillette

GALE,

Harry B. of Warren m. Laura E. **Libby** of Warren 1/2/1910 in
Warren; H - 28, laborer, b. Warren, s/o William Gale (Warren,
butcher); W - 17, housework, b. Warren, d/o Nelson Libby
(farmer)

GALLANT,

Thomas T. of Warren m. Florence J. **Balch** of Warren 12/24/1904 in
Warren; H - 26, mill man, b. Canada, s/o Thomas Gallant
(Canada, railroading); W - 19, domestic, b. Goffstown, d/o
Charles Balch (Johnson, VT, mechanic)

GANSZ,

Christopher Werner of Warren m. Karen Mariana **Lamarre** of
Warren 7/21/2001 in Warren; H - 27, s/o Werner William
Gansz and Dolerita Stubbs; W - 24, d/o Bruce Lee Lamarre
and Julie Mitchell Simpson

GARLAND,

W. W. of Warren m. Rachel P. **Nason** of Benton 7/15/1894 in
Benton; H - 67, farmer, 2nd, b. Grantham, s/o Simeon Garland;
W - 66, housekeeper, 3rd

GARRAND,

Brian Dean of Warren m. Michele Lorraine **Hadley** of Warren
6/28/1980 in Bradford, VT; H - 24, s/o Roderick Garrand and
Susan Delgrego; W - 22, d/o Joseph Allen and Ellen Smith

GARRETT,
Eugene E., Jr. of Warren m. Ethel E. **McKee** of Orford 6/21/1958 in Orfordville; H - 26, laborer, s/o Eugene E. Garrett, Sr. and Laura M. Cummings; W - 18, at home, d/o Kenneth W. McGee and Frances E. Foote

Eugene E., Jr. of Warren m. Eleanor Marie **Marshall** of Center Harbor 5/10/1969 in Moultonboro; H - 37, s/o Eugene Garrett, Sr. and Laura May Cummings; W - 39, d/o Peter Marshall

GATHERCOLE,
James C. of Warren m. Mrs. Elysa **Keysar** of Warren 6/6/1910 in Warren; H - 50, farmer, 3rd, b. Clarksville, s/o John Gathercole (England, retired); W - 53, nurse, 2nd, b. Colebrook, d/o John Moses

GEORGE,
Thomas I. of Woodsville m. Shirley R. **Stark** of Warren 9/26/1981 in Warren; H - 21, s/o Ernest P. George and Helen Brown; W - 19, d/o Gary Stark and Audrey Ames

GLEASON,
Fred C. of Warren m. Ettie L. **Prescott** of Warren 9/1/1892 in Warren; H - 26, merchant, b. Warren, s/o Orange S. Gleason (Plymouth, farming); W - 26, housekeeper, b. N. Haverhill, d/o Lucian W. Prescott (Bridgewater, clergyman)

GODVILLE,
James of Warren m. Edna **Short** of Warren 11/7/1926 in Warren; H - 29, laborer, b. Russia; W - 28, at home, b. Warren, d/o William Short (Newfoundland, laborer) and Mabel Gould (Warren, housewife)

GOODALE,
Scott Gregory of Warren m. Pamela Jane **Ball** of Warren 7/20/1996; H - 25, s/o Kenneth Goodale and Norma Witten; W - 21, d/o Bert Peter Ball and Judy Ann Thompson

GOODMAN,
Nathan of Bayonne, NJ m. Phyllis Lila **Aaronson** of New York, NY 8/6/1948 in Warren; H - 37, executive, b. Bayonne, NJ, s/o Julius Goodman (New York, NY, retired) and Rose Wynd

131

(Austria, housewife); W - 24, buyer, b. New York, NY, d/o Irving
Aaronson (PA, deceased) and Sadye Siegel (New York, NY,
housewife)

GOODWIN,
Everett W. of Warren m. Helen V. **Gale** of Warren 4/28/1934 in
Gilford; H - 23, truck driver, b. Orford, s/o Harry L. Goodwin
(Warren, F&G warden) and Bertha G. Gale (MA, at home); W -
24, stenographer, b. Warren, d/o Harry B. Gale (Warren, F&G
emp.) and Laura E. Libbey (Warren, at home)
Raymond of Littleton m. Flora H. **Young** of Warren 10/25/1920 in
Littleton; H - 26, chauffeur, b. Hanover, MA, s/o Archie Goodwin
(Hanover, MA) and Addeline Waterman (Hanover, MA); W - 18,
housework, b. Waterford, VT, d/o George Young (Sheffield, VT)
and Harriette Gero (Canada)

GORDON,
Wilbur C. of Warren m. Lillian L. **Noyes** of Warren 6/15/1890 in
Warren; H - 26, railroad conductor, b. Benton, s/o Horace W.
Gordon (produce dealer); W - 24, 2nd, d/o Joseph W. Little

GOSLAY,
Thomas of Warren m. Salomie **Ash** of W. Burke, VT 2/10/1902 in
Warren; H - 24, lumberman, b. Newark, VT, s/o Peter Goslay
(Canada, farmer); W - 17, domestic, 2nd, b. Newark, VT, d/o
Martin Ash (farmer)

GOULD,
Al O. of Warren m. Alice M. **Swain** of Meredith 9/11/1909 in Warren;
H - 22, engineer, b. Warren, s/o Francis L. Gould (Haverhill,
farmer); W - 19, housekeeper, b. Meredith, d/o George Swain
(Meredith, farmer)
Eugene H. of Warren m. Mertie B. **Heath** of Warren 11/23/1904 in
Warren; H - 28, farmer, b. Warren, s/o William Gould (Cape
Breton, farmer); W - 14, domestic, b. Haverhill, d/o Alba B.
Heath (laborer)
Henry B. of Warren m. Belle F. **Moses** of Warren 12/24/1887 in
Warren; H - 67, farmer, s/o William Gould (Cape Briton, NS,
deceased) and Sophia Butler (Cape Briton, NS, deceased); W -
32

Llewellyn Leon of Warren m. Dorothy Laura **Leonard** pf Haverhill 5/13/1950 in Woodsville; H - 29, student, b. Warren, s/o Leon Roscoe Gould (NH) and Clara Rebecca Buzzell (Canada); W - 24, bookkeeper, b. Haverhill, d/o John Francis Leonard (NH) and Harriet Etta Burton (Bath)

GOVE,
Donald Langdon of Wentworth m. Bernadette Theo **Kasheta** of Warren 6/19/1948 in Plymouth; H - 23, engineer construction, b. Wentworth, s/o Lewis Gove (Wentworth, construction foreman) and Pearl Terpening (Summit, NJ, housewife); W - 19, at home, b. Brooklyn, NY, d/o Francis J. Kasheta (Lawrence, MA, physician) and Bernadette Sasner (McKees Rocks, PA, housewife)

GRADY,
Darrin of Warren m. Sherry **Stevens** of Warren –/–/2003 in Warren

GRAVES,
Robert C. of Warren m. Janet W. **Hobart** of Plymouth 7/12/1952 in Warren; H - 19, truck driver, s/o Ronald J. Graves and Ethel M. Little; W - 16, at home, d/o Laurence Hobart and Marion Danforth
Ronald J. of Berlin m. Ethel M. **Little** of Warren 10/15/1927 in Warren; H - 22, machinist, b. Berlin, s/o Wallace L. Graves (NB, sup. water) and Annie Morrison (PEI, housewife); W - 20, clerk, b. Warren, d/o Charles F. Little (Warren, RR oper.) and Mary Howard (Lyme, housewife)

GREEN,
John P. of Warren m. Deborah L. **Bancroft** of Warren 11/2/1991 in Warren; H - 28, s/o Peter Green and Katherine Fitzgerald; W - 33, d/o Kenneth Bancroft and Elizabeth Brown
Milton L. of E. Haverhill m. Lillian **Merrill** of Warren 3/8/1936 in N. Haverhill; H - 21, farm work, b. Lubec, ME, s/o John Green and Rheta Chase; W - 18, at home, b. Warren, d/o Ernest Merrill and Mildred Merrill

GULLAGE,

Donald Robert of Billerica, MA m. Patricia Ann **Fuller** of Lowell, MA 7/2/1956 in Warren; H - 22, laborer, s/o William Gullage and Louise M. Stairs; W - 18, office clerk, d/o Clyde Fuller and Margaret Perkins

HAINES,

Wilbur N. of Newmarket m. Cora A. **Morrison** of Warren 9/21/1933 in Gilford; H - 31, mail clerk, b. Newmarket, s/o Herbert R. Haines (Newmarket, deceased) and Celia MacMillan (Fredericton, NB, housewife); W - 25, clerk, b. Warren, d/o Rodney Morrison (NS, laborer) and Cora A. Merrill (housewife)

HAIR,

Allan W. of Warren m. Jean **Towle** of Warren 8/10/1985 in Chesterfield; H - 39, s/o Walter Hair and Doris Desmarais; W - 29, d/o Wesley Towle and Marjorie Bragdon

Allen Walter of Warren m. Sandra Lee **Howard** of Warren 3/28/1969 in Warren; H - 23, s/o Walter Hair and Doris Desmarais; W - 26, d/o Kenneth Whitcher and Marion Cotton

Jeremy D. of Warren m. Sandra L. **Griffin** of Franklin 8/28/1999 in Franklin; H - 24, s/o Allen Walter Hair and Sandra Hair; W - 24, d/o Richard Griffin and Gale McNabb

HALEY,

Elmer Clifford, Jr. of ncx m. Jill Christine **Whitcher** of Warren 8/29/1992 in Plymouth; H - 25, s/o Elmer Clifford Haley, Jr. and Evelyn Rebecca Parent; W - 20, d/o David Ralph Whitcher and Judy Lee King

HALLETT,

Wallace S. of Centerville, MA m. Dorothy E. **Carbee** of Warren 1/27/1930 in Warren; H - 22, civil engineer, b. Centerville, MA, s/o Joseph P. Hallett (Centerville, MA, architect) and Nellie B. Kelly (Centerville, MA, housewife); W - 18, telephone oper., b. Warren, d/o Edgar S. Carbee (Hooksett, electrician) and Alice Head (Warren, housewife)

HAMILTON,

Scott of Warren m. Amy **Sackett** of Warren –/–/2003 in Warren

HAMMOND,
Lester F. of E. Jaffrey m. Gladys Julia **Lavoie** of E. Haverhill
4/27/1928 in Warren; H - 23, forest ranger, b. Newbury, VT, s/o
Ruben Hammond (Winchester, factory worker) and Rosena
Hahn (Ellington, CT, housewife); W - 18, tel. operator, b.
Rutland, VT, d/o Joseph Lavoie (Manchester, RR man) and
Myrtle Buskey (Rutland, VT, housewife)

HANCOCK,
Scott of Warren m. Sara **Jenkins** of W. Fairlee, VT –/–/2003 in
Warren

HANLEY,
Scott R. of Littleton m. Anna P. **Alessandrini** of Warren 7/2/1983 in
Woodsville; H - 21, s/o Robert L. Hanley and Georgia A.
Quimby; W - 19, d/o Simeone Alessandrini and Eleanor Chase

HANNETT,
Alfred Robert of Haverhill m. Carolyn A. **Whitney** of Warren
6/30/1960 in Warren; H - 18, laborer, s/o Robert James
Hannett and Edna M. Hanerford; W - 14, at home, d/o Percy L.
Whitney and Evelyn L. Hilliard
Ricky A. of Warren m. Dawnette M. **Coy** of Warren 1/1/1998 in
Lyman; H - 38, s/o Alfred R. Hannett and Corolyn A. Whitney;
W - 21, d/o Don M. Coy and Janice A. Clough

HANSEN,
Mark D. of Rockland, ME m. Lois Ann **Jones** of Rockland, ME
5/1/1999 in Warren; H - 41, s/o Melvin Hansen and Joanne E.
Veon; W - 39, d/o Orman B. Jones, Jr. and Arlene T. Spear

HARMON,
Everett B. of Warren m. Clara Celestia **Shortt** of Warren 8/27/1915
in Warren; H - 22, teamster, b. Island Pond, VT, s/o Stephen M.
Harmon (Buckston, ME) and Roxanna Stephens (Island Pond,
VT); W - 18, housemaid, b. Warren, d/o William Shortt and
Mabel M. Gould (Warren)
Frank James of Island Pond, VT m. Cynthia Rose **Philbrook** of
Warren 4/20/1946 in Plymouth; H - 24, US Army, b. Fairlee, VT,
s/o Everett Harmon (Island Pond, VT) and Clara Shortt
(Warren, housewife); W - 22, student, b. Warren, d/o William A.

Philbrook (Wytopitlock, ME, carpenter) and Kathleen Pike (Warren, housewife)

HARRIMAN,
Alton Merton of Edna Maxine **Ball** of Warren 5/12/1948 in Warren; H - 24, waiter, 2nd, b. Littleton, s/o Elroy Waldo Harriman (Whitefield, sawyer) and Margaret Elmira Adams (Danville, VT, housewife); W - 19, nurse attendant, b. Glencliff, d/o Bert L. Ball (Landaff, millman) and Eva Irene Moulton (Landaff, housewife)

HARRINGTON,
E. E. of Manchester m. Lena I. **Kydd** of Warren 7/3/1934 in Brattleboro, VT; H - 22, shoe worker, s/o Ernest Harrington (Thetford, VT) and Ethel Knight (Manchester); W - 21, b. Warren, d/o David Kydd (Scotland) and Lena McLauchlan (Scotland)

HARVEY,
Henry of Warren m. Nancy **Houghton** of Warren 5/30/1899 in Warren; H - 20, laborer, b. Manchester, s/o J. W. Harvey and Lucy Casey; W - 18, domestic, b. Manchester, d/o Edw. L. Houghton and Belle Wolcott
Wilmont M., III of Beverly, MA m. Donna M. **White** of Warren 4/10/1982 in Warren; H - 18, s/o Wilmont M. Harvey, Jr. and Sylvia Dudley; W - 18, d/o Lawrence R. White and Elizabeth Chase

HASKELL,
Harry A. of Poland, ME m. Lillian **Adams** of Boston, MA 10/24/1904 in Warren; H - 33, landlord, b. Wakefield, MA, s/o Henry Haskell (manufacturer); W - 29, telegraph oper., 2nd, b. Rumney, d/o Edgar A. Adams (Plymouth, tanner)

HATCH,
Stephen Wilder of Glencliff m. Sharon Ann **Babbit** of Wentworth 10/16/1976 in Warren; H - 25, s/o Vernon Hatch and Dorothy Mitchell; W - 20, d/o Robert C. Babbit and Carol Cole

HAZELTON,

Walter of Warren m. Helen Louise **Hutchins** of Rumney 7/22/1935 in Alfred, ME; H - 28, woodsman, b. Manchester, VT, s/o Ralza Hazelton and Sadie Place; W - 20, housekeeper, b. Rumney, d/o Nelson K. Hutchins and Susie R. Goodwin

HEAD,

Archie A. of Warren m. Mabelle S. **Gerald** of Warren 10/29/1902 in Warren; H - 25, bookkeeper, b. Hooksett, s/o George H. L. Head (Hooksett, landlord); W - 22, domestic, b. Hyde Park, MA, d/o Francis L. Gerald (Warren, physician)

Charles W. of Warren m. Alice M. **Bartlett** of Warren 11/25/1895 in Warren; H - 22, clerk, b. Boone, IA, s/o G. H. L. Head (Hooksett, landlord); W - 20, sch. teacher, b. Bath, d/o A. F. Bartlett (Whitefield, miller)

HEATH,

Anderson of Warren m. Ardella M. **Keysar** of Meredith 2/7/1920 in Meredith; H - 25, teamster, b. Warren, s/o Albert Heath (St. Johnsbury, VT) and Mary Howland (Piermont); W - 31, operative, 2nd, divorced, b. Ashland, d/o Charles S. Rankin (Bridgewater) and Alice A. Greenleaf (Ashland)

Arthur G. of Warren m. Robin J. **Russell** of Ashland 6/28/1980 in Warren; H - 22, s/o Elmer H. Heath and Jennie Raymond; W - 22, d/o Leonard N. Russell and Ruth Parr

Arthur G. of Warren m. Roberta J. **Hunter** of Warren 10/8/2005 in Plymouth

David E. of Warren m. Sylvia Jo **Trask** of Warren 5/11/1996; H - 25, s/o Donna Marie Heath; W - 34, d/o Leland Willard Trask and Evalyn Ann Shaw

Elmer H. of Warren m. Jennie M. **Raymond** of Warren 8/26/1938 in Claremont; H - 24, laborer, b. Warren, s/o Etta May Heath (Warren); W - 20, tel. operator, b. Leominster, MA, d/o Joseph L. Raymond (Canada) and Jenney G. Palmer (Rochester, VT)

Raymond, Jr. of Warren m. Rebecca J. **Torsey** of Warren 8/1/1999 in Warren; H - 34, s/o Raymond Heath, Sr. and Irma I. Angers; W - 43, d/o Horace Boynton and Rebecca A. Page

Raymond E. of Warren m. Irma Irene **Angers** of Warren 6/6/1964 in Warren; H - 21, press operator, s/o Elmer H. Heath and Jennie May Raymond; W - 20, factory worker, d/o Wallace C. Angers and Irene Mildred Bailey

HEATLEY,

Grant Ross of Seabrook m. Sandra Mae **Roulx** of Warren 2/1/1975 in Warren; H - 21, s/o Gordon Heatley and Rose Grant; W - 21, d/o Oscar Roulx and Mabel Godville

HEITZ,

Julian Michael of Warren m. Rebecca Jo **Palmer** of Woodsville 7/15/1980 in N. Haverhill; H - 19, s/o George J. Heitz and Ann Marley; W - 18, d/o Calvin W. Palmer and Joyce B. Nelson

HENSON,

Matthew E. of Warren m. Jessica P. **Carr** of Warren 6/12/1999 in Warren; H - 18, s/o Steven Henson, Sr. and Diana Barnes; W - 16, d/o Roy Edward Carr III and Katherine Palmer

HEYWOOD,

Fred, III of Warren m. Joy Inez **Smith** of Warren 8/27/1985 in Warren; H - 39, s/o Fred Heywood, Jr. and Evelyn Garside; W - 28, d/o Earle Leroy Smith and Nell Whitten

HIBBARD,

Clarence George of Warren m. Maude **McClosky** of Warren 6/2/1946 in Plymouth; H - 51, lumberman, 2nd, b. Orford, s/o George A. Hibbard (Piermont) and Emma A. Witham (Concord); W - 54, housewife, 2nd, b. Wentworth, d/o George McClosky and Susan Harris

Lawrence Lloyd of Warren m. Kimberly Jayne **Burnham** of Rumney 8/18/1979 in Rumney; H - 23, s/o Lloyd C. Hibbard and Eudora Wetherbee; W - 19, d/o Royal S. Burnham and Nancy Keniston

Lloyd C. of Warren m. Eudora M. **Wetherbee** of Warren 4/17/1954 in Haverhill; H - 33, truck driver, b. Piermont, s/o Clarence G. Hibbard (Piermont) and Maud McCloskey (Wentworth); W - 22, domestic, b. Warren, d/o Walter H. Wetherbee (Haverhill) and Lois M. Merrill (Warren)

HICKS,

Arthur J. of Glencliff m. Clara C. **Doane** of Warren 8/4/1932 in Ctr. Haverhill; H - 37, laborer, 2nd, b. Lawrence, MA, s/o Edward Hicks (Lawrence, MA, deceased) and Carrie Snell (Methuen, MA, deceased); W - 48, nurse, 2nd, b. Bridgeport, CT, d/o

Charles M. Davis (Bridgeport, CT, deceased) and Mary E. Pratt (Thompson, CT, deceased)

HIGGINS,
James Anthony of Warren m. Vicki Lee **Finneron** of Warren 2/11/1978 in Warren; H - 19, s/o Robert D. Higgins and Mary Louise Castaldo; W - 19, d/o Richard Finneron and Carole Leupold
Michael W. of Bradford, VT m. Jane A. **Boutin** of Warren 6/25/2005 in Warren

HIGHT,
Arthur of Warren m. Shirley **Manion** of Warren 12/15/1935 in N. Haverhill; H - 20, laborer, b. Lisbon, s/o William R. Hight and Iva Smith; W - 20, housework, b. W. Rumney, d/o Elwyn Manion and Ethel A. Colburn
George E. of Warren m. Orilene E. **Millette** of Warren 10/12/1941 in Warren; H - 21, mechanic, b. W. Topsham, VT, s/o William R. Hight (W. Topsham, VT) and Iva D. Smith (Warren); W - 20, tel. operator, b. Dover, d/o James Millette (Canada) and Hazel Pineo (Dover)
George Thomas of Warren m. Gladys Donna **Coburn** of Plymouth 8/17/1968 in Plymouth; H - 26, s/o George E. Hight (VT) and Oraline Jones (NH); W - 21, 2nd, b. NH, d/o Edward Latuch (NH) and Lillian Martin (NH)
George Thomas of Warren m. Patricia Ann **Hurlbutt** of Warren 4/10/1976 in Warren; H - 33, s/o George Hight and Orilene Millette; W - 23, d/o Vernon Pease and Jane Hay
William of W. Topsham, VT m. Iva **Smith** of Warren 9/24/1913 in Warren; H - 20, laborer, b. W. Topsham, s/o George Hight (Peacham, VT, mill man); W - 18, domestic, b. Warren, d/o Zebulon Smith (Littleton, farmer)
William R., Jr. of Warren m. Nancy J. **Sleeper** of Laconia 8/23/1952 in Lebanon; H - 25, manager, s/o William R. Hight and Iva D. Smith; W - 19, secretary, d/o Clarence W. Sleeper, Sr. and Sadie E. Connell

HILDRETH,
Charles L. of Haverhill m. M. Electa **Boynton** of Warren 8/9/1900 in Warren; H - 21, laborer, b. Haverhill, s/o Edward Hildreth

(Haverhill, mechanic); W - 16, student, b. Warren, d/o George N. Boynton (Warren, farmer)

David Wayne of Warren m. Patricia Ellen **Smith** of Warren 2/1/1969 in Warren; H - 19, s/o Harold L. Hildreth and Doris A. Perry; W - 15, d/o Chester F. Smith and Muriel Bevin

Edwin L. of Warren m. Thelma May **Ames** of Warren 8/25/1938 in N. Haverhill; H - 21, laborer, b. Warren, s/o William Hildreth (Warren) and Margaret Veasey (Bristol); W - 18, at home, b. W. Thornton, d/o William M. Ames (Bancroft, ME) and Sadie McCormick (Providence, ME)

Harold L. of Warren m. Doris Audrey **Perry** of Warren 10/23/1942 in Warren; H - 20, emp. highway, b. Warren, s/o William E. Hildreth (Warren) and Margaret Veasey (Bristol); W - 18, housework, b. Franklin, d/o John James Perry (Franklin) and Helen Perry

Harry L. of Warren m. Hazel F. **Plastridge** of Warren 5/18/1952 in Warren; H - 26, dyer, s/o Bryan K. Avery and Beatrice Brown; W - 31, housewife, d/o Ernest L. Batchelder and Lillian McLure

HILLIARD,

Joseph N. of Warren m. Leona H. **Short** of Warren 9/29/1923 in Warren; H - 21, laborer, b. Hill, s/o Nathan Hilliard (Hill, dead); W - 18, at home, b. Warren, d/o William J. Short (Newfoundland, laborer)

HO-SING-LOY,

Paul A. of Mission Viejo, CA m. Jane E. **Mauchly** of Warren 6/5/1982 in Plymouth; H - 22, s/o Vivian Ho-Sing-Loy and Gwendolyn Beverly McGie; W - 19, d/o James Thomas Mauchly and Flora Jane Hand

HOISINGTON,

Douglas A. of Glencliff m. Meredith L. **Ball** of Glencliff 6/3/2000 in Glencliff; H - 29, s/o Charles H. Hoisington and April D. Amaral; W - 26, d/o Edward J. Ball and Norma L. Clark

HOLMES,

Norris DeWitt of Woodstock m. Martha Jane **Mathews** of Warren 7/31/1914 in Rutland, VT; H - 24, electrician, b. Columbia, s/o Willis Holmes (Twin Mt.) and Ella E. Kimball (Madison); W - 30,

2, divorced, b. Warren, d/o Aaron Page (Bow) and Viola N. Flanders (Dorchester)

HOUGHTON,
Harry of Warren m. Helen **Chasson** of Warren 11/14/1924 in Warren; H - 20, laborer, b. Cabot, VT, s/o Dan Houghton (Cabot, VT, laborer); W - 19, at home, b. Warren, d/o Fred Chasson (NB, laborer)
Herbert W. of Warren m. Grace M. **Wilkins** of Plymouth 10/23/1921 in Warren; H - 30, tel. lineman, b. Warren, s/o Edward L. Houghton (Thetford, VT) and Delia A. Wolcott (Concord); W - 25, tel. operator, b. Whitefield, d/o Joseph F. Wilkins (Lawrence, MA) and Susie Mae Haley (Brunswick, ME)

HOWARD,
Noel Jay of Pine Plains, NY m. Sandra L. **Whitcher** of Warren 9/14/1963 in Warren; H - 20, student, s/o Harry William Howard and Anna M. Leach; W - 21, student, d/o Kenneth E. Whitcher and Marion Smith Cotton

HOWLAND,
Edgar of Warren m. Lucy J. **Prescott** of Warren 6/14/1888 in Warren; H - 39, millwright, 2nd, b. Landaff, s/o Samuel Howland; W - 38, 2nd, b. Piermont, d/o Amos Rodmer (Piermont)
John A. of Warren m. Mary H. **Eastman** of Henniker 11/9/1892 in Henniker; H - 24, miller, b. Woodstock, VT, s/o John Howland (Woodstock, VT, farmer); W - 23, teacher, b. Henniker, d/o George A. Eastman (Hopkinton, farmer)

HUBBARD,
Danny C. of Warren m. Jane A. **Smith** of Warren 3/15/1989 in Glencliff; H - 42, s/o Willy R. Hubbard and Lavern C. Carter; W - 35, d/o Joseph N. Boutin and Priscilla T. Paradie

HUBERDEAU,
Claude Roland of Canada m. Yolande Marguerite **Brochu** of Warren 3/18/1972 in Warren; H - 25, s/o Marc A. Huberdeau and Wilhelmine Brabant; W - 23, d/o Omer Brochu and Denise LeBourdais

HUCKINS,

Chad Ryan of Warren m. Jennifer Anne **Cilley** of Lebanon 7/13/1996; H - 25, s/o Robert Herman Huckins and Danette Alexia Danforth; W - 23, d/o Alan John Cilley and Joyce Brosius

Robert H. of Warren m. Deborah A. **Schofield** of Warren 12/23/1991 in Warren; H - 49, s/o Quintin Huckins and Doris Prescott; W - 40, d/o Charles Sladen and Emily Beck

HUNKINS,

Dana of Groton m. Eva **Blake** of Warren 8/21/1910 in Warren; H - 20, excelsior maker, b. Groton, s/o Willard Hunkins (Groton, farmer); W - 18, domestic, b. Piermont, d/o James Currie (Canada, farmer)

HURLBUTT,

William H. of Warren m. Mary E. **Judd** of Norwich, VT 7/3/1985 in Orford; H - 59, s/o Ebson Hurlbutt and Jeantte Barbaer; W - 48, d/o Russell S. Jamieson and Gretchen J. Campbell

William H., Jr. of Warren m. Patricia A. **Pease** of Wentworth 2/17/1972 in Wentworth; H - 19, s/o William H. Hurlbutt and Lucille B. Friend; W - 19, d/o Vernon C. Pease and Jane A. Hay

William H., Jr. of Warren m. Anne N. **LaBrie** of N. Woodstock 5/2/1974 in Warren; H - 21, s/o William Hurlbutt and Lucille Friend; W - 23, d/o Joseph LaBrie and Frances Shortt

HURLEY,

Michael M. of Manchester-by-the-Sea, MA m. Bernadette M. **Lupien** of Warren 2/12/1955 in Manchester; H - 29, lab technician, s/o Michael F. Hurley and Helena McGrath; W - 28, reg. nurse, d/o Edward R. Lupien and India Elliott

INGALLS,

Guy H. of Warren m. Eva **Short** of Warren 6/14/1904 in Warren; H - 27, carpenter, b. Hereford, PQ, s/o S. C. Ingalls (Warren, farmer); W - 17, domestic, d/o Edward Short (England, mason)

IZATT,

Arthur of Saco, ME m. Florence M. **Hanson** of Warren 5/17/1920 in Warren; H - 36, laborer, b. Saco, ME, s/o George Izatt (Mateland, NS) and Annie ----- (Saco, ME); W - 26, housekeeper, 3rd, widow, b. W. Topsham, VT, d/o Daniel Page and Esta Gilman (Molton Hill)

JACKSON,

Frank Curtice of Lyme m. Edith Belle **Colby** of Warren 6/4/1902 in Warren; H - 25, farmer, b. Belfast, ME, s/o Charles Curtice (Haverhill, MA); W - 22, compositor, b. Whitefield, d/o Ira M. Colby (Whitefield, farmer)

William C. of Warren m. Blanche R. **Kelley** of Warren 5/4/1904 in Warren; H - 26, laborer, b. Sullivan, ME, s/o Calvin P. Jackson (ME, laborer); W - 16, domestic, b. Warren, d/o John H. Kelley (Ellsworth, farmer)

JENNINGS,

Ralph E. of Warren m. Effie E. **Hutchins** of Warren 8/25/1926 in Laconia; H - 26, laborer, b. Digby, NS, s/o James Jennings (Yarmouth, NS, lumberman) and Jennett Smith (Digby, NS, housewife); W - 46, housewife, 3rd, b. Fairlee, VT, d/o David Copp (Piermont, retired) and Elizabeth Copp (Masina, NY, housewife)

JESSEMAN,

Elmer C. of Warren m. Ora May **Barry** of Warren 6/20/1929 in Woodsville; H - 22, laborer, b. Newbury, VT, s/o Irving Jesseman (Bethlehem, farmer) and Elizabeth LaFrance (Canada, housewife); W - 20, stenographer, b. Warren, d/o Charles F. Barry (Rumney, ladder rd. mfr.) and Ora May Smith (Sanbornton, housewife)

Elmer W. of Warren m. Hazel E. **Buskey** of Warren 8/11/1945 in Woodsville; H - 22, US Navy, b. Warren, s/o Raymond Jesseman (Plymouth, RR patrolman) and Marguerite Whitcher (Warren, housewife); W - 19, at home, b. E. Haverhill, d/o Henry Buskey (Derby Line, VT, NH fish & game) and Emma Dargie (Haverhill, housewife)

Elmer Whitcher of Warren m. Arlene Frederica **Laythe** of Warren 12/26/1976 in Plymouth; H - 53, s/o Raymond Jesseman and Marguerite Whitcher; W - 59, d/o Eugene Laythe and Gertrude Brooks

Raymond of Warren m. Marguerite **Whitcher** of Warren 8/6/1918 in Warren; H - 22, trackman, b. Plymouth, s/o William A. Jesseman (Dorchester) and Jennie Littlefield (Ellsworth); W -

143

19, housemaid, b. Warren, d/o Frank A. Whitcher (Warren) and
Laura E. Clement (Warren)

Raymond, Jr. of Warren m. Dorothy Eunice **Libbey** of Warren
6/21/1947 in Plymouth; H - 27, laborer, b. Warren, s/o
Raymond Jesseman (Plymouth, patrolman, B&M) and
Marguerite Whitcher (Warren, housewife); W - 23, school
teacher, b. Warren, d/o Natt E. Libbey (Warren, carpenter) and
Florence Balch (Goffstown, housewife)

Stanley William of Warren m. Mildred Lydia **Dooley** of NY 7/10/1971
in Warren; H - 39, s/o Raymond Jesseman and Marguerite
Whitcher; W - 28, d/o Howard Stanley and Dorothy Fox

JEWELL,

Frank E. of Warren m. Eva **Cross** of Warren 9/6/1887 in Plymouth;
H - 28, laborer, b. Wa—, VT, s/o Levi F. Jewell (millwright) and
Mariah Copp (housekeeper); W - 18

Frank E. of Warren m. Etta M. **Hadley** of Warren 7/4/1904 in
Warren; H - 46, carpenter, 2nd, b. Warren, s/o Levi F. Jewell
(millwright); W - 48, housekeeper, 3rd, b. Hereford, PQ, d/o
Chester A. Beecher (W. Stewartstown, carpenter)

Frank E. of Warren m. Martha J. **Brown** of Ashland 6/27/1922 in
Meredith; H - 64, sawyer, 3rd, b. Warren, s/o Levi F. Jewell
(Warren, millwright) and Mariah W. Copp (housewife); W - 67,
housekeeper, 2nd, b. Hanover, d/o Stillman Griffin (Hanover,
farmer) and Mary E. Fox (Hanover, housewife)

JEWETT,

Walter Harry of Rumney m. Nancy Helen **Simmons** of Warren
11/4/1978 in Rumney; H - 55, s/o Harry Jewett and Ona May
Balla; W - 30, d/o Edna Louise Dimond

JOHNSON,

Charles P. of Warren m. Tatyana **Yusopova** of Russia 7/6/2002; H -
45, s/o Thomas F. Johnson and Bernease Smith; W - 57, d/o
Viktor Ofcucnko and Maria Kotova

Jay C. of Warren m. Christine A. **Pelletier** of Warren 10/12/1990 in
Warren; H - 40, s/o Clifford H. Johnson and Norma Flynn; W -
35, d/o William E. Pelletier and Louise Hamlen

JONES,

Theodore of Plymouth m. Pauline **Harvey** of Warren 11/25/1933 in Bristol; H - 24, cook, b. Philadelphia, PA, s/o John Jones (Sharon Hill, PA, laborer) and Jenny Wensell (Chester, PA, housewife); W - 17, b. Warren, d/o Henry Harvey (Chazy, NY, fireman) and Nancy Houghton (Manchester, NY, housewife)

JOYCE,

Herbert W. of Moultonboro m. Deborah L. **Howe** of Meredith 10/19/1963 in Warren; H - 45, caretaker, s/o Albert A. Joyce and Mary V. Dulong; W - 37, weaver, d/o Oliver E. Howe and Mildred V. Sawyer

JUDKINS,

Amos H. of Warren m. Minnie M. **Kelley** of Warren 3/23/1903 in Warren; H - 24, farmer, b. Warren, s/o Harvey Judkins (farmer); W - 15, domestic, b. Warren, d/o John Kelley (farmer)

JULIAN,

Joseph of Warren m. Mary **Gagne** of Warren 5/9/1898 in Laconia; H - 26, laborer, b. Canada, s/o Oliver Jolian (Canada, farmer); W - 16, domestic, b. Bath, d/o Peter Gagne (Canada, farmer)

KAMINSKY,

Eric Robert of Warren m. Shirley Loraine **Bixby** of Warren 6/21/1975 in Warren; H - 18, s/o William P. Kaminsky and Doris Wetzler; W - 18, d/o Robert Bixby and Margaret Kramer

William Philip, Jr. of Warren m. Esther Joann **Wyatt** of Laconia 11/17/1973 in Laconia; H - 20, s/o William P. Kaminsky, Sr. and Doris I. Wetzler; W - 15, d/o Richard D. Wyatt and Edith I. Colby

KELLEY,

John H. of Warren m. Mary L. **Bennett** of Warren 1/7/1895 in Warren; H - 31, laborer, 2nd, b. Ellsworth, s/o William H. Kelley; W - 19, d/o George M. Bennett

KELLY,

Edwin of Warren m. Belle **Newton** of Campton 4/1/1913 in Warren; H - 57, farmer, 2nd, b. Lowell, MA, s/o William Kelly (Ellsworth, farmer); W - 25, domestic, b. Newbury, VT, d/o George Newton

Harry John of Warren m. Inez **Leavitt** of Claremont 9/7/1917 in
    Wentworth; H - 21, laborer, b. Warren, s/o John H. Kelly
    (Ellsworth) and Mary E. Bennette (Thornton); W - 33,
    housemaid, b. Claremont, d/o Elmer J. Leavitt (Grantham) and
    Carrie E. Blish (Winooski, VT)
John H. of Warren m. Della E. **Bennett** of Warren 8/27/1937 in
    Warren; H - 73, retired, b. Ellsworth, s/o William H. Kelly and
    Anne H. Wright; W - 69, housekeeper, b. Ellsworth, d/o George
    W. Bennett and Betsy McLintock

KENISION,
Stanley of Warren m. Tracie **Ferland** of Warren –/–/2003 in
    Piermont

KENNEDY,
Nelson L., Jr. of Warren m. Carol A. **Barclay** of Warren 11/23/1985
    in Warren; H - 26, s/o Nelson Kennedy and Loralee Whitcher;
    W - 26, d/o Rudolph Harvey Barclay and Zandra Uanalase
Nelson Leo, Jr. of Warren m. Kim Marie **Reid** of Swampscott, MA
    3/28/1979 in Warren; H - 20, s/o Nelson L. Kennedy and
    Loralee Whitcher; W - 19, d/o William C. Reid and Ann E. Horth

KENNEY,
Sidney Robert of Plymouth m. Edith Gould **Shortt** of Warren
    9/28/1956 in Warren; H - 44, tel. repair man, s/o Sidney R.
    Kenney and Adess E. Kinley; W - 40, tel. operator, d/o William
    J. Shortt and Mabel Gould

KESEK,
David Paul of Warren m. Laurel Lynne **Mason** of Warren
    10/22/1995; H - 36, s/o Walter A. Kesek and Mary Fluery; W -
    33, d/o Roderick A. Macdonald, Jr. and Linda Lee Hazelton

KEYES,
William F. of Haverhill m. Anna M. **Cotton** of Warren 4/14/1906 in
    Warren; H - 20, engineer, b. Haverhill, s/o Frank Keyes
    (Haverhill, foreman); W - 19, teacher, b. Concord, d/o Henry L.
    Cotton (Warren, farmer)

KEYSAR,

Donald Berkley of Warren m. Meca Ann **Williams** of Wentworth 5/13/1972 in Warren; H - 23, s/o Miles H. Keysar and Bertha N. Snelgrove; W - 21, d/o Fred W. Williams and Maude M. Bryant

Miles H. of Warren m. Bertha **Snelgrove** of Wentworth 9/19/1933 in Orford; H - 36, laborer, 2nd, b. Colebrook, s/o Berkley Keysar (Clarksville, carpenter) and Eliza Moses (Clarksville, housework); W - 18, nurse, b. Wentworth, d/o Frank Snelgrove (Moncton, NB, section hand) and Edna Wright (Piermont, housewife)

Royal E. of Hudson m. Marion L. **Averill** of Warren 9/20/1914 in Warren; H - 22, clerk, b. Colebrook, s/o Berkeley Keysar (Clarksville) and Eliza Moses; W - 20, compositor, b. Lakeport, d/o Chester B. Averill (Mount Vernon) and Edith M. Leonard (Warren)

KILPATRICK,

John of Lowell m. J. M. E. **Clifford** of Warren 9/9/1896 in Warren; H - 28, carpenter, b. Scotland, s/o T. Kilpatrick (Scotland, carpenter); W - 20, b. Lowell, d/o R. S. Clifford (Warren, jeweler)

KIMBALL,

Elmer R. of Warren m. Mary A. **Bergman** of Dover 6/29/1935 in Fairlee, VT; H - 29, forester, b. Middleton, s/o Oscar F. Kimball and Florence Runnells; W - 28, b. Dover, d/o Michael Conway and Helene Stevens

KING,

Gilbert of Warren m. Angelle **Ruel** of Warren 9/15/1891 in Warren Summit; H - 60, laborer, 2nd, b. Canada, s/o John King; W - 47, housekeeper, 2nd, b. Canada

James Russell of Warren m. Elizabeth Gertrude **White** of Warren 7/5/1988 in Warren; H - 44, s/o Linden A. King and Martha G. Powell; W - 49, d/o Howard E. Chase and Helen M. Curran

John Maurice, Jr. of Wentworth m. Suanne Jeanette **Clark** of Warren 6/2/1973 in Tilton; H - 19, s/o John M. King and Marion Verril; W - 21, d/o Wilbur O. Clark and Ingrid Hecketheer

Joseph D. of Warren m. Barbara C. **Fitts** of Warren 5/15/1998 in Warren; H - 36, s/o Joseph B. King and Phyllis E. Fredette; W - 35, d/o Ralph N. Fitts and Dorothy A. Chapman

Russell Frederick, Jr. of MA m. Janice Marie **Gherardi** of MA
9/2/1972 in Warren; H - 30, s/o Russell F. King and Myrtle L.
Murphy; W - 24, d/o Gerald Gherardi and Frances Sprago

KINGSBURY,
Karlton of Warren m. Amber **Stark** of Warren –/–/2003 in Warren

KITTREDGE,
Carl S. of Warren m. Julia N. **Morse** of Warren 9/28/1895 in
Warren; H - 28, merchant, b. Walden, VT, s/o J. W. Kittredge
(Walden, VT, merchant); W - 22, domestic, b. Chester, d/o S.
S. Morse (Chester, farmer)
Enos F. of St. Johnsbury, VT m. Sadie E. **Annis** of Warren
7/20/1910 in Warren; H - 22, clerk, b. Lyndon, VT, s/o George
Kittredge (Walden, VT, carpenter); W - 24, domestic, b.
Warren, d/o Perley Annis (Warren)

KNIGHTON,
Ivan L. of Warren m. Thelma **Dustin** of Warren 4/26/1941 in
Newbury, VT; H - 24, laborer, b. Bath, s/o Samuel Knighton
(Bath) and Gertrude Corey (Bath); W - 19, b. Easton, d/o
Charles Dustin (Farmington, ME) and Jennie Welch
(Farmington, ME)

KOWALEWSKI,
Walter Joseph of Bridgewater m. Olive Ellen **Howes** of Warren
4/26/1992 in Warren; H - 80, s/o Joseph Kowalewski and Julia
Marciniak; W - 71, d/o Joseph Arsenault and Emma Pelkey

KROL,
Paul of Stafford Springs, CT m. Eda Mae **Shortt** of Warren
10/6/1946 in Warren; H - 33, beltmaker, b. Stafford Springs,
CT, s/o Paul Krol (Czechoslovakia, lumbering) and Magdalena
Danick (Czechoslovakia, housewife); W - 22, grinder ppr., b.
Warren, d/o George A. Shortt (Walpole, farmer) and Nellie
Wright (Piermont, housewife)

KRUSE,
Donald Ray of Duluth, MN m. Carole Anne **Rogers** of Warren
7/15/1956 in Wentworth; H - 23, US Air Force, s/o Rudolph

Kruse and Mabel Lind; W - 19, US Air Force, d/o Ronald M.
Rogers and Alice M. Millican

KWEDOR,
Daniel of Warren m. Angela **Conkey** of Warren –/–/2003 in Warren

LAAUWE,
Brandt of Warren m. Denise **Bean** of Warren –/–/2003 in Warren

LABONTA,
Fred of Warren m. Delphine **Tangen** of Canada 10/20/1896 in
Woodsville; H - 24, laborer, b. Canada, s/o G. LaBonta
(Canada, laborer); W - 24, domestic, b. Canada, d/o N. Tangen
(Canada, laborer)
Peter of Warren m. Dellina **Fousiner** of Franklin 7/19/1900 in
Franklin; H - 25, painter, b. St. Clare, PQ, s/o Zephion LaBonta
(sailor); W - 24, housekeeper, b. St. Justine, PQ, d/o Jean
Fousiner (farmer)

LABOUNTY,
Joseph of Albany, NY m. Barbara **Green** of Warren 4/28/1961 in
Warren; H - 31, labor foreman, s/o Earl S. LaBounty and
Dorothy Lamere; W - 25, waitress, d/o Maurice A. Whitcher and
Helen Ball

LAFLAME,
Louis of Warren m. Eva **Austin** of Warren 1/13/1904 in Warren; H -
30, laborer, b. Canada, s/o Thomas Laflame (Canada, farmer);
W - 20, domestic, b. Bradford, VT, d/o Richard Austin
(truckman)

LAFLEUR,
John Edmond of NY m. Evangeline Lacorte **Amores** of NY 9/5/1993
in Warren; H - 35, s/o Louis Edmond Lafleur and Chritie
Poindexter; W - 34, d/o Vincente Amores and Elena Lacorte

LAMB,
Wilfred W. of Warren m. Daisy M. **Fales** of Warren 3/31/1903 in
Warren; H - 24, sawyer, b. St. John, NB, s/o Whitney S. Lamb
(St. John, NB, farmer); W - 22, domestic, b. Rumney, d/o
William Fales (Rumney, lumber dealer)

LAMOTHE,

Peter Edward of Warren m. Josephine V. **Florence** of Haverhill
11/1/1958 in Haverhill; H - 21, carpenter, s/o Roderick A.
Lamothe and Bernice M. Lupien; W - 36, unemployed, d/o
Willie P. Rollins and Mary E. Taylor

Peter Edward of Warren m. Marie D. **Thompson** of Campton
4/21/1962 in Wentworth; H - 25, carpenter, s/o Roderick G.
LaMothe and Bernice M. Lupien; W - 18, mach. operator, d/o
George W. Thompson and Delia L. Comeau

Roderick of Winchendon, MA m. Bernice M. **Lupien** of Warren
4/30/1934 in Plymouth; H - 27, forester, b. Winchendon, MA,
s/o Peter Lamothe (St. Jude, PQ, wood dealer) and Georgiana
Ledoux (St. Jude, PQ, at home); W - 23, at home, b. Warren,
d/o Edward R. Lupien (Newbury, VT, manufacturer) and India
Elliott (Warren, at home)

LAMSDEN,

George of New York City m. Gertrude M. **Kubler** of New York City
9/12/1922 in Warren; H - 27, machinist, b. Scotland, s/o
Andrew Lamsden (Brooklyn, NY, laborer) and Margarete Smith
(Brooklyn, NY, housewife); W - 19, silk worker, b. New York
City, d/o Alvis Kubler and Emilie Leblanc (Wentworth,
housekeeper)

LANDMESSER,

William Henry of ME m. Susan Gail **Walter** of VT 6/26/1977 in
Warren; H - 25, s/o Charles Landmesser and Jessie Jeffers; W
- 22, d/o Richard Walter and Carol Goodman

LAVOIE,

George J. of Glencliff m. Bernice **Swift** of Glencliff 9/4/1918 in
Woodsville; H - 32, carpenter, b. Benton, s/o Louis Lavoie
(Canada) and Adeline Caron (Canada); W - 27, housemaid,
2nd, b. Benton, d/o Henry Buskey (Canada) and Julia Graham
(Canada)

Leo L. of Warren m. Audrey M. **Dearborn** of Woodsville 8/23/1925
in Woodsville; H - 21, truck driver, b. Manchester, s/o Peter
Lavoie (Groton, VT, lumber dealer) and Lydia Derosia (Groton,
VT, housewife); W - 19, at home, b. Canada, d/o Guy Dearborn
(E. Haverhill, farmer) and Julia Sherman (Canada, housewife)

LAWRENCE,

Charles J. of Winchester m. Darlene G. **Bent** of Warren 12/22/1984
    in Plymouth; H - 38, s/o F. William Lawrence and Doris Porter;
    W - 16, d/o Norman Bent and Claire Hurlbutt

LEAVITT,

Ira W. of Hanover m. B. Blanche **Annis** of Warren 1/2/1907 in
    Warren; H - 21, clerk, b. Sanbornton, s/o George A. Leavitt
    (Sanbornton, farmer); W - 26, teacher, b. Warren, d/o Perley R.
    Annis (Warren)

LEONARD,

Ernest, Jr. of New York City m. Emma **Moulton** of New York City
    12/20/1923 in Warren; H - 22, laborer, b. New York City, s/o
    Ernest Leonard (New York City, tannery); W - 21, school
    teacher, b. New York City, d/o Orice Moulton (New York City,
    farmer)

F. F. of Providence m. Alice V. **Pillsbury** of Warren 6/19/1895 in
    Warren; H - 38, bookkeeper, b. Amesbury, MA, s/o A. C. J.
    Leonard (Piermont); W - 27, school teacher, b. Warren, d/o A.
    M. Pillsbury (Warren, farmer)

LEROY,

Herbert of Lisbon m. Cathy **Short** of Warren 3/15/1898 in Piermont;
    H - 22, laborer, b. Lisbon, s/o Anson Leroy (miner); W - 19,
    domestic, b. England, d/o William Short (England, laborer)

LESTER,

John G. of Warren m. Sarah C. **Fabian** of Warren 10/2/1982 in
    Wolfeboro; H - 27, s/o Richard Lester and Marjorie Wood; W -
    32, d/o Robert Fabian and Dorothy Crane

LEWIS,

Ralph W. of Andover m. Florence J. **Moses** of Warren 12/31/1935 in
    Wilmot; H - 26, truck driver, b. Andover, s/o Harold Lewis and
    Ethel Seavey; W - 18, housework, b. Warren, d/o Clarence
    Moses and Lucy Fisher

LIBBEY,

Earl B., Jr. of Warren m. Carlene D. **Thomason** of Hebron
11/30/1969 in Warren; H - 42, s/o Earl B. Libbey and Elsie
McCloud; W - 30, d/o Lawrence Jewell and Mildred Rice

Harold L. of Wentworth m. Barbara A. **Derosia** of Warren 6/29/1952
in Wentworth; H - 24, mechanic, s/o Earl B. Libbey and Elsie E.
McLoud; W - 19, housework, d/o Louis J. Derosia and Flossie
Rollins

Millard A. of Warren m. Nyra J. **Savage** of Lynn, MA 6/8/1935 in
Warren; H - 26, 1st Lt., FA Res., b. Portland, ME, s/o Clifford W.
Libby and Mabel A. Luce; W - 25, school teacher, b. Coplin Plt.,
ME, d/o Albion L. Savage and Louise Denico

Natt Everett of Warren m. Florence B. **Gallant** of Warren
11/22/1918 in Warren; H - 30, laborer, 2nd, widower, b. Warren,
s/o Ira N. Libbey (Warren) and Lucia Whitman (Warren); W -
30, housekeeper, 2nd, divorced, b. Goffstown, d/o C. S. Balch
(Johnson, VT) and Mary Moses (Riverdale)

Otis R. of Warren m. Lucy Ellen **Blake** of Wilder, VT 4/17/1917 in
W. Lebanon; H - 25, laborer, b. Warren, s/o Ira N. Libbey
(Warren); W - 17, housemaid, b. Haverhill, d/o Joseph H. Blake
(Haverhill) and Addie G. Dow (Concord)

Ralph of Warren m. Eda R. **Gramont** of Warren 1/28/1902 in
Warren; H - 32, farmer, b. Warren, s/o Robert Libbey (Warren,
farmer); W - 17, domestic, b. Orford, d/o George D. Gramont
(France, chopper)

Ralph of Warren m. Alice M. **Walsh** of Boston 1/21/1919 in
Wentworth; H - 49, farmer, 2nd, divorced, b. Warren, s/o Robert
M. Libbey (Warren) and Mary E. Page (Bow); W - 37,
housemaid, b. Boston, d/o Ambrose W. Walsh (PEI) and
Elizabeth A. Hayden (St. Johns, NF)

LIBBY,

Albert Earl of Warren m. Melissa Sue **Wetherbee** of Warren
4/23/1971 in Warren; H - 32, s/o Almer Libby and Vera Ball; W
- 21, d/o Walter Wetherbee and Lois Merrill

Grover Almer of Warren m. Harriet Sadie **Ames** of Warren
7/25/1953 in Warren; H - 25, truck driver, s/o Almer Libby and
Vera Ball; W - 18, at home, d/o Spurgeon Ames and Della
Libby

Grover Basil of Warren m. Vicki Gay **Brooks** of Pike 12/14/1974 in Warren; H - 19, s/o Grover A. Libby and Harriet S. Ames; W - 18, d/o Victor A. Brooks and Emily Gay

Natt E. of Warren m. Lillian **Smith** of Laconia 7/10/1910 in Warren; H - 21, teamster, b. Warren, s/o Ira N. Libby (Warren, carpenter); W - 29, domestic, 2nd, b. Amesbury, MA

LINDSAY,

Everest of Warren m. Inez G. **Eldrich** of Laconia 8/9/1892 in Warren; H - 21, carpenter, b. MN, s/o Loyd Lindsay (carpenter); W - 18, b. Laconia, d/o Nathan Eldrich

LITTLE,

John R. of Warren m. Mattie L. **Howard** of Orford 2/22/1902 in Orford; H - 24, telegraph oper., b. Warren, s/o Henry A. Little (Warren, justice); W - 25, dressmaker, b. Lyme, d/o R. A. Howard (Lyme, laborer)

William H. of Warren m. Annie Nurse **Reside** of Littleton 8/28/1920 in Warren; H - 47, engineer, 2nd, widower, b. London, England, s/o Isaac John Little (Corsham, England) and Emma Williams (Warwickshire, England); W - 42, housewife, 2nd, widow, b. Littleton, d/o Samuel Nurse (Bangor, ME) and Mary Eastman (York State)

William H. of Warren m. Mary J. **Clark** of E. Braintree, MA 9/2/1929 in Wentworth; H - 56, eng. & painter, 2nd, b. London, England, s/o Isaac John Little (Warwickshire, England, detective) and Emma Williams (Warwickshire, England, dressmaker); W - 46, hairdresser, 2nd, b. Bradford, VT, d/o William H. Noyes (Tunbridge, VT, real estate) and Alice K. Chamberlin (W. Bradford, VT, housewife)

William Henry of Warren m. Ida B. **Newell** of Manchester 3/12/1904 in Piermont; H - 31, engineer, b. England, s/o Isaac J. Little (London, England, stone cutter); W - 32, dressmaker, b. Plymouth, d/o Henry Newell (Rochester, MA, machinist)

LOCKE,

Henry E. of Warren m. Meney M. **Elliott** of Warren 4/20/1897 in Warren; H - 24, laborer, b. Concord, s/o E. Locke (Loudon, engineer); W - 27, housewife, 2nd, b. Warren, d/o H. D. Whitcher (Warren, farmer)

Morrill H. of Monroe m. Julia E. **Coates** of Glencliff 9/29/1922 in Monroe; H - 26, carpenter, b. Bath, s/o Harvey E. Locke (Floural, farmer) and Ella Smith (Floural, housekeeper); W - 18, housemaid, b. Haverhill, d/o William Coates (Glencliff, farmer) and Etta Sealy (Glencliff, housekeeper)

LORENCE,
Larry Vlastimil of New York City m. Susan **Gadd** of New York City 6/13/1970 in Warren; H - 47, s/o Jaroslav Lorence and Antonie Sotonova; W - 29, d/o Charles Gadd and Blanche Schimmel

LOUGEE,
Walter E. of Warren m. Sadie D. **Cutting** of Warren 4/25/1921 in Warren; H - 41, laborer, 2nd, divorced, b. Bradford, VT, s/o Sylvester J. Lougee (Lakeport) and Orlancy Kemp (PQ); W - 39, dressmaker, 2nd, divorced, b. Warren, d/o E. Emery Flanders (Warren) and Martha Moody (Sugar Hill)

LUCE,
Bernard of W. Rumney m. Edith M. **Ramsay** of Warren 9/12/1933 in Rumney; H - 26, chauffeur, b. N. Thetford, VT, s/o Leslie F. Luce (Tunbridge, VT, at home) and Rose Hubbard (Canada, deceased); W - 32, housework, 2nd, b. Glencliff, d/o James Belyea (NB, deceased) and Mary Fifield (Glencliff, housework)

LUGTON,
Russell Earl of Warren m. Eleanor M. **Shanna** of Warren 9/15/1991 in Franconia; H - 40, s/o Ralph Everett Lugton and Ruth Blasser Sheppard; W - 40, d/o Vernon Smith and Waneta Hawes

LUPIEN,
Edward R., Jr. of Warren m. Judith L. **Bickford** of Warren 4/30/1958 in Plymouth; H - 29, logger, s/o Edward R. Lupien, Jr. and India M. Elliott; W - 18, at home, d/o James R. Bickford and Aurelia M. Kingsley
Edwin R. of Warren m. India **Elliott** of Warren 4/30/1908; H - 22, b. Newbury, VT, s/o Napoleon Lupien (carpenter); W - 21, b. Warren, d/o Charles Elliott

MACCINI,

Peter Donald of Woodsville m. Lisa Marie **Ramsay** of Warren 6/17/1978 in Warren; H - 21, s/o Joseph R. Maccini and Evangeline A. Merrill; W - 21, d/o Dale V. Ramsay and Estella C. Cushing

MACDONALD,

Barry S. of Warren m. Kathy L. **Cass** of Warren 5/4/1991 in Warren; H - 26, s/o John H. MacDonald and Grace H. Tewksbury; W - 21, d/o Robert Peter Cass, Sr. and Barbara J. Hutchins

David L. of Warren m. Patricia J. **Deangelis** of Warren 12/12/1987 in Wentworth; H - 29, s/o Roger MacDonald and Audrey Weeden; W - 22, d/o Ronald Deangelis and Nancy Keeley

John Herbert, Jr. of Warren m. Grace Helen **Tewksbury** of Warren 3/1/1947 in Warren; H - 21, mill foreman, b. Warren, s/o John H. MacDonald (Bath, board sawyer) and Eva Lovett (Plymouth, housewife); W - 20, bobbin counter, b. Plymouth, d/o Clarence Tewksbury (Bath, bobbin mill s. pltr., Bath) and Lydia Bailey (Warren, housewife)

John Herbert, 3d of Warren m. Carol Anne **Rannacher** of Lincoln 10/27/1967 in Warren; H - 20, mill worker, s/o John Herbert MacDonald and Grace H. Tewksbury; W - 21, mill worker, d/o Ray William Rannacher and Ella Anne

MACKENZIE,

James A. of Warren m. Kellie K. **Loughlin** of Warren 6/30/1990 in Dover; H - 24, s/o James H. MacKenzie and Gail V. Arendt; W - 24, d/o Bernard Loughlin and Irene Morin

MAGNEN,

Henry J. of Warren m. Annie **Gagney** of Warren 2/11/1896 in Warren; H - 22, laborer, b. France, s/o A. L. Magnen (Paris, France, clerk); W - 23, domestic, b. Canada, d/o Peter Gagney (Canada, laborer)

MAHER,

Thomas M. of Warren m. Janine S. **Leduc** of Warren 10/31/1987 in Dunbarton; H - 23, s/o Thomas S. Maher and Margaret Mitten; W - 24, d/o Julien Leduc and Sandra Meattey

MALONE,
Cyril H. of Enfield, CT m. Frances V. **Duncan** of Wethersfield, CT
7/14/1952 in Warren; H - 45, truck driver, s/o Edward A. Malone
and Mary A. Allen; W - 25, secretary, d/o Edward L. Duncan
and Adelaide Stonebridge

MALTAIS,
David Arthur of Concord m. Elaine Marie **Hibbard** of Warren
8/4/1972 in Epsom; H - 23, s/o Arthur L. Maltais and Virginia M.
Jackson; W - 18, d/o Lloyd C. Hibbard and Eudora M.
Wetherbee

MANSUR,
Arthur J., Cpl. of Bristol m. Priscilla D. **Cutting** of Warren 9/23/1948
in Bristol; H - 22, US soldier, b. Lawrence, MA, s/o John W.
Mansur (Lawrence, MA, truck driver) and Agnes Reich
(Methuen, MA, woolen mill work); W - 18, at home, b. Warren,
d/o Charles E. Cutting (Piermont, woodsman) and Mary Dyer
(RI, at home)

MARDIN,
Clement of Warren m. Jennie **Plant** of Haverhill 2/28/1920 in
Warren; H - 35, lumberman, 2nd, divorced, b. Lisbon, s/o Willard
Mardin (Lisbon) and Elva Quimby (Lisbon); W - 30,
housekeeper, 2nd, divorced, b. Bath, d/o Sylvanus Moses
(Burlington, VT) and Emma Barney (Burlington, VT)

MARQUIS,
Joseph of Warren m. Janice L. **McKinnon** of Warren 10/26/1957 in
Plymouth; H - 39, woodsman, s/o Denise Marquis and Anna
Soucy; W - 20, housewife, d/o Charles E. Cutting and Margaret
Dyer

MARSTON,
Neil C. of Warren m. Dianne L. **Palmer** of Northwood 11/30/1985 in
Andover; H - 25, s/o Theodore Marston and Gladys
Featherstone Payne; W - 26, d/o Joseph Heath and Ruth Kay
Neil C. of Warren m. Julie B. **Labbie** of Warren 10/8/2005 in Warren

MARTIN,

Dean W. of MN m. Elva M. **Eastman** of Warren 10/16/1920 in Warren; H - 32, forester, b. Minneapolis, s/o Henry S. Martin (Danville, VT) and Blanche Woodmansee (Cincinnati, OH); W - 22, b. Warren, d/o George C. Eastman (Warren) and Margaret McCutcheon (St. Johns, NB)

Richard A. of Pike m. Elizabeth C. **Ames** of Warren 7/3/1959 in Warren; H - 22, laborer, s/o Rosario Edward Martin and Rena Rebecca Fuller; W - 19, at home, d/o Spurgeon McC. Ames and Adella Tilley

Walter B. of Warren m. Eliza M. **White** of Warren 8/13/1916 in Woodstock; H - 64, horse dealer, 4th, b. Grafton, s/o John Martin (Rumney) and Elvira Avery (Rumney); W - 34, housekeeper, 3rd, b. Thornton, d/o Charles Ham and Martha Wallace (Thornton)

William Joseph. Jr. of Glencliff m. Louise G. **Stengel** of Medfield, MA 6/8/1953 in Rumney; H - 28, mechanic, s/o William J. Martin and Grace MacLeod; W - 48, domestic, d/o Frank P. Stengel and Louise Guething

MASSE,

Robert J. of Franklin m. Charlotte **Wistner** of Warren 9/12/1939 in Fairlee, VT; H - 21, laborer, b. Franklin, s/o Herman Masse (St. Gertrude, Canada) and Alma Morrisy (St. Gertrude, Canada); W - 18, b. Haverhill, d/o Charles Wistner (Rockaway, NJ) and Catherine Short (St. Johns, NF)

MATSON,

James L. of Warren m. Donna L. **Roy** of Warren 4/26/1969 in Warren; H - 25, s/o John M. Matson and Viney Strojny; W - 21, d/o Kenneth Bancroft and Elizabeth Brown

James Louis of Warren m. Jean Margaret **Marston** of Warren 10/5/1974 in Plymouth; H - 30, s/o John M. Matson and Viney Strojny; W - 22, d/o Theodore Marston and Gladys Featherstone

Jon Milton of Warren m. Jeannette F. **Olivier** of Berlin 4/12/1969 in Berlin; H - 25, s/o John M. Matson and Viney Strojny; W - 18, d/o Laurier Olivier and Florence Dusault

MAUNULA,

Toivo John of Warren m. Ardeth Mae **Stimson** of Warren 4/12/1948 in Woodsville; H - 20, none, b. Norwood, MA, s/o Toivo Harold Maunula (Norwood, MA, laborer) and Helen Ann Mattson (Duluth, MN, housewife); W - 20, none, b. Woodsville, d/o Elmer Gerald Stimson (Woodsville, laborer) and Lilla Mae Martin (Glencliff, housewife)

McCAULEY,

James F. of Richford, VT m. Shirley H. **Adams** of Newport, VT 11/24/1904 in Warren; H - 25, mill operator, 2nd, b. Lebanon, s/o James McCauley (Canada, blacksmith); W - 18, domestic, b. Coventry, VT, d/o George Adams (laborer)

McCLAIN,

Frank of Warren m. Pauline L. **Picanso** of Warren 9/18/2004 in Plymouth

McGARY,

Angus Ross of Warren m. Gladys Evelyn **Smith** of Bradford, VT 12/4/1943 in Bradford, VT; H - 45, laborer, b. Linreau, ME, s/o John Lamble McGary (Linreau, ME) and Mary Catherine Shields (Linreau, ME); W - 40, housework, b. Newbury, VT, d/o Christopher Millette (Canada) and Mary Stanton (Ireland)

McGUY,

Thomas M. of Warren m. Laurel A. **Kapplain** of Warren 7/18/2002; H - 49, s/o James E. McGuy and Dorothy Snow; W - 43, d/o Edward W. Kapplain and Mary A. Tefft

McHUGH,

James D. of Warren m. Bree **Heward** of Warren 8/14/2004 in Warren

McISAAC,

Henry of Warren m. Mabel L. **Eastman** of Warren 11/14/1895 in Warren; H - 24, teamster, b. Cape Briton, s/o Dan McIsaac (Cape Briton, tailor); W - 21, housekeeper, b. Warren, d/o B. F. Eastman (Warren, farmer)

Henry E. of Warren m. Natalie M. **Gallant** of Warren 9/30/1924 in Wentworth; H - 27, laborer, b. Warren, s/o Henry McIsaac

158

(Cape Breton, laborer); W - 19, tel. oper., b. Warren, d/o
Thomas Gallant (Canada, laborer)

Henry E. of Warren m. Elizabeth A. **Glode** of Plymouth 7/5/1980 in
Plymouth; H - 55, s/o Henry E. McIsaac, Sr. and Natalie
Gallant; W - 45, d/o Henry D. Elliott and Eleanor M. Ramsay

McKENNA,

Christipher S. of Glencliff m. Kathy A. **Moore** of Glencliff 11/22/1986
in Warren; H - 34, s/o John P. McKenna and Eileen M. Davis;
W - 28, d/o Lamoine Moore and Rose Maloof

McKIERNAN,

Matthew Erwin of Tolland, CT m. Marie Elizabeth **DeJohn** of
Tolland, CT 10/15/2002; H - 44, s/o Vincent T. McKiernan and
Dorothy M. Whitcher; W - 48, d/o Anthony J. DeJohn and
Margaret Gedeon

McKINLEY,

Ralph of Warren m. Susie E. **Whitney** of Warren 4/4/1903 in
Warren; H - 19, laborer, b. NS, s/o George McKinley (St. John,
NB, laborer); W - 16, domestic, b. Lancaster, d/o E. F. Whitney
(mechanic)

McKINNON,

Norman of Warren m. Eva **McKevie** of Rumney 6/18/1904 in
Warren; H - 26, laborer, b. Bangor, ME, s/o Roderick McKinnon
(Scotland, farmer); W - 17, domestic, b. MA

Paul W. of Warren m. Janice L. **Cutting** of Warren 8/6/1955 in
Warren; H - 23, paper maker, s/o Theodore R. Ames and
Helen Chandler; W - 18, at home, d/o Charles E. Cutting and
Margaret Dyer

McLAUGHLIN,

James of Warren m. Mary J. **McLeod** of Milton, MA 7/31/1891 in
Warren Simmit; H - 24, clergyman, b. PEI, s/o Laughlin
McLaughlin (PEI); W - 23, b. PEI, d/o James McLeod (PEI)

Robert A. of Wentworth m. Sarah E. **Swain** of Warren 9/13/1903 in
Warren; H - 24, mechanic, b. Sherbrooke, PQ, s/o John
McLaughlin (Sherbrooke, PQ, farmer); W - 18, domestic, b.
Warren, d/o Darius O. Swain (Warren, gentleman)

McNAMARA,

Wallace E. of Island Pond, VT m. Christina F. **Clifford** of Warren 1/27/1915 in Warren; H - 27, marker, b. Westmore, VT, s/o Edward E. McNamara (Inverness, Canada) and Annie Agnes Hinton (Westmore, VT); W - 19, housemaid, b. Boston, MA, d/o Iolas C. Clifford (Warren) and Annie Cameron (Boston, MA)

McNERLIN,

William L. of Charlestown, MA m. Frances E. **Conolly** of Charlestown, MA 8/8/1920 in Warren; H - 34, foreman, b. Charlestown, MA, s/o Hugh H. McNerlin (Boston) and Annie Foley (Halifax, NS); W - 25, bookkeeper, b. Charlestown, MA, d/o Patrick Connolly (Charlestown, MA) and Margaret Malanavy (Charlestown, MA)

McVETTY,

William of Warren m. Emma E. **French** of Warren 6/30/1898 in Warren; H - 60, farmer, 2nd, b. Canada; W - 42, domestic, 2nd, b. Warren

MELLO,

Frank R., Jr. of Centerville, MA m. Marilyn Ann **Hight** of Warren 10/26/1963 in Warren; H - 27, laborer, s/o Frank R. Mello and Elsie Nan Mederios; W - 23, bookkeeper, d/o Arthur L. Hight and Shirley E. Mannion

MERRILL,

Clinton J. of Warren m. Florence F. **Miclon** of W. Thornton 4/5/1923 in Plymouth; H - 25, RR emp., b. Warren, s/o Fred J. Merrill (Warren, farmer); W - 17, at home, b. Warren, d/o Orin Miclon (Warren, sect. fore.)

Craig A. of Warren m. Janet A. **Cortes** of Bristol 11/15/1987 in Warren; H - 32, s/o Ralph Merrill and Kathrine Dudley; W - 33, d/o Cleon Barton and Mildred Stafford

Ernest E. of Warren m. Mildred G. **Fifield** of Warren 12/24/1914 in Warren; H - 25, laborer, b. Warren, s/o Fred J. Merrill (Rumney) and Lizzie B. Cummings (Warren); W - 18, housemaid, b. Warren, d/o Ethelbert Fifield (Warren) and May Miriam Morrison (Lawrence, MA)

Jesse H. of Warren m. Lois M. **Cate** of Hooksett 6/29/1940 in Manchester; H - 26, Swift & Co., b. Warren, s/o John B. Merrill

(Warren) and Hattie M. Elliott (Warren); W - 26, teacher, b. Hooksett, d/o George E. Cate (Hooksett) and Anna M. Farnham (Salem, MA)

John of Warren m. Hattie **Elliott** of Warren 4/18/1910 in Warren; H - 28, lineman, b. Warren, s/o Jesse Merrill (Warren, farmer); W - 21, housewife, d/o Charles Elliott

John S. of Warren m. Emily J. **Blake** of Warren 8/13/1897 in Warren; H - 60, mechanic, 2nd, b. Andover, s/o John Merrill (Bristol, farmer); W - 56, housewife, 2nd, b. Orange, d/o Ezekiel Collins (farmer)

Lyman G. of Warren m. Fannie S. **Fifield** of Warren 5/3/1911 in Warren; H - 24, teamster, b. Warren, s/o Fred J. Merrill (Rumney, farmer); W - 20, school teacher, b. Warren, d/o Ethelbert Fifield (Warren, farmer)

Lyman G. of Warren m. Myrtie B. **Gould** of Warren 2/11/1920 in Woodsville; H - 32, laborer, 2nd, widower, b. Warren, s/o Fred J. Merrill (Rumney) and Lizzie D. Cummings (Warren); W - 30, housekeeper, 2nd, widow, b. Haverhill, d/o A. Heath and Mary Howland (Easton)

Paul Ranville of Warren m. Winnie M. **Perry** of Warren 9/30/1917 in Wentworth; H - 25, shipping clerk, b. Hampton, s/o Samuel Albert Merrill (Warren) and Emeline C. Hirsch (Germany); W - 23, sch. teacher, b. Warren, d/o Onslow D. Perry (Chichester) and Bertha Ana Leighton (Haverhill)

Sam A. of Warren m. Millie **Hirsch** of Hampton 6/15/1889 in Warren; H - 36, farming, 2nd, b. Warren, s/o G. W. Merrill and Elizabeth Merrill; W - 34, b. Hampton, d/o George F. Hirsch

MEYERS,

E. H. B. of Cleveland, OH m. Miriam K. **Bard** of Rheems, PA 8/15/1927 in Warren; H - 33, physical dr., b. PA, s/o Christian Meyers (PA) and Mary Blemley (PA); W - 27, teacher, b. PA, d/o Andrew S. Bard (PA, RR oper.) and Mary Kraybill (PA, housewife)

MICHAUD,

Joseph A. of Marblehead, MA m. Elizabeth A. **Lausier** of Marblehead, MA 8/9/1980 in Warren; H - 18, s/o Joseph N. Michaud and Janice Noyes; W - 19, d/o Paul L. Lausier and Elizabeth Trefry

MILLER,

David Dwain of Riverview, FL m. Germaine Norman **Roulx** of
Warren 9/30/1967 in Woodsville; H - 19, Army, s/o Theo Miller
and Joyce V. Lafave; W - 19, service, d/o Oscar A. Roulx and
Mabel S. Godville

David Karl of Haverhill m. Sharon Lee **MacDonald** of Warren
5/13/1967 in Woodsville; H - 20, mill, s/o William Karl Miller and
Irene Tomko; W - 16, at home, d/o John Herbert MacDonald
and Grace Helen Tewksbury

MILNE,

Francis John of Washington, DC m. Eleanor M. **Keysar** of Warren
6/14/1941 in Warren; H - 24, gov't clerk, b. Barre, VT, s/o John
Milne (Aberdeen, Scotland) and Elizabeth Naughton (Barre,
VT); W - 25, stenographer, b. Warren, d/o Royal E. Keysar
(Colebrook) and Marion L. Averill (Lakeport)

MITCHELL,

Joseph James of Warren m. Carol Ann **Hazen** of Warren 10/1/1988
in Warren; H - 34, s/o Richard Mitchell and Pearl L. Joyce; W -
31, d/o Everett L. Vincellette, Sr. and Blanche I. Libby

MONTAGNE,

Clifford of Bozeman, MT m. Joan Lansing **Weed** of Hanover
8/31/1968 in Warren; H - 21, b. WY, s/o John Montagne (NY)
and Phoebe Corthell (WY); W - 22, b. DC, d/o Walker T. E.
Weed, II (NJ) and Hazel Schofield (GA)

MOODY,

Kenneth V. of S. Tamworth m. Marion F. **Whitcher** of Warren
11/20/1922 in Warren; H - 18, laborer, b. Albany, s/o William
Moody (Brownfield, ME, laborer) and Mabel Moore (S.
Tamworth, housekeeper); W - 16, at home, b. Warren, d/o
George Whitcher (Warren, laborer) and Sarah N. Stickney
(Warren, housewife)

Lyle Clayton of Warren m. Jean Gertrude **Lumsden** of Wentworth
2/24/1946 in Wentworth; H - 22, veteran, b. Warren, s/o
Kenneth Moody (Albany, carpenter) and Marion Whitcher
(Warren, housewife); W - 20, stenographer, b. Bronx, NY, d/o
George Lumsden (Edinborough, Scotland, painter) and
Gertrude Kubler (New York City, housework)

Owen K. of Warren m. Eleanor L. **MacDonald** of Rumney 8/27/1955 in Rumney; H - 21, student, s/o Kenneth V. Moody and Marion Whitcher; W - 20, clerk, s/o Harold C. MacDonald and Thelma M. Moses

Stephen Ross of Warren m. Marlene **Stevens** of Warren 7/3/1967 in Warren; H - 20, construction, s/o Kenneth V. Moody and Marion F. Whitcher; W - 18, none, d/o Wallace A. Stevens and Althea June Gould

MOONEY,
Fergus T. of Branford, CT m. Laurel H. **Owen** of Branford, CT 5/5/1987 in Warren; H - 31, s/o F. Mooney and Anne Fitzgerald; W - 29, d/o Edward Owen and Ruth Yoder

MORIN,
Leon F. of Manchester m. Mary A. **Raymond** of Warren 11/9/1920 in Woodsville; H - 23, druggist, b. Concord, s/o Henry Morin (Canada) and Matilda Pincence (Canada); W - 21, millwork, b. Woodsville, d/o Francis F. Raymond (Canada) and Matilda Boucher (Canada)

MORRISON,
Everett A. of Warren m. Anna F. **Benson** of Warren 8/15/1932 in Littleton; H - 24, forest guard, b. Warren, s/o Rodney Morrison (laborer) and Cora A. Merrill (Warren, housekeeper); W - 20, teacher, b. S. Portland, ME, d/o John J. Benson (Biddeford, ME, seaman) and Annie F. Owen (Portland, ME, housekeeper)

Louis R. of Warren m. L. Riddell **Clifford** of Warren 10/18/1894 in Warren; H - 24, tel. operator, b. Monford, WI, s/o F. M. Morrison (Roxbury, MA, scale builder); W - 18, housekeeper, b. Colebrook, d/o George C. Clifford (Warren, boarding)

Rodney of Warren m. Cora A. **Batchelder** of Warren 1/24/1906 in Warren; H - 36, fireman, b. NS, s/o Neil Morrison (Scotland, carpenter); W - 31, housekeeper, 2nd, b. Warren, d/o Asa Merrill (Warren, farmer)

MORSE,
George W. of Warren m. Nellie V. **Campbell** of Warren 11/20/1893 in Woodsville; H - 27, carpenter, b. Cabot, VT, s/o Nelson Morse (farmer); W - 18, b. Hudson

163

Ira H. of Warren m. Lillian **Little** of Cambridge, MA 9/7/1898 in
Warren; H - 23, clerk, b. Chester, s/o Samuel S. Morse
(Chester, farmer); W - 27, student, b. Manchester, d/o William
Little (Warren, lawyer)
Ira H. of Warren m. Lillian R. **Dunbar** of Warren 6/26/1943 in
Concord; H - 68, shoe merchant, b. Chester, s/o Samuel S.
Morse (Chester) and Luella H. Merrill (Warren); W - 50, at
home, b. Somerville, MA, d/o Wilbur A. Whitcomb (Springfield,
VT) and Annie B. MacLennan (NS)
Ira Herbert of Reno, NV m. Julie B. **Mahoney** of W. Roxbury, MA
3/12/1932 in Warren; H - 56, merchant, 2nd, b. Chester, s/o
Samuel S. Morse (Chester) and Luella Helen Merrill (Warren);
W - 37, at home, 2nd, b. Lowell, d/o John C. Burke (Liverpool,
England, lawyer) and Gertrude Dow (Albany, VT, at home)
Philip M. of Lowell, MA m. Jane C. **Wolfe** of Miami, FL 6/20/1955 in
Warren; H - 52, shoe merchant, s/o Ira H. Morse and Lillian
Little; W - 32, secretary, d/o William J. Callery and Grace
Conway

MORTON,
Wallace Edward of Fairlee, VT m. Althea Mary **Fadden** of Fairlee,
VT 2/11/1966 in Warren; H - 24, machinist, s/o Eugene W.
Morton and Myrtle M. Elliott; W - 21, hairdresser, d/o Robert E.
Fadden and Priscilla M. Horton

MOSES,
Clarence of Warren m. Lucy **Fisher** of Brookline, MA 9/30/1912 in
Warren; H - 27, teamster, 2nd, b. Warren, s/o Lubian Moses
(Colebrook, farmer); W - 28, waitress, b. Manchester, England,
d/o George Fisher (England)
Clarence H. of Warren m. Lena M. **Foote** of Warren 1/31/1907 in
Laconia; H - 21, laborer, b. Warren, s/o Lubian Moses
(Colebrook, laborer); W - 17, housekeeper, b. Warren, d/o
Charles G. Foote (Warren, farmer)
Elmer O. of Warren m. Winnie B. **Glines** of Warren 4/20/1895 in
Haverhill; H - 24, railroad, b. Warren, s/o John Moses (Warren,
lumber); W - 21, compositor, d/o G. A. Glines
Fred A. of Lynn, MA m. Setlla A. **Boynton** of Warren 11/22/1894 in
Wentworth; H - 20, pop corn, b. Warren, s/o John B. Moses
(Chichester, pop corn); W - 17, d/o John L. Boynton (laborer)
(note - groom's name given as Fred A. Morse)

MOSHOLDER,

Daniel D. of Warren m. Debra J. **Hathaway** of Merrimack 3/29/1980 in Merrimack; H - 19, s/o Kenneth R. Mosholder and Shirly Dewolf; W - 21, d/o Malcolm R. Hathaway and Patricia Racette

MOULTON,

Alvah of E. Concord m. Mae I. **Foster** of Lunenburg 4/4/1908; H - 21, b. Bath, s/o Sherman Moulton (carpenter); W - 18, b. Bath, d/o E. P. Foster (St. Johns, NB, farmer)

George F. of Warren m. Linnie C. **County** of Rumney 11/1/1892 in Warren; H - 25, horse trainer, b. Burke, VT, s/o H. H. Moulton (Ellsworth, farmer); W - 17, b. Canaan, d/o Dennis County (Lowell, MA)

MOUNCEY,

Harold Alton, Jr. of Warren m. Barbara Frances **Perry** of Pike 11/5/1949 in Warren; H - 31, truck driver, 2nd, b. Jersey City, NJ, s/o Harold A. Mouncey (Jersey City, NJ) and Laura Nash (Jericho, VT); W - 21, at home, b. Hingham, MA, d/o Carleton Perry (Hingham, MA) and Ruth Wing (Weymouth, MA)

MUDGETT,

John H. of Warren m. Lill **Ford** of Warren 4/4/1895 in Warren; H - 23, med. student, 2nd, b. Holderness, s/o John I. Mudgett; W - 27, domestic, b. Warren, d/o Isiah F. Ford (Warren)

MUGFORD,

Thomas Lester of Hooksett m. Bernadette Victoria **Currier** of Warren 6/26/1971 in Warren; H - 26, s/o Thomas Mugford and Ernestine Hudson; W - 21, d/o John D. Currier and Frances Kasheta

MUNROE,

Peter Paul of Watertown, MA m. Ann Marie **Phillips** of Watertown, MA 8/12/1992 in Warren; H - 24, s/o Robert Munroe and Helen Bowes; W - 24, d/o Kenneth Phillips and Mary DiGiacomandrea

MURPHY,

Douglas W., Jr. of Moultonboro m. Myrtie M. **Heath** of Warren 10/12/1991 in Warren; H - 23, s/o Douglas Murphy, Sr. and Linda Colt; W - 20, d/o Raymond Heath and Irma Angers

165

MYERS,

Robert J., Jr. of Warren m. Nanci-Beth **Hurst** of Warren 4/30/1988 in Warren; H - 27, s/o Robert J. Myers, Sr. and Irene L. Spinazzola; W - 26, d/o Russell N. Hurst, Sr. and Jeanne Dawkins

NADEAU,

Gene of Warren m. Norma **Nadeau** of Warren –/–/2003 in Warren
Gene Howard of Warren m. Norma Jean **Parenteau** of Warren 7/1/1995; H - 53, s/o A. J. Nadeau and Sara M. Leplante; W - 30, d/o Wilfred A. Parenteau, Sr. and Barbara V. Rollins

NEDEAU,

Charles of Ashland m. Hattie **Nedeau** of Warren 6/9/1928 in Warren; H - 55, trackman, 2nd, b. Canada, s/o Antoine Nedeau (Canada, section man) and Ellen Derosia (Canada, housewife); W - 64, housekeeper, 2nd, b. Bethlehem, d/o William Dexter (Bethlehem, farmer) and Dorinda Eaton (Friberg, ME, housewife)

NELSON,

Daniel Mark of Hanover m. Deborah Heller **Bacon** of Sparks, MD 6/5/1976 in Warren; H - 23, s/o Charles E. Nelson and Marilon Saxby; W - 22, d/o John Foster Bacon and Phoebe Follmer
Edward J. of N. Woodstock m. Eva D. **Kelly** of Warren 11/28/1923 in Warren; H - 30, pharmacist, b. Rumney, s/o William S. Nelson (Underhill, VT, laborer); W - 28, clerk, 3rd, b. Warren, d/o John H. Kelly (Littleton, farmer)

NEWTON,

Jason M. of Warren m. Kendra L. **Kuntz** of Warren 8/6/2005
Jeffrey S. of Warren m. Penny L. **Shortt** of Warren 10/10/1987 in Warren; H - 19, s/o Robert H. Newton and Sylvia Carlson; W - 19, d/o Stanley F. Shortt and Marjorie L. Libby
Robert H. of Wentworth m. Sylvia Ann **Carlson** of Warren 8/24/1963 in Wentworth; H - 21, set up man, s/o Mervin K. Newton and Helen D. Rollins; W - 20, staff maid, d/o Paul C. Carlson and Jennie P. Nelson

166

NICOL,

Berkeley Charles of Warren m. Shirley L. **Bigelow** of N. Haverhill 6/20/1964 in N. Haverhill; H - 23, student, s/o John Henry Nicol and Marjorie B. Nicol; W - 22, teacher, d/o Leon H. Bigelow and Mary Plant Bigelow

John H. of Warren m. Marjorie A. **Brown** of Wentworth 6/27/1932 in N. Haverhill; H - 25, clerk, b. Warren, s/o William B. Nicol (Bathurst, NB, laborer) and Alice M. Libbey (Warren, housewife); W - 27, teacher, b. Wentworth, d/o Charles H. Brown (Wentworth, farmer) and Eva M. Breck (Wentworth, housewife)

John Laurence of Warren m. Carol Jane **Matson** of Warren 9/19/1959 in Plymouth; H - 22, pressman, s/o John Henry Nicol and Marjorie A. Brown; W - 21, secretary, d/o John M. Matson, Sr. and Viney T. Strojny

Mark A. of Warren m. Shirley A. **Matson** of Warren 5/7/1960 in Warren; H - 25, accountant, s/o John Henry Nicol and Marjorie A. Brown; W - 21, secretary, d/o John Milton Matson and Viney T. Strojny

NOLAN,

Courtney Lee of Warren m. Susan Lynn G. **Farnham** of Warren 9/12/1992 in Orford; H - 28, s/o Lee Nolan and Jean Smith; W - 26, d/o Bruce S. Farnham and Sondra E. Clifford

NUTTER,

Theodore L. of Warren m. Susan F. **Nolan** of Warren 7/8/2005 in Warren

NYSTROM,

Alden Edmond of Glencliff m. Karen Lee **Smith** of Orford 7/2/1977 in Orford; H - 21, s/o Robert Nystrom, Sr. and Marcella Horton; W - 19, d/o Stanley Smith, Sr. and Mary Cummings

Carl Edwin of Haverhill m. Loretta Rose **Asselin** of Warren 3/13/1976 in Haverhill; H - 21, s/o Robert E. Nystrom and Marcella J. Horton; W - 17, d/o Henry T. Asselin and Sheila E. Moore

OLDING,

Paul B., Jr. of Plymouth, MA m. Kathleen **Cahill** of Plymouth, MA 11/9/1991 in Warren; H - 36, s/o Paul Olding, Sr. and Anna May Franey; W - 29, d/o Richard G. Cahill and Eileen June McLaughlin

PAIGE,

Jack E. of Wentworth m. Gayle E. **Mansur** of Warren 6/5/1971 in Warren; H - 21, s/o Arthur C. Paige and Francese E. Knowles; W - 22, d/o Arthur Mansur and Priscilla D. Cutting

PALMER,

Stanley Wilson of Durham m. Flora Belle **Palmer** of Warren 6/20/1945 in Epping; H - 34, US Army, b. Durham, s/o Roscoe Palmer (Durham, retired) and Lillian Arsenault (Durham, housewife); W - 30, teacher, 2nd, b. Epping, d/o Willie Rollins (Epping) and Mary E. Rollins (Fall River, MA, housewife)

PANUS,

Michael E. of Warren m. Julie A. **Sicks** of Warren 9/2/2000 in Warren; H - 45, s/o Chester S. Panus and Mary Lou Butler; W - 33, d/o Jon L. Sicks and Jane D. Hunt

PATTERSON,

Ralph Russell of Warren m. Mary Ellen **Strout** of Warren 11/4/1978 in Warren; H - 32, s/o Harold Patterson and Hazel Anstey; W - 30, d/o Harold Hildreth and Doris Perry

PEASE,

Edwin S. of Warren m. Florence M. **Pease** of Warren 11/9/1935 in Lisbon; H - 64, merchant, b. Wentworth, s/o Samuel J. Pease and Sarah J. Randall; W - 51, domestic, b. Lynn, MA, d/o Edward Edgerly and Stella M. Combs

PERRY,

George D. of Warren m. Gladys T. **Clifford** of Warren 6/21/1919 in Warren; H - 25, RR sta. agent, b. Jefferson, s/o George E. Perry (Bennett's Landing) and Addie E. Berry (Jefferson); W - 21, store clerk, b. Medford, MA, d/o Iolas C. Clifford (Warren) and Annie C. Cameron (Boston)

PETELLE,
Douglas Ray of Tilton m. Brenda Lee **Marshall** of Warren 7/30/1988 in Warren; H - 35, s/o Harold C. Petelle and Elizabeth A. Clark; W - 21, d/o Arthur D. Marshall and Elizabeth A. Demella

PETITO,
Andrew of Warren m. Leona **Pike** of Warren 7/17/1913 in Warren; H - 22, laborer, b. NY, s/o Alexander Destino (Italy, laborer); W - 16, b. Warren, d/o Arthur Pike (Warren, laborer)

PHAIR,
William Thomas of Warren m. Mildred M. **Comings** of Durham 12/26/1914 in Lakeport; H - 20, farmer, b. Laconia, s/o Thomas W. Phair (County Cork, Ireland) and Josephine Flanders (Warren); W - 23, school teacher, b. Durham, d/o Albert Comings (Boston, MA) and Emma J. Dow (Joliet, IL)

PHILBROOK,
William A. of Warren m. Katherine Ruby **Pike** of Warren 11/21/1921 in Woodsville; H - 19, laborer, b. Springfield, ME, s/o Alfred I. Philbrook (Omaha, NE) and Maude M. Cessar (Carrol, NE); W - 17, at home, b. Warren, d/o Joseph W. Pike (Warren) and Jennie F. Tibbetts (Benton)

PICKARD,
Milton A. of Warren m. Katherine **Applebee** of N. Haverhill 7/25/1934 in Warren; H - 22, laborer, b. W. Newbury, MA, s/o John A. Pickard (Groveland, MA, farmer); W - 20, housework, b. N. Haverhill, d/o George Applebee (Jefferson, laborer) and Gertrude M. Clement (Canada, housework)

PICKNELL,
Frank Edward of Tilton m. Sharon Marie **Asselin** of Warren 8/17/1974 in Franklin; H - 21, s/o Albert Picknell and Irene Robert; W - 17, d/o Henry T. Asselin and Sheila Moore

PIKE,
Arthur L. of Warren m. Eva **Judkins** of Warren 6/1/1887 in Warren; H - 24, laborer, b. Warren, s/o Walter F. Pike (deceased) and Sarah Swain (housekeeper); W - 17, b. Dan----

Clarence W. of Warren m. Eva Della **Kelly** of Warren 6/18/1914 in
Warren; H - 24, laborer, b. Warren, s/o Arthur L. Pike (Warren)
and Eva G. Judkins (Danville, VT); W - 18, housemaid, b.
Warren, d/o John K. Kelly (Ellsworth) and Dilla Bennett
(Ellsworth)

Clarence W. of Warren m. Christin M. **Woodward** of Quincy
1/18/1919 in Warren; H - 28, trackman, 2nd, divorced, b.
Warren, s/o Arthur L. Pike (Warren) and Eva G. Judkins
(Danville, VT); W - 22, housemaid, b. Milan, d/o Edward S.
Woodward (Holland, VT) and Alice L. ----- (Bethel, ME)

Joseph W. of Warren m. Jennie F. **Tibbetts** of Warren 6/21/1892 in
Warren; H - 22, farmer, b. Warren, s/o Walter Pike; W - 17, b.
Benton, d/o Delden H. Tibbetts (sect. boss)

Lanson James of Warren m. Dorothy Irene **Morey** of Warren
8/30/1919 in Warren; H - 22, laborer, b. Warren, s/o Arthur L.
Pike (Warren) and Eva Judkins (Danville, VT); W - 17,
housemaid, b. Orford, d/o Irving W. Morey (Union Village, VT)
and Annie V. McIntire (Canada)

Lawrence H. of Warren m. Eva D. **Kelly** of Warren 2/22/1920 in
Warren; H - 25, laborer, b. Warren, s/o Arthur L. Pike (Warren)
and Eva G. Judkins (Danville, VT); W - 24, 2nd, divorced, b.
Warren, d/o John H. Kelly and Della A. Bennett

Lawrence H. of Warren m. Rose A. **McAuley** of Warren 9/10/1923
in Warren; H - 29, chauffeur, 2nd, b. Warren, s/o Arthur L. Pike
(Warren, laborer); W - 24, at home, 2nd, b. Warren, d/o George
Stubbard (Sidney, NS, steamfitter)

Leon B. of Haverhill m. Arlene **Washburn** of Warren 4/14/1914 in E.
Haverhill; H - 21, brakeman, b. Dedham, MA, s/o Charles E.
Pike (Meredith) and Lula A. Bixby (Warren); W - 16, student, b.
Newbury, VT, d/o Horace H. Washburn (Canaan) and Lilla -----

Michael Shane of Warren m. Traci Lyn **Sackett** of Warren
10/6/2001 in Glencliff; H - 26, s/o Michael Earl Pike and Kathryn
Althea Garrett; W - 19, d/o Charles Nelson Sackett and Tammy
Lyn Irwin

Richard Alanson of Warren m. Barbara May **Gove** of Wentworth
12/27/1946 in Plymouth; H - 27, state emp., b. Warren, s/o
Alanson J. Pike (Warren, farmer) and Dorothy I. Pike (Orford,
housewife); W - 21, teacher, b. Wentworth, d/o Earl Gove
(Wentworth, farmer) and Beatrice Downing (Wentworth,
housewife)

170

Richard Morey of Warren m. Sandra Jane **Stallings** of Warren
7/7/1972 in Warren; H - 25, s/o Richard A. Pike and Barbara
Gove; W - 24, d/o David Caverhill and Helen Hildreth

POITRAS,
Clarence Louis of Rumney m. Hazel Beatrice **Deblois** of Warren
9/16/1950 in Warren; H - 20, millhand, b. Warren, s/o Louis
Poitras (Rumney) and Almina Demerritt (VT); W - 18, at home,
b. St. Johnsbury, VT, d/o Melvin Deblois (Lowell, VT) and
Beatrice Irwin (St. Johnsbury, VT)

PORTER,
John Dale, Jr. of Warren m. Ernestine Beatrice **Perkins** of
Skowhegan, ME 8/26/1947 in Skowhegan, ME; H - 27, farming,
b. Readville, MA, s/o John D. Porter (Topeka, KS, locomotive
eng.) and Grace E. Morrell (Long Island, NY, housewife); W -
21, at home, b. Skowhegan, ME, d/o Chester Ross Perkins
(Blanchard, ME, laborer) and Olive Caleay (Skowhegan, ME,
housewife)

POWELL,
David Franklin of Warren m. Suzanne Marie **Bixby** of Warren
10/9/1993 in Pike; H - 37, s/o Franklin Powell and Madeline
Adel Demers; W - 26, d/o Reginald Wayne Bixby and Jeanette
Marie Haines

PRESCOTT,
Roscoe C. of Warren m. Vivian Alice **Channell** of St. Johnsbury, VT
6/5/1935 in Orford; H - 30, forester, b. Lebanon, s/o Harry F.
Prescott and Minie J. Kelly; W - 30, reg. nurse, b. Bolton, PQ,
d/o Charles Channell and Alma Manning

PROUTY,
John of Warren m. Winifred **Haartz** of Thornton 10/3/1982 in
Campton; H - 72, s/o Clement J. Prouty and Bessie W. Clapp;
W - 73, d/o G. Weston Elliott and Edna Pratt

PROVENCHER,
Kevin J. of Warren m. Kimberly **White** of Warren 9/18/1982 in
Warren; H - 26, s/o Michael C. Provencher and Patricia C.
Grey; W - 20, d/o Lawrence R. White and Elizabeth G. Chase

PUSHEE,
Clarence Leslie of Warren m. Sharon Lee **Bancroft** of Warren 12/19/1992 in Warren; H - 54, s/o Clarence Leslie Pushee, Sr. and Evelyn T. Tattersall; W - 44, d/o Innon B. Conley and June C. McCullough

PUTNAM,
Robert E. of Plymouth m. Bertha E. **Prescott** of Warren 8/15/1937 in Conway; H - 23, forest service, b. Worcester, MA, s/o Arthur P. Putnam and Mary K. Owens; W - 22, NE Tel. & Tel., b. Peacham, VT, d/o Grover C. Prescott and Ester Rollins

QUIMBY,
Roger C. of Dorchester m. June C. **Weeks** of Warren 2/27/1938 in Warren; H - 20, mechanic, b. Dorchester, s/o Custer Quimby (Dorchester) and Bertha Parker (Dorchester); W - 18, servant, b. Rumney, d/o Vallie J. Weeks (Warren) and Lillian M. Dennis (Boscawen)

RAMSAY,
Brian William of Warren m. Barbara A. **Cunningham** of Warren 5/14/1988 in Hebron; H - 37, s/o Sherburn C. Ramsay and Sally A. Robinson; W - 24, d/o Charles M. Cunningham and Ruth A. Jilson
Earl Edwin of Piermont m. Edith May **Belyea** of Warren 11/28/1917 in Haverhill; H - 24, engineer, b. Haverhill, s/o Alex. Ramsay (PEI) and Josephine Newcomb (PEI); W - 18, housemaid, b. Warren, d/o James Belyea (NB) and May Fifield (Benton)
Thomas H. of Warren m. Judy L. **Chase** of Warren 2/14/1998 in Lochmere; H - 56, s/o Harry T. Ramsay and Thomasena L. Porter; W - 32, d/o Leon E. Chase and Edna Dimond

RAMSEY,
Dale Vernon of Warren m. Estella Clarissa **Cushing** of Warren 9/16/1947 in Warren; H - 20, laborer, b. Pike, s/o Earl Ramsey (Pike, laborer) and Edith Belyea (Piermont, housewife); W - 20, beautician, b. Warren, d/o Irving G. Cushing (Freeport, ME, merchant) and Pearl E. Batchelder (Warren, housewife)
Earl E. of Warren m. Eunice M. **Moses** of Haverhill 1/12/1942 in Rumney; H - 21, US Air Corps, b. Warren, s/o Earl Ramsay (Pike) and Edith M. Belyea (Warren); W - 18, at home, b.

Haverhill, d/o Harry Moses (W. Rumney) and Dell Downing (Orford)

RANDALL,
Cameron G. of Warren m. Susan **Ball** of Warren –/–/1997; H - s/o Gary W. Randall and Linda Lee Harnett; W - d/o John W. Simmons

Vincent G. of Warren m. Susan M. **Libby** of Warren 12/24/1990 in Warren; H - 26, s/o Gary W. Randall and Linda L. Randall; W - 19, d/o Albert E. Libby and Melissa S. Wetherbee

RAY,
Alex Eastman of Ashland m. Ellen Ann **White** of Warren 5/26/1979 in Warren; H - 19, s/o Bill Ray and Adelia M. Eastman; W - 19, d/o Lawrence R. White and Elizabeth G. Chase

Donald G. of Wentworth m. Donna L. **Bancroft** of Warren 11/6/1965 in Wentworth; H - 18, laborer, s/o George S. Ray and Mamie M. Hilliard; W - 18, at home, d/o Kenneth Bancroft and Elizabeth Brown

Floyd R. of Warren m. Doris H. **Rowell** of Warren 6/28/1934 in Bristol; H - 21, clerk, b. Dorchester, MA, s/o Edward E. Ray (W. Rumney, farmer) and Sadie Stark (Boston, MA, housewife); W - 29, school teacher, b. Meredith, d/o Frank C. Rowell (Bristol, mechanic) and Agnes Hoyt (Meredith, librarian)

George Stanley of Warren m. Mamie Madeline **Hilliard** of Warren 10/4/1946 in Rumney; H - 18, truck driver, b. E. Otis, MA, s/o George Roy (Lebanon) and Alice LaPorte; W - 1-, at home, b. Warren, d/o Joseph Hilliard (Hill, RR section) and Leona Shortt (Warren, housewife)

RAYMOND,
Alfred J. of Warren m. Lydia Jennie **Short** of Warren 7/4/1920 in Warren; H - 18, laborer, b. Woodsville, s/o Frank Raymond (Derby Line, PQ) and Matilda Bushee (Kinsley, PQ); W - 18, housekeeper, b. Warren, d/o Will J. Shortt (Newfoundland) and Mabel Gould (Warren)

READE,
Amos L., Jr. of Warren m. Eleanor I. **Euiler** of W. Rumney 1/7/1955 in Plymouth; H - 24, truck driver, s/o Amos L. Reade, Sr. and

Minnie McLeod; W - 24, stewardess, d/o Paul W. Euiler and
Eleanor Sagendorph

REMICK,
William F. of Warren m. Myrtie **Miller** of Warren 3/9/1909 in Warren;
H - 43, teamster, b. Gorham, s/o Orrin Remick; W - 32,
housekeeper, b. Groveton, d/o John Astol

REYNOLDS,
Ernest G. of Hardwick, VT m. Ethel M. **Mitchell** of Warren
7/28/1928 in Wells River, VT; H - 23, farmer, b. Burke, NY, s/o
George Reynolds (Burke, NY) and Mova Greenway (Canada);
W - 23, b. Burke, NY, d/o Will Mitchell (Burke, NY) and Bertha
Wood (Burke, NY)

John D. of Warren m. Evelyn Wanda **Roth** of Portland, ME 8/4/1928
in Warren; H - 21, X-ray technician, b. Warren, s/o Berturn
Reynolds (laborer) and Lottie Pero; W - 22, at home, b.
Scranton, PA, d/o Frank Roth (Hungary, electrician) and Mary
Beranza (Hungary, housewife)

RICE,
Donald Arthur of Bristol m. Phyllis Ann **Keysar** of Warren 3/19/1955
in Warren; H - 22, moulder, s/o Wallace A. Rice and Blanche
Gage; W - 20, typist, d/o Miles H. Keysar and Bertha Snelgrove

RICHARDS,
Charles V. of Littleton m. Kathy J. **Spinelli** of Littleton 3/6/1972 in
Warren; H - 23, s/o Charles V. Richards and Eva Ella Adams;
W - 22, d/o William Spinelli and Edith Blais

Richard Orin of Warren m. Rita Louise **McCoy** of Warren 6/30/1977
in Warren; H - 47, s/o Raymond L. Richards and Doris Sargent;
W - 41, d/o Frank McCoy and Lulu Tattersall

RICHARDSON,
Craig E. of Warren m. Kimberly J. **Hubbard** of Laconia 7/9/1989 in
Laconia; H - 32, s/o Harold Richardson and Theresa Booklauz;
W - 29, d/o Royal S. Burnham and Nancy Keniston

Edwin of Warren m. Flora **Lovernway** of Wilmington, VT
10/11/1902 in Warren; H - 23, laborer, b. Worcester, MA, s/o
Leon Richardson (Worcester, MA, laborer); W - 18, domestic,
b. NY State

Fred W. of Benton m. Rachel L. **Townsend** of Warren 3/22/1888 in Warren; H - 35, minister, b. Greenport, NY, s/o L. O. Richardson; W - 33, teacher, b. Broome, PQ, d/o Abner Townsend

ROBERTS,
Kenneth E. of Chelsea, VT m. Ethel M. **Avery** of Warren 10/2/1936 in Rumney; H - 25, cook, b. Warren, AZ, s/o Elmer C. Roberts and Alma St. John; W - 36, at home, b. Warren, d/o Hasting Avery and Della Batchelder

ROBERTSON,
Paul S. of FL m. Debra S. **Brueggemann** of FL 10/3/1991 in Warren; H - 20, s/o Thomas A. Robertson; W - 21, d/o David Brueggemann and Claudia Earhardt

ROBIDOUX,
Fernand Edward of Lincoln, RI m. Ethel Barbara **Medeiros** of Warren 4/3/1948 in Providence; H - 28, asst. engineer, b.. Albion, RI, s/o Napoleon Robidoux (Fall River, MA) and Clara Lusignant (Canada); W - 28, jewelry worker, 2nd, b. Warren, d/o Eugene Whitcher (NH) and Elsie Lindsey (NS)

ROCA WHU,
Christian J. of Warren m. Jenny M. **Maviki** of Bristol 5/1/2005 in Warren

ROCK,
Harold Albert of Woodsville m. Esther E. **Boardman** of Glencliff 5/6/1944 in Haverhill; H - 27, painter, b. Morrisonville, NY, s/o Albert G. Rock (Morrisonville, NY) and Eva May Fortune (Woodsville); W - 21, unemployed, b. Haverhill, d/o George R. Boardman (N. Troy, VT) and Mary L. Brown (Orford)

ROMANO,
Gino Joseph of Hyde Park, MA m. Pauline Martha **Doherty** of Roslindale, MA 6/20/1970 in Warren; H - 34, s/o Luigi Romano and Onorina Sbardella; W - 30, d/o Kenneth Bancroft and Elizabeth Brown

ROMON,

Antenio of Miami, FL m. Marie M. F. **Roulx** of Warren 11/4/1961 in Bradford, VT; H - 21, houseman, s/o Sugendo Romon and Rosa Rodugez; W - 16, none, d/o Oscar A. Roulx and Mabel L. Godville

ROSS,

George S., Jr. of Portsmouth m. Debra L. **Bixby** of Warren 2/14/1986 in Portsmouth; H - 24, s/o George S. Ross, Sr. and Carole Mornechuk; W - 25, d/o Reginald W. Bixby and Jeanette Haines

ROULX,

Oscar Alphonse of Warren m. Mabel Louise **Godville** of Warren 6/9/1945 in Rumney; H - 38, lumbering, b. Canada, s/o Joseph Roulx (Canada, farmer) and Anaisse Caron (Canada); W - 24, housewife, b. Warren, d/o James Godville (Lithuania, laborer) and Edna Shortt (Warren, housewife)

ROY,

George of Warren m. Grace E. **French** of Warren 6/2/1898 in Warren; H - 35, laborer, 2nd, b. Canada, s/o Lewis Roy (Canada, farmer); W - 20, domestic, b. Warren, d/o Osco French (Rumney, laborer)

RUDOLPH,

Fulton J. of Warren m. Judy L. **Chase** of Warren 11/2/1991 in Warren; H - 21, s/o Fulton E. Rudolph and Marjorie Blake; W - 26, d/o Leon E. Chase and Edna Dimond

RUELL,

Joseph of Warren m. Mary **Valler** of Lakeport 10/16/1906 in Woodsville; H - 27, farmer, b. Canada, s/o Lawrence Ruell (Canada, farmer); W - 24, b. Lakeport, d/o Joe Valler (Canada, laborer)

ST. CROIX,

John W. of White River Jct., VT m. Marion H. **Hilliard** of Warren 11/22/1951 in White River Jct., VT; H - 39, clerk, s/o Joseph E. St. Croix and Elmira Picard; W - 27, waitress, d/o Joseph N. Hilliard and Leona Shortt

SACKETT,

Charles Nelson of Erie, PA m. Janice Marie **Ball** of Warren 7/2/1960 in Warren; H - 22, laborer, s/o Nelson George Sackett and Marie T. Jackson; W - 20, at home, d/o Leslie Albert Ball and Doris Mary Leger

Charles Nelson of Warren m. Tammy Lyn **Irwin** of N. Haverhill 11/11/1978 in Warren; H - 19, s/o Charles N. Sackett and Janice M. Ball; W - 17, d/o Charles A. Irwin and Everdene A. Reed

Norman Leslie of Warren m. Carol Beth **Cardin** of Haverhill 6/18/1988 in Warren; H - 27, s/o Charles N. Sackett, Sr. and Janice M. Ball; W - 26, d/o Normand Cardin and Emme J. Marshall

Terry Joseph of Warren m. Jennifer Grace **Vincent** of Warren 6/4/1988 in Warren; H - 21, s/o Charles N. Sackett, Sr. and Janice M. Ball; W - 18, d/o Ronald A. Vincent and Georgia Bower

Timothy J. of Warren m. Lorie A. **Warbin** of Warren 9/18/1986 in Plymouth; H - 21, s/o Charles Nelson Sackett and Janice Marie Ball; W - 24, d/o Nelson L. Kennedy and Loralee Whitcher

SANBORN,

Gregory Allen of Rumney m. Rhonda Colleen **Cushing** of Warren 3/18/1971 in Rumney; H - 19, s/o Roger Sanborn and Mary Murdough; W - 18, d/o Irving B. Cushing and Avis Huckins

Jerrie T. of Franklin m. Millie **Day** of Warren 12/20/1897 in Warren; H - 23, clerk, b. Franklin, s/o V. M. Sanborn (Franklin, farmer); W - 20, teacher, b. Cincinnati, OH, d/o Alonzo Day (Boscawen, shoemaker)

SANDSTIM,

August L. of ME m. Marcia **Boulresse** of ME 8/20/1907 in Warren; H - 21, laborer, b. Sweden, s/o Olaf Sandstim (millwright); W - 21, b. VT, d/o Amos Boulresse (NY, laborer)

SCHIFF,

Dayton A. of Albuquerque, NM and Darlene D. **Dooley** of Warren 5/1/1985 in Warren; H - 20, s/o Duane A. Schiff and Dorothea J. Adcox; W - 20, d/o Thomas F. Dooley and Mildred L. Jesseman

SCHLEICHER,
Michael D. of Warren m. Dolores Ann **Wood** of Warren 3/22/1977 in
Warren; H - 33, s/o Michael A. Schleicher and Catherine Zerby;
W - 34, d/o William D. Wood and Anna Ball

SEELEY,
William R. of Warren m. N. Leona **Edwards** of Whitman 8/4/1920 in
Warren; H - 35, farmer, b. Underhill, VT, s/o R. Seeley
(Underhill, VT) and Florence Story (Underhill, VT); W - 38,
shoeshop, b. Brockton, MA, d/o Frank W. Edwards
(Cambridge, MA) and Carrie E. French (Glencliff)

SHANTY,
Frederick C. of Newport, VT m. Jessie A. **Lambert** of Warren
8/25/1952 in Lyme; H - 53, engineer, s/o Joseph Shanty and
Eliza O. Towner; W - 57, beautician, d/o Archibald M. Wright
and Dora McIntyre

SHARON,
William of Warren m. Mabel E. **Stratton** of Boston 9/23/1907 in
Warren; H - 36, farmer, 2nd, b. N. Woodstock, s/o Stephen
Sharon (Somerville, MA, hotel keeper); W - 32, nurse, b. NY,
d/o Ernest Stratton (Boston, bookkeeper)

SHEEHAN,
Christopher of Rumney m. Darlene Ball **Butson** of Glencliff
2/16/1974 in Warren; H - 21, s/o Dennis A. Sheehan and
Therese C. Phaneuf; W - 18, d/o Clifford Ball and Ardeth
Stimson

SHORT,
Edward of Warren m. Lela L. **Whitcher** of Warren 10/31/1908; H -
26, b. Fairlee, VT, s/o Edwin Short (Manchester, England,
mason); W - 35, b. Warren, d/o Henry Whitcher (Warren,
farmer)
Edward B. of Warren m. Ethel Flora **Timson** of Warren 5/26/1945 in
Warren; H - 60, inspector, 2nd, b. Fairlee, VT, s/o Edwin Shortt
(Manchester, England, mason) and Laura A. Warner (Bradford,
VT); W - 35, nurse, 2nd, b. Ellsworth, d/o Melvin Allard
(Whitefield, fireman) and Mary Norton (Whitefield)

George A. of Warren m. Georgianna **Walbridge** of Warren 8/5/1911 in Warren; H - 26, laborer, b. Wakefield, s/o William Short (Dorchester, England, farmer); W - 25, housework, 2nd, divorced, b. Orford, d/o George D. Gramo (Montreal, farmer)

Will J. of Warren m. Mabel M. **Gould** of Warren 4/8/1896 in Warren; H - 21, laborer, b. Newfoundland, s/o William Short (England, laborer); W - 17, b. Warren, d/o Lewis Gould (Warren, laborer)

SHORTT,

Arron William of Warren m. Geneva Emily **Simpson** of Plymouth 10/20/1946 in Plymouth; H - 24, mechanic, b. Warren, s/o George A. Shortt (Walpole, farmer) and Nellie Wright (Piermont, housewife); W - 23, factory emp., b. Wentworth, d/o Harry Clarence Simpson (Piermont, retired) and Lura Brown (Wentworth, housewife)

George A. of Warren m. Nellie M. **Bean** of Warren 5/11/1920 in Rumney; H - 35, laborer, 2nd, divorced, b. Walpole, s/o William Shortt (Dorchester, England) and Rose Weymouth (Newfoundland); W - 26, housekeeper, 2nd, widow, b. Piermont, d/o Ximenes P. Wright (Groton, MA) and Emmagene Harris (Warren)

Leland Phillie of Warren m. Regina Arlene **Huckins** of Wentworth 11/17/1946 in Rumney; H - 20, mechanic, b. Warren, s/o George A. Shortt (Walpole, farmer) and Nellie Wright (Piermont, housewife); W - 1-, at home, b. Wentworth, d/o Harvey W. Huckins (New Hampton, mechanic) and Marjorie Smith (Gilford, housewife)

Leon Hazen of Warren m. Doris Alice **Huckins** of Ashland 8/14/1963 in Plymouth; H - 58, mill worker, s/o William J. Shortt and Mabel L. Gould; W - 43, seamstress, d/o Grover C. Prescott and Della F. Hardy

Lewis William of Warren m. Evelyn Florence **Heath** of Ashland 8/7/1953 in Tilton; H - 40, foreman paper mill, s/o William J. Shortt and Mabel L. Gould; W - 28, housewife, d/o Arthur Ralph Dicey and Ellen L. Cross

Stanley F. of Warren m. Marjorie L. **Libbey** of Warren 8/19/1952 in Warren; H - 21, mechanic, s/o George A. Shortt and Nellie M. Wright; W - 16, domestic, d/o Almer M. Libbey and Vera Ball

179

SIMMONS,

Fred E. of Hudson m. Kimberly A. **Leonard** 2/14/1998 in Warren; H - 32, s/o John W. Simmons and Nancy Simmons; W - 24, d/o Donna L. Bancroft

John of Bath m. Nancy H. **Dimond** of Warren 8/4/1964 in Newbury, VT; H - 49, mechanic, s/o John W. Simmons and Phyllis Gay; W - 16, d/o Edna Dimond

SIMPSON,

Curtis Henry of Plymouth m. Margery Stewart **Dunbar** of Warren 7/1/1946 in Warren; H - 27, US Army, b. Wentworth, s/o Harry C. Simpson (Piermont, retired) and Lura Brown (Wentworth, housewife); W - 22, curator, b. Cambridge, MA, d/o Robert W. Dunbar (New York, NY) and Lillian Whitcomb (Boston, MA, housewife)

Ernest Cedric of Warren m. Ernestine Perry **Asselin** of Warren 6/–/1946 in Exeter; H - 30, laborer, 2nd, b. Wentworth, s/o Harry C. Simpson (Piermont, retired) and Lura A. Brown (Wentworth, housewife); W - 30, housework, b. Medford, MA, d/o George Perry (St. John, NB, painter) and Mary McCarthy

Harry C. of Warren m. Lulu A. **Brown** of Wentworth 8/2/1902 in Warren; H - 23, laborer, b. Haverhill, s/o Henry D. Simpson (Haverhill, laborer); W - 19, domestic, b. Wentworth, d/o George Brown (farmer)

SMITH,

A. Leroy of Warren m. Lena O. **Merrill** of Warren 5/1/1901 in Warren; H - 22, clerk, b. W. Topsham, VT, s/o Arthur T. Smith (W. Topsham, farmer); W - 21, domestic, b. Warren, d/o Amos L. Merrill (farmer)

Benjamin W. of Warren m. Stella Alice **Drouin** of Warren 1/29/1942 in Haverhill; H - 37, farmer, b. Lyme, s/o Carlton A. Smith (Lyme) and Ida May Brissette (Hanover); W - 41, pastry cook, b. N. Stratford, d/o Irving M. Barnet (Columbia) and Elizabeth Foster (Ball'ph'ps, NB)

Carl W. of Warren m. Louise R. **Abler** of Warren 10/18/1941 in Warren; H - 39, farmer, b. Guilford, s/o Claude R. Smith (New Hampton) and F. M. Wilkinson (Laconia); W - 35, at home, b. W. Newark, NJ, d/o Charles W. Abler (New York, NY) and Minnie Kstein (W. Newark, NJ)

Charles H., Jr. of Warren m. Gwendolyn I. **Brown** of Wentworth
8/27/1946 in Rumney; H - 31, farmer, b. New Canaan, CT, s/o
Charles H. Smith (Norwalk, CT, farmer) and Emma Person
(Werum, Sweden, housewife); W - 16, waitress, b. Wentworth,
d/o Oscar W. Brown (Wentworth, farmer) and Gladys Ridgewell
(Providence, RI, housewife)

Charles H., Jr. of Warren m. Gwendolyn I. **Smith** of Warren
5/26/1952 in Woodsville; H - 36, laborer, s/o Charles H. Smith
and Emma T. Parson; W - 22, housewife, d/o Oscar W. Brown
and Gladys L. Ridgewell

Charles N. of Warren m. Nellie O. **Jaques** of Tilton 5/10/1888 in
Laconia; H - 30, farmer, b. Warren, s/o Sullivan Smith
(Sanbornton); W - 21, b. Tilton, d/o Henry C. Jaques

George E. of Warren m. Rose Maria **Emery** of Concord 4/15/1919 in
Warren; H - 49, grain merchant, 2nd, widower, b. Plymouth, s/o
Obadiah G. Smith (N. Groton) and Elvira J. Grant (N. Groton);
W - 48, tailoress, b. London, England, d/o William Emery
(London, England) and Jane Allen (Darking, England)

Guy W. of Warren m. Belle **Hildreth** of Warren 10/5/1910 in
Plymouth; H - 24, farmer, b. Woodstock, s/o Warren Smith
(Woodstock, farmer); W - 24, domestic, b. Warren, d/o Elroy
Hildreth (Haverhill, carpenter)

Harry of Warren m. Goldie M. **Palmer** of Woodsville 6/22/1908; H -
23, b. Woodsville, s/o George F. Smith (Milo, ME, RR cond.);
W - 21, b. Whitefield, d/o F. H. Palmer (Littleton, painter)

James P. of New Haven, CT m. Barbara **Norcia** of New Haven, CT
6/1/1985 in Warren; H - 53, s/o James P. Smith and Marie
Gallo; W - 47, d/o Merlin J. Smith and Amelia Turner

Osborne W. of Ashland m. Tavie W. **Little** of Warren 12/24/1901 in
Warren; H - 20, laborer, b. Ashland, s/o William B. Smith
(Campton, farmer); W - 19, domestic, b. Warren, d/o Henry A.
Little (Warren, justice)

Paul Steven of Wentworth m. Charlene Ann **Downing** of Warren
3/15/1969 in Fairlee, VT; H - 19, s/o Stafford Smith and June
Stevens; W - 16, d/o Lewis Downing and Lorraine Ames

Richard I. of Warren m. Marie F. **Smith** of Warren 2/2/1982 in
Warren; H - 36, s/o Stafford I. Smith and June E. Stevens; W -
37, d/o Oscar A. Roulx and Mabel Shortt

Richard Irving of Wentworth m. Marie Mabel Floret **Roman** of
Warren 3/4/1967 in Wentworth; H - 20, Army, s/o Stafford Irving

Smith and June Erma Stevens; W - 22, machine operator, d/o
Oscar Roulx and Mabel S. Godville

Richard Irving of Warren m. Nancy Lee **Steele** of Warren 7/10/1994
in Warren; H - 47, s/o Stanford I. Smith and June Esma
Stevens; W - 29, d/o Albert Russell Conkey and Ethel Marble
Walker

Walter P. of Warren m. Nellie M. **Upton** of Warren 10/26/1887 in
Warren; H - 33, farmer, s/o Joshua P. Smith (Enfield, farmer)
and Eveline H. Smith (Bristol, housekeeper); W - 32, b. Pla-----

Warren A. of Warren m. Mary F. **Daniels** of Warren 11/6/1889 in
Warren; H - 34, farming, b. Warren; W - 38, 2nd, b. Chichester

Wendell A. of Glencliff m. Bonnie L. **Taylor** of Glencliff 3/14/1982 in
Warren; H - 19, s/o Wendell A. Smith and Grace H. Gausa; W -
16, d/o Walter C. Taylor and Charlotte Dumas

SNAY,
Albert F., Jr. of White River Jct., VT m. Lorraine B. **Dimick** of White
River Jct., VT 6/22/1940 in Warren; H - 25, med. student, b.
Somerville, MA, s/o Albert F. Snay (Berkshire, VT) and Viola E.
Lang (Boston, MA); W - 20, stenographer, b. White River Jct.,
VT, d/o Rollo L. Demick (W. Hartford, VT) and Maud E.
Blaisdell (Underhill, VT)

SORELL,
Frank of Warren m. Della **Ruell** of Warren 5/30/1888 in Warren; H -
34, laborer, b. Northfield, VT, s/o Marshall Sorell; W - 18, b.
St—d, PQ, d/o Lourent Ruel

Lewis of Warren m. Levine **Ruel** of Warren 5/30/1888 in Warren; H -
22, laborer, b. Stanstead, PQ, s/o Marshall Sorell; W - 15, b.
St—d, PQ, d/o Lourent Ruel

SPENCER,
Edward C. of Warren m. Marie W. **Blanchard** of Warren 6/12/1975
in Orford; H - 24, s/o Hugh Spencer and Evelyn Stetson; W -
31, d/o Fred White and Irene Eldridge

John C. of Warren m. Laura J. **Weeks** of Warren 11/14/1925 in
Warren; H - 20, laborer, b. Watervaliet, s/o Clarence Spencer
(NY, laborer) and Ida Zukorosi (NY, housewife); W - 21, at
home, b. Warren, d/o Henry E. Weeks (Warren, painter) and
Elvira Smith (Barton, VT, housewife)

182

Michael David of Warren m. Pamela Jo **Kinne** of Warren 7/13/1996;
   H - 26, s/o Edward Clinton Spencer and Marie Elaine White; W
   - 26, d/o Frank Bradford Kinne and Mary Jo Astle

STALLINGS,
Erik A. of Warren m. Sandra J, **Caverhill** of Warren 6/25/1966 in
   Glencliff; H - 18, paper maker, s/o Peter M. Stallings and Muriel
   Ida Sullivan; W - 18, at home, d/o David Caverhill and Helen
   Jane Hildreth

STARK,
Wayne Douglas of Warren m. Monica Lynn **Valdes** of Warren
   9/15/1979 in Warren; H - 19, s/o Gary Stark and Audrey Ames;
   W - 17, d/o George Manuel Valdes and Dolores Wood
Wayne Douglas of Warren m. Sarah Jean **Cate** of Warren 7/1/1995;
   H - 35, s/o Gary G. Stark and Audrey E. Ames; W - 28, d/o
   Lloyd D. Cate and Anita S. Butson

START,
Allen Richard of Warren m. Denise **Parenteau** of Warren 7/6/1991
   in Warren; H - 33, s/o Marvin W. Start and Betty Ann Heselton;
   W - 24, d/o Wilfred Parenteau and Barbara Rollins
John Steven of Warren m. Loretta Lee **Parenteau** of Warren
   10/30/1993 in W. Rumney; H - 25, s/o Marrin Start and Betty
   Ann Hazelton; W - 20, d/o Wilfred Arthur Parenteau and
   Barbara V. Rollins

STEARNS,
Raymond H. of Cambridge, MA m. Margaret **Morrill** of Warren
   6/26/1915 in Warren; H - 25, clerk, b. Cambridge, MA, s/o John
   P. Stearns (Paris, ME) and Caroline V. Hayden (Roxbury, MA);
   W - 22, stenographer, b. Portland, ME, d/o Edmund N. Morrill
   (Portland, ME) and Charlotte W. Safford (Charlestown, MA)

STEELE,
Arthur H. of Worcester, MA m. Margaret F. **Roberts** of Warren
   1/9/1916 in Warren; H - 22, teamster, b. Fiskdale, MA, s/o
   Abram J. Steele (Lonsdale, RI) and Margaret D. Gray
   (Providence, RI); W - 21, nurse, b. Ashland, d/o Arthur Roberts
   (Ashland) and Ada Curtis (Parsonsfield, ME)

STEVENS,

Charles E. of Warren m. Avis J. **Batchelder** of Warren 2/6/1939 in Warren; H - 25, truck driver, b. Warren, s/o Walter Stevens (Coventry, VT) and Pearl Whitcher (Warren); W - 20, housewife, b. Warren, d/o A. N. Batchelder (Warren) and Nettie Merrill (Warren)

Walter of Warren m. Pearl **Whitcher** of Warren 6/3/1911 in Warren; H - 27, laborer, b. Coventry, VT, s/o Eben Stevens (Canada, carpenter); W - 18, b. Warren, d/o Arthur Whitcher (Warren, farmer)

Wayne Earl of Warren m. Barbara A. **Michaud** of Salem, MA 12/30/1962 in Glencliff; H - 22, shipping clerk, s/o Wallace A. Stevens and Althea June Gould; W - 21, nurses aide, d/o Wilfred G. Michaud and Cecil Mae Cheney

STIMSON,

Delton Gerald of Warren m. Rita Mae **Chase** of Woodsville 1/19/1949 in Woodsville; H - 21, laborer, b. Woodsville, s/o Elmer Gerald Stimson (Haverhill) and Lilla Mae Marn (Warren); W - 18, at home, b. Woodsville, d/o Forrest Ray Chase (NH) and Georgia Arlene LaFrance (VT)

STODDARD,

Francis A. of Haverhill m. Sylvia Louise **Hatch** of Glencliff 11/16/1963 in N. Haverhill; H - 23, farmer, s/o Frederick A. Stoddard and Lorree Rosa Cassady; W - 18, student, d/o Vernon Hatch and Dorothy M. Mitchell

STROUT,

Leslie Jackson of Lyme m. Mary Ellen **Hildreth** of Warren 6/15/1968 in Lyme; H - 24, 2nd, b. NH, s/o Gerald Strout (ME) and Elizabeth Wilmont (NH); W - 20, b. NH, d/o Harold Hildreth (NH) and Doris A. Perry (NH)

STUBBARD,

George of Sydney, NS m. Carrie M. **Day** of Warren 9/28/1887 in Warren; H - 28, engineer, b. Sydney, NS, s/o Matthew Stubbard and Amelia Stubbard (deceased); W - 35, 2nd

SUSEE,
Joseph P. of Wentworth m. Winifred B. **Buskey** of Warren 6/1/1938 in Rumney; H - 49, board sawyer, b. Frenchville, ME, s/o William Susee (ME) and Helen Brunelle (Canada); W - 31, housewife, b. Lisbon, d/o James Tuttle (Springfield, MA) and Minnie Cutting (Haverhill)

SWAIN,
Charlie I. of Laconia m. S. Grace **Little** of N. Haverhill 10/4/1893 in Haverhill; H - bag man, b. Warren, s/o Ira C. Swain; W - 20, b. Warren, d/o Frank P. Little (Warren, farmer)
Elmer E. of Warren m. Martha J. **Page** of Warren 10/29/1887 in Warren; H - 23, mill hand, s/o Samuel E. Swain (farmer) and Mary J. Gale (Warren); W - 17, b. Warren
Elmer E. of Warren m. Eva L. **Upton** of Warren 5/2/1895 in Warren; H - 31, farmer, 2nd, b. Warren, s/o Samuel Swain; W - 21
Willie H. of Warren m. Flora M. **Brooks** of Easton 12/31/1887 in Warren; H - 22, fireman, 2nd, s/o William M. Swain (farmer) and Sarah Caswell; W - 27

SWARTZ,
John of Cleveland, OH m. Edna Mae **Valley** of Warren 10/20/1956 in Plymouth; H - 27, auditor, s/o Paul D. Swartz and Anna Molloy; W - 18, at home, d/o Clifton W. Valley and Velma Litz

SWEENEY,
Waldo F. of Warren m. Evelyn Dorothy **Rollins** of Haverhill 7/1/1944 in Haverhill; H - 30, bulldog operator, b. Keene, s/o John P. Sweeney (Phillipston, MA) and Idella Lancey (Phillipston, MA); W - 22, telephone operator, b. Warren, d/o Louise J. Derosia (Benton) and Florence M. Rollins (Wentworth)

TANGUAY,
Nobert of Warren m. Mintae **Sorrell** of Warren 1/2/1905 in Ashland; H - 19, laborer, b. Canada, s/o Theadore Tanguay (Canada, farmer); W - 16, domestic, b. Warren, d/o Lewis Sorrell (Canada, farmer)

TATHAM,

Joel Howard of Wentworth m. Pamela Ann **Green** of Warren 4/8/1977 in Nashua; H - 20, s/o Wilfred Tatham and Ruth Keneson; W - 22, d/o William Green and Barbara Whitcher

Stephen Paul of Warren (RFD) m. Sara Jane **Ireland** of Plymouth 9/28/1974 in Plymouth; H - 20, s/o Wilfred Tatham and Ruth Keneson; W - 24, d/o Chester Ireland and Lois Yeaton

TAYLOR,

Walter Charles of Warren m. Evelyn Ella **Ryan** of Warren 12/20/1988 in Glencliff; H - 48, s/o Harold F. Taylor and Myrtle F. Thayer; W - 38, d/o Ernest W. Wentworth and Marjorie P. Durgin

Walter D. of Orford m. Lisa M. **Lamothe** of Warren 9/3/1983 in Orford; H - 22, s/o Elmer Taylor, Sr. and Phyllis Royston; W - 18, d/o Peter Lamothe and Marie Thompson

TEWKSBURY,

Clarence of Warren m. Lydia **Eastman** of Warren 7/26/1924 in Haverhill; H - 25, laborer, b. Swiftwater, s/o Merrill Tewksbury (Swiftwater, farmer); W - 30, housekeeper, 2nd, b. Warren, d/o Russell Bailey (Warren, farmer)

Roscoe Merrill of Warren m. Nellie Etta **Curtis** of Warren 10/30/1949 in Bristol; H - 24, laborer, b. Warren, s/o Clarence Tewksbury (Bath) and Lydia Bailey (Warren); W - 27, housewife, 2nd, b. W. Fairlee, VT, d/o Allan Farr (Bradford, VT) and Dora Bythrow (Bradford, VT)

THISTLE,

William of Chelsea, MA m. Emma P. **Harper** of Warren 5/26/1940 in Seabrook; H - 50, milk salesman, b. Newfoundland, s/o James Thistle (Newfoundland) and Clara Allen (Newfoundland); W - 53, chef, b. Warren, d/o Anslow Perry (Chichester) and Anna Leighton (Pike)

William of Glencliff m. Olive **Tracy** of Glencliff 5/31/1955 in Bradford, VT; H - 64, institution wkr., s/o James Thistle and Clara Allen; W - 59, housekeeper, d/o Hervey Jordan and Addie Potter

THOROUGHGOOD,
Allan Wesley of Warren m. Diana Joy **Devine** of Warren 2/18/1995;
H - 32, s/o George W. Thoroughgood and Lula E. Varney; W -
35, d/o Victor A. Brooks and Emily J. Gay

TIBBETTS,
Carl E. of Warren Summit m. Mrs. Jennie M. **Prior** of Warren
Summit 5/27/1910 in Warren Summit; H - 19, laborer, b.
Warren, s/o Delden Tibbetts (sec. foreman); W - 24, nurse, 2nd,
b. NS, d/o Henry Iram (England)

TILLEY,
William of Warren m. Sarah J. **Merrill** of Warren 6/26/1895 in
Warren; H - 27, farmer, b. Canada, s/o William H. Tilley
(Canada, school teacher); W - 17, b. Warren, d/o Asa B. Merrill
(Warren, farmer)

TITUS,
Calvin A. of Warren m. Cornelia Ann **Chase** of Orford 3/24/1956 in
Orford; H - 19, air line mech., s/o Calvin A. Titus and
Genevieve MacDougall; W - 19, domestic, d/o Maurice Chase
and Irene Mack

TOWER,
David M. of Hampton Falls m. Agnes Hattie **Avery** of Warren
12/12/1929 in Portsmouth; H - 42, dealer, b. Lincoln'e Bh, ME,
s/o Martin V. B. Tower (Lincoln'e Bh, ME) and Albina Richards
(Lincoln'e Bh, ME); W - 36, teacher, b. Warren, d/o Hastings H.
Avery (Ellsworth, laborer) and Della Batchelder (Warren,
housewife)

TRANFAGLIA,
Henry L. of Revere, MA m. Evelyn Foster **Dyer** of Boston, MA
7/28/1940 in Warren; H - 30, druggist, b. Revere, MA, s/o
Vincent Tranfaglia (Italy) and Annie Tranfaglia (Italy); W - 34,
sales girl, b. Portsmouth, d/o George A. Foster (Gardner, ME)
and Lula E. Keysar (Clarksville)

TRASK,
Frank E. of Glencliff m. Natalie Alberta **Perry** of Glencliff 4/12/1928
in Warren; H - 21, laborer, b. NS, s/o Oscar Trask (NS,

fisherman) and Dora Stanton (NS, housekeeper); W - 18, housewife, b. Haverhill, d/o Charles A. Perry (Whitefield, laborer) and Inez C. Lindsey (Benton, housewife)

TRUELOVE,
Henry J. of Warren m. Cora **Elliott** of Warren 12/15/1903 in Warren; H - 26, laborer, b. NJ, s/o John Truelove (NJ); W - 20, domestic, b. Warren, d/o Charles Elliott

VALLEY,
Clifton H., Jr. of Warren m. Marilyn Ann **Balch** of Lyme Center 10/29/1960 in Lyme Center; H - 18, printer, s/o Clifton H. Valley and Velma Mae Litz; W - 19, secretary, d/o Raymond H. Balch and Esther E. Smith
John of Warren m. Alma **Copp** of Warren 8/4/1901 in Warren; H - 22, farmer, b. Lunenburg, VT, s/o Henry Valley (Canada, carpenter); W - 40, housekeeper, divorced, b. Warren, d/o Addison Gerald (farmer)

VARNUM,
Clarence of Warren m. Bertha **Chase** of Warren 8/26/1929 in Wentworth; H - 37, laborer, b. Gloucester, MA, s/o John L. Varnum (Essex, MA, laborer) and Lizzie B. Roberts (Gloucester, MA, housewife); W - 19, housework, b. Bath, d/o Frank Chase (Bath) and Phoebe Wright (MI, housewife)

VIGENT,
Joseph Purdy of Ryegate, VT m. Patricia Ann **Bancroft** of Warren 8/19/1967 in Warren; H - 22, Army, s/o Leo Fremont Vigent and Gladys Esther Smith; W - 20, at home, d/o Lewis Earl Bancroft and Dorothy E. Young

VINCELETTE,
Everett L., Sr. of Glencliff m. Brenda L. **Dickinson** of Glencliff 8/27/1983 in Glencliff; H - 57, s/o Edmond Vincelette and Alice Ketchum; W - 43, d/o Richard W. Frizzell and Cleona Demers
Everett L., Sr. of Warren m. Betty L. **Foster** of Wichita, KS 6/2/2002; H - 78, s/o Edwin Vincelette and Alice Ketchum; W - 48, d/o Johnny Foster and Anniebell Allen
Everett Lloyd of Warren m. Blanche Irene **Libbey** of Warren 4/26/1950 in Warren; H - 23, bobbin mill lbr., b. Warren, s/o

Edmund Vincelette (Canada) and Alice Ketchum (Fairlee, VT);
W - 19, at home, b. Warren, d/o Almer Libbey and Vera Ball

Everett Lloyd, Jr. of Warren m. Hollis Marie **Hurd** of Warren
11/22/2001 in Warren; H - 46, s/o Everett Lloyd Vincelette, Jr.
and Blanche Irene Libby; W - 35, d/o Chester Edward Hurd and
Patricia B. Demarais

Jedediah of Warren m. Jessica **Thompson** of Warren —/--/2003 in
Gilford

Robert J. of Warren m. Tina L. **Huff** of Warren 4/17/1996; H - 28,
s/o Everett L. Vincelette and Blanche I. Libby; W - 35, d/o David
H. Ramsey and Arlene J. Marshall

WALCOTT,

George S. of Warren m. Emeline E. **Moore** of Pembroke 9/15/1892
in Warren; H - 75, carpenter, 2nd, b. Barnet, VT, s/o Salmon
Walcott; W - 73, 2nd, b. Pembroke

WALKER,

Charles H. of Warren m. Grace E. **Myers** of Warren 9/18/1938 in
Warren; H - 18, laborer, b. Franklin, s/o Charles Walker (New
Hampton) and Z. V. Purrington (Manchester); W - 20, at home,
b. Quincy, MA, d/o John I. Myers (Brockton, MA) and Grace E.
Myers (Woodstock, CT)

WARBIN,

Richard C. of Warren m. Lorie A. **Kennedy** of Warren 6/20/1981 in
Warren; H - 20, s/o Richard E. Warbin and Isabell Ramig; W -
18, d/o Nelson L. Kennedy, Sr. and Loralee Whitcher

WASHBURN,

Claude D. of Warren m. Glenna M. **Houghton** of Warren 8/5/1951
in Rumney; H - 25, office mgr., s/o Claude W. Washburn and
Violet M. Smith; W - 26, teacher, d/o Harry B. Houghton and
Helen R. Chasson

Clyde Winslow of Warren m. Madeline Vera **Dickey** of Warren
2/5/1946 in Haverhill; H - 44, fireman, 2nd, b. Wytopitlock, ME,
s/o Daniel B. Washburn (Wytopitlock, ME) and Bertha B. Irish;
W - 32, pastry cook, b. Newbury, VT, d/o Peal M. Dickey
(Bradford, VT) and Marion W. MacAllister (Manchester, retired)

Harvey H. of Orford m. Marlene S. **Whitcher** of Warren 11/24/1955
in N. Haverhill; H - 18, farming, s/o Harvey L. Washburn and

Bernice Horton; W - 18, at home, d/o Maurice A. Whitcher and Helen M. Ball

WEBBER,
Charles G. of Warren m. Geraldine **Hatch** of Haverhill, MA 12/6/1935 in Salem; H - 26, gas station attendant, b. Somerville, MA, s/o William H. Webber and Marion G. Webber; W - 19, b. Warren, d/o Fairfax Hatch and Claribel Clark

WEEKS,
Brian H. of New Hampton m. Charlene M. **Caverhill** of Warren 11/12/1983 in Warren; H - 22, s/o Harold Weeks and Ethel Drake; W - 23, d/o David Caverhill and Helen Hildreth
Carlyle of Warren m. Alma E. **Jacques** of Warren 5/3/1958 in Bradford, VT; H - 21, laborer, s/o Henry E. Weeks and Jessie M. Spencer; W - 18, none, d/o Peter L. Jacques and Myrtle M. Roper (see following entry)
Carlyle R. of Warren m. Alma E. **Jacques** of Warren 5/8/1958 in Warren; H - 20, laborer, s/o Henry Edgar Weeks and Jesie Mae Spencer; W - 16, at home, d/o Peter Louis Jacques and Myrtle May Roper (see preceding entry)
Charles L. of Warren m. Sarah **French** of Haverhill 11/10/1888 in Warren; H - 24, teamster, b. Warren, s/o Ira M. Weeks (Warren); W - 18, b. Haverhill, d/o Bert French
Clinton S. of Warren m. Bessie **Lewis** of Bath 11/8/1934 in Woodsville; H - 22, laborer, b. Somerville, MA, s/o Sidney C. Weeks (Warren, farmer) and Elizabeth Streeter (Tilton, housewife); W - 21, at home, b. Windsor, VT, d/o Ernest A. Lewis (Newport, VT, farmer) and Alice Doe (S. Deerfield, housewife)
H. Edgar of Warren m. Jessie M. **Spencer** of Warren 10/29/1927 in Warren; H - 20, teamster, b. Warren, s/o Henry E. Weeks (Warren, painter) and Elvira L. Smith (Barton, VT, housewife); W - 17, at home, b. NY, d/o Clarence N. Spencer (Warren, laborer) and Ida May Zouwskie (NY, housewife)
Ira M. of Warren m. Eliza **Pickering** of Warren 9/23/1908; H - 22, b. Warren, s/o Henry Weeks (Warren, painter); W - 18, b. Haverhill, d/o George Pickering (farmer)
Natt C. of Warren m. Marion H. **Mills** of Warren 12/11/1925 in Plymouth; H - 36, laborer, b. Warren, s/o Henry E. Weeks (Warren, painter) and Elosia Smith (Barton, VT, housewife); W

190

- 26, tel. op., b. Lebanon, ME, d/o Jesse F. Mills (ME, laborer) and Carrie B. Mason (ME, housewife)

Sidney C. of Warren m. Sarah E. **Streeter** of Northfield 7/7/1909 in Warren; H - 21, farmer, b. Warren, s/o Henry E. Weeks (Warren, painter); W - 19, domestic, b. Franklin, d/o Walter W. Streeter (carpenter)

Wayne Alvin of Orford m. Louella J. **Godville** of Orford 7/1/1955 in Orford; H - 18, st. highway, s/o Charles A. Weeks and Lillian E. Marsh; W - 18, at home, d/o James Godville and Edna Shortt

Wilbur R. of Warren m. Margaret **Prescott** of Warren 7/30/1927 in Rumney; H - 25, painter, b. Warren, s/o Henry E. Weeks (Warren, painter) and Elvira L. Smith (Barton, VT, housewife); W - 18, housekeeper, b. Newbury, VT, d/o Grover C. Prescott (Newbury, VT, teamster) and Esther Mary Rollins (Campton, housewife)

William Rexford of Warren m. Emma Elizabeth **Hatch** of Woodsville 8/14/1946 in Rumney; H - 45, painter, 2nd, b. Warren, s/o Henry E. Weeks (Warren, painter) and Elvira L. Smith (Orleans, VT); W - 37, housework, 2nd, b. Newbury, VT, d/o Emerson Perrin (Canada, farmer) and Mary Millette (Canada, manicurist)

WETHERBEE,

Bernard O. of Warren m. Gloria J. **Caverhill** of Warren 9/5/1964 in Warren; H - 21, barber, s/o Walter H. Wetherbee and Lois M. Merrill; W - 19, secretary, d/o David W. Caverhill and Helen E. Hildreth

Cary B. of Warren m. Mary B. **Elder** of Warren 6/23/2001 in Lyme Ctr.; H - 33, s/o Bernard O. Wetherbee and Gloria J. Caverhill; W - 32, d/o Don Edward Elder and Julia Mae Balch

Hue Owen, Jr. of Warren m. Hailey Kristin **Noury** of Warren 12/1/2004 in Canaan

Walter of Haverhill m. Lois **Merrill** of Warren 7/25/1929 in Canaan; H - 23, carpenter, b. Haverhill, s/o William G. Wetherbee (Haverhill, carpenter) and Prudy Pelton (Lyme, housewife); W - 18, at home, b. Warren, d/o John Merrill (Warren, carpenter) and Hattie Elliott (Warren, housewife)

WHITCHER,

Arthur D. of Warren m. Eleanor **Short** of Fairlee, VT 8/9/1890 in Bradford, VT; H - 29, laborer, b. Warren, s/o Henry D. Whitcher; W - 20, d/o William Short

191

Charles A. of Warren m. Lucasta **Boynton** of Warren 11/13/1895 in
Warren; H - 44, farmer, 2nd, b. Warren, s/o Joseph Whitcher
(Warren, farmer); W - 55, housekeeper, 2nd, b. Warren, d/o -----
(Lyman, blacksmith)

Charlie H. of Warren m. Bertha May **Hildreth** of Warren 3/16/1914
in Warren; H - 22, teamster, b. Warren, s/o Arthur O. Whitcher
(Warren) and Nellie E. Shortt (England); W - 16, b. Warren, d/o
Elroy E. Hildreth (Haverhill) and Ida S. Flanders (Warren)

Chester R. of Warren m. Esther B. **Cooper** of Lincoln 12/5/1942 in
Lincoln; H - 31, US Army, b. Warren, s/o E. R. Whitcher
(Warren) and Elsie Lindsay (DeBrt. Sta., NS); W - 26, school
teacher, b. Lincoln, d/o Leslie G. Cooper (Bloomfield, VT) and
Maude Marshall (Lancaster)

Christopher M. of Warren m. Jaime A. **Goodwin** of Warren 8/7/2004
in Warren

Clayton of Warren m. Vera A. **Newling** of Dover 12/24/1921 in
Warren; H - 24, farmer, b. Warren, s/o George W. Whitcher
(Warren) and Sarah Stickney (Campton); W - 24, waitress, b.
Dover, d/o Charles Newling (Effingham Falls) and Etta Straw
(Center Barnstead)

Clayton S. of Warren m. Margaret P. **Weeks** of Warren 4/23/1938 in
E. Haverhill; H - 39, carpenter, b. Warren, s/o George Whitcher
(Warren) and Sarah Stickney (Campton); W - 26, housework,
b. Newbury, VT, d/o Grover Prescott (Bradford, VT) and Esther
Rollins (Campton)

Clifton L. of Warren m. Bertha Belle **Tibbetts** of Warren 5/9/1914 in
Glencliff; H - 20, laborer, b. Warren, s/o George W. Whitcher
(Warren) and Sarah N. Stickney (Campton); W - 15,
housemaid, b. Warren, d/o Leon B. Tibbetts (Benton) and
Carrie Fifield (Warren)

Edward of Warren m. Esther I. **Ball** of Glencliff 8/4/1939 in Wells
River, VT; H - 24, saw mill, b. Warren, s/o Eugene Whitcher
(Warren) and Elsie Lindsay (NS); W - 21, b. Bath, d/o Bert Ball
(Landaff) and Eva Ball (Landaff)

Eugene R. of Warren m. Elsie E. **Lindsey** of Boston, MA 3/27/1909
in Tilton; H - 32, farmer, b. Warren, s/o Samuel Whitcher
(Warren, farmer); W - 26, dress maker, b. Boston, d/o Samuel
Lindsey (farmer)

Eugene R., Jr. of Warren m. Jeanne E. **Stafursky** of Warren
10/10/1981 in Warren; H - 34, s/o Eugene R. Whitcher and
Margaret Gove; W - 31, d/o Paul S. Engley and Lucille Andrews

Eugene Rand of Warren m. Margaret Lucille **Gove** of Wentworth
12/23/1945 in Wentworth; H - 21, US Navy, b. Warren, s/o
Eugene R. Whitcher (Warren, lumberman) and Elsie Lindsey
(NS, housewife); W - 20, waitress, b. Plymouth, d/o Martin L.
Gove (Wentworth, RR engineer) and Viola C. Taylor (Lynn, MA)
Eugene Rand of Warren m. Jane Ellen **Chase** of Warren 4/30/1993
in Warren; H - 46, s/o Eugene Rand Whitcher and Margaret
Lucille Gove; W - 51, d/o Wright L. Towers and Alida Mae Bixby
Eugene Rand, Jr. of Warren m. Gloria Louise **Blake** of Haverhill
2/28/1970 in Haverhill; H - 22, s/o Eugene Rand Whitcher and
Margaret Gove; W - 22, d/o Earl R. Blake, Jr. and Gloria Louise
Cassady
Fred J. of Warren m. Nellie J. **Ladd** of St. Johnsbury 2/11/1898 in
Warren; H - 29, laborer, b. Warren, s/o Samuel Whitcher
(Warren, farmer); W - 34, domestic, 2nd
George W. of Warren m. Sarah N. **Stickney** of Campton 10/25/1888
in Warren; H - 24, farmer, b. Warren, s/o Joseph Whitcher
(Warren); W - 24, b. Campton, d/o Samuel Stickney (New
Hampton)
George W. of Warren m. Sarah N. **Whitcher** of Campton 1/16/1902
in Warren; H - 37, carpenter, 2nd, b. Warren, s/o Joseph
Whitcher (Cornish, VT, farmer); W - 37, domestic, 2nd, b.
Campton, d/o Samuel Stickney (farmer)
Henry L. of Warren m. Etta H. **Avery** of Warren 1/12/1892 in
Warren; H - 21, laborer, b. Warren, s/o Henry D. Whitcher
(farmer); W - 26, 2nd, b. Warren, d/o William Currier (carpenter)
K. E. of Warren m. Marion S. **Cotton** of Warren 7/12/1941 in
Warren; H - 23, mill work, b. Warren, s/o H. A. Whitcher
(Warren) and Mildred Libbey (Boston, MA); W - 27, teacher, b.
Warren, d/o Ralph P. Cotton (Warren) and Mary E. Moran
(Chestnut Hill, PA)
Maurice A. of Warren m. Helen M. **Ball** of Glencliff 1/1/1935 in
Salem; H - 26, laborer, b. Warren, s/o Harry A. Whitcher and
Mildred Libbey; W - 20, housework, b. Landaff, d/o Bert Ball
and Eva Moulton
Neil C. of Warren m. Daisy Ann **Weeks** of Belmont 9/7/1960 in
Belmont; H - 21, carpenter, s/o William H. Whitcher and Vera
Leona Bixby; W - 21, nurse's aid, d/o Sumner Ivo Weeks and
Elise R. Thompson

Philip B. of Warren m. Jennifer J. **Burke** of Warren 7/18/1999 in
Piermont; H - 24, s/o David R. Whitcher and Judy K. King; W -
23, d/o Stephen C. Burke and Susan R. Harrington
Ronald Martin of Warren m. Mary Louise **Boutin** of Woodsville
1/11/1975 in Warren; H - 21, s/o Eugene R. Whitcher and
Margaret Gove; W - 18, d/o Joseph Boutin and Priscilla Paradie
William H. of Warren m. Vera L. **Bixby** of Wentworth 10/6/1934 in
Wentworth; H - 27, laborer, b. Warren, s/o Harry A. Whitcher
(Warren, deceased) and Mildred Libbey (Boston, MA,
housewife); W - 20, at home, b. Alberta, Canada, d/o Willard M.
Bixby (Warren, farmer) and Hattie Currie (Canada, housewife)

WHITE,
Frederick of Glencliff m. Lorraine **Bullard** of Glencliff 6/15/1953 in
Newbury, VT; H - 30, X-ray, s/o Frederick White and Adeline
Souza; W - 33, R.N., d/o Edwin C. Wallace and Mary Bunce
James Robert of Glencliff m. Doreen Joyce **Wiggins** of Haverhill
7/19/1968 in Haverhill; H - 24, b. NH, s/o Robert Franklin White
(NH) and Lottie Boardman (NH); W - 20, b. NH, d/o Charles
George Wiggins (VT) and Beatrice Pressey (MA)

WHITEMAN,
Fred L. of Warren m. Della E. **Spooner** of Benton 10/1/1890 in
Warren; H - 25, laborer, b. Warren, s/o John Whiteman; W -
19, b. Benton, d/o Alonzo Spooner
Will A. of Warren m. Viney **Burke** of Warren 4/2/1898 in N.
Haverhill; H - 35, laborer, 2nd, b. Warren, s/o John Whiteman
(Canada, laborer); W - 37, house keeper, 2nd

WHITNEY,
Earle H. of Warren m. Cora E. **Flanders** of Warren 1/28/1924 in
Warren; H - 22, laborer, b. Lancaster, s/o Benjamin F. Whitney
(Groveton, laborer); W - 15, at home, b. Warren, d/o Leonard
M. Flanders (Warren, lumberman)
Percy L. of Rumney m. Evelyn **Hilliard** of Warren 3/5/1944 in
Rumney; H - 43, woodsman, b. Lincoln, s/o Benjamin F.
Whitney (Northumberland) and Edith Remick (Groveton); W -
19, at home, b. Warren, d/o Joseph Hilliard (Keene) and Leona
Short (Warren)

WHITTEN,

Philip H. of Keene m. Mary J. **Eastman** of Warren 4/9/1944 in
Warren; H - 39, shovel operator, b. Chester, s/o Frank Whitten
(E. Boston, MA) and Della Todd (Dorchester, MA); W - 23, at
home, b. Woodstock, VT, d/o Edward V. Eastman (Providence,
RI) and Lydia M. Bailey (Warren)

WILKINS,

Henry E. of Warren m. Ida **Walker** of Warren 8/5/1917 in Bath; H -
30, laborer, 2nd, divorced, b. Wolcott, VT, s/o Joseph L. H.
Wilkins (Dorchester) and Jessie Partlow (Portland, ME); W -
27, housekeeper, 2nd, divorced, b. Manchester, d/o Arthur
Walker and Mary Farrington (Plattsburgh, NY)

WILLEY,

Alfred Smith of Pike m. Joan Gay **Bowles** of Warren 1/1/1949 in
Littleton; H - 20, unemployed, b. Pike, s/o Harry Allen Willey
(Topsham, VT) and Amy Morrill (Bradford, VT); W - 18,
unemployed, b. Warren, d/o Kenneth Bowles (Haverhill) and
Eva Lovett (Plymouth)

WILLIAMS,

Dave B. of Wentworth m. Suzanne M. **LaRochelle** of Warren
1/19/1974 in Warren; H - 18, s/o Fred Williams and Maureen
Bryant; W - 15, d/o Raymond LaRochelle and Patricia Douillard

WILMOT,

Troy Alan of Warren m. Vicki Lynn **Clark** of Warren 7/15/1995; H -
28, s/o Merle K. Wilmot and Linda Horton; W - 25, d/o Douglas
A. Clark and Janice S. Urbaniak

WILSON,

Albert C. of Rutland, VT m. Patricia Ann **Mannetho** of Warren
7/22/1995; H - 69, s/o Albert C. Wilson, Sr. and Agnes Sarah
Jones; W - 65, d/o Henry G. Mannetho and Helen E. Starke

WISTNER,

Charlie A. of Warren m. Kate **Bowles** of Warren 6/19/1909 in
Wentworth; H - 23, electrician, b. Edison, NJ, s/o A, Wistner
(Sweden, machinist); W - 26, housekeeper, 2nd, b.
Newfoundland, d/o William Short (England, farmer)

Floyd Alfred of Warren m. Evelyn Rose **Lucius** of Lyme 1/24/1949 in Lyme; H - 38, merchant, 2nd, b. Warren, s/o Charles Augustus Wistner (Patterson, NJ) and Katherine Short (Newfoundland); W - 29, clerk, 2nd, b. Lyme, d/o Guy A. Roberts (Bradford, VT) and Jennie Hobart (Lyme)

WOLCOTT,

Archie R. of Warren m. Ethel Mae **Sargent** of Warner 9/17/1902 in Warren; H - 29, railroading, b. Lancaster, s/o George S. Wolcott (Barnet, VT, carpenter); W - 22, housekeeper, b. Warner, d/o Frank M. Sargent (Webster, farmer)

WOOD,

William D. of Warren m. Anna Mae **Ball** of Warren 12/25/1941 in Rumney; H - 22, painter, b. Warren, s/o William L. Wood (St. Johnsbury, VT) and Amy Smith (Warren); W - 16, at home, b. Bath, d/o Bert Ball (Landaff) and Eva I. Moulton

WOODARD,

Montague W. of Warren m. Marie E. **Skalla** of Boston, MA 3/23/1936 in Concord; H - 24, US Navy, b. Waterbury, VT, s/o Burt O. Woodard and Mabel Jenkins; W - 23, nurse, b. Trenton, NJ, d/o Julius Skalla and Julia Singlarsky

WOODS,

John V. of Hollis m. Eliza M. **Clifford** of Warren 9/1/1891 in Warren; H - 24, carpenter, b. Hollis, s/o John L. Woods (Pepperell, MA, farmer); W - 24, b. Warren, d/o George C. Clifford (blacksmith)

WORDEN,

John E. of Enfield m. Janet G. **Clark** of Glencliff 6/26/1999 in Glencliff; H - 45, s/o Shirley Worden and Ruth Curtis; W - 45, d/o Arthur F. Clark and Gertrude Feeley

WRIGHT,

Arthur G. of Warren m. Ethel E. **Downing** of Warren 4/13/1946 in Rumney; H - 63, laborer, 2nd, b. Piermont, s/o Ximinis P. Wright (Lowell, MA, farmer) and Emmagene Harris (Warren, housewife); W - 54, housework, 2nd, b. Orford, d/o Willie E. Downing (Wentworth) and Lena M. Poor (Orford)

Carl E. of Haverhill m. Glenna M. **Hight** of Warren 6/25/1955 in
Warren; H - 19, janitor, s/o Forrest E. Wright and Althea Dow;
W - 19, secretary, d/o Arthur L. Hight and Shirley Manion
Clarence F. of Warren m. Freda E. **Dame** of Lakeport 10/15/1921 in
Lebanon; H - 20, butcher, b. Warren, s/o Frank N. Wright
(Piermont) and Sarah P. Smith (Warren); W - 20, at home, b.
Lakeport, d/o John C. Dame (Guilford) and Mattie S. Perkins
(Guilford)
Fay E. of Warren m. Joan **Caverhill** of Warren 1/29/1949 in
Woodstock; H - 23, laborer, b. Warren, s/o Arthur G. Wright
(Piermont) and Nancy Flanders (Warren); W - 18, factory
worker, b. Cornwall, CT, d/o Ulysses Caverhill (NB) and Mary
Beeman (NH)
George I. of Haverhill m. Martha M. **Foote** of Warren 2/15/1929 in
Warren; H - 24, laborer, b. Wentworth, s/o Tilden B. Wright
(Haverhill, farmer) and Mary E. Page (Haverhill, housewife); W
- 17, at home, b. Warren, d/o Harry L. Foote (Warren, farmer)
and Emma C. Wright (Piermont, housewife)
Glenn G. of Warren m. Gertrude A. **Lebrun** of Lebanon 10/30/1965
in Lebanon; H - 22, truck driver, s/o George I. Wright and
Martha Foote; W - 20, waitress, d/o Carl E. Johnson and
Gertrude A. Ducharme
Harry T. of Warren m. Lorraine Ann **Ball** of Warren 11/24/1962 in
Warren; H - 22, farmer, s/o George E. Wright and Martha May
Foote; W - 18, factory worker, d/o Leslie Albert Ball and Doris
Mary Ledger
Lawrence R. of Warren m. Barbara J. **Hamilton** of Warren
3/14/1987 in Warren; H - 20, s/o Fay Wright and Joan
Caverhill; W - 26, d/o Donald Hamilton and Barbara Gleason
Leslie I. of Warren m. Tammy S. **Roy** of Warren 10/18/1991 in
Warren; H - 27, s/o Harry T. Wright and Lorraine Ball; W - 22,
d/o Robert D. Roy and Connie Lale
Lewis of Warren m. Mamie L. **Harris** of Warren 4/8/1896 in Warren;
H - 21, laborer, 2nd, b. Warren, s/o George Wright (Mason,
farmer); W - 22, b. Warren, d/o P. E. Harris (farmer)
Michael W. of Warren m. Marlene **Moody** of Warren 8/12/1972 in
Warren; H - 22, s/o Wallace F. Wright and Isabell Dunleavey;
W - 23, d/o Wallace A. Stevens and Althea Gould
Richard A. of Warren m. Rita Louise **Menard** of Benton 5/26/1956 in
Benton; H - 20, truck driver, s/o George Wright and Martha
Foote; W - 20, at home, d/o Forrest Clark and Lulu Tattersall

197

Tilden George of Warren m. Ellen Mary **Grafton** of Lincoln
1/28/1978 in Wentworth; H - 21, s/o Richard Wright and Rita
McCoy; W - 22, d/o George E. Grafton and Olive Hill

YORK,
Omah L. of Plymouth m. Iva E. **Reed** of Warren 10/31/1911 in
Warren; H - 26, teamster, 2nd, divorced, b. Belmont, s/o Morrill
York (teamster); W - 19, domestic, b. Wentworth, d/o Frank
Reed (Canterbury, laborer)

YOUNG,
Gerald R. of Bath m. Kathryn P. **Gray** of Warren 6/4/1932 in
Warren; H - 22, truck driver, b. Bath, s/o Homer Young (Bath,
farmer) and Amy Wheeler (Orfordville, housewife); W - 19,
housework, b. E. Jaffrey, d/o Frank Gray (Alexandria, farmer)
and Mary Borner (New Hampton, housewife)
Gerald R. of Haverhill m. Catherine A. **Lavoice** of Glencliff
12/13/1941 in N. Haverhill; H - 32, truck driver, b. Bath, s/o
Homer Young (Bath) and Amy Wheeler (Lyme); W - 25,
housework, b. Haverhill, d/o Fred Lavoice (Stillwater, NY) and
Marguerite White (Wells River, VT)
Rufus B. of Warren m. Electa Mae **Bailey** of Warren 6/3/1922 in
Warren; H - 23, mechanic, b. Waterford, VT, s/o George M.
Young (Sutton, VT, laborer) and Hattie G. Gero (Milborn, PQ,
housewife); W - 18, at home, b. Contoocook, d/o William
Byraque (Contoocook, sawyer) and Josie D. Dwinnelle
(Manchester, housewife)

Aaronson, Phyllis Lila - Goodman, Nathan
Abler, Louise R. - Smith, Carl W.
Adams, Lillian - Haskell, Harry A.
Adams, Shirley H. - McCauley, James F.
Alessandrini, Anna P. - Hanley, Scott R.
Allen, Virginia C. (Paige) - DeForest, William Edward, Jr.
Ames, Elizabeth C. - Martin, Richard A.
Ames, Harriet Sadie - Libby, Grover Almer
Ames, Thelma May - Hildreth, Edwin L.
Ames, Viola Fay - Brown, Clyde Francis
Amores, Evangeline Lacorte - LaFleur, John Edmond
Anderson, Alberta Alice - Cail, Harry Arthur
Anderson, Esther Jane - Belyea, Roland Roy
Anderson, Leonetta H. - Aubrey, Mark J.
Anderson, Natasha M. - Campbell, Carl A.
Angers, Irma Irene - Heath, Raymond E.
Annis, B. Blanche - Leavitt, Ira W.
Annis, Bessie - Derosia, Fred
Annis, Nettie - Dow, Levi
Annis, Sadie E. - Kittredge, Enos F.
Applebee, Katherine - Pickard, Milton A.
Arnold, Jessie E. A. (Atchison) - Bonazzi, Charles
Ash, Salomie - Goslay, Thomas
Asselin, Ernestine Perry - Simpson, Ernest Cedric
Asselin, Loretta Rose - Nystrom, Carl Edwin
Asselin, Sharon Marie - Picknell, Frank Edward
Austin, Eva - Laflame, Louis
Averill, Marion L. - Keysar, Royal E.
Avery, Agnes Hattie - Tower, David M.
Avery, Ethel M. - Roberts, Kenneth E.
Avery, Etta H. (Currier) - Whitcher, Henry L.

Babbit, Sharon Ann - Hatch, Stephen Wilder
Bacon, Deborah Heller - Nelson, Daniel Mark
Bailey, Electa Mae - Young, Rufus B.
Bailey, Lydia M. - Eastman, Edward V.
Balch, Florence J. - Gallant, Thomas T.
Balch, Marilyn Ann - Valley, Clifton H., Jr.
Balch, Mary (Moses) - Faley, John
Ball, Anna Mae - Wood, William D.
Ball, Edna Maxine - Brown, Walter Henry

Ball, Edna Maxine - Harriman, Alton Merton
Ball, Esther I. - Whitcher, Edward
Ball, Helen M. - Whitcher, Maurice A.
Ball, Janice Marie - Sackett, Charles Nelson
Ball, Lorraine Ann - Wright, Harry T.
Ball, Meredith L. - Hoisington, Douglas A.
Ball, Nancy May - Fagnant, Fernand R.
Ball, Pamela Jane - Goodale, Scott Gregory
Ball, Sarah Renee - Davis, Jeffrey Lyle
Ball, Susan (Simmons) - Randall, Cameron G.
Ball, Wanda Lee - Bassler, Allen Eugene
Balsamo, Elaine Marie - Faletra, Peter Paul
Bancroft, Cynthia M. - Conrad, Peter L.
Bancroft, Deborah L. - Green, John P.
Bancroft, Donna L. - Ray, Donald G.
Bancroft, Patricia Ann - Vigent, Joseph Purdy
Bancroft, Sharon Lee (Conley) - Pushee, Clarence Leslie
Barclay, Carol A. - Kennedy, Nelson L., Jr.
Bard, Miriam K. - Meyers, E. H. B.
Barry, Ora May - Jesseman, Elmer C.
Bartlett, Alice M.- Head, Charles W.
Batchelder, Avis J. - Stevens, Charles E.
Batchelder, Cora A. (Merrill) - Morrison, Rodney
Batchelder, Marcia E. - Anderson, Fayne E.
Beamis, Sheila Agnes (French) - Darling, Clifford Calvin
Bean, Denise - Laauwe, Brandt
Bean, Elaine Marie (Spencer) - Ball, James Edward
Bean, Nellie M. (Wright) - Shortt, George A.
Belanger, E. Millie - Bilodeau, William
Belyea, Edith May - Ramsay, Earl Edwin
Belyea, Olive M. (Flanders) - Bates, Kenneth Ray
Bennett, Shirley Mae - Evans, Wayne Lloyd
Bennett, Della E. - Kelly, John H.
Bennett, Mary L. - Kelley, John H.
Benson, Eleanor Arlene (Howard) - Boulet, William Lawrence
Benson, Anna F. - Morrison, Everett A.
Bent, Darlene G. - Lawrence, Charles J.
Bergman, Mary A. (Conway) - Kimball, Elmer R.
Bickford, Judith L. - Lupien, Edward R., Jr.
Bigelow, Shirley L. - Nicol, Berkeley Charles
Bixby, Verona Louise - Blake, Ernest Raymond, Jr.

Bixby, Suzanne - Flagg, Brian
Bixby, Shirley Loraine - Kaminsky, Eric Robert
Bixby, Debra L. - Ross, George S., Jr.
Bixby, Vera L. - Whitcher, William H.
Bixby, Suzanne Marie - Powell, David Franklin
Blake, Emily J. (Collins) - Morrill, John S.
Blake, Gloria Louise - Whitcher, Eugene Rand, Jr.
Blake, Maude E. B. (Brooks) - Derosia, Phillip
Blake, Eva - Hunkins, Dana
Blake, Lucy Ellen - Libbey, Otis R.
Blake, Lucy (Hardy) - Derosia, Phillip
Blanchard, Marie W. (White) - Spencer, Edward C.
Blanchard, Marie Elaine (White) - Davidson, David Allen
Boardman, Esther E. - Rock, Harold Albert
Boulresse, Marcia - Sandstim, August L.
Boutin, Angela Ruth - Clark, Daniel Jay
Boutin, Mary Louise - Whitcher, Ronald Martin
Boutin, Jane A. - Higgins, Michael W.
Bowles, Alice May - Everett, Joseph Alexander
Bowles, Kate (Short) - Wistner, Charlie A.
Bowles, Joan Gay - Willey, Alfred Smith
Boynton, Lucasta - Whitcher, Charles A.
Boynton, M. Electa - Hildreth, Charles L.
Boynton, Stella A. - Moses, Fred A.
Brar, Ramandeep Kaur - Davis, Scott Stephen
Brochu, Yolande Marguerite - Huberdeau, Claude Roland
Brooks, Vicki Gay - Libby, Grover Basil
Brooks, Flora M. - Swain, Willie H.
Brown, Martha J. (Griffin) - Jewell, Frank E.
Brown, Lulu A. - Simpson, Harry C.
Brown, Marjorie A. - Nicol, John H.
Brown, Gwendolyn I. - Smith, Charles H., Jr.
Brown, Nellie A. - Averill, Ray R.
Brueggemann, Debra S. - Robertson, Paul S.
Bryant, Patricia - Brown, Theodore, Jr.
Bullard, Lorraine (Wallace) - White, Frederick
Burke, Hattie - Beede, William C.
Burke, Jennifer J. - Whitcher, Philip B.
Burke, Viney - Whiteman, Will A.
Burnham, Valerie Jean - Dyson, William James
Burnham, Kimberly Jayne - Hibbard, Lawrence Lloyd

Bushaw, Barbara M. - Davis, John R.
Bushey, Eglantine - Bowles, Roy E.
Bushor, Judith A. (Manfield) - Belyea, Ronald R.
Buskey, Hazel E. - Jesseman, Elmer W.
Buskey, Winifred B. (Tuttle) - Susee, Joseph P.
Butson, Darlene (Ball) - Sheehan, Christopher
Buttrick, Pamela Susan - Bancroft, Kenneth Albert, Jr.
Buttrick, Sheryl Ann - Diamond, Allen Fred
Buttrick, Debra Suzanne - Brochu, Joseph Charles Guy

Cahill, Kathleen - Olding, Paul B., Jr.
Calcagny, Clorinda - Duke, Horace
Camp, Linda Lee - Brochu, Denis Omer
Campbell, Nellie V. - Morse, George W.
Carbee, Dorothy E. - Hallett, Walter S.
Cardin, Carol Beth - Sackett, Norman Leslie
Carlson, Sylvia Ann - Newton, Robert H.
Carr, Jessica P. - Henson, Matthew E.
Cass, Kathy L. - MacDonald, Barry S.
Cate, Lois M. - Merrill, Jesse H.
Cate, Sarah Jean - Stark, Wayne Douglas
Caverhill, Charlene M. - Weeks, Brian H.
Caverhill, Sandra J. - Stallings, Erik A.
Caverhill, Gloria J. - Wetherbee, Bernard O.
Caverhill, Joan - Wright, Fay E.
Channell, Vivian Alice - Prescott, Roscoe C.
Charles, Angelia - Balch, William
Chase, Jane Ellen (Towers) - Whitcher, Eugene Rand
Chase, Beulah F. - Eaton, Edgar F.
Chase, Andrea V. - Canterbury, David S.
Chase, Judy L. - Ramsay, Thomas H.
Chase, Bertha - Varnum, Clarence
Chase, Rita Mae - Stimson, Delton Gerald
Chase, Cornelia Ann - Titus, Calvin A.
Chase, Judy L. - Rudolph, Fulton J.
Chase, Eleanor - Alessandrini, Simeone
Chasson, Helen - Houghton, Harry
Cheney, Kathleen Lea - Bushaw, Jesse Edward
Chenez, Renee L. - Bourassa, Andrew G.
Cilley, Jennifer Anne - Huckins, Chad Ryan
Clark, Janet G. - Worden, John E.

Clark, Mary J. (Noyes) - Little, William H.
Clark, Vicki Lynn - Wilmot, Troy Alan
Clark, Suanne Jeanette - King, John Maurice, Jr.
Claro, Lynneth O. - Derosia, Leo F.
Clement, Vernie D. - Barber, Frank W.
Clement, Gladys F. - Bradbury, Lester Ray
Clifford, L. Riddell - Morrison, Louis R.
Clifford, Eliza M. - Woods, John V.
Clifford, J. M. E. - Kilpatrick, John
Clifford, Christina F. - McNamara, Wallace E.
Clifford, Gladys T. - Perry, George D.
Clifford, Sibbell (Whitcher) - Frazer, George
Coates, Julia E. - Locke, Morrill H.
Coates, Florence - Bowles, Albert W.
Coburn, Gladys Donna (Latuch) - Hight, George Thomas
Colby, Edna M. - Caswell, Charlie E.
Colby, Kathy A. - Bixby, Steven V.
Colby, Edith Belle - Jackson, Frank Curtice
Cole, Luane C. - Clark, Douglas A.
Comings, Mildred M. - Phair, William Thomas
Conkey, Angela - Kwedor, Daniel
Conolly, Frances E. - McNerlin, William L.
Cook, Lauren Elizabeth - Belyea, Philip Roy
Cooper, Esther B. - Whitcher, Chester R.
Copeland, Grace G. (Goss) - Boynton, Elmer W.
Copp, Alma (Gerald) - Valley, John
Corliss, Elizabeth (Chamberlin) - Anderson, James W.
Cortes, Janet A. - Merrill, Craig A.
Cotton, Marion S. - Whitcher, K. E.
Cotton, Edith M. - Blake, John W.
Cotton, Anna M. - Keyes, William F.
County, Lizzie O. - Moulton, George F.
Couture, Pearl (Shores) - Dyke, Horace Henry
Coy, Dawnette M. - Hannett, Ricky A.
Cross, Eva - Jewell, Frank E.
Cummings, Lillian (Gale) - Blake, Robert
Cunningham, Barbara A. - Ramsay, Brian William
Currie, Hattie L. - Bixby, W. M.
Currie, Grace A. - Adams, B. S.
Currier, Bernadette Victoria - Mugford, Thomas Lester
Curtis, Nellie Etta (Farr) - Tewksbury, Roscoe Merrill

Cushing, Pearl (Batchelder) - Collier, Otis Floyd
Cushing, Estella Clarissa - Ramsey, Dale Vernon
Cushing, Rhonda Colleen - Sanborn, Gregory Allen
Cutting, Priscilla D. - Mansur, Cpl. Arthur J.
Cutting, Janice L. - McKinnon, Paul W.
Cutting, Sadie D. (Flanders) - Lougee, Walter E.

Dame, Freda E. - Wright, Clarence F.
Daniels, Mary F. - Smith, Warren A.
Davis, Mary A. - Clement, Edward E.
Davis, Angela D. - Ball, Kevin R.
Davis, Lori A. (Bowen) - Clark, Chester L.
Day, Millie - Sanborn, Jerrie T.
Day, Carrie M. - Stubbard, George
Day, Carol S. (McCall) - Cosine, Michael J.
Deangelis, Patricia J. - MacDonald, David L.
Dearborn, Grace M. - Brown, George E.
Dearborn, Audrey M. - Lavoie, Leo L.
Deblois, Hazel Beatrice - Poitras, Clarence Louis
DeJohn, Marie Elizabeth - McKiernan, Matthew Erwin
DeLorenzo, Rosanne M. - Brown, Gregory Alan
DeRoehn, Barbara Ann (Shortt) - DeForest, Frank Croxford
Derosia, Lydia Ella - Belyea, Roland Mearl
Derosia, Barbara A. - Libbey, Harold L.
Devine, Diane Joy (Brooks) - Thoroughgood, Allan Wesley
Diamond, Edna L. - Chase, Leon E.
Dickey, Madeline Vera - Washburn, Clyde Winslow
Dickinson, Brenda L. (Frizzell) - Vincelette, Everett L., Sr.
Dimick, Lorraine B. - Snay, Albert F., Jr.
Dimond, Nancy H. - Simmons, John
Doane, Clara C. (Davis) - Hicks, Arthur J.
Doherty, Pauline Martha (Bancroft) - Romano, Gino Joseph
Dooley, Darlene D. - Schiff, Dayton A.
Dooley, Mildred Lydia (Stanley) - Jesseman, Stanley William
Downing, Ethel E. - Wright, Arthur G.
Downing, Charlene Ann - Smith, Paul Steven
Dowse, Ellen A. - Flanders, Leonard M.
Draper, Mabel Merrill (Hussey) - Avery, Raymond A.
Drouin, Stella Alice (Barnet) - Smith, Benjamin W.
Duffy, Patricia J. - Bradley, Jack Louville
Dunbar, Margery Stewart - Simpson, Curtis Henry

Dunbar, Lillian R. (Whitcomb) - Morse, Ira H.
Duncan, Frances V. - Malone, Cyril H.
Dustin, Thelma - Knighton, Ivan L.
Dyer, Evelyn (Foster) - Tranfaglia, Henry L.

Eastman, Elva M. - Martin, Dean W.
Eastman, Alice L. - Eaton, Ezra B.
Eastman, Mabel L. - McIsaac, Henry
Eastman, Mary H. - Howland, John A.
Eastman, Mary J. - Whitten, Philip H.
Eastman, Lydia (Bailey) - Tewksbury, Clarence
Edwards, N. Leona - Seeley, William R.
Edwards, Thelma Mabel - Belyea, Robert Leo
Elder, Mary B. - Wetherbee, Cary B.
Eldrich, Inez G. - Lindsay, Everest
Elliott, Meney M. (Whitcher) - Locke, Henry E.
Elliott, Cora - Truelove, Henry J.
Elliott, Hattie - Merrill, John
Elliott, India - Lupien, Edwin R.
Emery, Rose Maria - Smith, George E.
Euiler, Eleanor I. - Reade, Amos L., Jr.

Fabian, Sarah C. - Lester, John G.
Fadden, Althea Mary - Morton, Wallace Edward
Fales, Daisy M. - Lamb, Wilfred W.
Fales, Eva D. - Foster, Fred L.
Farnham, Susan Lynn G. - Nolan, Courtney Lee
Ferland, Tracie - Kenision, Stanley
Field, Susan Elaine - Ball, Daniel Joseph
Fifield, Fannie S. - Merrill, Lyman G.
Fifield, Mildred G. - Merrill, Ernest E.
Finneron, Vicki Lee - Higgins, James Anthony
Fisher, Lucy - Moses, Clarence
Fitts, Barbara C. - King, Joseph D.
Fitts, Barbara A. - Bolduc, Michael W.
Flanders, Cora E. - Whitney, Earle H.
Flanders, Sadie D. - Cutting, F. D.
Florence, Josephine V. (Rollins) - Lamothe, Peter Edward
Foote, Martha M. - Wright, George I.
Foote, Lena M. - Moses, Clarence H.
Ford, Lill - Mudgett, John H.

Forrest, Susan May - Bancroft, Earl Robert
Foster, Mae I. - Moulton, Alvah
Foster, Betty L. - Vincelette, Everett L., Sr.
Foster, Lula M. - Blake, Alvah C.
Fousiner, Dellina - LaBonta, Peter
Fowler, Susan (Whiteman) - Derway, Joseph
Franusiak, Penny Lee - Beamis, Herbert Glen
French, Sarah - Weeks, Charles L.
French, Sheila A. - Beamis, Harold G.
French, Hannah B. - Eaton, William F.
French, Una Violet - Avery, Raymond A.
French, Grace E. - Roy, George
French, Emma E. - McVetty, William
French, Brandy Lee - Crawford, Sumner J., III
Fuller, Patricia Ann - Gullage, Donald Robert

Gadd, Susan - Lorence, Larry Vlastimil
Gagne, Mary - Julian, Joseph
Gagney, Annie - Magnen, Henry J.
Gale, Lena - Bickford, Arthur
Gale, Martha C. - Chandler, Allen L.
Gale, Lillian L. - Cummings, Maynard
Gale, Helen V. - Goodwin, Everett W.
Gallant, Natalie M. - McIsaac, Henry E.
Gallant, Florence B. (Balch) - Libbey, Natt Everett
Garrett, Yvonne M. - Blodgett, Scott M.
Gerald, Mabelle S. - Head, Archie A.
Geraw, Shirley Elizabeth - French, Glenn Robert
Gherardi, Janice Marie - King, Russell Frederick, Jr.
Glines, Winnie B. - Moses, Elmer O.
Glode, Elizabeth A. (Elliott) - McIsaac, Henry E.
Godville, Mabel Louise - Roulx, Oscar Alphonse
Godville, Louella J. - Weeks, Wayne Alvin
Gohde, Nancy Jean - Frei, Steven Allen
Goodwin, Jean G. - Demorest, Cornelius G.
Goodwin, Jaime A. - Whitcher, Christopher M.
Gould, Althea June - Brown, George C.
Gould, Hildegarde C. - Brown, Earland V.
Gould, Jo-Ann - Alessandrini, Bernadino L., Jr.
Gould, Mabel M. - Short, Will J.
Gould, Myrtie B. (Heath) - Merrill, Lyman G.

Gould, Bell - French, A. V.
Gove, Margaret Lucille - Whitcher, Eugene Rand
Gove, Barbara May - Pike, Richard Alanson
Govoni, Jennifer - Chase, David
Gowen, Gloria Jean - Ball, David Harry
Grafton, Ellen Mary - Wright, Tilden George
Graham, Lillian - Clark, Frank W.
Gramont, Eda R. - Libbey, Ralph
Gray, Kathryn P. - Young, Gerald R.
Gray, Avis - Clark, Enos I.
Green, Pamela Ann - Tatham, Joel Howard
Green, Barbara (Whitcher) - LaBounty, Joseph
Greenwood, Pauline E. (Cloutier) - Cutting, Charles F.
Griffin, Charlotte M. - Ball, Reginald H.
Griffin, Sandra L. - Hair, Jeremy D.
Griffin, Sadie Julina - Barry, Everett F.

Haartz, Winifred (Elliott) - Prouty, John
Hadley, Michele Lorraine (Allen) - Garrand, Brian Dean
Hadley, Etta M. (Beecher) - Jewell, Frank E.
Hall, Catherine M. - Bixby, Lawrence P.
Hamel, Cynthia Marie - Dussault, Thomas Michael
Hamilton, Barbara J. - Wright, Lawrence R.
Hanson, Florence M. (Page) - Izatt, Arthur
Hapsis, Karen L. (Helleberg) - Asselin, David B.
Hardy, Blanche - Arnold, Walter J.
Harper, Emma P. (Perry) - Thistle, William
Harris, Mamie L. - Wright, Lewis
Harris, Maud E. - Blodgett, Charles N.
Harvey, Pauline - Jones, Theodore
Hatch, Sylvia Louise - Stoddard, Francis A.
Hatch, Geraldine - Webber, Charles G.
Hathaway, Debra J. - Mosholder, Daniel D.
Hayward, Maud M. - Bartlett, Charles C.
Hazen, Carol Ann (Vincelette) - Mitchell, Joseph James
Head, Alice M. - Carbee, Edward S.
Heath, Donna Marie - Bagley, Donald Bixby
Heath, Evelyn Florence (Dicey) - Shortt, Lewis William
Heath, Florence L. (Strickland) - Cummings, Maynard E.
Heath, Mertie B. - Gould, Eugene H.
Heath, Etta - Andrews, Harold V.

Heath, Mary (Howland) - Davis, John E.
Heath, Effie May - Fifield, Melvin B.
Heath, Sally M. (Merrill) - Clark, Stephen K.
Heath, Myrtie M. - Murphy, Douglas W., Jr.
Heath, Rhonda Marie - Bloom, Brian George
Heath, Emma Elizabeth (Perrin) - Weeks, Wilbur Rexford
Henderson, Pollyanna - Cobb, Russell B.
Heward, Bree - McHugh, James D.
Hibbard, Elaine Marie - Maltais, David Arthur
Highland, Florence A. (Spooner) - Chapman, Allan H.
Hight, Mary Elizabeth - Amsden, Paul A.
Hight, Marilyn Ann - Mello, Frank R., Jr.
Hight, Glenna M. - Wright, Carl E.
Hildreth, Helen Elizabeth - Caverhill, David Wayne
Hildreth, Belle - Smith, Guy W.
Hildreth, Bertha May - Whitcher, Charlie H.
Hildreth, Blanche I. - Adams, Martin B.
Hildreth, Mary Ellen - Strout, Leslie Jackson
Hildreth, Evelyn B. - Carter, William M.
Hilliard, Evelyn - Whitney, Percy L.
Hilliard, Mamie Madeline - Ray, George Stanley
Hilliard, Marion H. - St. Croix, John W.
Hirsch, Millie - Merrill, Sam A.
Hobart, Janet W. - Graves, Robert C.
Hollinrake, Elizabeth Louise (Meserve) - Bancroft, Robert Allison
Hopkins, Arlene Agusta (Amer) - Bean, Ray Charles
Houghton, Ella A. - Chasson, Frederick J. H.
Houghton, Nancy - Harvey, Henry
Houghton, Glenna M. - Washburn, Claude D.
Howard, Mattie L. - Little, John H.
Howard, Sandra Lee (Whitcher) - Hair, Allen Walter
Howe, Deborah L. - Joyce, Herbert W.
Howes, Olive Ellen (Arsenault) - Kowalewski, Walter Joseph
Hubbard, Kimberly J. (Burnham) - Richardson, Craig E.
Huckins, Avis Marjorie - Cushing, Irwin Beecher
Huckins, Regina Arlene - Shortt, Leland Phillie
Huckins, Doris Alice (Prescott) - Shortt, Leon Hazen
Hudson, Carol I. - Brown, Kevin S.
Hudson, Christine N. - Ball, Scott A.
Huff, Tina L. (Ramsey) - Vincelette, Robert J.
Hunter, Roberta J. - Heath, Arthur G.

Hurd, Hollis Marie - Vincelette, Everett Lloyd, Jr.
Hurlbutt, Patricia Ann (Pease) - Hight, George Thomas
Hurlbutt, Isadore - Breer, Charles
Hurlbutt, Annette Marie - Ballester, Michael David
Hurst, Nanci-Beth - Myers, Robert J., Jr.
Hutchins, Helen M. - Barker, Carl E.
Hutchins, Effie E. (Copp) - Jennings, Ralph E.
Hutchins, Helen Louise - Hazelton, Walter

Ingalls, Eva B. (Short) - Flanders, Leonard M.
Ireland, Sara Jane - Tatham, Stephen Paul
Irwin, Tammy Lyn - Sackett, Charles Nelson
Isaacs, Ruth - Cotton, Norris H.

Jacques, Alma E. - Weeks, Carlyle R.
Jaques, Nellie O. - Smith, Charles N.
Jasmer, Ramona Leigh - Dillon, Robert Erwin
Jenkins, Sara - Hancock, Scott
Jewell, Flossie B. - Comette, Warren L.
Jewett, Nancy - Boynton, Lester W.
Jones, Celia Mae - Ball, Herman George
Jones, Lois Ann - Hansen, Mark D.
Judd, Mary E. (Jamieson) - Hurlbutt, William H.
Judkins, Eva - Pike, Arthur L.

Kapplain, Laurel A. - McGuy, Thomas M.
Kasheta, Bernadette Theo - Gove, Donald Langdon
Keith, Blanche I. - Bartlett, Homer E.
Kelley, Blanche R. - Jackson, William C.
Kelley, Minnie M. - Judkins, Amos H.
Kelly, Eva D. - Nelson, Edward J.
Kelly, Eva Della - Pike, Clarence W.
Kelly, Eva D. - Pike, Lawrence H.
Kemp, Helen Eva - Evans, Reginald S.
Keniston, Nancy D. - Burnham, Royal S.
Keniston, Joanne M. - Britton, Thomas Allen
Kennedy, Lorie A. - Warbin, Richard C.
Kerr, Grace H. (Barber) - Cates, William H.
Keysar, Ardella M. (Rankin) - Heath, Anderson
Keysar, Phyllis Ann - Rice, Donald Arthur
Keysar, Mrs. Elyza (Moses) - Gathercole, James C.

Keysar, Shirley Marie - Collier, Freeman W.
Keysar, Eleanor M. - Milne, Francis John
Kinne, Pamela Jo - Spencer, Michael David
Kittredge, Lillian B. - Frye, Lewis A.
Koski, Mary Lynn - Foote, Charles Avery
Kubler, Gertrude M. - Lamsden, George
Kuntz, Kendra L. - Newton, Jason M.
Kydd, Mary Helen - Franks, Robert D.
Kydd, Lena I. - Harrington, E. E.

Labbie, Julie B. - Marston, Neil C.
LaBrie, Anne N. - Hurlbutt, William H., Jr.
Ladd, Nellie J. - Whitcher, Fred J.
Lamarre, Karen Mariana - Gansz, Christopher Werner
Lambert, Jessie A. (Wright) - Shanty, Frederick C.
Lamothe, Lisa M. - Taylor, Walter D.
Landon, Gloria (Parris) - Cummings, Vance
Langston, Sandra K. - Clancey, Daniel J.
LaRochelle, Suzanne M. - Williams, Dave B.
LaRochelle, Dany Marie - Butson, Donald Arthur
Lausier, Elizabeth A. - Michaud, Joseph A.
Lavoice, Catherine A. - Young, Gerald R.
Lavoie, Gladys Julia - Hammond, Lester F.
Lavoie, Blanch M. - Belyea, Llewellyn
Laythe, Arlene Frederica - Jesseman, Elmer Whitcher
Leavitt, Inez - Kelly, Harry John
Leblance, Celina (Lavoie) - Derosia, Dominac
Lebrun, Gertrude A. (Johnson) - Wright, Glenn G.
Ledger, Doris M. - Ball, Leslie Albert
Leduc, Janine S. - Maher, Thomas M.
Lee, Effie May - Foote, Leslie M.
Leonard, Dorothy Laura - Gould, Llewellyn Leon
Leonard, Kimberly A. - Simmons, Fred E.
Lewis, Bessie - Weeks, Clinton S.
Libbey, Blanche Irene - Vincelette, Everett Lloyd
Libbey, Ada E. - Cross, Horace H.
Libbey, Dorothy Eunice - Jesseman, Raymond, Jr.
Libbey, Audrey Jane - Dunklee, Kenneth C.
Libbey, Marjorie L. - Shortt, Stanley F.
Libby, Susan M. - Randall, Vincent G.
Libby, Laura E. - Gale, Harry B.

Lindsey, Elsie E. - Whitcher, Eugene R.
Little, S. Grace - Swain, Charlie I.
Little, Lillian - Morse, Ira H.
Little, Tavie W. - Smith, Osborne W.
Little, Anna G. - French, Lewis E.
Little, Ethel M. - Graves, Ronald J.
Loehr, Diane Alvern Grace (Barnes) - Clark, Michael John
Lord, Ida W. - Emery, Charles A.
Loughlin, Kellie K. - MacKenzie, James A.
Lovernway, Flora - Richardson, Edwin
Lucius, Evelyn Rose (Roberts) - Wistner, Floyd Alfred
Lumsden, Jean Gertrude - Moody, Lyle Clayton
Lupien, Bernadette M. - Hurley, Michael M.
Lupien, Bernice M. - Lamothe, Roderick

MacDonald, Catherine - Adams, David M.
MacDonald, Sharon Lee - Miller, David Karl
MacDonald, Eleanor L. - Moody, Owen K.
MacDonald, Eva (Lovett) - Bowles, Kenneth H.
Macomber, Lolita - Ball, Brian
Mahoney, Julie B. (Burke) - Morse, Ira Herbert
Manion, Shirley - Hight, Arthur
Mannetho, Patricia Ann - Wilson, Albert C.
Manning, Mildred E. (Brogan) - Alessandrini, Simeone
Mansfield, Ilene C. (Woodard) - Gage, Charles E.
Mansur, Gayle E. - Paige, Jack E.
Marland, Audrey Lynn - Asselin, Michael Dearborn
Marsh, Paula Jean - Boutin, Robert James
Marshall, Eleanor Marie - Garrett, Eugene E., Jr.
Marshall, Brenda Lee - Petelle, Douglas Ray
Marston, Jean Margaret - Matson, James Louis
Martin, Ina Florence (Brown) - French, Benjamin H.
Martin, Barbara E. - Brown, James R.
Mason, Laurel Lynne (Macdonald) - Kesek, David Paul
Mathews, Martha Jane (Page) - Holmes, Norris DeWitt
Matson, Carol Jane - Nicol, John Laurence
Matson, Shirley A. - Nicol, Mark A.
Mauchly, Mary L. - Asselin, Daniel M.
Mauchly, Jane E. - Ho-Sing-Loy, Paul A.
Maunula, Ardeth M. (Stimson) - Ball, Clifford E.
Maviki, Jenny M. - Roca Whu, Christian J.

McAuley, Rose A. (Stubbard) - Pike, Lawrence H.
McClosky, Maude - Hibbard, Clarence George
McCoy, Rita Louise - Richards, Richard Orin
McCrillis, Myra E. - Eastman, Edmund
McCutcheon, M. - Eastman, George C.
McCutcheon, Annie Mae - Dobson, Walter E.
McGuire, Edith - Cano, Jose
McIsaac, Mabel L. (Eastman) - Fifield, Harry A.
McKee, Ethel E. - Garrett, Eugene E., Jr.
McKevie, Eva - McKinnon, Norman
McKinnon, Janice L. (Cutting) - Marquis, Joseph
McLeod, Mary J. - McLaughlin, James
Medeiros, E. Barbara (Whitcher) - Bond, Francis J.
Medeiros, Ethel Barbara (Whitcher) - Robidoux, Fernand Edward
Menard, Rita Louise (Clark) - Wright, Richard A.
Merrill, Lillian - Green, Milton L.
Merrill, Susie Belle - Flanders, Fred J.
Merrill, Blanche - Baker, Earle L.
Merrill, Sarah J. - Tilley, William
Merrill, Cora A. - Batchelder, C. W.
Merrill, Ruth - Derosia, Leo F.
Merrill, Nettie A. - Carpenter, Frank A.
Merrill, Lena O. - Smith, A. Leroy
Merrill, Nettie M. - Batchelder, Albert N.
Merrill, Lois - Wetherbee, Walter
Meuse, Marsha L. (Flagg) - Downs, Jean P.
Michaud, Barbara A. - Stevens, Wayne Earl
Miclon, Florence F. - Merrill, Clinton J.
Miller, Myrtie (Astol) - Remick, William F.
Millette, Orilene E. - Hight, George E.
Mills, Marion H. - Weeks, Natt C.
Mitchell, Ethel M. - Reynolds, Ernest G.
Molway, Mabel E. - French, Charles B.
Moody, Marlene (Stevens) - Wright, Michael W.
Moore, Kathy A. - McKenna, Christipher S.
Moore, Emeline E. - Walcott, George S.
Moran, Mary E. - Cotton, Ralph P.
Morey, Dorothy Irene - Pike, Lanson James
Morrill, Margaret - Stearns, Raymond H.
Morrison, Cora A. - Haines, Wilbur N.
Morrison, Joan L. - Ames, Roy H., Jr.

Morse, Julia N. - Kittredge, Carl S.
Moses, Eunice M. - Ramsey, Earl E.
Moses, Lizzie M. - Cotton, Henry L.
Moses, Jennie H. - Belyea, George N.
Moses, Elmeda May - Boynton, Carl M.
Moses, Florence J. - Lewis, Ralph W.
Moses, Belle F. - Gould, Henry B.
Motta, June - Dooley, David P.
Moulton, Emma - Leonard, Ernest, Jr.
Myers, Grace E. - Walker, Charles H.

Nadeau, Shirley (Lowell) - Flanders, Carl L.
Nadeau, Norma - Nadeau, Gene
Nason, Rachel P. - Garland, W. W.
Nedeau, Hattie (Dexter) - Nedeau, Charles
Nelson, Beverly B. - Ellingson, William Roger
Newell, Sandra M. - Donahue, Sean T.
Newell, Ida B. - Little, William Henry
Newling, Vera A. - Whitcher, Clayton
Newton, Belle - Kelly, Edwin
Nickerson, Mary T. (MacKea) - Frye, Simeon Cheney
Nicol, Victoria E. - Dreghorn, Samuel
Nolan, Susan F. - Nutter, Theodore L.
Norcia, Barbara (Smith) - Smith, James P.
Noury, Hailey Kristin - Wetherbee, Hue Owen, Jr.
Noyes, Lillian L. (Little) - Gordon, Wilbur C.
Nystrom, Heather L. - Chase, Timothy

Olin, Emily May - Evans, Gerald W.
Oliver, Marion - Alessandrini, Bernardino L.
Olivier, Jeannette F. - Matson, Jon Milton
Ordway, Pamela Ethel - Deres, Richard Bernard
Owen, Laurel H. - Mooney, Fergus T.

Page, Martha J. - Swain, Elmer E.
Palmer, Rebecca Jo - Heitz, Julian Michael
Palmer, Goldie M. - Smith, Harry
Palmer, Dianne L. (Heath) - Marston, Neil C.
Palmer, Flora Belle (Rollins) - Palmer, Stanley Wilson
Palmeter, Lettie A. (Morgan) - Carpenter, Frank A.
Papio, Michele - Adams, Donald Linwood

Parenteau, Norma Jean - Nadeau, Gene Howard
Parenteau, Denise - Start, Allen Richard
Parenteau, Loretta Lee - Start, John Steven
Parenteau, Norma J. - Bent, Anthony G.
Pease, Pamela Jean - Cummings, George Charles
Pease, Florence M. (Edgerly) - Pease, Edwin S.
Pease, Patricia A. - Hurlbutt, William H., Jr.
Pelletier, Christine A. - Johnson, Jay C.
Perkins, Ernestine Beatrice - Porter, John Dale, Jr.
Perry, Barbara Frances - Mouncey, Harold Alton, Jr.
Perry, Helen I. - Belyea, William H.
Perry, Winnie M. - Merrill, Paul Ranville
Perry, Doris Audrey - Hildreth, Harold L.
Perry, Natalie Alberta - Trask, Frank E.
Perry, Ernestine E. - Asselin, Henry D.
Petito, Leona May (Pike) - Batchelder, Arthur M.
Philbrook, Cynthia Rose - Harmon, Frank James
Phillips, Ann Marie - Munroe, Peter Paul
Picanso, Pauline L. - McClain, Frank
Pickering, Eliza - Weeks, Ira M.
Pierson, Carol Ann - Ball, Allan Max
Pike, Leona - Petito, Andrew
Pike, Katherine Ruby - Philbrook, William A.
Pillsbury, Alice V. - Leonard, F. F.
Plant, Jessica A. - Carter, Michael J.
Plant, Jennie (Moses) - Mardin, Clement
Plastridge, Hazel F. (Batchelder) - Hildreth, Harry L.
Prescott, Ettie L. - Gleason, Fred C.
Prescott, Gracia - Cummings, Walker F.
Prescott, Lucy J. (Rodmer) - Howland, Edgar
Prescott, Margaret - Weeks, Wilbur R.
Prescott, Annie E. - Crosby, Arthur
Prescott, Bertha E. - Putnam, Robert E.
Prior, Mrs. Jennie M. (Iram) - Tibbetts, Carl E.
Prue, Wyllian E. - French, Richard J.
Pushee, Fawn Marie - Carter, Derrick Noel

Ramsay, Sandra M. - Burgess, Hollis A., Jr.
Ramsay, Kimberly P. - Conrad, Philip R.
Ramsay, Earline M. - Derosia, Louis B.
Ramsay, Lisa Marie - Maccini, Peter Donald

Ramsay, Edith M. (Belyea) - Luce, Bernard
Ramsdell, Thelma M. - Cartwright, David N.
Rannacher, Carol Anne - MacDonald, John Herbert, 3rd
Raptis, Susan Denise (Brassard) - Ball, Brian Bert
Raymond, Mary A. - Morin, Leon F.
Raymond, Jennie M. - Heath, Elmer H.
Reed, Iva E. - York, Omah L.
Reid, Kim Marie - Kennedy, Nelson Leo, Jr.
Reside, Annie (Nurse) - Little, William H.
Roberts, Margaret F. - Steele, Arthur H.
Robertson, Judith Ann (Lemner) - Blanchard, Robert Allen
Robertson, Sheila Lee - Foote, Charles Avery
Rocchi, Paula M. - Cate, Nicholas L.
Rogers, Carole Anne - Kruse, Donald Ray
Rollins, Evelyn Dorothy (Derosia) - Sweeney, Waldo F.
Rollins, Flossie M. - Derosia, Louis J.
Roman, Marie Mabel Floret (Roulx) - Smith, Richard Irving
Roth, Evelyn Wanda - Reynolds, John D.
Roulx, Marie M. F. - Romon, Antenio
Roulx, Sandra Mae - Heatley, Grant Ross
Roulx, Germaine Norma - Miller, David Dwain
Rowell, Doris H. - Ray, Floyd R.
Roy, Donna L. (Bancroft) - Matson, James L.
Roy, Tammy S. - Wright, Leslie I.
Ruel, Levine - Sorell, Lewis
Ruell, Angelle - King, Gilbert
Ruell, Della - Sorell, Frank
Ruell, Lougee - Fountain, Paul
Russell, Robin J. - Heath, Arthur G.
Ryan, Evelyn Ella (Wentworth) - Taylor, Walter Charles

Sackett, Traci Lyn - Pike, Michael Shane
Sackett, Amy - Hamilton, Scott
Sampson, Belle - Fifield, Alva E.
Sanborn, Jennie H. - Caswell, Charles H.
Sargent, Ethel Mae - Wolcott, Archie R.
Sargent, Josephine (Ellis) - Blake, Eugene
Savage, Nyra J. - Libbey, Millard A.
Schieber, Brenda Lee (Vincelette) - Bartlett, Robert William
Schofield, Deborah A. (Sladen) - Huckins, Robert H.
Sears, Martha Lee - Chamberlain, Wilbur

Seifert, Marie Margaret - Bushnell, Horace Llewellyn
Shanna, Eleanor M. (Smith) - Lugton, Russell Earl
Sharer, Sarah Elizabeth - Curley, Roger Damien
Short, Edna - Godville, James
Short, Lydia Jennie - Raymond, Alfred J.
Short, Eva - Ingalls, Guy H.
Short, Eleanor - Whitcher, Arthur D.
Short, Cathy - Leroy, Herbert
Short, Leona H. - Hilliard, Joseph N.
Shortt, Penny L. - Newton, Jeffrey S.
Shortt, Bonnie Lee - Cook, Wesley Norman
Shortt, Edith Gould - Kenney, Sidney Robert
Shortt, Muriel Barbara - Dicey, Arthur Ralph
Shortt, Eda Mae - Krol, Paul
Shortt, Clara Celestia - Harmon, Everett B.
Sicks, Julie A. - Panus, Michael E.
Simard, Christina A. - Collette, Donald David
Simmons, Susan - Ball, Loren R.
Simmons, Nancy Helen - Jewett, Walter Harry
Simpson, Martha A. - Blake, Harry I.
Simpson, Geneva Emily - Shortt, Arron William
Simpson, Edith - Chase, Warren
Skalla, Marie E. - Woodard, Montague W.
Sleeper, Nancy J. - Hight, William R., Jr.
Smith, Joy Inez - Heywood, Fred, III
Smith, Melanie A. (Carr) - Benedict, Royce
Smith, Lillian - Libby, Natt E.
Smith, Karen Lee - Nystrom, Alden Edmond
Smith, Gwendolyn I. (Brown) - Smith, Charles H., Jr.
Smith, Marie F. (Roulx) - Smith, Richard I.
Smith, Patricia Ellen - Hildreth, David Wayne
Smith, Jane A. (Boutin) - Hubbard, Danny C.
Smith, Gladys Evelyn (Millette) - McGary, Angus Ross
Smith, Iva - Hight, William
Snelgrove, Bertha - Keysar, Miles H.
Sorrell, Mintae - Tanguay, Nobert
Spencer, Jessie M. - Weeks, H. Edgar
Spencer, Marcia L. - Belyea, Jay L.
Spencer, Elaine M. - Bean, Stuart K.
Spencer, Laurie-Anne M. - Foley, Edward W.
Spinelli, Kathy J. - Richards, Charles V.

Spooner, Della E. - Whiteman, Fred F.
Spoonor, Nora B. (Burke) - Flanders, Leonard M.
Stafursky, Jeanne E. (Engley) - Whitcher, Eugene P., Jr.
Stallings, Sandra Jane (Caverhill) - Pike, Richard Morey
Stark, Shirley R. - George, Thomas I.
Stark, Amber - Kingsbury, Karlton
Steele, Nancy Lee (Conkey) - Smith, Richard Irving
Stein, Anita Theresia - Bancroft, Steven Allison
Stengel, Louise G. - Martin, William Joseph, Jr.
Stevens, Sherry - Grady, Darrin
Stevens, Marjorie A. - Brown, Edward William
Stevens, Marlene - Moody, Stephen Ross
Stickney, Sarah N. - Whitcher, George W.
Stimson, Pamela Gail - Ball, Anthony Herbert
Stimson, Ardeth Mae - Maunula, Toivo John
Stimson, Noreen Ellen - Chase, Robert Cecil
Stratton, Mabel E. - Sharon, William
Streeter, Sarah E. - Weeks, Sidney C.
Strickland, Annemarie - Dennis, Craig M.
Strout, Mary Ellen (Hildreth) - Patterson, Ralph Russell
Swain, Sarah E. - McLaughlin, Robert A.
Swain, Alice M. - Gould, Al O.
Swain, Annie L. - Foote, Charles G.
Swan. Helen E. (Emery) - Avery, Clifton A.
Sweet, Dorothy M. - Clark, Wilbur A.
Swift, Bernice (Buskey) - Lavoie, George J.

Taggart, Nancy L. (Najarian) - Foote, Charles A.
Tangen, Delphine - LaBonta, Fred
Taylor, Teresa-Ann - Fellows, Jeffrey M.
Taylor, Marie L. - Belyea, Jay L.
Taylor, Bonnie L. - Smith, Wendell A.
Tetley, Ruby Lee - Finerty, Frank
Tewksbury, Grace Helen - MacDonald, John Herbert, Jr.
Thomason, Carlene D. (Jewell) - Libbey, Earl B., Jr.
Thompson, Jessica - Vincelette, Jedediah
Thompson, Judy Ann - Ball, Bert Peter
Thompson, Marie D. - Lamothe, Peter Edward
Thompson, Leslie Martha (Johnston) - Fassnacht, Eugene T.
Thornhill, Linda Pauline - Chase, Ronald Arthur
Tibbetts, Nellie M. - Derosia, Zebulon

Tibbetts, Millie Ann - Derosia, William Joseph
Tibbetts, Jennie F. - Pike, Joseph W.
Tibbetts, Elizabeth - Bringhurst, Arthur Wesley
Tibbetts, Bertha Belle - Whitcher, Clifton L.
Tilley, Adella - Ames, Spurgeon
Timson, Ethel Flora (Allard) - Short, Edward B.
Torsey, Rebecca J. (Boynton) - Heath, Raymond, Jr.
Towle, Jean - Hair, Allan W.
Townsend, Rachel L. - Richardson, Fred W.
Tracy, Olive (Jordan) - Thistle, William
Trask, Sylvia Jo - Heath, David E.
Trudou, Albina (Charist) - Charist, Louis
Turner, Myrtie M. - Caswell, George H.

Upton, Eva L. - Swain, Elmer E.
Upton, Nellie M. - Smith, Walter P.

Valdes, Monica Lynn - Stark, Wayne Douglas
Valler, Mary - Ruell, Joseph
Valley, Edna Mae - Swartz, John
Vincent, Jennifer Grace - Sackett, Terry Joseph

Walbridge, Georgianna (Gramo) - Short, George A.
Walker, Ida - Wilkins, Henry E.
Wallace, Marguerite A. - Belyea, George A.
Walsh, Alice M. - Libbey, Ralph
Walter, Susan Gail - Landmesser, William Henry
Warbin, Lorie A. (Kennedy) - Sackett, Timothy J.
Washburn, Arlene - Pike, Leon B.
Washburn, Sharyn M. - Acquistapace, Mark L.
Watts, Rozella E. - Batchelder, William H.
Weed, Joan Lansing - Montagne, Clifford
Weeks, Daisy Ann - Whitcher, Neil C.
Weeks, June C. - Quimby, Roger C.
Weeks, Margaret P. (Prescott) - Whitcher, Clayton S.
Weeks, Marion E. - Bishop, Harold L.
Weeks, Laura J. - Spencer, John C.
Wetherbee, Stacey D. - Cass, Bobby James
Wetherbee, Sylvia A. - Brill, James Allen
Wetherbee, Eudora M. - Hibbard, Lloyd C.
Wetherbee, Melissa Susan - Libby, Albert Earl

Wheeler, Doris E. - Avery, Raymond A.
Wheeler, Christie (Cretinon) - DeOliveira, Dennis
Whitcher, Marlene S. - Washburn, Harvey H.
Whitcher, Jennie T. - Foote, Bert L.
Whitcher, Marion F. - Moody, Kenneth V.
Whitcher, Sarah N. (Stickney) - Whitcher, George W.
Whitcher, Sandra L. - Howard, Noel Jay
Whitcher, Lela L. - Short, Edward
Whitcher, Pearl - Stevens, Walter
Whitcher, Jill Christine - Haley, Elmer Clifford, Jr.
Whitcher, Marguerite - Jesseman, Raymond
White, Ellen Ann - Ray, Alex Eastman
White, Kimberly - Provencher, Kevin J.
White, Donna M. - Harvey, Wilmont M., III
White, Eliza M. (Ham) - Martin, Walter B.
White, Elizabeth Gertrude (Chase) - King, James Russell
Whitney, Susie E. - McKinley, Ralph
Whitney, Carolyn A. - Hannett, Alfred Robert
Wiggett, Mabel E. - Connaughton, F. E.
Wiggins, Doreen Joyce - White, James Robert
Wilkins, Grace M. - Houghton, Herbert W.
Wilkins, Jessie (Portlaw) - Demeritt, Lester C.
Williams, Meca Ann - Keysar, Donald Berkley
Williams, Betty M. - Bell, Richard A.
Wistner, Charlotte - Masse, Robert J.
Wistner, Mazie P. - Cummings, George W.
Wistner, Charlotte P. - Burt, Alden L.
Wolfe, Jane C. (Callery) - Morse, Philip M.
Wood, Elaine Marie - Ames, Wesley T.
Wood, Dolores Ann - Schleicher, Michael D.
Woodward, Christin M. - Pike, Clarence W.
Woodward, Janette P. - Ball, Albert Leslie
Wright, Bernice A. - Blake, Wyman W.
Wright, Emma Cora - Foote, Harry Lee
Wyatt, Esther Joann - Kaminsky, William Philip, Jr.

Young, Flora H. - Goodwin, Raymond
Yusopova, Tatyana (Ofcucnko) - Johnson, Charles P.

WARREN
DEATHS

ABBOTT,

Horace D., d. 11/26/1915 at 88/0/2 in Warren; teacher; single; b. Bath; Charles Abbott (Andover, MA) and Anna Lang (Bath)

Nancy F., d. 4/11/1890 at 71/10/27 in Warren; heart disease; b. Bath; Charles Abbott (deceased) and Anna S. Lang

ADAMS,

Blancard I., d. 10/28/1994 at 64 in Plymouth; nurses aid; b. Warren; Elwin Hildreth and Marguerite Veasey

Ellery R., d. 7/25/1943 at 63/5/29; glazier; widower; b. Franklin; James Adams (Franklin)

George Samuel, d. 9/15/1950 at 71 in Warren; farmer; married; b. Hanover; Frank Ames and Clara Davis

Martin B., d. 11/1/2003 in Plymouth; Harold Martin and Gladys Barnard

ALDERMAN,

Annie L., d. 9/21/1996 at 75 in Warren; homemaker; b. Winsted, CT; Walter Slater and Ollie Lamson

Arthur W., d. 2/27/1986 at 77 in Haverhill; manager; b. Torrington, CT; Herbert Alderman and Addie Hubby

Laura E., d. 9/7/2001 in Plymouth; Arthur DeMar and Olive Lamson

Robert H., d. 12/16/1981 at 63 in White River Jct., VT; WW II vet.; b. CT; Herbert Alderman and Addie Hubby

ALDRICH,

Dorothy S., d. 10/27/2003 in Plymouth; Earl Howard and Amy Sanders

Henry, d. 6/25/1978 at 73 in Barre Town, VT; claims manager; b. NH; Hiram Aldrich and Agnes Southard

ALESSANDRINI,

Mildred, d. 1/6/1963 at 65 in Hanover; housewife; married; b. Ashland; Edward Brogan and Mabel Jewell

Mura, d. 6/10/1956 at 48 in Hanover; housewife; married; b. Westbrook, ME; James H. Dorsett and Margaret Chick

Simeone V., d. 3/3/1994 at 96 in Haverhill; b. Italy

ALLEN,

Chelsea Elexis, d. 2/23/1995 at 2 in Glencliff; b. Plymouth; Mark D. Allen and Caron E. Heselton

AMES,

son, d. 2/22/1934 at –; b. Warren; Spurgeon Ames (Warren) and
Lillian Graham (Fernandina, FL)

Addie Powers, d. 9/4/1978 at 77 in Plymouth; housewife; b. Groton;
Daniel Powers and Evelyn Moulton

Adella E., d. 3/2/2003 in Warren; William Tilley and Sarah Morrill

Edward H., d. 2/4/1906 at 0/0/16 in Warren; cong. of lungs; b.
Warren; William Ames (ME) and Sadie McCormick (NB)

Fred Manford, d. 2/14/1977 at 77 in Plymouth; bobbin maker; b.
Kinsman, ME; William M. Ames and Sadie McCormick

Sadie Jane, d. 10/17/1971 at 91 in Plymouth; b. ME; George
McCormick and Augusta Delong

Shirley L., d. 5/20/1952 at 15 in Plymouth; student; single; b.
Wentworth; Spurgeon Ames and Adella Tilley

Spurgeon McCormick, d. 1/8/1983 at 76 in Woodsville; logger; b.
Warren; William Ames and Sadie McCormick

Theodore R., d. 3/10/1965 at 60 in Warren; bobbin mill; divorced; b.
Warren; William Ames and Sadie McCormack

William C., d. 3/19/1938 at 0/0/1; b. Wentworth; Spurgeon Ames
(Warren) and Della Tilley (Warren)

William Manlord, d. 8/7/1957 at 87 in Warren; lumberman; married;
b. Bancroft, ME; William Ames and Martha Lee

ANDERSEN,

John, d. 12/29/1974 at 67 in Hanover; truck driver; b. NY; Niles
Andersen and Sophie Sorensen

ANDERSON,

Arnold A., d. 8/6/1994 at 78 in White River Jct., VT; cabinet maker;
b. Cook, IL; Peter Anderson and Stella Bouche

Ernest W., d. 10/3/1929 at 21/9/2; laborer; single; Carl Anderson
(Sweden) and Bertha G. Cook (Sweden)

Fayne, d. 3/29/1977 at 73 in Haverhill; self-employed carpenter; b.
ME; Fred Anderson and Pansy Collier

Marcia E., d. 7/16/1987 at 82 in Plymouth; homemaker; b. Warren;
Albert Batchelder and Nettie Merrill

ANDREWS,

daughter, d. 2/27/1925 at 0/0/1 in Warren; b. Warren; Harry V.
Andrews and Etta Heath (Warren)

Donald A., d. 1/13/1992 at 75 in St. Cloud, FL; construction; b.
    Warren; Harold V. Andrews and Etta M. Heath
Etta M., d. 4/19/1990 at 93 in St. Cloud, FL; nurse; b. Piermont;
    Joshua Heath and Ada M. Chase
Eva M., d. 3/26/1915 at 36/4/23 in Warren; housewife; married; b.
    Franklin; Joseph P. Gilman (N. Sanbornton) and Rosanna C.
    Cole (Hill)
Henry, d. 10/29/1943 at 79/11/24; laborer; widower; b. Canada;
    Norris Andrews (Canada) and Martha Cheney
Martha J., d. 6/24/1911 at 75/6/24 in Warren; ascetis; housewife;
    married; b. Bradford; Stilman Cheney and Eliza Cheney
Norris, d. 7/1/1917 at 86/4/24 in Warren; laborer; b. Danville;
    Augustus Andrews

ANGERS,
Irene, d. 3/29/2001 in Laconia; Eldred Bailey and Myrtie Smith
Wallace Charles, d. 7/25/1985 at 69 in Hartford, VT; truck driver; b.
    NH; Walter J. Angers, Sr. and Irma Labbe

ANNIS,
daughter, d. 1/20/1889 at – in Warren; b. Warren; Perley Annis and
    Lovilla Swain

ARNOLD,
Charles H., d. 11/22/1913 at 67 in Warren; chronic nephritis; married

ASSELIN,
Henry D., d. 5/17/1939 at 30/0/13; laborer; married; b. Warren; John
    B. Asselin (St. John, NB) and Ruth Whitcher (Warren)
John, d. 11/18/1929 at 64; carpenter; b. Canada
Michael D., d. 6/24/1994 at 38 in New Ipswich; b. Ft. McPherson;
    Henry T. Asselin and Sheila Asselin
Ruth, d. 4/25/1916 at 31/9/17 in C. Haverhill; housewife; married; b.
    Warren; Samuel Whitcher (Warren) and Almina Whitcher
    (Warren)

AVERILL,
Chester B., d. 12/5/1941 at 74/10/18; merchant, manuf.; married; b.
    Mont Vernon; Joseph Averill (Mont Vernon) and S. Baldwin
    (Mont Vernon)

Edith M., d. 12/29/1947 at 72/7/25 in Plymouth; housewife; widow; b. Warren; Charles K. Leonard (Warren) and Emily S. Swain (Warren)

Joseph W., d. 2/9/1908 at 78/2/8; acute indigestion; laborer; widower

AVERY,

Della, d. 3/15/1930 at 63/9/8; housewife; married; b. Warren; Reuben Batchelder (Orford) and Laura Osborn (Warren)

Doris Elaine, d. 3/18/1935 at 26/8/11 in Warren; nurse; married; b. Newport; Robert Wheeler and Annie Burpee

Hastings, d. 9/26/1937 at 78/10/13 in Haverhill; widower; b. Ellsworth; Joseph Avery and Johana Hill

Orrin C., d. 4/23/1917 at 74/8/28 in Warren; retired; widower; b. Campton; Aaron Avery and Fannie Jacobs

Raymond Albert, d. 11/11/1977 at 69 in Concord; farming; b. Warren; Hasting Avery and Delia Batchelder

Wilhelma, d. 6/16/1913 at 1/10/22 in Plymouth; epilepsy; b. Plymouth; Charles Avery (Campton) and Emma Perry (Warren)

BACHELDER,

Harriet E., d. 12/3/1945 at 85/3/28 in Plymouth; retired; widow; b. Manchester; Charles Tufts and Adelaide Wright

BACON,

Elmer T., d. 4/24/1897 at 0/7/3 in Warren; cerebral meningitis; b. Warren; Fred S. Bacon and Ida J. Perry

BADGER,

Charles M., d. 10/1/1900 at 74/6 in Warren; cystitis; blacksmith; married; b. Warner; Jonathan Badger (Warren) and Ariah Bodwell (Methuen, MA)

Mary A., d. 2/25/1906 at 70/7/6 in Concord; heart disease; housewife; widow; b. Warren; Isaac Fifield (ME) and Mary Downing (Holderness)

BAILEY,

Albert A., d. 4/7/1891 at 3/11/17 in Warren; poisoning; b. E. Haverhill; R. W. Bailey (Warren, painter) and Mary B. Wright (Benton)

Florence, d. 10/5/1947 at 78/8/4 in Haverhill; housewife; widow; b. Haverhill; John C. Shelby (Haverhill) and Mina T. Ward (Haverhill)

Harry, d. 12/25/1953 at 70 in Concord; laborer; divorced; b. Warren; Russell Bailey and Mary Wright

Hosea, d. 6/4/1963 at 79 in Laconia; janitor; single; b. Warren; Russell Bailey and Mary Wright

Laura Ellen, d. 8/8/1938 at 53/0/4; housekeeper; married; b. Meredith; Charles Clark (Laconia) and Annie Miles (Laconia)

Mary Blanch, d. 12/24/1945 at -2/5/10 in Warren; housewife; widow; b. Benton; Gilbert Wright (Hebron) and Phoebe Marston (Benton)

Russell W., d. 4/1/1940 at 81/2; farmer-painter; married; b. Glencliff; Winslow R. Bailey (Glencliff) and Mr'a Whitcher (Glencliff)

BAKER,
Blanche E., d. 7/13/1905 at 20/2 in Warren; pneumonia; housewife; married; b. Warren; Fred J. Merrill (W. Rumney) and Lizzie Cummings (Warren)

BALDWIN,
Paul E., d. 10/3/1929 at 20/0/24; laborer; single; b. Bradford, VT; Edward G. Baldwin (Barton, VT) and Daisy Chase (Calais, VT)

BALL,
son, d. 4/23/1941 at 1 hr.; b. Woodsville; Reginald H. Ball (Landaff) and C. M. Griffin (Tilton)

Alice Mary, d. 10/18/1941 at 0/0/1; b. Warren; Leslie A. Ball (Landaff) and Doris Ledger (Westminster, MA)

Allan M., d. 9/14/1986 at 48 in Haverhill; maint. foreman; b. Woodsville; Reginald Ball and Charlotte Griffin

Burt L., d. 2/15/1947 at 70/6/15 in Warren; mill man; married; Herbert Ball (Landaff) and Sophie M. Clifford (Landaff)

Doris, d. 8/3/2003 in Warren; Florian Ledger and Delina Joillett

Ethelyn, d. 1/18/2005 in Plymouth; Robert Hillock and Eliza Black

Eva, d. 6/29/1975 at 86 in Haverhill; retired & housewife; b. NH; Edwin Moulton and Ida Williams

Leslie A., d. 2/26/1995 at 77 in Plymouth; farmer; b. Landaff; Bert L. Ball and Eva Moulton

Reginald H., d. 5/17/1988 at 78 in Glencliff; fireman; b. Landaff; Bert L. Ball and Eva Moulton

225

Vincent Bruce, d. 5/23/1959 at 24 in Warren; mining; married; b. Burlington, VT; Helen M. Ball

BANCROFT,
Chester R., d. 8/10/1981 at 74 in Hanover; lumber grader; b. NH; Fred L. Bancroft and Ida M. Fitzgerald
Elizabeth, d. 4/17/1983 at 61 in Warren; seamstress; b. Shelburne; James Brown and Myrtle Parker
Fred L., d. 9/17/1994 at 53 in Lebanon; tax collector; b. Littleton; Lewis E. Bancroft and Dorothy Young
Lewis Earl, d. 4/3/1992 at 77 in Lebanon; construction; b. Hollis; Fred L. Bancroft and Ida M. Fitzgerald
Marjorie P., d. 5/13/1987 at 60 in Warren; home; b. Nashua; Earl Moore and Vesta Harris
Verona, d. 3/11/1972 at 59 in Hanover; housewife; b. NY; Verne Aldrich and Ella May White

BANFILL,
Fred F., d. 2/28/1966 at 87 in Warren; farmer; married; b. Dixville, PQ; William Banfill and Sarah Young

BARBER,
Frank W., d. 11/17/1960 at 81 in Milford; minister ret.; married; b. Hancock; Alfred Barber and Clara Weston

BARNEY,
Ellen, d. 10/24/1953 at 94 in Warren; housewife; widow; b. Essex, VT; Henry Roberts and Elizabeth Levine

BARRETT,
Arthur, d. 9/16/1992 at 84 in Woodsville; never employed; b. Hudson; Alfred Barrett and Hedwing Boutin

BARRY,
Charles Freeman, d. 5/18/1947 at 86/2/18 in Warren; ladder rung mfg.; married; b. Rumney; Erastus Barry and Helen Tyler
Ora Smith, d. 4/5/1963 at 73 in Haverhill; housewife; widow; b. Sanbornton; Zebulon Smith and Eva Flanders

BARTLETT,

Alonzo F., d. 4/10/1906 at 66/8/7 in Warren; fatty degen. of heart; sheriff; widower; b. Whitefield; Ephram Bartlett

Luvia, d. 1/12/1902 at 62/3/4 in Warren; bronchial pneumonia; housewife; married; b. Bath; Movanda Wh'tch and Rosann H. Childs (Bath)

Silas S., d. 6/3/1917 at 66/10/18 in Warren; farmer; married; b. Sutton, VT; Joseph L. Bartlett (Sutton, VT) and Phebe Noyes (Landaff)

BARTON,

Janice M., d. 5/1/2001 in Woodsville; Joseph Galanck and Marguerite Davis

BATCHELDER,

daughter, d. 8/4/1898 at 0/0/7 in Warren; premature birth; b. Warren; C. W. Batchelder

daughter, d. 8/16/1901 at – in Warren; neph. on part mthr; b. Warren; Joel I. Batchelder (Warren) and Stella A. Clifford (Warren)

Albert N., d. 4/2/1925 at 55/11/19 in Warren; lumberman; married; b. Warren; Charles Batchelder (Warren) and Mary J. Ingles (Plymouth)

Arthur Merrill, d. 7/9/1970 at 75 in Plymouth; retired; b. NH; Charles Batchelder and Cora Merrill

Belinda I., d. 11/24/1945 at 71/8/27 in Warren; school teacher; widow; b. Warren; John W. Batchelder (Coventry) and Nancy E. Ingalls (Warren)

Charles H., d. 10/4/1902 at 64/2/27 in Warren; apoplexy; farmer; widower; b. Warren; John S. Batchelder (Northfield) and Susan Cate (Canterbury)

Charles W., d. 11/1/1904 at 43/7/24 in Warren; dermatis serpati; farmer; married; b. Warren; Charles H. Batchelder (Warren) and Mary J. Ingalls (Plymouth)

Clarence, d. 6/3/1887 at 21/5/22; brakeman; single; b. Warren; John W. Batchelder (Coventry, VT) and Nellie Ingalls (Warren)

Estella A., d. 11/9/1928 at 63/1/4; housewife; married; b. Warren; George C. Clifford (Warren) and Sybil Whitcher (Benton)

Frank W., d. 5/9/1929 at 70/6/23; farmer; single; b. Warren; Reuben Batchelder (Orford) and Laura Osborn (Warren)

Hannah W., d. 11/11/1888 at 50/2 in Warren; married; b. Warren;
 W. S. Cleasby and Mary Weeks
Joel I., d. 4/5/1937 at 73/5/13 in Warren; retired; widower; b.
 Warren; Charles Batchelder and Mary Jane Ingalls
John, d. 11/5/1938 at 73/0/14; none; widower; b. Warren; Charles
 Batchelder (Warren) and Mary Ingalls (St. Johnsbury, VT)
John W., d. 4/18/1927 at 91/4/15; carpenter; widower; b. Coventry;
 John Batchelder and Susan Cate
Laura, d. 1/6/1902 at 74/3/27 in Warren; bronco pneumonia;
 housewife; married; b. Warren; Samuel Osborne (Piermont)
 and Dulane Pope (Exeter)
Leona M., d. 10/1/1960 at 62 in Franklin; housewife; married; b.
 Warren; Arthur Pike and Eva Judkins
Marcia N., d. 1/29/1903 at 0/0/5 in Warren; inanition; b. Warren;
 Albert Batchelder (Warren) and Nettie M. Merrill (Warren)
Martha E., d. 10/13/1940 at 80/6/0; housekeeper; single; b. Warren;
 Reuben Batchelder and Laura Osborne
Mary J., d. 2/9/1900 at 61/4/11 in Warren; inflammation bowels;
 housekeeper; married; b. Plymouth; Joel Ingalls and Belinda
 Blake
Maynard, d. 1/1/1906 at 23/5/7 in Warren; appendicitis; engineer;
 single; J. W. Batchelder (Coventry) and Nancy Ingalls (Warren)
Nancy E., d. 11/4/1910 at 66/6/24 in Warren; abscess of brain;
 housewife; married; b. Warren; Joel Ingalls and Belinda
 Batchelder (Andover)
Nettie, d. 9/6/1938 at 58/10/12; housewife; widow; b. Warren; Jesse
 Merrill (Warren) and Emily Hartwell (Piermont)
Nettie, d. 12/27/1938 at 69/6/16; rug maker; widow; b. E. Haverhill;
 George Austin and Nellie DeGoosh
Reuben, d. 7/3/1904 at 80/10/14 in Warren; gastro-enteritis; farmer;
 widower; b. Orford; Ward Batchelder and Hannah Putney
Wayland, d. 3/22/1953 at 73 in Haverhill; caretaker; single; b.
 Warren; John W. Batchelder and Nancy Ingalls
William H., d. 1/12/1930 at 70/1/2; farmer; widower; b. Warren;
 Reuben Batchelder (Orford) and Laura Osborn (Warren)

BATES,
Lena, d. 5/9/1970 at 72 in Haverhill; b. NH; Thomas Phair and
 Josephine Flanders
Mary, d. 8/3/1893 at 84/6 in Warren; old age; housekeeper; Samuel
 Kittredge (Waldon, VT) and ----- Folsom

BATTIS,

Lydia A., d. 9/30/1919 at 77/2/1 in Warren; housekeeper; widow; b. Warren; Samuel Whitcher (Warren) and Mary Richardson (Warren)

BEAMIS,

Ethel M., d. 4/7/1896 at 0/2 in Warren; spinal meningitis; b. Warren; William H. Beamis and Bertha M. Crane

Harold G., d. 11/2/1998 at 77 in Plymouth; highway; b. Haverhill; Herbert Beamis and Mary Flanders

Priscilla D., d. 11/15/2001 in Warren; Charles Cutting and Mary -----

BEAUDOIN,

Aime, d. 11/8/1958 at 50 in Warren; furniture mfg.; married; b. Manchaug, MA; Napoleon Beaudoin and Marie Sevigny

BEAULIEU,

daughter, d. 6/1/1919 at – in Warren; b. Warren; Alex. J. Beaulieu (Three Rivers) and Lucy G. Copp (Warren)

Alexis, d. 4/24/1961 at 77 in Haverhill; RR laborer; widower; b. Canada; Thomas Beaulieu and Leda Cote

Lucy, d. 1/5/1937 at 44/9/7 in Haverhill; housewife; widow; b. Warren; Byron Copp and Alma Gerald

Mary A., d. 11/16/1907 at 18/11/19 in Warren; eclampsia; housekeeper; married; b. Warren; Byron Copp (Haverhill) and Almer M. Gerald (Warren)

BEAUREGARD,

Doris Florence, d. 11/3/1982 at 70 in Haverhill; homemaker; b. Newmarket; Raymond A. Otis and Lumina M. Laderbush

BELEVANCE,

son, d. 10/8/1903 at – in Warren; placenta pralvia; b. Warren; Archie Belevance (Canada) and Delena Bosahua (Canada)

BELYEA,

son, d. 1/10/1930 at – in Glencliff; b. Glencliff; George A. Belyea (Benton) and Marguerite Wallace (Meredith)

Alberta, d. 12/28/1994 at 90 in Concord; homemaker; b. Tilton; Henry B. Harriman and Ida Hall

Anne Marie, d. 10/14/1974 at 3 in Glencliff; b. NH; Charles Neal
   Belyea and Carol Ann Wright
Blanche M., d. 8/29/1982 at 79 in Haverhill; laundress; b.
   Manchester; Peter LaVoie and Leola Desrosier
Charles M., d. 3/1/1980 at 75 in Woodsville; retired postmaster; b.
   NH; George N. Belyea and Jennie N. Moses
George Alfred, d. 9/7/1960 at 52 in Laconia; carpenter; married; b.
   Haverhill; George Belyea
George Nathaniel, d. 1/5/1943 at 77/4/30; retired; widower; b,.
   Olenville, NB
Harry Roy, d. 9/4/1921 at – in Haverhill; laborer; single; b. Warren;
   James Belyea (NB) and Mary M. Fifield (Warren)
Helen Inez, d. 2/17/1993 at 85 in Woodsville; cook; b. Haverhill;
   Charles Alvin Perry and Inez C. Lindsay
James Isaac, d. 2/5/1929 at 66/9/8; laborer; married; b. Queens Co.,
   NB; George S. Belyea (NB) and Emily E. McKeel (NB)
Leslie Elmer, d. 4/27/1954 at 55 in Plymouth; NH Highway Dept.;
   widower; b. Benton; George Belyea and Jennie Moses
Lewellyn, d. 9/17/1959 at 57 in Plymouth; laborer; b. Warren; James
   Belyea and Mary Fifield
Marguerite W., d. 6/7/1974 at 64 in Laconia; cook; b. NH; Harry
   Wallace and Alma H. Ardrich
Mary Melinda, d. 10/3/1946 at 77/5/5 in Glencliff; housewife; widow;
   b. Glencliff; Lorenzo Fifield (Glencliff) and Jane Moody
Roland M., d. 2/22/1994 at 72 in Holyoke, MA; boiler fireman; b.
   Glencliff; Roy B. Belyea
William H., d. 6/21/1979 at 78 in Haverhill; laborer; b. Benton;
   George Belyea and Jennie Moses

BENNETT,
Betsy, d. 4/28/1923 at 90/8/3 in Warren; widow
George W., d. 12/9/1902 at 67 in Warren; softening of brain; farmer;
   married; b. Orange; David Bennett and Mary Cole
James J., d. 6/4/1978 at 86 in Haverhill; laborer; b. New York, NY

BENSON,
Alexander P., d. 3/22/1967 at 58 in Windsor, VT; real estate;
   married; b. St. John, NF; Eric Benson and Agnes Ryan

230

BERRY,

Effie May, d. 7/22/1903 at 28/5 in Wentworth; pulmonary
tuberculosis; housewife; married; b. Haverhill; Timothy Webber
(Rumney) and Alma C. Fifield (Warren)

Ruth Foster, d. 8/10/1954 at 40 in Warren; housewife; married; b.
Weld, ME; Harry Foster and Ella Kitridge

BICKFORD,

James R., d. 3/7/1969 at 52 in Warren; locomotive engineer; b. CT;
James A. Bickford and Gertrude Prosser

BIEER,

William R., d. 1/16/1925 at 9/1/8 in Warren; b Warren; James Bieer
(Sheldon, VT) and Minnie Clark (Warren)

BIXBY,

Albert L., d. 9/30/1904 at 79/8/12 in Warren; pneumonia;
expressman; widower; b. Warren; Benjamin Bixby (MA) and
Mary Cleasby

Anna C., d. 8/15/1913 at 77/5 in Warren; arterio sclerosis; b.
Warren; Benjamin Bixby (Topsham, VT) and Polly Crosby
(Concord)

Dorilla, d. 2/15/1914 at 87/1/25 in Concord; widow; b. Wilmot;
Benaih Bean (NH) and Susan Morey (NH)

Eliza S., d. 7/4/1911 at 69/1/12 in Warren; apoplexy; housewife;
married; b. Salem, MA; Benjamin Symonds (Salem, MA) and
Eliza Shatswell (Salem, MA)

Fred L., d. 12/14/1894 at 23/11/18 in Warren; phthisis pulm.; laborer;
b. Warren; Solomon C. Bixby (Warren) and Addie Danforth

Grace C., d. 12/24/1951 at 10 in Hanover; student; b. Piermont;
Vernon Bixby and Gertrude Walls

James Martin, d. 10/8/1903 at 76/2/14 in Warren; valvular dis. heart;
farmer; married; b. Warren; Samuel B. Bixby (Fairlee, VT) and
Nancy C. Martin (Epsom)

Maurice H., d. 2/14/1954 at 54 in Warren; manufacturer; married; b.
Warren; Willard Bixby and Hattie Currie

Mildred A., d. 6/25/1981 at 73 in Warren; housewife; b. NH; Willard
H. Hunkins and Eva Pinda

Sarah M., d. 9/18/1896 at 75/3/20 in Warren; pneumonia; housewife;
b. Warren; Samuel H. Boynton and Mehitable Clark

Solomon, d. 3/17/1901 at 68/0/14 in Laconia; consumption; farmer; married; b. Warren; Benjamin Bixby (Salem) and Mary Clisby (Concord)

William, d. 12/24/1951 at 14 in Thetford, VT; student; b. Warren; Vernon Bixby and Gertrude Walls

William C., d. 4/28/1894 at 79/6/19 in Warren; consumption; minister; b. Warren; Benjamin Bixby and Mary B. Cleasby

BLAKE,

daughter, d. 4/12/1901 at – in Warren; childbirth; b. Warren; Harry L. Blake (Warren) and Martha A. Simpson (Haverhill)

Dillie, d. 2/10/1973 at 62 in Concord; retired; b. NH; Edwin Blake and Mary Houghton

Edith Cotton, d. 11/1/1942 at 59/4/4; housewife; married; b. Warren; Edward D. Cotton (Warren) and F. A. Pillsbury (Warren)

Eugene, d. 7/5/1927 at 63/2/9 in Laconia; RR man; married; b. Ellsworth; Oscar Blake (W. Thornton) and Emily Collins

Frank, d. 12/24/1936 at 81/11/8 in Concord; farmer; married; b. Kingsley, Canada; Moses Blake and Caroline Lovelock

Henry Austin, d. 8/11/1942 at 83/4/1; laborer; single; b. PQ; Moses Blake (England) and C. Lovelock (England)

Irvin I., d. 1/4/1913 at 22/11/3 in Warren; laborer; single; b. Ellsworth; Eugene Blake (Ellsworth)

Isaac, d. 2/6/1898 at 67/4/14 in Warren; catarrh of stomach; farmer; married; b. Salem, VT; William H. Blake

John Wesley, d. 9/26/1968 at 86 in Plymouth; ret. telegrapher; b. NH; W. Frank Blake and Mary Wesley

Lula M., d. 7/9/1898 at 26/9/15 in Warren; phthisis; housewife; married; b. Wentworth; Alvah Foster

Mary A., d. 2/22/1941 at 88/9/29; housewife; widow; b. Bethlehem; John Wesley (Chatum, England) and R. Clauson (Augusta, ME)

Mary E., d. 3/14/1909 at 70/5/14 in Plymouth; apoplexy; widow; b. Warren; Daniel Marston (Warren)

Roy A., d. 5/6/1898 at – in Warren; bronchitis; b. Warren; Alvah Blake

BLOOD,

Cornelia A., d. 1/15/1900 at 66 in Warren; cancer; housewife; married; b. Amherst; James Lovejoy (Claremont) and ----- (Amherst)

BOURQUE,
Patricia, d. 8/25/2004 in Woodsville; Henry Asselin and Ernestine Perry

BOWL,
Robert W., d. 9/18/1936 at 5/11/14 in Warren; b. Somerville, MA; Harry W. Bowl and Eleanor Graham

BOWLES,
Clarence H., d. 11/12/1932 at 50/11/1; state emp. at fish hatchery; married; b. Franconia; George H. Bowles (Lisbon) and Hattie Dexter (Bethlehem)

Eglantine Eva, d. 3/8/1986 at 87 in Bradford, VT; burial permit

Eva, d. 7/27/1994 at 87 in Hanover; housewife; b. Plymouth; Lyman Lovett and Nellie Andrew

Harriet Alice, d. 3/13/1928 at 1/0/11; b. Warren; Clarence H. Bowles (Franconia) and Adeline A. Adams (Milton, MA)

James H., d. 6/27/1932 at 63/3/15; farmer; married; b. Lisbon; Anson Bowles (Lisbon) and Lois Judd (Easton)

Kenneth Herbert, d. 4/5/1970 at 64 in Plymouth; carpenter; b. NH; Herbert Bowles and Catherine Shortt

Roy E., d. 2/23/1972 at 69 in Plymouth; retired; b. NH; Herbert Bowles and Catherine Short

BOYNTON,
David M., d. 1/21/1900 at 80 in Warren; cancer; farmer; b. Warren

George N., d. 4/25/1929 at 75/2/22; farmer; married; b. Warren; Joseph G. Boynton and Mary Burnham

Joseph P., d. 9/4/1894 at 84/4/20 in Warren; heart disease; farmer; b. Orford; Stephen Boynton and Betsey Palmer

May A., d. 9/11/1932 at 75/0/21; widow; b. Concord; George Wolcott (Barnet, VT) and Electa Beebe

BOZARTH,
Ruth Olive, d. 1/8/1966 at 72 in Plymouth; teacher; widow; b. Gillum, IL; George S. Bozarth and Belle Downes

BREER,
James, d. 5/8/1964 at 82 in Franklin; farmer; widower; b. Sheldon, VT; Charles Breer and Nancy Perry

Minnie E., d. 1/17/1931 at 50/1/25; housewife; married; b. Warren;
   Walter Clark (Montpelier, VT) and Lucy Clark (Chichester)

BROWN,
George E., d. 12/12/1958 at 83 in Warren; mail carrier; married; b.
   Lowell, MA; George H. Brown and Anne M. Foster
James Alfred, d. 1/26/1943 at 77/7; carpenter; married; b.
   Plattsburgh, NY; Jerry Brown (Ireland) and Annie Rock Brown
Luann Lyn, d. 3/1/1969 at 12 in Warren; student; b. Littleton; Clyde
   F. Brown and Fay Ames
Nettie Merrill, d. 12/24/1977 at 96 in Plymouth; housewife; b. NH;
   Henry N. Merrill and Sally C. Libby
Rosie A., d. 6/22/1917 at 58/1/12 in Warren; housewife; married; b.
   Westmon, VT; Welcome Daniels (Wheelock, VT) and Elec.
   Humphrey (Burke, VT)
Viola F., d. 12/13/2003 in Plymouth; Roy Ames and Helen Crafts
Vivia, d. 5/6/1960 at 89 in Warren; housewife; widow; b. Abbott, ME;
   ----- and Sylvia Weeks

BRUCE,
Ella May, d. 6/20/1950 at 73 in Plymouth; housewife; married; b.
   Montpelier, VT; Ephraim Pierce and Mariva Bruce

BRYANT,
Laura Annis, d. 4/1/1973 at 90 in Laconia; lunch program; b. NH;
   Perley Annis and Lovilla Swain

BRYSON,
Gerald R., d. 10/31/1967 at 29 in Warren; chef; divorced; b.
   Franklin; Louis Bryson and Florence Jordan

BUCK,
Margaret G., d. 3/19/1930 at 0/0/12; b. Warren; Archie Buck
   (Newport, VT) and Flora Russell (Grantham)

BUCKLEY,
daughter, d. 4/19/1904 at – in Warren; premature birth; b. Warren;
   John H. Buckley (Concord) and Nellie Fifield (Thetford, VT)

BUISA,
Angie L., d. 8/11/1923 at 20/2/29 in Glencliff; housewife; married; b. Barre, VT; Joseph Rugo (Italy) and Mannel Buisa (Italy)

BURGESS,
Edmund P., d. 9/19/1987 at 52 in Plymouth; lineman; b. Bangor, ME; William Burgess and Alice Ashford

BURKE,
Laura, d. 8/30/1910 at 56/11/10 in Warren; chronic nephritis; housewife; married; b. Canada; Joseph Gannett (Canada) and Laura Stone (Canada)
Patrick, d. –/–/1908 at 44; internal hemorrhage

BURLEIGH,
Catharine, d. 10/14/1902 at 78 in Warren; jaundice; housewife; married; b. Warren
Charles W., d. 4/19/1904 at 68 in Warren; chron. rheumatism; laborer; widower; b. Newmarket

BURNELL,
son, d. 1/23/1915 at – in Warren; b. Warren; Chester A. Burnell (St. Armond, PQ) and Sadie Marie Ellis (Brentwood)
Fred, d. 5/27/1906 at 36 in Warren; heart disease; laborer; single; b. Stratford; Frank Burnell (Canada) and Mary Rivers (Canada)

BURNHAM,
Richard Amon, d. 3/2/1979 at 62 in Warren; storekeeper; b. Orford; Amon B. Burnham and Vernie M. Pease

BURRILL,
John T., d. 3/21/1915 at 80/3/9 in Warren; painter; widower; b. Newburyport, MA; John Burrill (Newburport) and Mary Toppan (Newburyport)

BURT,
Harold J., d. 3/25/1934 at 39/10/0; laborer; married; b. Lyman; Merritt E. Burt (Lyman) and Hannah Sanborn (Kirby, VT)

BUSHAW,
Jesse Edward, d. 6/21/1987 at 66 in Wolcott, VT; retired; b. VT;
    Fred E. Bushaw and Edna B. Gilbert

BUSKEY,
Albert J., d. 3/19/1936 at 47/5/19 in Warren; mechanic; married; b.
    Sutton Flats, Canada; Henry Buskey and Julia Manning
Emma M., d. 10/30/1986 at 85 in Haverhill; housewife; b. Haverhill;
    Peter Dargie and Rose Cantin
Henry, d. 10/11/1976 at 75 in Hanover; b. VT; Harry Buskey and
    Julia Manning
Myron Albert, d. 2/10/2004 in Glencliff; Albert J. Buskey and Fannie

BUTTRICK,
Lois Joyce, d. 6/14/2004 in Warren; Frank Carbone and Evelyn
    Gerry

BYRON,
Evelyn S., d. 2/18/1988 at 90 in Haverhill; social worker; b. Medford,
    MA; Aldanus Soderland and Alfreda Fried

CADRETT,
Isabelle R., d. 9/22/2001 in Lebanon; Delmore Pelletier and Rose
    Chicoine

CAMPBELL,
Wallace E., d. 1/4/1902 at 43/10/16 in Warren; pneumonia;
    overseer; married; b. NB; Calvin Campbell (Scotland) and -----
    (Ireland)

CARBONNEAU,
Lena, d. 11/6/1993 at 91 in Woodsville; labor; b. Littleton; Francis
    Carbonneau and Evenlyn Gadbois

CARLETON,
Mattie B., d. 10/29/1946 at 80/8/28 in Warren; housewife; widow; b.
    Haverhill; John Shelly (Haverhill) and Mina F. Ward (Haverhill)

CARLSON,
Dorothy, d. 11/8/1999 at 90 in Glencliff; b. Somerville, MA; John
    Gould, Sr. and Abbe Mcdona

Jennie, d. 2/22/1976 at 72 in Woodsville; housewife; b. MI; John
Nelson and Inga Swanson
Paul C., d. 12/21/1981 at 80 in White River Jct., VT; construction; b.
IL; Carl Carlson and Olivia Borstell

CARPENTER,
Frank A., d. 2/1/1937 at 61 in Hanover; farmer; widower; b. Warren;
William Carpenter and Ella Clough
Mrs. Ora E., d. 7/9/1914 at 63/8/17 in Warren; married; b. Warren;
Aaron Jewett Clough (Warren) and Martha Thompson (Pittston,
ME)
Nellie A., d. 6/13/1915 at 35/9/24 in Warren; housewife; married; b.
Dorchester; John S. Merrill (WI) and Emma Streeter (NH)
Ora E., d. 6/13/1915 at – in Warren; b. Warren; Frank A. Carpenter
(Vershire, VT) and Nellie A. Merrill (Dorchester)
William E., d. 12/17/1929 at 77/7/17; widower; b. Benton; Charles B.
Carpenter and Nancy A. Goodwin

CARSON,
Frank, d. 1/21/1904 at – in Warren; stillborn; b. Warren; Frank
Carlson (Bangor, NY) and Julia M. Lontine (Westmore, VT)

CARTER,
Evelyn B., d. 1/4/1982 at 72 in Concord
Harry William, d. 2/17/1923 at 0/0/0 in Warren; b. Warren; William I.
Carter (Lunenburg, VT) and Evelyn B. Hildreth (Warren)
Marion Louise, d. 4/17/1979 at 83 in Warren; homemaker; b.
Charlestown, MA; Fred Pitman and Louise -----

CARTWRIGHT,
Byron K., d. 5/16/1958 at 11 weeks in Warren; b. Plymouth; David
Cartwright and Thelma Ramsdell

CASSADY,
Henry J., d. 1/28/1980 at 54 in Manchester; sign painter; b. IN;
Harley Cassady and Pauline Flynn

CASWELL,
Addie J., d. 1/13/1923 at 82/8/24 in Glencliff; widow; b. Warren;
Jonathan Little (Canaan) and Mary Currier (Warren)

Alfreda B., d. 2/27/1900 at 48/10/21 in Warren; paralysis;
  housekeeper; married; b. Warren; Eben Swain and Nancy
  Libbey
Clarence A., d. 1/2/1928 at 69/9/21; mail messenger; widower; b.
  Warren; William Caswell (Warren) and Addie Little (Warren)
Edward T., d. 6/8/1915 at 70/8 in Warren; retired; widower; b.
  Haverhill; Newell Caswell (Moultonboro) and Mary Parsley
  (Moultonboro)
Mary, d. 12/17/1890 at 84/7/1 in Warren; tuberculosis of intestines;
  b. Moultonborough; Humphrey Hodgdon (Berwick, ME,
  deceased) and Lydia Brown (Moultonborough)
Nellie E., d. 7/30/1893 at 31 in Warren; phthisis pul.; housekeeper;
  Joseph Patch
Nellie M., d. 2/27/1946 at 76/3/3 in Warren; postmaster; widow; b.
  Greensboro, VT; Joseph Hale Clark (Stannard, VT) and Jane
  Folsom (Wheelock, VT)
Susie E., d. 2/7/1887 at 27/11/19; housewife; married; Albin N. Nash
  and Mary A. Haley
William H., d. 4/28/1910 at 75/8/27 in Warren; apoplexy, acute
  indigestion; farmer; married; b. Warren

CATE,
Lloyd, d. 12/23/2005 in Woodsville; George Cate and Ruth Edmunds

CAVERHILL,
Helen C., d. 12/11/2003 in Warren; William Hildreth and Marguerite
  Veasey
Mary S., d. 5/19/1967 at 70 in Haverhill; housewife; married; b.
  Laconia; Charles Beaman and Sarah Clement
Ulysses Raymond, d. 3/10/1973 at 75 in Warren; paper worker; b.
  Canada; Peter Caverhill and Joan Fox
Wayne P., d. 5/25/1990 at 38 in Hanover; boiler man; b. Plymouth;
  David Caverhill and Helen E. Hildreth

CHADBOURNE,
Clifton, d. 6/27/2003 in Glencliff; Clifton Chadbourne and Irene
  Brackley

CHAMPNEY,
Jody E., d. 11/21/2003 in Plymouth; Henry Champney and Bonnie
  Russell

CHANDLER,
Allen, d. 5/7/1978 at 94 in Bradford, VT
Martha A., d. 1/31/1899 at 60/7/9 in Warren; pneumonia;
    housekeeper; widow; b. Hanover; Aden Sweet
Martha Gale, d. 10/31/1977 at 87 in Berlin; housewife; b. NH;
    William Gale and Belle K. Simpson

CHAPMAN,
Harold B., d. 3/20/1905 at 17/6/23 in Warren; chron. nephritis;
    laborer; single; b. Orford; Perley Chapman (Ludlow, MA) and
    Marietta Willis (Warren)

CHAREST,
Leo, d. 10/12/1972 at 70 in Concord; caretaker; b. NH; Jarome
    Charest and Norma LaRiviere

CHASE,
Amos L., d. 3/25/1951 at 84 in Warren; farming; married; b.
    Piermont; Henry Chase and Zilpah A. Wright
Frank Edward, d. 1/26/1929 at 42/7; married; b. Bath; Fred Chase
    (Bath) and Maggie Hazelton (Plattsburg, NY)

CHASSON,
Ella A., d. 1/10/1961 at 73 in Haverhill; housewife; widow; b. Warren;
    Edward Houghton and Delia Wolcott
Esther D., d. 8/11/1994 at 89 in Grinnell, IA; teacher; b.
    Bloomington, IL; Robert T. Chasson and Belle Downs
Frederick J., d. 6/8/1958 at 73 in Haverhill; groundsman; married; b.
    Middletown, NB; Hector Chasson and Rebecca Ross
Paul Edward, d. 11/5/1936 at – in Plymouth; b. Plymouth; Edward
    Chasson and Esther Bozarth

CHENEY,
Donald Wayne, d. 12/29/1993 at 47 in Woodsville; self employed; b.
    Haverhill; Irvin Cheney and Rita Horton

CHRISTOU,
Paul Joseph, d. 9/15/1995 at 77 in Haverhill; laborer; b. Lowell, MA;
    Joseph Christoun and Pauline Mayhew

CHRONIAK,
Patricia, d. 4/24/1985 at – in Concord; burial permit

CHRYSTIE,
Richard, d. 5/15/2004 in Chocorua; Richard Chrystie and Helen
Hammond

CLARK,
daughter, d. 6/3/1926 at – in Warren; b. Warren; Enos I. Clark
(Warren) and Avis Gray (Centre Harbor)
Albert W., d. 5/5/1922 at 31/0/2 in Benton; RRA agent; single; b. Fall
River, MA; Thomas Clark and Emma Morse
Avis May, d. 5/19/1950 at 49 in Wolfeboro; at home; widow; b.
Center Harbor; Frank Gray and Mary Bonner
Dorothy M., d. 4/30/1980 at 74 in Concord; retired; b. VT; Charles
Sweet and Melissa -----
Enos I., d. 9/5/1947 at 69/7/13 in Ashland; lumberman; married; b.
Warren; Walter Clark (Montpelier, VT) and Lucy Moses
(Chichester)
John L., d. 3/22/1902 at 78/0/15 in Warren; peritonitis; farmer;
married
John P., d. 9/7/1915 at 35 in Warren; tel. operator; single; b.
Campton, PQ; Matthew Clark (Canada) and Bridget Lynch
(Ireland)
Lucy M., d. 11/22/1929 at 68/4/2; housekeeper; widow; b.
Chichester; William Moses and N. Fellows
Martha R., d. 2/5/1892 at 61/2/11 in Warren; consumption;
housewife; b. Monroe; Rev. P. Mason (Munroe) and Betsy
Johnson
Sallie M., d. 3/31/1909 at 76 in Warren; old age; housewife; widow
Sarah J., d. 12/7/1918 at 83/3/4 in Warren; retired; widow; b. Gilford
Stevens K., d. 9/7/1894 at 69/10 in Warren; paralysis; carpenter;
John Clark (Piermont) and Mary Knight
Thomas Joseph, d. 5/16/2004 in Warren; Stanley Clark and Minerva
Orser
Wilbur A., d. 7/6/1983 at 77 in Plymouth; carpenter; b. Meredith;
Frank Clark and Zella Reed
Wilbur O., d. 2/1/2000 in Ix; Wilbur Clark and Dorothy Sweet
Zell A., d. 5/25/1907 at 20/9 in Warren; bron. consumption;
housekeeper; married; b. Tilton; O. S. Reed (Grafton) and Alice
Berry (MI)

CLEMENT,

Alpha, d. 10/18/1909 at 74/0/23 in Warren; atoxic panapligia; engineer; widower; b. Warren; Benjiman Clement and Dolly Aikin

Amos, d. 12/17/1887 at 67/0/9; farmer; married; Moses Clement and Hannah Little

Burgess, d. 12/31/1901 at 74/5 in Warren; bron. pneumonia; farmer; single; b. Warren; Benjamin Clement (Warren) and Dolly Aiken

Daniel Q., d. 12/31/1901 at 75/7 in Concord; arteriosclerosis; farmer; married; b. Warren; Moses H. Clement and Tamar Little

Eunice E., d. 11/23/1916 at 90/0/2 in Warren; retired; widow; b. Warren; Jonathan Clough (Warren) and Sally Pillsbury (Warren)

Frank C., d. 11/3/1919 at 66 in Warren; produce dealer; married; b. Warren; Joseph Clement (Warren) and Eunice Clough (Warren)

Grace W., d. 5/7/1930 at 84/10/23 in Concord; retired; widow; b. Dorchester

Joseph, d. 8/6/1890 at 72/4/3 in Warren; dysentery; farmer; b. Warren; Moses H. Clement (Warren, deceased) and Tamor Little (Warren)

Leigh A., d. 11/12/1940 at 63/0/12; retired; single; b. Warren; Daniel O. Clement (Warren) and G. Woodworth (Dorchester)

Mary Alice, d. 1/20/1929 at 56/7/10; housewife; widow; b. Warren; John Davis (Haverhill) and Sarah Eastman (Orange, VT)

Mary C., d. 4/29/1914 at 84/2/21 in Warren; widow; b. Warren; Samuel L. Merrill (Warren) and Sally Noyes (Atkinson)

Philoxena, d. 9/29/1904 at 66/0/27 in Warren; manition; housewife; married; b. Wentworth; Hazen Libby (Benton) and Mehitable Clifford (Dorchester)

Warren L., d. 6/14/1933 at 56/9/26; retired; married; b. Woburn, MA; Albert A. Clement (Warren) and Emily Page (Pepperell, MA)

William, d. 10/1/1910 at 83/2/8 in Warren; cystitis; engineer; married; b. Warren

CLEVELAND,

Anna M., d. 5/29/1941 at 46; housewife; married; b. Laconia; William Gale (Warren) and Belle Simpson

CLIFFORD,

Emma J., d. 12/29/1928 at 83/8/7; housekeeper; widow; b. Vasileboro, ME

George C., d. 3/10/1901 at 55/3/15 in Warren; locomotor ataxia; landlord; married; b. Warren; Simeon Clifford (Warren) and Sally Boynton (Orford)

Hannah C., d. 12/25/1942 at 72/5/21; housewife; widow; b. Boston, MA; John B. Cameron (Scotland) and C. McDonald

Iolas C., d. 9/27/1932 at 67/10; barber; married; b. Warren; William Clifford (NH) and Abbie Hazelton (NH)

Iolas W., Jr., d. 10/21/1929 at 3/10/3; b. Woodsville; Iolas William Clifford (Warren) and Louise Rosa (VT)

Louise C., d. 11/16/1928 at 25/6/21; housework; married; b. S. Ryegate, VT; John Rosa (Italy) and Florence Sanarvo (Italy)

Marion W., d. 3/27/1925 at 75 in Warren; widow; b. Cambridge; Charles Tucker

Russell S., d. 8/8/1897 at 52/7 in Warren; Bright's disease; jeweler; married; b. Wentworth; Russell F. Clifford and Sarah Fitts

Sarah, d. 1/24/1900 at 93/0/10 in Warren; old age; houusekeeper; b. S. Hampton; Joseph Fitts (S. Hampton) and Sarah French (S. Hampton)

William, d. 4/14/1917 at 76/4/8 in Warren; pensioner; married; Russell F. Clifford and Sarah Fitz

Zechariah Loren, d. 10/5/1935 at 86/1/8 in Warren; retired; single; b. Warren; Russell Clifford and Sarah Fitts

CLINE,

Lois, d. 8/15/1995 at 86 in Haverhill; telephone worker; b. Broken Bos, NB; William Cline and Lily Mast

CLOGSTON,

Marjorie P., d. 2/18/2004 in Warren; Lucien Parris and Violet Parris

CLOUGH,

Chester A., d. 7/25/1970 at 68 in Hanover; dyer; b. NH; Birt Clough and Edna Eldbridge

George M., d. 5/2/1908 at 81/3/19; paralysis; carpenter; single; b. Warren; Amos Clough (Warren) and Ora Jewett (Beverly, MA)

Mary A., d. 10/6/1915 at 90/7/26 in Warren; housewife; widow; b. Wentworth; John Pillsbury (Wentworth) and Mehitable Clifford (Wentworth)

Mattie M., d. 3/18/1938 at 70; teacher; single; b. Warren; Jewett
　　Clough (ME)
Millard C., d. 12/1/1932 at 76/6/23
Minnie B., d. 3/27/1887 at 22/0/14; housewife; married; b.
　　Washington, VT; Harvey Williams (Bridgewater, VT) and Mary
　　Havendon (Randolph, VT)
Pearl Lucille, d. 11/16/1961 at 69 in Hanover; housewife; married; b.
　　Warren; Arthur Whitcher and Eleanor Shortt

COLBY,
Olcott, d. 4/16/1893 at 89/11 in Warren; old age; farmer; b. Hill;
　　Isaac Colby
Olcott, d. 7/21/1912 at 73/4/4 in Warren; ulcer; laborer; widower; b.
　　Warren; Olcott Colby (Hill) and Abigail Barker (Warren)
Richard W., d. 4/4/1999 in Haverhill; Leon Colby and Irene Voloscak

COLEMAN,
Elizabeth, d. 9/27/1900 at 78/4 in Warren; old age; housekeeper;
　　widow; b. Warren; Daniel Merrill (Warren) and Abigail Pillsbury
　　(VT)

COLLIER,
Otis F., d. 8/13/1966 at 73 in Haverhill; married; b. Wytopitlock, ME;
　　Lorenzo Collier and May Pierce
Pearl B., d. 1/3/1974 at 76 in Haverhill; teacher & storekeeper; b.
　　NH; Joel I. Batchelder and Estella A. Clifford

COLSON,
Alice M., d. 2/19/1973 at 69 in Warren; housewife; b. MA; Allen O.
　　Goodman and Ada Yates

COMSTOCK,
Arthur C., d. 6/2/1973 at 89 in Warren; b. VT; William H. Comstock
　　and Carrie Robinson

CONNOR,
Louisa, d. 5/9/1921 at –; housekeeper; widow
Stephen, d. 5/1/1921 at 74/9/1 in Warren; farmer; married; b. Willey
　　House, Crawford Notch; James Connor (Wolfeboro) and
　　Elizabeth Cook (ME)

CONVERSE,

Frank, d. 12/4/1901 at 38 in Warren; accidental; laborer; widower; b. Canada; Asa C. Converse (Canada)

COOKE,

Marion, d. 3/28/1978 at 75 in Concord; hairdresser; b. Japan; Alou Cooke and Alice Smith

Stanley Neil, d. 8/15/1931 at 0/0/7; b. Plymouth; Alfred Cooke (New Britain, CT) and Mary Brandaburg (Elizabeth, NJ)

COOMBS,

Harold E., d. 8/15/1985 at 68 in Laconia; lumberman; b. Henniker; John L. Coombs and Julia Jameson

COPP,

Elizabeth M., d. 3/20/1924 at 78/5/16 in Warren; housewife; married; b. Massina, NY; Thomas Reed (Massina, NY) and Thebet'l Uyhengal (Fairlee, VT)

COTTON,

Anna M., d. 1/3/1897 at 31/6/1 in Warren; heart disease; housewife; married; b. Vineland, NJ; Samuel Blood and Juliet Hall

Dudley B., d. 9/17/1888 at 69/10 in Warren; married; b. Wentworth; Solomon Cotton and Anna Bixby

Edward D., d. 1/16/1929 at 72/4/2; farmer; married; b. Warren; Dudley B. Cotton (Warren) and Martha Abbott (Bath)

Edward Dean, d. 2/18/1944 at 25/7/22 in Warren; woodsman; single; b. Warren; Ralph P. Cotton (Warren) and Mary E. Moran (Philadelphia, PA)

Elizabeth M., d. 4/17/1951 at 69 in Plymouth; housewife; widow; b. Warren; John B. Moses and Viola B. Merrill

Flora Ayer, d. 7/10/1944 at 79 in Plymouth; widow; b. Warren; Anson Pillsbury and Elizabeth Ford (1962)

Henry L., d. 3/9/1940 at 79/4/29; dep. sheriff; married; b. Warren; Dudley B. Cotton (Bath) and Martha Abbott (Bath)

Mary E., d. 11/17/1975 at 84 in Hanover; b. PA; James T. Moran and Emily C. Smith

Polly C., d. 12/12/1910 at 94/7/24 in Warren; debility incident to old age; housewife; widow; b. Corinth, VT; Amos Sanborne (Corinth, VT) and Sally Clement (Corinth, VT)

Ralph P., d. 12/12/1964 at 75 in Warren; farmer; married; b. Warren; Edward D. Cotton and Flora Ayer Pillsbury

COUNTS,
Timothy L., d. 3/31/1991 in Washington, DC; salesperson; b. Bristol, TN; Billy A. Counts and Margaret Thompson

COVELL,
Roger, d. 3/27/2000 in Glencliff; Corliss Covell and Nora Mayberry

COVERT,
Emily C., d. 9/21/1971 at 71 in Haverhill; retired; b. MA; Warren Clement and Sigrid Johnson

COWING,
Wilbur F., d. 5/2/1888 at 39/5/3 in Warren; brakeman; married; b. Lisbon; E. B. Cowing and Eliza Turner

CREED,
Bertha M., d. 8/10/1967 at 70 in Henniker; at home; widow; b. Boston, MA; Peter Perry and Alice S. Perry
Harold S., d. 10/21/1966 at 71 in Concord; shipyard sup.; married; b. Rockland, ME; Andrew S. Creed and Jessie Sutherland

CRESS,
Ellen A., d. 3/14/1889 at 35/8/26 in Warren; consumption; housekeeping; married; b. Chichester; William Moses and Ellen
-----

CRIMMINGS,
John, d. 10/17/1897 at 65/10 in Warren; degeneration; farmer; widower; b. Ireland; John Crimmings

CROSS,
Ada, d. 5/13/1912 at 34 in Warren; apoplexy; housewife; married; b. Warren; Ira N. Libby (Warren) and Lucy Whiteman (Warren)
Frances Sarah, d. 4/2/1927 at 86/5/29 in Grafton; home; widow; b. Norwich, VT; Walden T. Cross (Acworth) and Mary L. Lord (Thetford, VT)
Seth M., d. 1/31/1887 at 1/11/9; b. Warren; E. H. Cross and E. A. Moses

CUMMINGS,

Ada, d. 5/29/1946 at 71/7/29 in Haverhill; housewife; widow; b. Gilford Ctr., VT; John William Davis and Lilla Armstrong

Carlos A., d. 1/28/1910 at 40 in VT; diabetes; laborer; single; b. Warren; John T. Cummings and Jennie Clark

Ellen H., d. 1/19/1899 at 54/11/6 in Warren; strangulated hernia; housewife; married; b. Benton; Gilbert P. Wright

Francis, d. 6/8/1913 at 78/11/15 in Warren; old age; farmer; widower; b. Chester, VT

George C., d. 12/14/1986 at 47 in Plymouth; burial permit

George William, d. 6/20/1973 at 62 in Haverhill; mason; b. NH; George W. Cummings and Ada Davis

John T., d. 11/2/1888 at 47/5/5 in Warren; farming; married; b. Warren; Calvin Cummings and Eva K. Sinclair

Martha L., d. 6/18/1895 at 16/8/10 in Warren; typhoid fever; scholar; b. Warren; F. C. Cummings (farmer) and Ellen M. Wright

Mazie Pearl, d. 10/22/1975 at 62 in Warren; housewife; b. NH; Charles Wistner and Catherine Shortt

Walker, d. 7/10/1969 at 91 in Warren; auditor; b. ME; Thomas Cummings and Ellen Barker

CURRIER,

Arvilla A., d. 1/26/1897 at 59/0/14 in Warren; consumption; housewife; married; Willard Pearson and Harriet Avery

Gertrude, d. 12/13/1986 at 77 in Franklin; burial permit

John S., d. 2/1/1955 at 90 in Sanbornton; farmer painter; married; b. Ashland; Edwin Currier and Mary Smith

William, d. 5/17/1899 at 68/10/12 in Warren; heart disease; carpenter; widower; b. Danbury; Willard Currier

CUSHING,

Irving Beecher, d. 5/16/1945 at 55/4/17 in Warren; merchant; married; b. Freeport, ME; Henry Cushing (Freeport, ME) and Evelyn Rogers (Freeport, ME)

Lexie Frances, d. 9/27/1990 at 75 in Woodsville; homemaker; b. Portland, ME; Leonard B. Cushing, Sr. and Annie Shores

CUTTING,

Charles E., d. 1/22/1985 at – in Rumney; burial permit

Mary M., d. 6/14/1974 at 75 in Franconia; housewife; b. CT; John G. Theurer and Clara E. Ladish

DALE,

Alfred H., d. 9/28/1958 at 86 in Haverhill; teamster; married; b. Rexton, NB; William Dale and Elizabeth Porter

DAMON,

Susan E., d. 2/7/1935 at 85/8/27 in Warren; housework; widow; b. Lyme; Louis Dimick

DANA,

Burage V., d. 4/15/1911 at – in Warren; heart disease; married

James P., d. 4/5/1890 at 42/4/15 in Warren; railroad accident; painter; b. Warren; Walcott Dana (Andover, MA, deceased) and Rhoda Fifield (Bath)

DAVIS,

son, d. 9/23/1895 at 0/0/4 in Warren; spasms; b. Warren; John E. Davis (laborer) and Effie L. Annis

Anna, d. 11/17/1910 at 68/8/23 in Haverhill; widow

Charles, d. 6/1/1905 at – in Warren; dis. of heart; farmer; married

Charles Henry, d. 6/27/1929 at 85/7; retired; widow; b. Haverhill; Daniel Davis (Haverhill) and Mary S. Rollins (Haverhill)

Effie, d. 12/29/1909 at 37/9 in Warren; carcinoma (uterus); housewife; married; b. Warren

Homer N., d. 6/1/1899 at 0/5/20 in Warren; malformation of heart; b. Warren; John E. Davis

John E., d. 3/1/1935 at 74/4/20 in Concord; RR section; married; b. E. Haverhill; Edith Colby

Lena Belle, d. 5/17/1978 at 66 in Franconia; housewife; b. Piermont; James White and Katherine Gildin

Mary, d. 2/12/1938 at 78/9/27; widow; b. Landaff; Samuel Howland and Lucinda Bowles

Mary H., d. 1/11/1902 at 53 in Concord; perunioces ana'ce; housewife; married; b. Dunbarton; John P. Tenney

Ralph Allan, d. 2/3/1995 at 93 in Haverhill; laborer; b. Haverhill, MA; Charles H. Davis and Etta G. Harmon

Sarah W., d. 6/21/1896 at 54/6/7 in Warren; spinal men.; housewife; married; b. Corinth, VT; Lyman Eastman and Polly Patch

William Alfred, d. 4/18/1946 at 75/9/1 in Warren; painter carp.; b. Warren; John William Davis (Williamstown, MA) and Lillian Armstrong (Hinsdale)

DEARBORN,

Howard S., d. 7/8/2001 in Woodsville; Henry Dearborn and Grace Silver

DEFOREST,

Marie E., d. 10/17/1983 at 64 in Hanover; housewife; b. Stamford, CT; Frank Croxford and Florence Rice

DELANEY,

James, d. 9/28/1894 at 58 in Warren; cardiac init.; laborer; b. Melborne, Canada; John Delaney (Ireland) and Mary Kilijile

DENNIS,

Fred W., d. 11/11/1900 at 33/2/9 in Warren; disease of heart; carpenter; married; b. N. Hatley, PQ; William Dennis (England) and Elizabeth Richards (England)

DEROSIA,

Bessie Lovella, d. 5/6/1973 at 80 in Plymouth; housewife; b. NH; John Davis and Effie -----

Flossie May, d. 2/19/1999 at 97 in S. Hadley, MA; home maker; b. Wentworth; Hiram B. Rollins and Addie Hammond

John, d. 3/29/1941 at 48/0/2; driller & quarry; widower; b. Benton; Dominie Derosia (Canada) and Phoebe Gilmin (Canada)

Leo, Jr., d. 10/9/1998 at 57 in Plymouth; residential builder; b. Newport, VT; Leo F. Derosia, Sr. and Ruth Merrill

Louis J., d. 12/31/1956 at 65 in Glencliff; lineman ret.; married; b. Benton; Joseph Derosia

Nillie, d. 5/25/1967 at 74 in Haverhill; married; b. Warren; Leon Tibbetts and Carrie Fifield

Zeb, d. 2/19/1976 at 89 in Glencliff; retired railroad; b. Canada; Joe Derosia and Josephine Lavoie

DERRICK,

George Edward, d. 8/26/1947 at 80/6/17 in Plymouth; woodsman; married; b. Troy, VT; Camel Derrick and Patience Boardman

DESCHENES,

Clairl, d. 2/22/1995 at 65 in Glencliff; none; b. Nashua; Joseph Deschenes and Adele Berube

DESROSIERS,
Robert, d. 11/17/1978 at 75 in Plymouth; never worked; b. Pembroke; Joseph Desrosiers and Marguerite Lacasse

DEVOID,
Earle Edward, d. 12/1/1923 at 1/9/26 in Warren; b. Lincoln, VT; George Devoid (N. Fren'g, VT) and Christine Sprague (Fram'ham)

DICEY,
Ella, d. 5/25/1930 at 31 in Hanover; married; b. Orford; Hyman Rollins (NH) and Addie ----- (NH)
Vernon Elwin, d. 5/12/1962 at 76 in Franklin; lumberman; widower; b. Alexandria; William Dicey and Levine Waldron

DIDSBURY,
Anne, d. 4/3/1976 at 52 in Laconia; sales mgr.; b. RI; Michael Babon

DOLE,
Margaret, d. 8/3/1896 at 10 in Warren; heart failure; b. Concord

DONALDSON,
Marilyn P., d. 6/1/1983 at 53 in Boston, MA; teacher; b. Newton, MA; Paul Merrill and Winifred Perry

DONNELLY,
Joseph B., d. 10/1/1939 at 35; Capt. CCC; married; b. Pittsfield, MA; Michael Donnelly (New Lebanon, NY) and Anna Nelson (Oconta, WI)

DOW,
J. M., d. 9/9/1893 at 84/6 in Warren; dysentery; farmer; b. Warren; James Dow (Plaistow) and Hannah Merrill
Louisa M., d. 9/27/1893 at 74/10 in Warren; unknown; housewife; b. Warren; Daniel Patch (Warren) and Betsey Hall

DOWNING,
Ann, d. 12/19/1913 at 83/5/16 in Warren; chronic nephritis; b. Littleton; Alfred Wright (Littleton) and Harriet Bowman (Littleton)

DUFFLEY,
Rita E., d. 3/15/2003 in Glencliff; James Duffley and Margaret Smith

DUFFY,
Willaim, d. 9/6/1999 in Woodsville; Willaim Duffy and Gracia Hardy

DUNBAR,
Robert W., d. 7/14/1940 at 46/7/26; selectman; married; b. New York, NY; John B. Dunbar (ME) and Jessie Cape (NY)

DUNN,
Kenneth M., d. 9/3/1900 at 0/11/18 in Warren; convulsions; b. Hooksett; Charles H. Dunn (New London, CT) and Phebe Martin (NS)

DURWAY,
Susan, d. 8/9/1912 at 56/3/23 in Warren; chronic endocarditis; housewife; b. Warren; Nicholas Whiteman (Warren) and Hannah Libby (Warren)

EAMES,
Mary E., d. 6/6/1912 at 48/1/12 in Warren; housewife; married; b. Wentworth; Amos Rollins (Wentworth) and Louise Rollins (Haverhill)

EASTMAN,
Addison W., d. 11/29/1888 at 65 in Warren; minister; widower
Arthur E., d. 9/10/1902 at 41/2/5 in Warren; nervous dyspepsia; conductor; married; b. Littleton; George W. Eastman (E. Concord) and Lois B. Elliott (Irasburg, VT)
Benjamin F., d. 3/7/1923 at 91/8/23 in Warren; retired; widower; b. Warren; Jesse Eastman and Sally Wyman
Damon Jesse, d. 6/1/1976 at 72 in Laconia; maintenance; b. NH; George Eastman and Margaret McCutcheon
Daymon Y., d. 11/12/1892 at 67/6/15 in Warren; dis. of heart; wheelwright; b. Warren; Jesse Eastman (Warren) and Sally Wyman
Edmund W., d. 8/15/1927 at 87/1/2; retired; widower; b. Orange, VT; Lyman Eastman (Orange, VT) and Polly N. Patch (Warren)
George C., d. 11/25/1952 at 94 in Lanham, MD; retired; widower; b. Warren; Benjamin F. Eastman and Lydia Upton

Lydia E., d. 6/1/1921 at 88/0/17 in Warren; domestic; married; b. Lyndeboro; Russell Upton and Lydia Grey (Wilton)

Lydia L., d. 8/6/1909 at 86/11/18 in Warren; debil. incident to old age; housekeeper; widow; b. Litchfield; Asa Patch and Mary Thompson

Martha J., d. 3/6/1897 at 56/9/6 in Warren; consumption; housewife; married; b. Topsham, VT; William Rogers and Sarah Colby

Myra, d. 6/12/1918 at 68/0/15 in Warren; housekeeper; married

Nellie D., d. 8/24/1903 at 39/0/13 in Warren; meningitis; housekeeper; widow; b. Warren; Damon Eastman (Warren) and Sophia B. Patch (Warren)

Sophia B., d. 11/28/1903 at 72/10/28 in Warren; anasarca; housekeeper; widow; b. Warren; Jacob Patch (Warren) and Sophia Brown (Wentworth)

EATON,

Alice E., d. 11/14/1929 at 79; retired; widow; b. E. Orange, VT; Lyman Eastman (E. Orange, VT) and Polly Patch

Ezra B., d. 9/5/1905 at 76/7/2 in Warren; cereb. scharosis; ret. merchant; married; b. Plymouth; Ezra B. Eaton (Plymouth) and Mary Currier (Wentworth)

Hannah, d. 2/1/1929 at 89/10/11; at home; widow; b. E. Warren; Joseph French and Mary Batchelder

Johnathan M., d. 8/5/1888 at 94/1/25 in Warren; b. Wentworth; Job Eaton (Plaistow) and Phebe Eaton (Kingston)

Melissa, d. 12/2/1902 at 67/2/3 in Warren; marmeary carcinoma; housewife; married; b. Warren; Thomas Pillsbury (Warren) and Sally Clement (Warren)

William F., d. 6/15/1916 at 82/0/13 in Warren; retired; married; b. Warren; Jonathan M. Eaton (Wentworth) and Betsey Merrill (Warren)

EDWARDS,

Carrie Emma, d. 4/15/1943 at 89/0/14; widow; b. Warren; John French (Warren) and Sarah Willey (Benton)

ERICKSON,

Paul, d. 1/11/2003 in Glencliff; Joseph Erickson and Naomi Johnson

EVANS,

Harry H., d. 10/6/1952 at 78 in Warren; sawyer; widower; b. Madbury; David Evans and Eliza Hayes

Helen K., d. 10/22/2003 in N. Haverhill; Clarence Kemp and Annie Smith

Reginald S., d. 3/8/1986 at 85 in Plymouth; fish & game; b. Madbury; Harry Evans and Bertha Swain

Robb S., d. 8/1/1990 at 17 in Hanover; student; b. Plymouth; Gerald Evans and Emily Olin

EVERETT,

Elwood S., d. 3/13/1937 at 55/3/13 in Warren; mechanic; married; b. Bath; Edward Everett and Mary Elliott

FAILEY,

Mary, d. 11/24/1939 at 76/3/22; housewife; married; b. Goffstown; Harrison Moses (Goffstown) and Matilda Whitcher (Goffstown)

FARINEAU,

Florence E., d. 9/18/1995 at 68 in Gardner, MA

FARNHAM,

Joseph B., d. 10/9/1887 at 90/5/26; farmer; widower

FARNSWORTH,

Austin, d. 8/4/1954 at 54 in Rumney; road agent; married; b. Rumney; Clarence Farnsworth and Winnie L. Farnsworth

FELLOWS,

Benjamin, d. 11/29/1938 at 12 hrs.; b. Wentworth; Carle J. Fellows (Rumney) and Hattie Schofield (Rochester, VT)

Charles F., d. 2/5/1929 at 77/11/23; farmer; married; b. Chichester; Ebenezer K. Fellows and Susan Haines

Ebenezer K., d. 2/24/1904 at 78/2/14 in Warren; val. dis. of heart; farmer; widower; b. Chichester; Ebenezer Fellows (Chichester) and Betsey Moses

Ellen A., d. 11/14/1942 at 90/0/12; housewife; widow; b. Haverhill; William Gould and O. M. Spooner

Irene Gladys, d. 11/9/1957 at 10 in Plymouth; student; b. Wentworth; Carl Fellows and Hattie Schofield

Luella M., d. 1/4/1940 at 0/0/7; b. Wentworth; Carl J. Fellows (E. Rumney) and H. H. Schofield (Lynn, MA)

FERGUSON,
Nancy E., d. 6/18/1900 at 56/2/3 in Warren; diabetes; housekeeper; married; b. Warren; Jared S. Blodgett (Wentworth) and Priscilla Noyes (Landaff)

FERNANDEZ,
Pamela, d. 12/17/2004 in Woodsville; Harold Killian and Patricia Robert

FERRIN,
Lydia, d. 6/4/1912 at 89/9/21 in Warren; old age; housewife; widow; b. Warren; Henry D. Whitcher and Ruth Hooper (Rumney)

FIFIELD,
stillborn son, d. 4/6/1908 at –; b. Warren; Ethelbert Fifield (Warren) and Marion Morrison (Lawrence, MA)
Clayton A., d. 6/22/1924 at 0/1/14 in Warren; b. Warren; Alba Fifield (Warren) and Belle Sampson (Portsmouth)
Edwin L., d. 3/19/1907 at 62 in Warren; paralysis; farmer; widower; b. Warren
Effie May, d. 11/9/1961 at 77 in Barnstead Parade; housewife; widow; b. Plymouth; Alba B. Heath and Mary Howland
Harry A., d. 9/15/1925 at 51/5/12 in Warren; farmer; married; b. Warren; Lorenzo Fifield (Warren) and Jane Hendry (Franconia)
Jane, d. 1/4/1910 at 67 in Warren; heart disease; housewife; married
Lorenzo D., d. 9/21/1924 at 77/8/13 in Glencliff; farmer; widower; b. Warren; Lorenzo D. Fifield (Warren) and Sarah Whitcher (Warren)
Mabel L. Eastman, d. 4/17/1944 at 69/10/25 in Warren; housewife; widow; b. Warren; Benjamin F. Eastman (Warren) and Lydia E. Upton (Warren)
Mary Ann, d. 11/6/1903 at 57/0/21 in Warren; valvular dis. heart; housekeeper; married; b. Warren; Addison Gerald (NY) and Mary H. Merrill (Warren)
Melvin B., d. 9/2/1953 at 74 in Warren; day labor; married; b. Warren; Edwin Fifield and Mary Ann Gerald

Miriam F., d. 10/15/1928 at 66/9; housework; widow; b. Manchester;
    Charles Morrison (NH)
Royal D., d. 8/14/1902 at 64/0/25 in Warren; cancer of stomach;
    farmer; married; b. Warren; Isaac Fifield (Holderness) and
    Mary Downing (Holderness)
Wilson, d. 9/16/1924 at 35/5/5 in Glencliff; farmer; single; b. Warren;
    Ethelbut Fifield (Warren) and Marion Morrison (Lawrence, MA)

FLANDERS,
son, d. 10/9/1899 at – in Warren; stillborn; b. Warren; Rufus
    Flanders
son, d. 11/1/1900 at – in Warren; stillborn; b. Warren; Rufus
    Flanders (Warren) and Lulla Bancroft (N. Benton)
Ellen, d. 8/11/1917 at 32/8/9 in Warren; housewife; b. Warren; Asa
    Dowse and Synthia -----
Emery F., d. 2/8/1923 at 78/5/23 in Warren; retired; married; b.
    Warren; Samuel Flanders and Annie Foote (Warren)
Emily J., d. 4/20/1940 at 75/10/11; house work; single; b. Warren;
    Sylvester Flanders and Sarah Willis
Fannie E., d. 2/21/1896 at 12/1/14 in Warren; consumption; b.
    Warren; Jason E. Flanders and S. J. Muchmore
Frank, d. 10/20/1945 at 89/7/1 in Wentworth; farmer; widower; b.
    Benton; Sylvester Flanders and Sarah Willey (Warren)
Harry H., d. 8/4/1951 at 77 in Haverhill; farmer; divorced; b. Warren;
    Sylvester Flanders and Sarah Willey
Jason E., d. 3/6/1922 at 85/5/29 in Warren; farmer; widower; b.
    Warren; Samuel Flanders (Warren) and Annie Foote
Jessie Josephine, d. 8/5/1944 at 85/8/12 in Wentworth; housewife;
    married; b. Warren; Joseph P. Boynton (Orford) and Mary S.
    Burnham (Canada)
Leonard M., d. 12/27/1934 at 56/8/24; farmer; married; b. Warren;
    Jason Flanders (Warren) and Sarah Muchmore (Orford)
Martha, d. 6/27/1926 at 89/10/3 in Warren; at home; b. Franconia
Mary, d. 2/12/1909 at – in Warren; stillborn; b. Warren; Nancy
    Flanders (Warren)
Myrie R., d. 8/11/1917 at 12/0/14 in Warren; school boy; b. Warren;
    Leonard Flanders (Warren) and Ellen Downs (Warren)
Myrtie Colburn, d. 8/31/1935 at 52/7/24 in Haverhill; housework;
    married; b. Piermont; Artemas Colburn and Elizabeth Brooks
Nora A., d. 3/28/1942 at 67/11/23; housewife; widow; b. Lewiston,
    ME; Napoleon Burke (Canada) and Laura -----

Raymond H., d. 12/11/1915 at 12/1/27 in Warren; schoolboy; b. Nashua; Ernest L. Flanders (Lyme) and Anne McCutcheon (NS)

Sarah A., d. 7/19/1922 at 89/6/24 in Warren; evangelist; widow; b. Warren; Nathan Willey and Mary French

Sarah J., d. 4/20/1915 at 72/6/13 in Warren; housewife; married; b. Orford; James Muchmore and Sarah J. Bunton

FOOTE,

Bert L., d. 4/2/1951 at 76 in Warren; farmer; widower; b. Warren; Charles G. Foote and Emma Eastman

Charles G., d. 11/11/1931 at 78/10/2; farmer; b. Warren; Samuel E. Foote and Abagail Swain

Charles Guy, d. 9/13/1956 at 80 in Orford; farmer; married; b. Warren; Charles G. Foote and Emma MacMurphy

Clarabel, d. 6/18/1946 at 74/8/3 in Warren; housewife; married; b. Denver, CO; Harry H. Felch

Elmer R., d. 8/29/1903 at 0/10/23 in Warren; cholera infantum; b. Warren; Bert L. Foote (Warren) and Jennie Whitcher (Warren)

Emma C., d. 1/19/1929 at 49/1/22; housewife; married; b. Wentworth; X. P. Wright and Emogene Harris (Wentworth)

Emma F., d. 12/13/1921 at 67/1/16 in Laconia; retired; divorced; b. Derry; James MacMurphy (Derry) and Lydia E. Patch

Everett W., d. 6/5/1965 at 68 in Haverhill; widow; b. Warren; Bert Foote and Jennie Whitcher

Grace B., d. 5/12/1946 at 63/4/1 in Haverhill; housewife; married; b. Pittsford, VT; Frank Allard and Emily Thurston

Harry Lee, d. 11/30/1973 at 92 in Warren; retired farmer; b. NH; Charles Foote and Emma McMurphy

Ray Frank, d. 12/4/1961 at 73 in Bradford, VT; opr. movies; single; b. Orford; George E. Foote and Sarah E. Libbey

Sarah Etta, d. 7/27/1950 at 83 in Hanover; none; widow; b. Fairlee, VT; George Emery and Sarah Libbey

Timothy B., d. 12/2/1920 at 72 in Lyme; farmer; widower; b. Thetford, VT; Ezra B. Foote (Warren) and Sarah Burnham

FOSS,

Henry F., d. 8/31/1904 at 0/1 in Warren; manition; b. Warren; Edward Foss (Benton) and Cora Veazey (Bradford, VT)

FOSTER,

Adolphus G., d. 7/1/1916 at 81/4/11 in Warren; retired; widower; b. Hancock; John Foster (Hancock) and Mary Fletcher (Peterboro)

Clarice B., d. 7/24/1910 at 2/9/24 in Warren; infantile paralysis; b. Rochester; George Foster (Garland, ME) and Lula Keysar (Clarksville)

George A., d. 4/11/1914 at 33/10/15 in Hudson; married; b. Garland, ME; Rev. C. G. Foster (Gray, ME) and Marinda Flanders (Alton)

Lula E., d. 11/12/1939 at 63/6/23; housework; widow; b. Clarksville; Berkley Keysar (Clarksville) and Eliza Moses (Colebrook)

FOWLER,

Alice B., d. 11/17/1941 at 84/1/7; single; b. Addison, ME; James E. Sawyer (Addison, ME) and Frances Reed (Addison, ME)

John W., d. 9/14/1888 at 40/6/8 in Warren; married; b. Bristol; John Fowler (Sanbornton) and Susan Ingall (Bristol)

FRASER,

Sybil, d. 11/4/1909 at 62/7/24 in Warren; chronic myocaditis; housewife; married; b. Benton; Joseph P. Whitcher (Benton) and Jane Eliza Albert (Canada)

FRENCH,

son, d. 5/16/1934 at –; b. Warren; Alvie Fry and Addline L. French (Haverhill)

Albert J., d. 3/28/1902 at 54 in Laconia; heart disease; farmer; single; b. Warren; Reubin French (Warren) and ----- Batchelder (Warren)

Benjamin F., d. 5/31/1925 at – in Warren; farmer; widowerl b. Warren; Joseph French (Warren) and Mary Batchelder (Warren)

Benjamin H., d. 5/9/1961 at 72 in Springfield; laborer; widower; b. Warren; Oscar French and Emma E. Page

Bertrand C., d. 8/1/2000 in Warren; Bertrand French and Hazel Blake

David, d. 6/13/1908 at 69/6/2; musician; married; b. Warren; D. C. French and Ruth S. Colby

Edna B., d. 6/15/1895 at 1/3/29 in Warren; chol. morbus; b. Warren; Herbert H. French (laborer) and Eva A. Whiteman

Elsie M., d. 2/9/1889 at 71/1/24 in Warren; liver trouble, old age; housekeeping; widow; b. Warren; W. C. Batchelder and Sally --

---

Eva, d. 3/15/1940 at 72/0/19; at home; widow; b. J'h'sville, PQ; William Whiteman and Elvira Coffrin (Johnsville, PQ)

Flora, d. 6/20/1950 at 76 in Concord; housewife; married; b. VT; John Smith and Lytetia Crawford

George W., Jr., d. 2/3/1935 at 19/3/14 in Warren; laborer; single; b. Warren; George W. French and Flora O. Smith

George Washington, d. 12/5/1948 at 76/9/27 in Franklin; laborer; married; b. Warren; Lorenzo French (Warren)

Ina Brown, d. 12/26/1955 at 66 in Haverhill; housekeeper; married; b. Hanover; T. Franklin Brown and Georgianna Hutton

John, d. –/–/1888 at 82 in Warren

Osco H., d. 1/26/1895 at 58/9/26 in Warren; laudanum; farmer; b. Warren; Reuben French and Elsie Batchelder

Reuben, d. 6/11/1940 at 52/4/19; mill hand; married; b. Auford, Canada; Caleb R. French (Haverhill) and Anice Dubois (Canada)

Sarah, d. 7/6/1901 at 84/4/23 in Warren; senile mania; housekeeper; widow; b. Benton; Nathan Willey (Stoneham) and Betsey Larabee

William Guy, d. 12/16/1927 at 3/8 in Glencliff; b. Warren; Ruben French (Canada) and Velma Ladeau

FURGUSSON,
Hilda, d. 2/11/1901 at 4/6/10 in Warren; conges. of lungs; b. Springfield, MA; Daniel Furgusson (Canada) and Edith Farlane (Canada)

GAGNON,
Beatrice B., d. 12/19/2002 in Benton; Dominic Belliveau and Philomene Boucher

GALE,
Alonzo, d. 10/18/1897 at 84/9/20 in Warren; shock; farmer; widower; b. Amesbury, MA; Reuben Gale and Lydia Folsom

Andrew F., d. 2/6/1917 at 81/10/30 in Wentworth; retired; widower; Jacob Gale and Mary Heath

Anna S., d. 8/6/1922 at 66/3/9 in Laconia; house wife; married; b. Wentworth; Amos Rollins (Haverhill) and Louisa Cutting (Wentworth)

Bell K., d. 12/8/1954 at 91 in Haverhill; housewife; widow; b. Haverhill; Orin Simpson and Martha Caswell

Burton N., d. 5/2/1920 at 0/3 in Warren; b. Warren; Harry B. Gale (Warren) and Laura E. Libbey (Warren)

Frank, d. 1/28/1908 at 54/1; heart failure; farmer; single; b. Warren; Jacob Gale (Alexandria) and Mary Heath (Alexandria)

Fred Andrew, d. 9/9/1945 at 89/4/4 in Meredith; married; b. Warren; Freeman A. Gale (Warren) and Amelia Stevens

Harry B., d. 8/9/1964 at 82 in Haverhill; laborer; married; b. Warren; William F. Gale and Belle Simpson

Hattie E., d. 10/19/1949 at 80 in Ashland; housewife; widow; b. Haverhill; Arin E. Simpson and Martha Caswell

Horace B., d. 4/28/1938 at 82/7/5; retired; widower; b. Warren; Alonzo B. Gale (Warren) and Rhoda Fogg (Bridgewater)

James H., d. 9/3/1940 at 90/0/7; railroad man; widower; b. Warren; Alonzo Gale (Warren) and Rhoda Fogg (Bridgewater)

Laura E. Libbey, d. 11/14/1976 at 83 in Plymouth; housewife; b. Warren; Ira Libbey and Lucia Libbey

Lizzie Jane, d. 3/24/1932 at 78/1/10; housewife; married; b. Wentworth; Emerson Pillsbury (Warren) and Mary Jane Harris (Warren)

Mary J., d. 1/28/1929 at 72/7/5; housewife; widow; b. Wentworth; Joseph Kimball (Wentworth) and Julia Chase (Wentworth)

Rhoda, d. 1/28/1894 at 74/10/2 in Warren; old age; b. Bridgewater

Violet R., d. 12/18/1989 at 94 in Plymouth; administrative assistant; b. Coxsackie, NY; Harriet Van Loon

William Frank, d. 1/24/1929 at 84/5/17; farmer; b. Warren; Alonzo Gale and Rhoda Fogg

GALLANT,
Ruth Balch, d. 2/27/1913 at 0/0/3 in Warren; b. Warren; Thomas Gallant (PEI) and Florence Balch (Goffstown)

GANNETT,
Zella May, d. 6/17/1950 at 79 in Warren; music teacher; widow; b. Victory, VT; Lewis Young and Hannah Sabin

GARLAND,

Lillian F., d. 6/23/1974 at 56 in Goffstown; Emp. Scovill Aerosol Prod.; b. NH; Ernest Merrill and Mildred Fifield

Rachel P., d. 10/5/1901 at 76/4/5 in Warren; inflam. of bowels; housekeeper; married; b. Waterville, VT

Ruth C., d. 3/29/1893 at 67/4 in Warren; pneumonia; housekeeper; b. Warren; Nathan Willey (Stoneham, MA) and Mar. French

William, d. 8/26/1912 at 86/3/25 in Warren; old age; farmer; widower; b. Enfield; Simeon Garland (Enfield) and Eliza Gage (Enfield)

GARRANT,

Maurice, d. 12/31/1973 at 73 in Concord; none; b. Canada

GARRETT,

Laura, d. 10/29/1967 at 60 in Hanover; housework; widow; b. Keene; George W. Cummings and Ada B. C. Davis

GAUTHIER,

Lawrence L., d. 5/10/1983 in VT

GEIST,

John C., d. 6/30/1973 at 77 in Haverhill; retired painter; b. NH; John E. Geist and K. Strobel

GERALD,

Alma, d. 3/3/1938 at 74/7; housekeeper; widow; b. Lincoln; Addison Gerald (NY) and Mary Merill (Warren)

Francis L., d. 4/5/1914 at 76/3/0 in Warren; married; b. Warren; Addison W. Gerald (NY State) and Mary H. Merrill (Warren)

Mary H., d. 7/3/1902 at 86/10/12 in Warren; old age; housekeeper; widow; b. Warren; Samuel Merrill (Warren) and Hannah Elliott

GEREMIA,

Anna G., d. 2/2/1993 at 70 in Plymouth; cook; b. Harrisville, RI; Thomas Creighton and Catherine Clavin

GILL,

William J., d. 8/2/2002 in Glencliff; Allan Gill and Esther Gardner

GILMAN,

Samuel W., d. 6/15/1932 at 83/9/2; none; widower; b. Bangor, ME; Jonathan Gilman and Lydia Brown

GLEASON,

Ettie L., d. 3/23/1953 at 87 in Warren; housewife; widow; b. N. Haverhill; Lucien W. Prescott and Julia French

Fred C., d. 8/23/1941 at 75/5/23; merchant; married; b. Warren; O. S. Gleason (Westmoreland) and Ruth Clifford (Warren)

Kenneth Prescott, d. 7/10/1946 at 45/11/21 in Plymouth; salesman; single; b. Warren; Fred C. Gleason (Warren) and Ettie L. Prescott (N. Haverhill)

Orange S., d. 8/3/1924 at 87/0/26 in Warren; farmer; widower; b. Plymouth; Solomon Gleason and Jerushia Willard

Ruth C., d. 11/24/1918 at 86/9/27 in Warren; housewife; married; b. Warren; Russell F. Clifford (Warren) and Sarah Fitz

Salmon, d. 9/9/1889 at 85/2 in Warren; concussion of brain; clergyman; married; b. Langdon

GLODE,

Francis E., d. 11/9/1989 at 81 in Woodsville; inspector; b. Littleton; Walter Glode and Emile Cushing

GODEK,

Edward, d. 7/25/2000 in Woodsville; John Godek and Julia Rose

GODVILLE,

Edna Susan, d. 12/19/1958 at 60 in Pike; housewife; widow; b. Warren; William Shortt and Mabel Gould

James Dominic, d. 11/14/1949 at 53 in Warren; laborer; married; b. Russia; Frank Godville

GONYER,

Madeline, d. 9/23/2000 in Glencliff; Frank Brigham and Fern Willey

GOODWIN,

son, d. 11/7/1899 at – in Warren; stillborn; b. Laconia (sic); Charles B. Goodwin

son, d. 5/25/1930 at –; b. Warren; Harry L. Goodwin (Warren) and Bertha G. Gale (MA)

Bertha, d. 5/21/1973 at 83 in Hanover; housewife; b. MA; Charles
    Gale and Mary Kimball (adoptive parents)
Blanche E., d. 10/21/1897 at 2/3/24 in Warren; pneumonia; b.
    Warren; Charles B. Goodwin and Nellie Morey
Brian W., d. 11/29/1989 at 25 in Warren; mechanic; b. Plymouth;
    Ronald E. Goodwin and Lorita Downing
Everett W., d. 5/2/1995 at 84 in Plymouth; hatchery worker, game
    warden; Harry Goodwin and Bertha -----
Harry L., d. 11/14/1981 at 91 in Laconia; conservation officer; b. NH;
    Walter Goodwin and Georgianna Pease
Helen V., d. 11/19/1995 at 85 in Rumney; bookkeeper; b. Warren;
    Harry Gale and Laura Libby
John, d. 5/14/1888 at – in Warren; farmer; married
Maude W., d. 8/5/1933 at 49/1/2; housewife; divorced; b. Irasburg;
    Henry Hill (Shelburne, VT) and Mary Merrill (Warren)

GORDON,
Cynthia J., d. 9/3/2003 in Glencliff; Samuel Gordon and Marjorie
    Dean
Lillian, d. 8/28/1934 at 68; housewife; married; b. Warren; Joseph
    Little (Hill) and Eliza Crockett (Warren)
Wilbur C., d. 4/24/1948 at 83/11/2 in Concord; brakeman; widower;
    b. Benton; Horace W. Gordon (Landaff) and Lucinda Witcher
    (Benton)

GOSS,
George S., d. 9/1/1925 at 78 in Hanover; farmer; married

GOULD,
daughter, d. 8/6/1912 at – in Warren; stillborn; b. Warren; Frank
    Gould (Warren) and Mabel Gould (Bradford, VT)
Almiria E., d. 1/27/1926 at 65/9/3 in Warren; housewife; b.
    Colebrook; Malcomb Swett and Phebe McKinnon
Belle, Mrs., d. 5/18/1928 at 73/3/16; housewife; widow; b. Concord;
    George Wolcott (VT) and Electa Burke (VT)
Clara R., d. 7/5/1984 in Plymouth; burial permit
Eddie Wesley, d. 1/31/1945 at 82/1/9 in Plymouth; single; b. Warren;
    Henry Gould (Hanover) and Mahala Ford
Eugene H., d. 8/11/1914 at 38/4/13 in Warren; married; b. Warren;
    William Gould (Cape Breton) and Olive M. Spooner (Haverhill)

Henry B., d. 12/13/1908 at 87/5; heart disease; farmer; married; b. Cape Breton; William Gould

Leon Roscoe, d. 11/3/1956 at 63 in Plymouth; carpenter; married; b. Stewartstown; Charles Gould and Elmira Swett

Mary F., d. 1/9/1915 at 59/9/26 in Warren; housewife; married; b. Chichester; Ebenezer K. Fellows and Susan Haynes

Mary H., d. 4/29/1900 at 34/2/17 in Warren; heart disease; housekeeper; married; b. Haverhill; William G. Wolcott and Helen M. Day

Olive M., d. 12/23/1915 at 84/2/1 in Warren; retired; widow; b. Benton; Chester Spooner

William, Jr., d. 8/23/1899 at 75/10/1 in Warren

GRANT,

Linda L., d. 10/21/1992 at 43 in Lebanon; homemaker; b. Auburn, NY; Emory Mallory and Rhoda Arnold

GRAVES,

Ethel, d. 4/17/1993 at 86 in Newton, CT; homemaker; b. Warren; Charles F. Little and Mary A. Howard

Ronald John, d. 11/28/1970 at 65 in Hanover; machinist; b. NH; Wallace Graves and Annie Morrison

GREEN,

Melvin J., d. 9/11/1900 at 61/11/22 in Warren; apoplexy; married; b. Sherburne, NY; Jeremiah Green (Sherburne, NY) and Sophronia Eaton (Sherburne, NY)

Winston George, d. 7/29/1929 at 0/3/18; b. Lisbon; Joseph Green (VT) and Dorothy Byron (VT)

GREENE,

Ernest William, d. 5/18/1955 at 0/4/18 in Holderness; b. NH; Milton E. Greene and Beverly J. Veasey

Roger Edward, d. 12/13/1945 at 45 mins. in Plymouth; b. Plymouth; Milton Lellan Greene (Lubeck, ME) and Lillian F. Merrill (Warren)

GREENOUGH,

Ethel L., d. 6/29/2003 in Glencliff; Carl Carlson and Hulda Lundburg

GREENWOOD,
Roger, d. 2/16/2000 in Glencliff; Corliss Greenwood and Edith Morrissette

GRIFFIN,
John, d. 7/28/1917 at 34 in Warren; lumber jack

GRIGAS,
Bernice, d. 3/7/1999 in Haverhill; John Grigas and Stefania Januskevich

GURNEY,
"child of Mr. Gurney", d. 10/22/1888

HADLEY,
Henry, d. 8/20/1957 at 78 in Warren; farmer; single; b. Barnet, VT; William Hadley and Ellen -----

HAINES,
Cora, d. 3/10/1982 at 74 in Franconia; housewife; b. Warren; Rodney Morrison and Cora Merrill
Wilbur N., d. 10/17/1980 at 78 in Woodsville; railway mail clerk; b. NH; Herbert R. Haines and Celia McMillan

HALL,
Eleazer M., d. 10/11/1909 at 90/11/16 in Warren; old age; carpenter; married; b. Hardwick, VT; James Hall (Swanzey) and Lurania Mason (Swanzey)
Myra P., d. 6/29/1910 at 88/6/23 in Warren; apoplexy; housewife; married; b. Orford; Charles Rogers (Orford) and Permelia Ramsay (Campton)

HALMAND,
Olive, d. 1/28/1918 at 49 in Warren; housekeeper; widow; b. Madison, ME; Sylvester Littlefield and Jane Roberts

HALNE,
Enert, d. 4/6/1918 at 28 in Warren; laborer; married; b. Kaylin, Finland; Kustaa A. Hanle (Kaylia, Finland) and Hilma Farsman (Kaylia, Finland)

HAM,
Horace John, d. 12/19/1916 at 28/9/5 in Warren; clothier; married; b. Portsmouth; Alfred H. Ham (Portsmouth) and Anna T. French (Portsmouth)

HANCOCK,
Bettyjo, d. 8/17/1990 at 34 in Plymouth; patient care technician; b. Danbury, CT; Donald K. Decker and Elizabeth B. Warren

HANNETT,
Robert J., d. 4/15/1987 at 63 in Haverhill; sawmill; b. Haverhill; Frank R. Hannett and Ethel Walker

HARDY,
Celia S., d. 7/6/1949 at 92 in Union, ME; housework; widow; b. Warren; Frank Steward and Sally Bixby
Paul, d. 12/6/2002 in Woodsville; Anna Hardy

HARPER,
Charles, d. 1/20/1935 at 63/8/6 in Boston, MA; hotel caretaker; married; b. England; Thomas Harper and Henrietta Banks
Lucy J., d. 1/23/1901 at 63/1/1 in Warren; cancer; housekeeper; divorced; b. W. Fairlee; Micah George (Vershire, VT) and Hannah Hutchins (Fryeburg, ME)

HARRIMAN,
Alton Merton, d. 3/19/1997 at 72 in Claremont; restaurant; b. Easton; Elroy Harriman and Maggie M. Adams
Ethel Una, d. 9/18/1992 at 66 in Lebanon; housekeeper; b. Jay, VT; Simon Amos Eldred and Vivian May Farrand
James M., d. 7/19/1898 at 70/1/11 in Warren; shock; blacksmith; married; b. Haverhill; James Harriman
Kenneth B., d. 8/24/1986 at 60 in Warren; bldg. contr.; b. Littleton; Elroy W. Harriman and Maggie Adams
Margaret, d. 4/6/1972 at 85 in Haverhill; housewife; b. VT; Mark Adams and Viola Peck
Sarah, d. 8/18/1899 at 54 in Warren; tumor uterus; housekeeper; widow; Russell Cady

HARRINGTON,

Frank H., d. 5/29/1948 at 74/6/1 in Warren; RR conductor; widower; b. Manchester; Charles M. Harrington (Manchester) and Cora Sinda (Manchester)

Grace Emily, d. 1/14/1947 at 74/2/21 in Plymouth; housewife; married; b. Plymouth; George B. Roby and Mary Sargent (Concord)

HARRIS,

Eugene, d. 10/26/1934 at 79/2/11; retired; divorced; b. Warren; Moses Eaton Harris (Warren) and Abigail Eaton (Lowell, MA)

Helen A., d. 8/2/1930 at 77/2; housewife; widow; b. Easton; Eben Eastman and Abbie Kendall

Lois Jane, d. 6/28/1958 at 65 in Glencliff; laundress; widow; b. Topsham, VT; Carlos Wright and Carrie Page

Minnie A., d. 10/13/1929 at 41/0/18; housewife; single; b. Littleton; Hiram Harris (Bridgewater) and Helen Eastman (NH)

Moses E., d. 2/24/1905 at 77/0/23 in Wentworth; metriae endec'ndts; farmer; married; b. Warren; Samuel Harris and Betsy Blanchard

Procter E., d. 1/27/1906 at 72/1 in Warren; heart disease; farmer; married; b. Warren; Samuel Harris (Warren) and Betsy Blanchard (Ashland)

HARTWELL,

Emeline, d. 4/8/1901 at 79/11/21 in Warren; heart failure; housekeeper; married; b. Piermont; Timothy Ladd and Esther Pillsbury

HARVEY,

Henry H., d. 4/26/1926 at 53/7/19 in Warren; fireman; b. Chazy, NY; Joseph B. Harvey (Peru, NY) and Dalphine Cassidy

HASSEN,

Eleanor, d. 7/2/1995 at 78 in Haverhill; housewife; b. Groton, MA; ----- Baker and Sarah -----

HAZZARD,

Gilbert E., d. 12/22/1933 at 0/4/17; b. Dunham, PQ; William Hazzard (Farnham's Corner, PQ) and Hilda Hazzard (Dunham, PQ)

HEAD,

Alice May, d. 11/15/1951 at 76 in Laconia; bookkeeper; widow; b. NH; Alonzo Bartlett and Luvia Whitcher

Archie A., d. 11/11/1922 at 45/2/20 in Warren; electrician; married; b. Hooksett; Cap. G. H. Head (Chichester) and Sarah Moses (Hooksett)

Bobby, d. 4/7/1908 at –; stillborn; b. Warren; Archie S. Head (Hooksett) and Mabel S. Gould (Hyde Park, MA)

Cecil James, d. 9/29/1899 at 0/2/1 in Warren; whooping cough; b. Warren; Charles W. Head

Charles W., d. 8/9/1901 at 28/1/7 in Warren; suicide by shooting; laborer; married; b. IA; George H. L. Head (Hooksett) and Sarah E. Moses (Chichester)

George H. L., d. 5/12/1909 at 65/8/12 in Warren; apoplexy; hotel keeper; married; b. Hooksett; Thomas Head (Hooksett) and Maryetta Dennison (Francestown)

Sarah E., d. 9/23/1910 at 65/2/21 in Warren; hepatic carcinoma; housewife; widow; b. Chichester; William Moses (Chichester) and Nancy Fellows (Chichester)

HEATH,

Ada Maria, d. 4/18/1938 at 67/2; housework; married; b. Wentworth; Henry Chase (Warren) and Zilpah Wright (Lowell, MA)

Albert, d. 1/13/1912 at 53 in Warren; carcinoma liver; married; b. S. Reading; Henry Heath and Lucinda Bowles

Bert, d. 9/9/1964 at 72 in Concord; laborer; single; b. Piermont; J. Merrill Heath and Ida Chase

Elmer H., d. 4/10/2002 in Lebanon; Etta Heath

Joshua M., d. 12/31/1939 at 71/0/6; farmer; widower; Caleb Heath and Sally Merrill

Lillian B., d. 2/2/1904 at 0/0/12 in Warren; disease of heart; b. Warren; J. Merrill Heath (Warren)

Trudy Lee, d. 4/29/1956 at – in Plymouth; b. Plymouth; Elmer Heath and Jennie Raymond

HEITZ,

George J., d. 12/19/1991 at 62 in Woodsville; auto mechanic; b. Brooklyn, NY; Julius Heitz and Anna Lucin

HENDEE,
William A., d. 5/4/1981 at 67 in Woodsville; salesman; b. VT; William
  Hendee and Luella Ayer

HENDERSON,
Harry T., d. 12/20/1958 at 82 in Warren; farmer; widower; b. Dover;
  Howard Henderson and Elizabeth Bickford
Howard R., d. 2/5/1957 at 65 in Hanover; stock room clerk; widower;
  b. Dover; Frank H. Henderson and Amelia Hamm
Lettie G., d. 12/12/1947 at 71/4/23 in Rumney; self; married; b.
  Dover; Jason Goodwin (Berwick, ME) and Marion Miles
  (Canada)

HENDRICKSON,
Oscar, d. 9/14/1949 at 76 in Haverhill; Carl Hendrickson and
  Christina Cotane

HERSCH,
August A., d. 2/17/1928 at 81/4; shoemaker; single; b. Whitten'g,
  Germany

HIBBARD,
Clarence G., d. 4/12/1962 at 67 in Plymouth; mill prop.; widower; b.
  Orford; George Hibbard and Emma -----
Lloyd Clarence, d. 8/10/1986 at 67 in Hartford, VT; truck driver; b.
  NH; Clarence Hibbard and Maude McCloskey

HICKS,
Arthur James, d. 1/14/1954 at 59 in Warren; laborer; widower; b.
  Lawrence, MA; Edward Hicks and Cary S. Richardson
Clara E., d. 6/15/1953 at 68 in Concord; housewife; married; b.
  Bridgeport, CT; Henry Davis
Edward J., d. 12/6/1924 at 58/8/20 in Warren; wool sorter; married;
  b. Methuen, MA; John T. Hicks and Elizabeth Waite
Fred Edward, d. 4/4/1950 at 69 in Warren; woodsman; single; b.
  Lawrence, MA; Edward Hicks and Clara Snell

HIGHT,
Arthur, d. 9/12/1996 at 81 in Warren; fish hatchery; b. Lisbon
George Edmund, d. 1/18/1973 at 52 in Plymouth; garage prop. &
  mech.; b. VT; William Hight and Iva Smith

George Henry, d. 1/1/1942 at 71/9/28; retired; widower; b. Barnet;
John Hight and Mary Kennedy
Iva Smith, d. 1/28/1971 at 75 in Franconia; housewife; b. NH;
Zebulon Smith and Eva Flanders
Shirley Etta, d. 6/20/1998 at 82 in Warren; self; b. Rumney; Elwyn
Manion and Ethel -----
William R., d. 1/8/1969 at 75 in Warren; retired; b. VT; George Hight
and Anna Eastman

HILDRETH,
Arden S., d. 2/20/1932 at 73/3/24; carpenter; divorced; b. Haverhill;
Edwin W. Hildreth (Haverhill) and Ann L. Haney (Hebron)
Doris A., d. 4/8/2000 in Warren; John Perry and Helen Hopkins
Elroy E., d. 6/12/1954 at 93 in Warren; carpenter; widower; b.
Haverhill; Edwin Hildreth and Ann Haney
George H., d. 9/2/1923 at 66/6/7 in Warren; const. eng.; married; b.
Cincinnati, OH; William J. Hildreth and Virginia Elliott (VA)
Gwendolin, d. 7/23/1902 at – in Warren; abnormal labor; b. Warren;
Charles L. Hildreth (Haverhill) and May E. Boynton (Warren)
Harold L., d. 12/4/1998 at 76 in Haverhill; highway dept.; b. Warren;
William E. Hildreth and Margaret Veasey
Ida S., d. 12/6/1949 at 83 in Warren; housewife; married; b. Warren;
Sylvester Flanders and Sarah Willey
Marguerite, d. 7/31/1961 at 63 in Haverhill; housewife; widow; b.
Bristol; Byron Veasey and Leliar Whitcher
Paula Y., d. 11/8/1976 at 7 in Manchester; b. NH; David Wayne
Hildreth and Patricia E. Smith
William E., d. 9/10/1968 at 73 in Haverhill; widower; b. NH; Elroy
Hildreth and Ida Flanders
William F., d. 5/20/1943 at 80/10/3; farmer; widower; b. Haverhill;
Edward W. Hildreth (Haverhill) and Lucinda A. Havey (Hebron)

HILL,
son, d. 3/26/1948 at 0/0/0 in Plymouth; b. Plymouth; Leslie H. Hill
(Castleton, VT) and Amelia Wheeler (Langdon)
Henry A., d. 11/8/1915 at 68/11/2 in Warren; farmer; married; b.
Sheldon, VT; Edward B. Hill (Burlington, VT) and Lucy Allen
(Burlington, VT)
Mary Ardelia, d. 1/19/1938 at 79/9/6; widow; b. Warren; Nathaniel
Merrill (Warren) and Adeline Moran

HILLIARD,
Edward J., d. 3/31/1933 at 0/1; b. Warren; Joseph N. Hilliard (Hill)
and Leona Hazel Shortt (Warren)
Joseph, d. 3/29/1957 at 55 in Warren; RR section hand; widower; b.
Hill
Leona H., d. 10/15/1956 at 51 in Warren; housewife; married; b.
Warren; William Shortt and Mabel Gould

HINES,
Edward M., d. 7/28/1911 at 84/1/5 in Warren; debil. inc. to old age;
retired; widower; b. St. Albans; Elija B. Hines and Merinda
Griswold

HINKLEY,
Frederick H., d. 12/29/1935 at 25/9/19 in Warren; single; b. Medfield;
John F. Hinkley and Una Waterman

HOGAN,
Kenneth, d. 1/3/1978 at 69 in Concord; b. NY; Patrick Hogan and
Victorice Turgeon

HOIT,
Mary F., d. 1/30/1911 at 82/9 in Littleton; widow; b. Littleton; Daniel
Hoit (Gilmanton) and Lucy Nourse (Littleton)

HOOD,
Ernest E., d. 3/7/1955 at 74 in Woodsville; laborer; married; Arthur
Hood and Elsie Goodwin
Katie J., d. 11/12/1963 at 81 in Woodsville; housewife; widow; b.
Corinth, VT; George Hood and Fannie Avery

HOPKINS,
Clifford Henry, d. 2/5/1989 at 59 in Plymouth; electronics; b.
Bridgewater, MA; Paul Hopkins and Emma Nicholas

HOSFORD,
Harvey W., d. 2/10/1967 at 82 in Haverhill; widower; b. Houlton, ME;
Joseph Hosford and Lydia Tazier

HOUGHTON,
Delia A., d. 2/9/1915 at 64/2/10 in Warren; housewife; widow; b. Concord; George S. Walcott (McIndoes, VT) and Electa Beebe (Lyndon, VT)
Edward L., d. 12/11/1906 at 67/9/19 in Warren; pneumonia; printer; married; b. Thetford; George Houghton (Newbury, VT) and Nancy Boynton (Orford)
Helen C., d. 2/6/1970 at 64 in Haverhill; b. NH; Fred Chasson and Ella Houghton
Herbert B., d. 10/27/1908 at 58/3/24; mitral regurgitation; shoe laster; single; b. Newbury, VT; George Houghton (Newbury, VT) and Nancy Boynton (Orford)

HOWARD,
Audrey, d. 7/25/2004 in Wentworth; Wilbur Clark and Dorothy Sweet
Flora Abbie, d. 5/19/1955 at 89 in Plymouth; housewife; widow; b. Plymouth; William Lowd and Sarah E. Morgan
George W., d. 11/23/1938 at 79/4/27; farmer; married; b. Lancaster; James Howard (Ludlow) and Augusta Walker (Lynn, MA)

HOWES,
Forrest Carter, d. 6/9/1983 at 72 in Warren; machinist; b. Brockton, MA; Ralph Howes and Gladys Crosier

HOWLAND,
Arvilla, d. 12/10/1887 at 39/9/4; housewife; married; b. Wentworth; Peter Clifford (Wentworth) and Helen ----- (Wentworth)
Edgar F., d. 11/20/1894 at 46/1/8 in Warren; diphtheria; millwright; b. Easton; Samuel Howland and Lucinda Bowles

HOWLETT,
Tonya Nicole, d. 6/30/1997 at 10 in Plymouth; b. Fall River, MA; Charles J. Howlett, Jr. and Lorna J. Rodgers

HOYT,
George G., d. 4/20/1914 at 68/9/20 in Warren; married; b. Moultonboro; William Hoyt

HUBBARD,
Daniel, d. 2/18/1911 at 71/3/5 in Warren; Brights disease; retired; widower; b. New London; Rodney Hubbard

HUCKINS,

Charles, d. 8/13/1917 at 78/8/13 in Warren; retired; single; b. Warren; Enos Huckins and Betsy Ingalls

Enos, d. 4/9/1893 at 57/7/29 in Plymouth; paralysis; physician; married; b. Warren; Enos Huckins (New Hampton) and Betsy Ingalls

Marjorie, d. 9/6/2004 in North Haverhill; Claude Smith and Flora Wilkinson

Robert, d. 4/27/2005 in Plymouth; Quinton Huckins and Doris Prescott

HUDON,

Emile, d. 11/16/1905 at 46/10 in Warren; conc. of brain; millman; married; b. Canada; Blaise Hudon (Canada) and R. Chamberland

HUGHES,

Anna Caroline, d. 5/10/1950 at 67 in Plymouth; children's nurse; married; b. Germany; Christian Heinrich Grotkop and Marie Caroline Rathjen

HUKALA,

John (Hietala), d. 7/31/1974 at 86 in Concord; b. Finland; Albert Hukala and Mary -----

HUNKINS,

Corinne E., d. 4/7/1926 at 0/0/1 in Warren; b. Warren; Dana Hunkins (Groton) and Eva Currier (Piermont)

Dana F., d. 5/19/1974 at 84 in Haverhill; fish hatchery; b. NH; Willard H. Hunkins and Adeline Hardy

Eva May, d. 11/17/1974 at 82 in Concord; housewife; b. NH; James Curry and Helen Dexter

John, d. 2/20/1912 at 79/8/20 in Warren; intestinal carcinoma; ret. farmer; widower; b. Sandown; Maynard Hunkins (Sandown) and Rhoda French (Sandown)

HUNNEWELL,

Grace, d. 5/15/2002 in Glencliff; Fred Hunnewell and Ethel Robinson

HURST,
Russell, d. 12/11/2005 in Plymouth; Russell Hurst and Jeanne Dawkins

HUTCHINS,
Jennie L., d. 3/15/1951 at 86 in Hanover; retired; widow; b. S. Deerfield, MA; Granville Wardwell and Ellen Jewett
John W., d. 4/19/1900 at 35 in Warren; pneumonia; married; b. Franklin, ME; John Hutchins (Fremont, ME) and Julia Clark (Franklin, ME)

INGALLS,
Joel, d. 11/25/1891 at 75/10/27 in Warren; uremic poisoning; mechanic; Satchel Ingalls (farmer) and Hannah Heath

INGRAHAM,
Shuah, d. 5/16/1896 at 85/6/23 in Warren; cer. degeneration; housewife; widow; b. Weare; David Philbrick

JACKSON,
Hamilton C., d. 11/22/1910 at 6/0/8 in Warren; accident; b. Warren; Frank C. Jackson (Belfast, ME) and Edith B. Colby (Whitefield)
Mrs. George, d. 3/4/1887 at 79/1/10; widow; b. Saco, ME; Joseph Coolbrith

JACQUES,
Reginald K., d. 11/24/1956 at 0 in Rumney; b. Rumney; Peter Louis Jacques and Myrtle May Roper

JESSEMAN,
daughter, d. 1/8/1934 at 0/0/1; b. Warren; Elmer Jesseman (Newbury, VT) and May Barry (Warren)
Arlene, d. 5/19/1989 at 72 at Wanda's Rest Home; housewife; b. Derby Line, VT; Eugene B. Lagthe and Gertrude Brooks
Clarice M., d. 4/20/1933 at –; b. Warren; Elmer Jesseman (Newbury, VT) and Ora May Barry (Warren)
Elizabeth, d. 2/27/1941 at 64/7/2; housewife; married; b. Durham, PQ; F. C. LaFrance (Canada) and M. Lawrence (Canada)
Elmer C., d. 6/19/1974 at 67 in Concord; retired carpenter; b. VT; Irvin Jesseman and Elizabeth LaFrance

Elmer W., d. 2/17/1993 at 69 in Woodsville; truck driver; b. Warren; Raymond Jesseman, Sr. and Marguerite Whitcher

Hazel E., d. 6/9/1982 at 56 in Warren; housewife; b. Haverhill; Henry E. Buskey and Emma E. Dargie

Irvin A., d. 9/9/1951 at 80 in Warren; farmer; widower; b. Bethlehem; Charles Jesseman

Marguerite L., d. 11/11/1983 at 84 in Warren; housewife; b. Warren; Frank Whitcher and Laura E. Clement

Neil E., d. 6/5/1982 at 44 in Lake Auburn, ME

Ora May, d. 12/26/1966 at 58 in Warren; homemaker; married; b. Warren; Charles F. Barry and Ora May Smith

Raymond, d. 5/7/1968 at 71 in Laconia; railroad patrolman; married; b. NH; William Jesseman and Jennie Littlefield

Raymond, Jr., d. 2/26/1998 at 76 in Woodsville; fish and game; b. Warren; Raymond Jesseman, Sr. and Marguerite Whitcher

Richard E., d. 8/17/1929 at 0/0/12; b/ Warren; Elmer C. Jesseman (Newbury, VT) and Ora May Barry (Warren)

JEWELL,
Fannie, d. 1/24/1896 at 85 in Glencliff; old age; housewife; single; b. Warren; Samuel Jewell and Sally Foote

James, d. 5/6/1903 at 68 in Warren; paralysis; lumberman; married; b. Warren; Levi F. Jewell

Levi F., d. 1/21/1903 at 86/5/21 in Warren; bron. pneumonia; carpenter; widower

Maria W., d. 3/15/1897 at 59/10 in Warren; Bright's disease; housewife; divorced; Elmer Copp

JEWETT,
Harriet M., d. 4/6/1904 at 73/3/7 in Warren; pneumonia; housewife; married; b. Warren; Joseph Farnham (Concord) and Betsey Merrill

Jeremiah S., d. 5/22/1909 at 86/5/27 in Warren; valv. disease of heart; merchant; widower; b. Laconia

JOHNSON,
Burton W., d. 10/23/1940 at 70/6/25; farmer; married; b. Orford; Wallace Johnson (Orford) and ----- Spencer (N. Stratford)

Jane R., d. 2/27/1908 at 73/8/27; cardiac dropsy; housekeeper; widow; b. Strafford; Louis Curtis and Rebecca Chase

John, d. 1/20/1912 at 0/0/18 in Warren; b. Warren; Burt Johnson
    (Orford) and Lucinda Bowles (Wentworth)
Laura, d. 2/16/1909 at 1/0/7 in Warren; acute bronchitis; b. Warren;
    Bert Johnson (Wentworth) and Evelyn Gove
Simon Eugene, Jr., d. 6/13/1988 at 70 in Warren; bus driver; b. W.
    Bridgewater, MA; Simon E. Johnson, Sr. and Ruth C. Stetson
William E., d. 10/3/1929 at 26; laborer; single

JONES,
Clarence, d. 3/14/2002 in Warren; Clarence Jones and Marie Day
Josephine Anne, d. 10/4/1951 at 12 hrs. in Warren; b. Warren;
    Daniel N. Jones and Dorothy V. Hildreth
Loretta W., d. 6/5/1965 at 71 in Stoneham, MA; housekeeper;
    widow; b. Lynn, MA; George A. Robinson and Bessie Fraser
Walter R., d. 3/2/1965 at 67 in Hanover; retired; married; b. Meriden,
    WI; Andrew J. Jones and Estella Rashare

JUDKINS,
Amos H., d. 6/14/1941 at 61/8/6; laborer; divorced; b. Barnet, VT;
    Harvey Judkins (Barnet, VT) and Nanissus Scott (Danville, VT)

JUTRAS,
Lydia Ora, d. 5/4/1986 at 82 in Haverhill; housewife; b. Wakefield;
    Charles Croteau and Mary Drouin

KALLMAN,
George, d. 2/27/1956 at 81 in Concord; farmer; single; b. Sweden; --
    --- Kallman and Sophia M. Wallstead

KARSTOCK,
Joseph W., d. 8/27/2002 in Glencliff; Joseph Karstock and Mary
    Souslough

KASHETA,
Beradette Sasner, d. 12/12/1993 at 87 in Haverhill; homemaker; b.
    McKees Rock, PA; John Sasner and Theo Breinz
Francis J., d. 4/4/1982 at 77 in Meredith; retired physician; b.
    Lawrence, MA; James Kasheta and Mary Akstin

KATSOK,
Elizabeth F., d. 10/20/2002 in Glencliff; Archie Willard and Mary
  Sweeny

KATZ,
Melville J., d. 6/25/1986 at 74 in Warren; ret. txtl. cons.; b. New York
  City, NY; Lenard Katz and Irene Alter

KELLEY,
Edward A., d. 3/7/1929 at 74; married; b. Lowell, MA; William Kelley
  (Derry) and Annie Wright (Littleton)

KELLY,
Delia E., d. 9/11/1950 at 78 in Warren; housework; widow; b.
  Ellsworth; George W. Bennett and Betsey McClentie
Fred W., d. 7/1/1947 at 89 in Ashland; carpenter; widower; b.
  Haverhill, MA; William H. Kelly (Haverhill) and Annie Wright
  (Middletown)
Georgia Anna, d. 3/28/1891 at 29/11/23 in Warren; blood poison; b.
  Rumney; George W. Elliott (Plymouth) and Lydia J. Moulton
  (Ellsworth)
Harriet Josephine, d. 4/18/1937 at 80/7/18 in Haverhill; housewife;
  married; b. Haverhill, MA; Joseph Brickett and Mary Lizzie
  Morse
Harry J., d. 10/12/1918 at 22/11/24 in Warren; married; b. Warren;
  John H. Kelly (Ellsworth) and Mary E. Bennett (Ellsworth)
John, d. 12/31/1948 at 85/0/21 in Warren; none; married; b.
  Ellsworth; William Kelly (MA) and Anne Wright (NH)
Mary L., d. 12/22/1911 at 37/3/24 in Warren; lymphatis; housewife;
  married; b. Thornton; George Bennett (Orange) and Betsy
  McClintock (Canterbury)

KEMP,
Annie B., d. 1/14/1969 at 83 in Haverhill; b. NH; Zebulon Smith and
  Eva Flanders
Clarence W., d. 6/9/1958 at 78 in Warren; millwright; married; b.
  Lyme; Wallace William Kemp and Helen M. Brown

KENNESON,
Gladys H., d. 5/1/1974 at 73 in Hanover; b. NH; George Howard and
  Flora Lowd

Mary A., d. 5/18/1948 at 91/5/22 in Warren; housewife; widow; b. Concord, VT; Albert J. Frye (Concord, VT) and Catherine Brown (Concord, VT)

KENNEY,
Christopher, d. 2/5/1911 at 42/4 in Warren; homicide; surveyor; single; b. PQ; John Kenney (Canada) and Elizabeth Smith (Canada)
Edith S., d. 6/9/1972 at 56 in Haverhill; NE Tel. operator; b. NH; William Shortt and Mabel Gould

KESER,
Amanda, d. 6/30/1889 at 62 in Warren; ulceration of bowels; housekeeping; Ezra B. Eaton and Mary Currier

KEYSAR,
son, d. 10/26/1937 at – in Warren; b. Warren; Miles H. Keysar and Bertha Snelgrove
Bertha, d. 8/11/2005 in Warren; Frank Snelgrove and Edna Wright
Eliza L., d. 11/22/1924 at 68/4/12 in Warren; housewife; widow; b. Colebrook; John Moses and Fanny Munn
Marion L., d. 2/7/1930 at 36/4/16; married; b. Lakeport; Chester B. Averill (Mt. Vernon) and Edith M. Leonard (Warren)
Miles H., d. 2/14/1966 at 70 in Haverhill; mechanic; married; b. Colebrook; Berkley Keysar and Eliza Moses
Royal Everett, d. 2/5/1944 at 52/0/7 in Warren; merchant; widower; b. Colebrook; Berkley Keysar (Clarksville) and Eliza L. Moses (Colebrook)

KIDD,
Lena McL., d. 1/15/1960 at 84 in Rochester; housewife; widow; b. Glasgow, Scotland; John V. McLauchlan and Mary P. Monroe

KIMBALL,
Albert, d. 11/23/1924 at 72/5/23 in Warren; farmer; single; b. Warren; Page Kimball and Eugernie Page
Dennis, d. 11/12/1926 at 67/11/4 in Warren; farmer; b. Warren; Page Kimball (Wentworth) and ----- Page (Warren)
Eugena, d. 10/27/1898 at 80/0/22 in Warren; pyaemia; housewife; widow; b. Warren; Samuel Page
Henry W., d. 5/21/1929 at 71; RR emp.; single; b. Warren

KING,
Eva E., d. 6/24/1973 at 52 in Hanover; tel. operator; b. MA; Joseph Raymond and Jennie Palmer
Thomas W., d. 7/30/1896 at 34/4 in Warren; consumption; blacksmith; single; Josiah King and Jane Kilpatrick

KIPLING,
Caroline H., d. 11/29/1951 at 65 in Hanover; housewife; married; b. Germany; Christian Grotkpp and Caroline Rothgen
Gretchen C., d. 2/13/1984 in Providence, RI; burial permit
Lionel, d. 12/2/1967 at 79 in Hanover; edge guilder; married; b. England; William Kipling and Elizabeth Ann Reilly

KNAPP,
Arthur, d. 11/19/1898 at 75 in Warren; bron. pneumonia; farmer; married
Mercy J., d. 12/6/1906 at 78/7/23 in Warren; mit. regurgitation; housekeeper; widow; b. Haverhill; Newell Caswell (Moultonboro) and Mary Hodgdon (Meredith)

KOHLMAN,
Laura, d. 7/30/1999 at 90 in Glencliff; domestic; b. Mexico, ME; Frank Kohlman and Sarah Adriance

KYDD,
David, d. 4/22/1936 at 68/2/5 in Warren; farmer; married; b. Dundee, Scotland; David Kydd and Magdaline Mackay
John David, d. 11/9/1936 at 0/2/10 in Manchester; b. Manchester; John V. Kydd and Mary Ann Remillard

LABBEE,
Michael R., d. 7/27/1985 at 80 in Haverhill; lumberman; b. Hingham, MA; Paul Labbee and Mary Libby

LABRIE,
Frances E., d. 3/31/1983 at 64 in New Haven, VT; housewife; b. Warren; William J. Shortt and Mabel M. Gould

LAFOE,
Beatrice L., d. 3/14/1917 at 0/0/18 in Warren; b. Warren; John Lafoe (Hartford, CT) and Rosie Morrison (Lemington, VT)

LAMOTHE,
Roderick A., d. 9/5/1963 at 56 in Warren; carpenter; married; b. Winchendon, MA; Peter Lamothe and Georgianna Ledoux

LANE,
Iantha B., d. 9/30/1920 at 59/6/19 in Warren; housewife; married; b. Warren; Joseph Whitcher (Warren) and Liza Jane Albert

LATSIS,
Mary Jane, d. 10/27/1997 at 70 in Plymouth; writing fictional books; b. Chicago, IL; John Latsis

LAVERTUE,
Antoine, d. 2/7/1954 at 60 in Warren; laborer; single; b. Canada; Laurent Lavertue and Henriette Tremblay

LAVOIE,
Battis, d. 10/14/1890 at 35 in Warren; heart disease; laborer; b. St. Dennis

LEAOR,
Rose A., d. 4/3/2000 in Glencliff; Alfred Larouche and Ernestine LaFrance

LEAVITT,
Blanche A., d. 12/15/1950 at 70 in Hanover; housewife; married; b. Warren; Perley Annis and Lovilla Swain
Ira W., d. 7/14/1954 at 69 in Hanover; retired; widower; b. Sanbornton; George Leavitt and Alice Woodman

LEBLANC,
Graziella M., d. 3/20/1986 at 88 in Haverhill; dresser; b. Canada

LECLAIR,
Joseph D., d. 10/3/1929 at 24/5/2; laborer; single; b. N. Grafton, MA; Joseph Leclair (Whitinsville, MA) and Catherine Glennon (Grafton, MA)

LEET,
Ruth Hazel, d. 11/19/1923 at 0/1/15 in Warren; b. Plymouth; Edward Leet (Holden, VT) and Flora Gove (Lincoln)

LEGAULT,
Joseph G., d. 9/20/1981 at 77 in Woodsville; NH Home for the
   Elderly; b. Canada; David Legault and Phoebe Vileveau

LEIGHTON,
Constance, d. 7/7/2000 in Plymouth; Alan Leighton and Rachel
   Courser
L. H., d. 7/12/1898 at 62/8/26 in Warren; uraemia; housewife;
   married; b. Orford; John Nason

LEONARD,
Charles K., d. 10/9/1925 at 83/4/30 in Warren; farmer; married; b.
   Warren; George E. Leonard (Barton, VT) and Mihitable Little
   (Warren)
Emily E., d. 4/16/1933 at 80/5/4; widow; b. Warren; Josiah Swain, Jr.
   (Sanbornton) and Sarah Eaton (Weare)
George E., d. 7/6/1892 at 82/1 in Warren; la grippe; farming; b.
   Winchester; John Leonard and Deborah E. -----
Mehitable, d. 3/30/1889 at 68/2 in Warren; inflammation of bowels;
   housekeeping; married; b. Warren; Benjamin Little and Sally ---

LEROY,
Joseph, d. 7/1/1904 at 35/3/27 in Warren; heart disease; miner;
   single; b. PQ; Joseph Leroy (Canada) and Adeline Nolet
   (Canada)

LEWIS,
Susie, d. 4/22/1967 at 80 in Hanover; retired; widow; b. Groveton;
   Benjamin Whitney and Edith Remick

LIBBEY,
Donald, d. 9/23/1941 at 20/6; clerking; single; b. Warren; Nat E.
   Libbey (Warren) and Florence Balch (Goffstown)
Elizabeth, d. 8/18/1899 at 57/8/2 in Warren; fracture of vertebra;
   housewife; widow; b. Warren
Eva K., d. 1/30/1907 at 95/7/7 in Meredith; acute bronchitis;
   housekeeper; widow; b. Mt. Holly; Francis Sinclair and -----
   Kilburn
Ezra B., d. 9/10/1905 at 76/1/21 in Warren; dis. of heart; farmer;
   married; b. Warren; John Libbey (Landaff) and Betsy Merrill
   (Warren)

Florence, d. 1/5/1967 at 81 in Haverhill; housewife; married; b.
Goffstown
George W., d. 5/14/1914 at 74/8/2 in Wentworth; married; b.
Warren; John Libbey and Betsey Merrill (Warren)
Ira Nelson, d. 3/7/1935 at 82/10/13 in Warren; carpenter; married; b.
Warren; Ira Libbey and Melissa French
L. O., d. 3/10/1897 at 54/1/3 in Warren; Bright's disease; housewife;
widow; b. Warren; Hazen Libbey and M. S. Clifford
Lucia Anna, d. 12/13/1950 at 92 in Warren; housewife; widow; b.
Warren; John Whiteman and Nancy Colby
Nathaniel, d. 9/25/1888 at 94 in Warren; widower
Natt, d. 12/14/1968 at 80 in Haverhill; widower; b. NH; Ira Nelson
Libbey and Lucia Whitman
Ralph, d. 7/13/1934 at 64/9/12; farmer; widower; b. Warren; Robert
Libbey (NH) and Elizabeth Page (ME)
Robert M., d. 8/18/1899 at 68/3/16 in Warren; fracture of skull;
farmer; widower; b. Warren; John Libbey
Susie A., d. 9/10/1941 at 81/0/14; housewife; widow; b. Dover, MA;
Monroe M. Morse (Boston, MA) and Lucy Shaw

LIBBY,
Albert, d. 2/24/1999 at 60 in Warren; heavy equip. sales; b.
Haverhill; Almer Morrill Libby and Vera Viola Ball
Almer Morril, d. 1/25/1970 at 66 in Plymouth; laborer; b. NH; David
Libby and Ellen Chase
Amos F., d. 11/18/1942 at 56/11/21; laborer; single; b. Warren; Ira
N. Libbey (Warren) and L. Whiteman (Warren)
Emma A., d. 12/14/1922 at 84/1/27 in Laconia; retired; widow; b. N.
Haverhill; Moses French (Haverhill) and Cest'a Wheeler
(Haverhill)
Otis R., d. 5/13/1966 at 74 in Hartford, VT; truck driver; divorced; b.
Warren; Nelson Libby and Lucy Whitman
Vera Viola, d. 10/25/1995 at 87 in Warren; laundress; b. Granville,
VT; Bert L. Ball and Eva Irene Moulton
William E., d. 6/17/1910 at 49/11/6 in Warren; nephritis; farmer;
married; b. Warren; Judith Libby (Warren)

LIETT,
Lewis, d. 1/15/1925 at 69 in Warren; married

LIFF,
Alexander, d. 10/26/1987 at 69 in Haverhill; b. Stockholm, Sweden; Jonas Liff and Raissa Israelitin

LITTLE,
daughter, d. 3/3/1897 at – in Warren; b. Warren; Ernest R. Little and Hattie Haywood

Charles Forrest, d. 9/8/1956 at 86 in Warren; RR sta. agent; widower; b. Warren; Frank P. Little and Martha S. Wright

D. K., d. –/–/1892 at 13/1 in Warren; infla. of bowels; b. Warren Summit; Henry A. Little (Warren) and Mary L. Ford

Frank Benton, d. 8/30/1944 at 82/7/30 in Warren; railroading; divorced; b. Norway, ME; Joseph M. Little (Warren) and Eliza Jane Crockett (Norway, ME)

George A., d. 5/10/1930 at 82/11/17; lawyer; widower; b. Warren; Jesse Little (Warren) and Susan Merrill (Warren)

George Melvin, d. 12/8/1903 at 56/8/12 in Warren; nephritis; clergyman; married; b. Warren; Jonathan Little (Warren) and Mary Currier (Canaan)

Henry A., d. 4/13/1920 at 77/7/18 in Warren; optician; married; b. Warren; Jonathan Little (Warren) and Mary Currier (Canaan)

John, d. 7/28/1917 at 38 in Haverhill; telegraph oper.; married; b. Warren; Henry Little (Warren) and Mary Ford

Jonathan, d. 11/30/1889 at 85/5 in Warren; old age; married; Joseph Merrill and Sarah Copp

Joseph M., d. 12/26/1914 at 84/1/28 in Warren; widower; b. Warren; Jesse Little (Warren) and Susan C. Merrill (Warren)

Mary, d. 10/25/1891 at – in Warren; bronchitis

Mary A. Howard, d. 2/3/1948 at 74/9/12 in Warren; housewife; married; b. Lyme; Anson Howard (Lyme) and Julia Cutting (Broome, Canada)

Mary N., d. 1/25/1952 at 69 in Warren; housewife; widow; b. Bradford, VT; William H. Noyes and ----- Chamberlin

Mattie E., d. 12/2/1949 at 73 in Plymouth; housewife; widow; b. Lyme; Anderson Howard and Julia Cutting

Susan C., d. 12/12/1889 at 81/4/12 in Warren; old age; housekeeping; widow; b. Warren

William Henry, d. 1/25/1950 at 77 in Warren; painter; married; b. London, England; Isaac John Little and Emma Williams

LIVESTON,
Bruce, d. 10/5/2004 in Whitefield; James Liveston and Kathleen Aldrich

LOCKE,
Henry E., d. 1/30/1926 at 55/4/6 in Warren; laborer; b. London; Leroy Locke and Hannah Ever
Meanie M., d. 6/3/1926 at 57/7/11 in Warren; at home; b. Warren; Henry D. Whitcher (Warren) and Hattie M. Caswell (Haverhill)

LOMBARD,
Merrill, d. 7/4/1970 at 76 in Concord; laborer; b. NH; Lyman Lombard and Angie Marshall

LOSIER,
Mary, d. 2/2/2001 in Woodsville; Larry Losier and Catherine Losier

LOTHROP,
Elizabeth, d. 6/25/1929 at 56/3/3; housework; widow; b. Stoneham, MA; Lorenzo French (VT)

LOUGEE,
Sadie, d. 3/18/1923 at 41/2/13 in Warren; housewife; married; b. Warren; Emery F. Flanders (Warren) and Martha Moody (Sugar Hill)
Walter, d. 1/24/1955 at 77 in Warren; retired; divorced; b. Bradford, VT; John S. Lougee and Olanda Kemp

LUCE,
Edith Madeline, d. 1/9/1944 at 43/3/15 in Warren; housewife; married; b. Glencliff; James Belyea (St. Johns, NB) and Mary Fifield (Glencliff)
Lester, d. 3/16/1937 at 68/7 in Haverhill; laborer; widower; b. Tunbridge; Jabez Luce and Mary Clark

LUND,
Almira, d. 9/16/1891 at 85/1/2 in Warren; dropsy; b. Hill; David Colby (Hill, farmer) and Sally Wells (Hill)
Cora A., d. 10/14/1925 at 62/8/18 in Warren; married; b. Warren; Dr. J. F. Willey (Warren) and Phila Godfrey (VT)

Edward A., d. 2/25/1941 at 82/1/18; widower; H. Batchelder and
Sarah Lund (Warren)
Frances A., d. 6/16/1921 at 74/8/9 in Warren; married; b. Lakeport;
John D. Swain
George W., d. 2/25/1909 at 79 in Warren; acute bronchitis; single; b.
Warren
James H., d. 11/8/1926 at 86/2/26 in Warren; shoe maker; b.
Wentworth; Joseph Lund (Bradford, VT) and Emily Gay
Ross M., d. 8/25/1906 at 3/1/1 in Warren; cholera infantum; b.
Warren; Edward A. Lund (Warren) and Cora Willey (Warren)

LUNDGREN,
Lillian, d. 1/10/1969 at 75 in Warren; housewife; b. IL; ----- Berntson
and Julia Haisher
Victor R., d. 10/18/1972 at 79 in Hartford, VT; unknown; b. MA

LUPIEN,
son, d. 4/21/1925 at 0/0/0 in Warren; b. Warren; Edward Lupien
(Newbury) and India Elliott (Warren)
Edw. Louis, d. 12/26/1918 at 5/9/27 in Warren; school boy; b.
Warren; Edward R. Lupien (Newbury, VT) and India M. Elliott
(Warren)
Edward R., d. 2/6/1965 at 79 in Haverhill; grit mfg.; married; b.
Newbury, VT; Napoleon Lupien and Romina Rowe
India M., d. 5/12/1985 at 98 in Peabody, MA; housewife; b. Warren;
Charles Elliott and Meanie Mahala Whitcher

MACDONALD,
Grace H., d. 3/19/2002 in Hartford, VT; Clarence Tewksbury and
Lydia Bailey
John H., Jr., d. 8/16/1997 at 72 in Warren; law enforcement; b.
Plymouth; John H. MacDonald, Sr. and Eva E. Lovett

MANNING,
Charles B., d. 2/11/1924 at 52/0/21 in Glencliff; civil engineer;
married; b. Annapolis, MD; Charles H. Manning (Baltimore,
MD) and Fanny Bartlett (Haverhill, MA)
Francis B., d. 2/11/1924 at 32 in Glencliff; married; b. Manchester;
Charles H. Manning (Baltimore, MD) and Fanny Bartlett
(Haverhill, MA)

Robert L., d. 2/11/1924 at 50/6/6 in Glencliff; lawyer; married; b. Annapolis, MD; Charles H. Manning (Baltimore, MD) and Fanny Bartlett (Haverhill, MA)

MARDEN,

Lyman A., d. 7/9/1896 at 85/6/14 in Warren; par. shock; farmer; married; Jonathan Marden

Mehitable, d. 8/10/1898 at 78/3/22 in Warren; shock; housewife; widow; b. Warren; John Flanders

MARSAL,

Charles Hines, d. 5/14/1979 at 89 in Plymouth; retired machinist; b. Czechoslovakia; Hynek Marsal and Albina -----

MARSH,

Ella Mae, d. 7/5/1948 at 79/6/18 in Warren; housewife; widow; b. Richford, VT; George W. Audette (Stanbridge, Canada) and Emily Cadorette (Phillipsburg, Canada)

Samual A., d. 11/9/1991 at 58 in Plymouth; woodcutting foreman; b. Orford; Walter Marsh and Gladys Elliott

MARSTON,

Emma J., d. 1/23/1899 at 39/2/11 in Warren; anaemia; housewife; married; b. Warren; Charles Batchelder

Ezra L., d. 10/30/1922 at 67/3/15 in Warren; farmer; married; b. Warren; Ezra Marston (Cornish) and Lousia Flower (Warren)

Helen Girty, d. 3/13/1959 at 84 in Plymouth; nurse; widow; b. Lyme; Wallace W. Kemp and Helen M. Brown

Mary A., d. 12/14/1903 at 64 in Wentworth; angina pectoris; married; b. Orford; John B. Stickney (Orford) and Salomy W. Ford (Orford)

Nellie E., d. 10/16/1961 at 73 in Norwood, MA; monotyper; single; b. Warren; Ezra Marston and Emma Batchelder

Theodore Ezra, d. 12/24/1980 at 66 in Norwood, MA; retired; b. NH; Ezra L. Marston and Helen G. Kemp

MARTIN,

Ellen S., d. 10/29/1918 at 67/3/11 in Warren; housekeeper; married; b. Machiasport, ME; Otis Wescot (ME)

Henry D., d. 10/25/1922 at 79/9/25 in Warren; farmer; widower; b. Haverhill; Stephen Martin (Warren) and Pat'a Whitcher (Haverhill)

Mary, d. 7/24/1999 at 90 in Glencliff; domestic; b. Glencliff; Patrick Martin and Elizabeth Fahey

Patience, d. 12/27/1887 at 77; widow; Dearborn Whitcher and Ruth - ----

MASON,

Ernest, d. 7/27/1978 at 80 in Concord; mill worker; b. Montreal, Canada; Oliver Mason and Olive Sanville

MATHEWSON,

Edward E., d. 1/9/1909 at 0/3/2 in Warren; mososmus; b. Warren; Charles C. Mathewson and Georgianna Eastman

Georgiana, d. 11/2/1908 at 41; cancer of bowels; housekeeper; married

Iva R., d. 6/15/1920 at 28/8/20 in Warren; housewife; married; b. Wentworth; Frank Reed (Canterbury) and Winnie Johnson (Orford)

MATSON,

Alexander, d. 11/30/1952 at 89 in Haverhill; farming; widower; b. Crawburn, Canada; William Matson and Margaret McLintock

Jennie Semple, d. 1/3/1948 at 83/7/12 in Glencliff; housewife; married; b. St. Giles, PQ; Douglas Semple (Scotland) and Catherine Smith (at sea)

John M., d. 7/29/1969 at 63 in Warren; caretaker; b. MA; Alexander Matson and Jennie Semple

Viney T., d. 1/16/2000 in Plymouth; Joseph Strojny and Theresa -----

McCLINTOCK,

Herbert M., d. 12/10/1954 at 84 in Berlin

McCUTCHEON,

Rebecca, d. 6/12/1902 at 42 in Warren; consumption; housekeeper; married

McDONALD,

Dorothy, d. 1/22/1979 at 78 in Hanover; housewife; b. Deerfield; Hebert Lerrill and Mary McDonald

McEASTMAN,

Margaret J., d. 2/22/1942 at 71/11/19; housewife; married; b. Welsford, NB; William McCutcheon (Scotland) and Sidney Boyle (England)

McELROY,

Jo-Ann, d. 2/5/2003 in Glencliff; Paul Delagrange and Esther Holloway

McISAAC,

Bessie, d. 1/19/1900 at 0/7 in Warren; spinal meningitis; b. Warren; Henry McIsaac (Cape Breton) and Mabel Eastman (Warren)

Henry, d. 11/1/1900 at 29 in Warren; consumption; laborer; married; b. Cape Breton; Donald McIsaac (Cape Breton) and Dorothy Murphy (Cape Breton)

Henry E., Sr., d. 2/2/1980 at 82 in Plymouth; retired carpenter; b. NH; Harry Fifield McIsaac and Mabel Eastman

Hugh, d. 8/16/1945 at 73 in Warren; lumberman

Natalie Mary, d. 5/18/1978 at 72 in Plymouth; housewife; b. Warren; Thomas Gallant and Florence Balch

McKAY,

Alexander, d. 7/21/1999 in Bradford, VT; William McKay and Emma Joel

McKEE,

Ethel, d. 1/14/1964 at 77 in Haverhill; housewife; widow; b. Canada; Fred Armstrong and Annie Flemming

Gordon, d. 2/13/1971 at 61 in Haverhill; mechanic; b. MA; William McKee and Ethel Armstrong

McKINLEY,

Hazel A., d. 9/10/1906 at 1/11/28 in Warren; b. Warren; Ralph McKinley (Windsor, NS) and Susie Whitney (Groveton)

Lawrence P., d. 6/23/1951 at 43 in Lincoln; divorced; b. Warren

McKINNON,

Harold, d. 7/30/1906 at 2 in Warren; acute indigestion; b. W. Rumney; N. McKinnon (Halifax, NS) and Eva Mactava (Lawrence, MA)

McLINN,
Blanche E., d. 7/28/1930 at 19/3/16; bookkeeper; single; b. Canaan, VT; D. H. McLinn (Groton) and Tillie D. Raymond (Lyndonville, VT)
Mathilda D., d. 3/5/1924 at 43/4/7 in Warren; housewife; married; b. Lyndonville, VT; John Raymond (Montreal, Canada) and Mathilda Gordon (Duham, Canada)

McMASTER,
Angus, d. 11/12/1936 at 66 in Warren; woodsman; single; b. Four Rivers, NS; John MacMaster and Mary Hepburn

McNAMARA,
Christina, d. 9/30/1967 at 72 in Haverhill; housewife; married; b. Medford, MA; Iolas Clifford and Annie Cameron
Wallace Eugene, d. 3/31/1975 at 89 in White River Jct., VT; barber; b. VT; Edward McNamara and Annie Hinton

McVETY,
Ella M., d. 3/8/1896 at 37/10/8 in Warren; gourtric; housewife; married; b. Canada; John Barker and Margaret McGinnis
Emma E., d. 10/19/1906 at 54/3 in Warren; inf. of bowels; housekeeper; married; b. Warren
Isabelle, d. 3/24/1894 at 54/6/15 in Warren; heart failure; housekeeper; b. Canada; P. Kerwin (Ireland) and Susan Kerwin
John E., d. 6/22/1938 at 84/5/15; laborer; married; b. Canada; James McVety (Ireland) and Annie Miles (Ireland)
William, d. 5/7/1918 at – in Warren; retired; widower

MERCHANT,
Clara Eva, d. 12/7/1937 at 81/9/19 in Glencliff; retired; widower; b. Newbury, VT; S. McKillips and Mary Stebbins

MERRILL,
Carrie Maud, d. 10/17/1894 at ½ in Warren; pneumonia; b. Warren; Fred Merrill and Lizzie Cummings
Clarence, d. 6/16/1986 at 75 in Haverhill; b. Deerfield; Albert D. Merrill and Nelley Clay
Elizabeth A., d. 10/20/1911 at 76/3/18 in Warren; strangulated hernia; widow; b. Ryegate, VT

Emily J., d. 6/19/1926 at 86/0/25 in Warren; housewife; b. Orange;
Ezekiel Collins
Emily Jane, d. 10/28/1922 at 72/7/18 in Warren; married; b.
Piermont; John Hartwell (Piermont) and Emeline Ladd
(Piermont)
Enoch, d. 11/12/1906 at 88 in Warren; old age; farmer; married; b.
Warren; Samuel Merrill (Warren) and Sallie Noyes (Landaff)
Ernest E., d. 1/15/1938 at 48/4/20; RR fireman; married; b. Warren;
Fred J. Merrill (Rumney) and E. Cummings (Warren)
Fannie S., d. 12/26/1917 at 26/7/20 in Warren; housewife; married;
b. Glencliff; Ethelbert Fifield (Glencliff) and Merriam Morrison
(Lawrence)
Fred J., d. 1/24/1932 at 74/7/6; farmer; widower; b. Rumney; George
L. Merrill (NH) and Emeline French (NH)
George B., d. 7/9/1921 at 76/0/27 in Warren; farmer; married; b.
Warren; Nathaniel Merrill (Warren) and Betsey Bixby (Warren)
George E., d. 5/11/1896 at 16/6/14 in Warren; conc. of brain; farmer;
single; b. Warren; George B. Merrill and F. Jane Wesley
George W., d. 2/19/1899 at 71/0/6 in Warren; malarial fever; farmer;
married; b. Warren; Samuel L. Merrill
Hannah, d. 11/12/1906 at 78 in Warren; senile dementia;
housekeeper; married; b. Warren; Hobart Wyatt and Sarah B.
Lowe
Harriet, d. 11/5/1911 at 87/11 in Warren; debil. inc. to old age;
widow; b. Montpelier; Samuel Osborne (Piermont) and Dulcena
Pope (Montpelier, VT)
Hattie M., d. 5/15/1973 at 84 in Hanover; b. NH; Charles Elliott and
Meanie Whitcher
Henry N., d. 3/30/1920 at 79/8/18 in Warren; undertaker; widower; b.
Warren; Nathaniel Merrill (Warren) and Judith Little (Warren)
J. Motley, d. 10/11/1906 at 59/2/11 in Warren; typhoid fever; farmer;
single; b. Cambridge; John Merrill (Warren) and Mary Wells
(Plymouth)
James F., d. 3/22/1906 at 64/11/28 in Warren; chronic nephritis;
carpenter; married; b. Warren; James S. Merrill (Warren) and
Judith Noyes
Jessie O., d. 2/2/1923 at 78/5/23 in Warren; retired; widower; b.
Warren; True Merrill (Warren) and Sally Clough (Warren)
John Bell, d. 8/28/1947 at 65/7/13 in Warren; painter; married; b.
Warren; Jesse Orrin Merrill (Warren) and Emily Jane Hartwell
(Piermont)

John S., d. 2/15/1919 at 81/8/21 in Warren; retired; married; b. Andover; John Merrill

Judith, d. 1/12/1896 at 85/10/17 in Warren; old age; housewife; widow; b. Warren; Amos Little

Mary L., d. 11/18/1907 at 70/2/23 in Warren; apoplexy; housekeeper; widow; b. Warren; Nathan Willey (Medford, MA) and Mary French (Rumney)

Mildred C., d. 12/19/1954 at 58 in Hanover; cook; widow; b. Warren; Thelbert Fifield and Merriam Morrison

Millie C., d. 10/22/1917 at 61/0/7 in Warren; housewife; married; b. Germany; August Hirsch

Mrs. True, d. 12/20/1888 at 82/0/8 in Warren; widow; b. Warren; Nathaniel Clough

Nathaniel, d. 3/28/1911 at 83/2/10 in Warren; shock; farmer; married; b. Warren; Nathaniel Merrill and Betsy Bixby (Warren)

Paul R., d. 9/30/1971 at 71 in Acton, MA; electronics engineer; b. MA; Samuel Merrill and Emile Hirsch

Phebe Jane, d. 10/27/1930 at 86/5/17 in Bradford; housewife; widow; b. Bethlehem; John Wesley (England) and ----- Blossom

Robert E., d. 1/15/1892 at 87/0/26 in Warren; la grippe; physician; b. Warren; Samuel Merrill (MA) and Hannah Elliott

Sam A., d. 7/10/1932 at 79/8/2; farmer; widower; b. Warren; George W. Merrill and Elizabeth Franklin

Sarah C., d. 3/5/1911 at 69/2/5 in Warren; pneumonia; housewife; married; b. Warren; Hazen Libbey (Warren) and Mehitable Clifford

Sarah Filden, d. 9/29/1922 at 80/4/9 in Warren; widow; b. Warren; Russell Clifford (N. Hampton) and Sarah Fitts (Wentworth)

Walter S., d. 3/27/1915 at – in Warren; laborer; single; b. Warren; Albert B. Merrill (Warren) and Martha J. Noyes

William, d. 6/2/1902 at 77/4/23 in Lowell; erysipelas; retired; married; b. Warren; Samuel L. Merrill (Warren) and Sally Noyes (Warren)

William S., d. 7/3/1896 at 76 in Warren; heart disease; clergyman; married; b. Meredith; John Merrill and Abby Ward

Winifred Perry, d. 12/5/1977 at 83 in Acton, MA; at home; b. Warren; Onslow Perry and Ann Leighton

Zelinda, d. 3/7/1914 at 86/9/2 in Warren; widow; b. Landaff; Francis Knight (Bath) and Katherine Moore (Champl'e, NY)

MERRY,

Gladys, d. 2/13/1938 at 40/5; housewife; married; b. Lincoln; Benjamin Whitney (Northumberland) and Edith Remick (Lancaster)

MERTSCH,

Emilie H., d. 12/21/1942 at 90/3/23; housewife; divorced; b. Lieberase, Germany

Otto, d. 4/8/1963 at 79 in Haverhill; retired; divorced; b. Forst, Germany; Carl Mertsch and Emily Muller

MERTSH,

William F., d. 8/10/1989 in Plymouth; teaching; b. Candia; Otto F. Mertsh and Hildried Merrifield

MEYETTE,

Willard, d. 1/1/1993 at 75 in Woodsville; self employed; b. Glocester, RI; Louis Meyette and Rosalie -----

MINNIS,

Rita P., d. 5/3/2003 in Glencliff; Ephriam Bulduc and Eva Roy

MITCHELL,

Alice, d. 4/7/1906 at 27/9/28 in Warren; tuberculosis; housewife; married; b. Canada; Joseph Gervais (Canada) and Flora Gosley (Canada)

MONTANO,

Joseph, d. 10/23/1977 at 81 in Haverhill; masonry contractor; Matthew Montano

MOODY,

Kenneth V., d. 3/23/1985 at 79 in Warren; woodsman, carpenter; b. Albany; William Moody and Mabel Moore

Marion, d. 2/3/1968 at 61 in Hanover; cook; married; b. NH; George Whitcher and Sarah Stickney

Thelma V., d. 9/23/1930 at 0/0/5; b. Warren; Kenneth V. Moody (Albany) and Marion F. Whitcher (Warren)

MOORE,

John, d. 5/26/1888 at 41 in Warren

MOREY,
Annie V., d. 2/15/1934 at 69/8/14; housewife; widow; b. Inverness, Canada; ----- McIntire

MORGAN,
Ralph S., d. 8/15/1989 at 79 in Woodsville; baking; b. Dorchester, MA; William Morgan and Elizabeth Redihough
William, d. 8/1/1969 at 84 in Warren; sheet metal; b. England; William E. Morgan and Susan Yudd

MORIN,
Fred, d. 11/17/1967 at 68 in Warren; laborer; single; b. Canada; Leon Morin and Leona Newbonne
James, d. 8/2/1999 at 90; b. Rudby, ND; Edwin Morin and Miella Tanguay

MORRISON,
son, d. 7/7/1917 at – in Warren; b. Warren; Rodney Morrison (NS) and Cora A. Merrill (Warren)
Alex, d. 3/3/1934 at 75/2/3; blacksmith; married; b. Sydney, NS; Alexander Morrison (Sydney, NS) and Margaret ----- (Halifax, NS)
Cora A., d. 11/11/1962 at 88 in Warren; housewife; widow; b. Warren; Asa B. Merrill and Chastina C. Merrill
Hannah, d. 2/2/1910 at 76/4/27 in Warren; la grippe; housewife; married; b. Warren; Dan Marston and Eliza Cross
Rodney L., d. 12/15/1942 at 76/11/15; fireman; married; b. NS
Tina L., d. 8/20/1932 at 20/6/18; housework; single; b. Warren; Rodney L. Morrison (Baddeck, NS) and Cora A. Merrill (Warren)

MORSE,
Hattie B., d. 5/7/1898 at 0/5/26 in Warren; bronchitis; b. Warren; George Morse
Ira Herbert, d. 7/20/1960 at 85 in Plymouth; shoe retailer; married; b. Chester; Samuel Morse and Luella Merrill
Julia B., d. 2/2/1942 at 48/8/5; writer housewife; married; b. Lowell, MA; John Burke
Lillian W., d. 12/8/1973 at 80 in Warren; world traveler; b. MA; Wilbur Whitecomb and ----- McGennon

Nellie V., d. 7/6/1898 at 23/6/22 in Warren; phthisis; housewife; married; b. Hudson

Philip M., d. 10/8/1991 at 89 in Plymouth; shoe; b. Nashua; Ira H. Morse and Lillian Little

MOSES,

son, d. 2/16/1919 at "few hours" in Warren; b. Warren; Clarence H. Moses (Warren) and Lucy Fisher (Manehst, England)

Clarence H., d. 11/17/1947 at 61/6/25 in Plymouth; farmer; divorced; b. Warren; Lubian E. Moses (Colebrook) and Merry J. Whitcher (Warren)

Fred, d. 11/3/1960 at 86 in Goffstown; farmer; married; b. Warren; John Moses and Viola Merrill

Gladys E., d. 6/30/1907 at 0/1/16 in Warren; nephrites; b. Warren; Clarence Moses (Warren) and Lena M. Foote (Warren)

Joseph Walter, d. 4/17/1945 at 23/6/2 in Warren; none; single; b. Warren; Clarence H. Moses (Warren) and Lucy Fisher (Manchester, England)

Lubian E., d. 6/25/1928 at 69/2/18; laborer; widower; b. Colebrook; John Moses and Fannie Munn

Mary J., d. 2/12/1924 at 66 in Warren; housewife; married; b. Warren; Joseph Whitcher and Jane Elbert

Ralph W., d. 1/24/1971 at 57 in Orford; carpenter; b. NH; George Moses and Anna Gale

MOSHOLDER,

Kenneth R., d. 3/1/1988 at 54 in Hanover; air traffic controller; b. Rochester, NY; Clifford Mosholder and Gladys Greening

MUDER,

Alice Jane, d. 4/8/1957 at 76 in Franklin; housewife; married; b. Cabott, PA; John Stepp and Nancy Cooper

NASH,

Alice G., d. 11/13/1959 at 84 in Manchester; housewife; widow; b. Penacook; Joseph C. A. Mercerve and Mary Harvey

Herman, d. 8/16/1895 at 41/3/2 in Warren; inflam. rheum.; painter; b. Northfield, MA; Albin N. Nash and Mary A. Haley

Mary J., d. 8/29/1925 at 73/5/14 in Warren; widow; b. Rutland, VT

NELSON,
Bernice Dorothy, d. 1/2/1973 at 70 in Laconia; housewife; b. NS; Rufus Mosher and Harriet -----

NETTLE,
Jane W., d. 1/28/1927 at 80/9/5 in Warren; b. Cornwall, England; Phillip Wilkins (England) and Martha Wilkins (England)

NICOL,
Alice M., d. 1/22/1970 at 89 in Plymouth; housewife; b. NH; Ira N. Libbey and Lucia Whiteman

Allan P., d. 9/16/1966 at 78 in Warren; blacksmith; widower; b. Robertsville, NB; John Nicol and Bertha Beck

Janet Alice, d. 5/4/1933 at –; b. Haverhill; John H. Nicol (Warren) and Marjorie A. Brown (Wentworth)

John Henry, d. 11/28/1988 at 83 in Plymouth; mail carrier; b. Warren; William B. Nicol and Alice Libby

Marjorie B., d. 11/29/1957 at 53 in Warren; housewife; married; b. Wentworth; Charles H. Brown and Eva M. Breck

William B., d. 3/26/1959 at 91 in Warren; blacksmith; married; b. Bathurst, NB; John Nicol and Bertha Beck

NIZIAKOWICZ,
Joseph, d. 7/24/1996 at 87 in Haverhill; shoe mfg.; b. Manchester; Joseph Niziakowicz and Sophie Twaioz

NORTH,
Catherine Fish, d. 6/9/1974 at 76 in Warren; teacher; b. OH

NORTON,
Mary E., d. 7/10/1950 at 64 in Concord; housewife; married; b. Warren; George N. Boynton and May Wolcott

NOYES,
Hattie Lottie, d. 7/15/1944 at 88/11/5 in Concord; retired; single; b. Warren; Joseph Noyes (Bath) and Elizabeth Blake (Sutton)

O'BRIEN,
William L., Jr., d. 10/11/2004 in Warren; William L. O'Brien, Sr. and Helen Flynn

O'MALLEY,
Margaret, d. 10/12/1980 at 80 in Warren; retired; b. MA; Michael O'Malley and Ellen O'Malley

OLIN,
Marion Teresa, d. 6/17/1901 at 28/11 in Warren; pneumonia; housewife; married; b. Chicopee, MA; Patrick Barry (Chicopee, MA) and Nellie York (Chicopee, MA)

OUELLETTE,
Helen, d. 6/17/1974 at 77 in Concord; none; b. NH; Alphonse Martineau and Pamela Kuroate

OWEN,
Ada, d. 7/23/1947 at 52/9/2 in Warren; widow; b. Wiggin Lan England; John Bennett and Eva Critchley

PAGE,
Luella S., d. 6/22/1928 at 69/8/25; home; widow; b. Warren; Walter Libbey and ----- Bixby

PAIGE,
William, d. 12/27/1993 at 67 in Woodsville; unknown; b. Manchester; Lester Randall Paige and Esther Bowman Seaver

PALMER,
Vincent, d. 8/21/1971 at 55 in Hanover; library technician; b. NY; Floyd Palmer and Mary Louise Newman

PARE,
Doris, d. 3/21/2003 in Glencliff; Edward Minkler

PARKER,
Almina, d. 9/16/1977 at 69 in Concord; housewife; b. NH; John Bassett and Edith Gibson
Gary P., d. 11/29/1989 at 30 in Warren; state trooper; b. Tarrytown, NY; Guy P. Parker and Barbara Miller
Lebina H., d. 11/13/1928 at 72/11/26; carpenter; widower; b. Benton; Prescott Parker (Lyman) and Martha Fitzpatrick (Ireland)

PARMENTER,
Mabelle E., d. 8/15/1961 at 82 in Plymouth; housewife; widow; b.
Whitefield; Edward L. Houghton and Delia Wolcott

PATRICK,
Wilfred H., d. 12/17/1980 at 52 in Warren; truck driver; b. Canada;
Thomas Patrick and Sarah -----

PATTERSON,
Melvin A., d. 4/7/1976 at 69 in Laconia; logger; b. NS; Fred
Patterson and Roxy Wall

PEASE,
Edwin Samuel, d. 8/18/1948 at 77/5/3 in Warren; merchant; married;
b. Wentworth; Samuel Pease (Ellsworth) and Sarah J. Randall
(Ellsworth)
Florence M., d. 5/1/1952 at 68 in Warren; rug maker; widow; b.
Franconia; Edward Edgerly and Stella M. Combs
Leonra, d. 5/22/1992 at 68 in Woodsville; housewife; b. Cocoa
Beach, FL; Ira Riley and Emma Harrington

PERKINS,
Rudy Alan, d. 11/24/1984 at 30 in Warren; carpenter; b. Plymouth;
Vernon J. Perkins and Marjorie Burnham

PERRY,
Anna B., d. 6/9/1943 at 74/3/13; housewife; widow; b. E. Haverhill;
William H. Leighton (Danville, VT) and Lucina Nason (Newbury,
VT)
Field C., d. 3/4/1987 at 86 in Woodsville; printing; b. Lebanon;
Charles L. Perry and Rose L. Matson
George D., d. 8/10/1970 at 76 in Haverhill; retired; b. NH; George E.
Perry and Aldeline E. Berry
Gladys T., d. 11/11/1970 at 73 in Haverhill; retired; b. MA; Iolas
Clifford and Annie Cameron
Lydia J., d. 12/2/1903 at 60/4/11 in Warren; cancer; housekeeper;
married; b. Deerfield
Onslow Davis, d. 3/3/19122 at 61/4/16 in Warren; stone man;
married; b. Chichester; Davis C. Perry (London) and Sarah
Haines (Portsmouth)

PETERSON,
Andrew, d. 2/5/1933 at 2/9/11; b. Charlestown, MA; Ernest Peterson (Denmark) and Anna Milloy (Everett, MA)

PHAIR,
Josephine, d. 6/12/1952 at 82 in Boston, MA; housewife; widow; b. Warren; Sylvester Flanders and Sarah Willey
Thomas William, d. 4/17/1937 at 71/5/12 in Warren; gardener; married; b. Ireland; William T. Phair and Rebecca Spillane

PHELON,
Ethel Ruth, d. 3/24/1983 at 88 in Haverhill; resident of state inst.; b. S. Glastonbury, CT; Robert W. Warren and Jennie Scranton

PHILBROOK,
Kathleen, d. 9/28/1986 at 86 in Dover; burial permit
William, d. 8/15/1967 at 65 in Haverhill; carpenter; married; b. Springfield, ME; Alfred Philbrook and Maude Cosser

PICKERING,
George W., d. 1/21/1920 at 70/7/15 in Warren; farmer; married; b. Italy; William Pickering and Elizabeth -----

PIERCE,
Ruth, d. 4/6/1972 at 73 in Concord; housework; b. MA; Caleb Morse and Addie B. Morse

PIKE,
Alanson James, d. 5/19/1978 at 82 in Plymouth; lumber grader; b. Warren; Arthur Livermore Pike and Eva Judkins
Arthur L., d. 9/9/1951 at 88 in Holderness; farmer; separated; b. Warren; Walter Pike
Dorothy Irene, d. 12/19/1978 at 76 in Plymouth; housewife; b. Orford
Eva G., d. 12/8/1953 at 83 in Warren; housewife; widow; b. Danville, VT; Harvey Judkins
Herbert, d. 11/19/1956 at 89 in Springfield, MA; chef; single; b. Warren; Walter Pike and Sarah Swain
James C., d. 10/1/1975 at 60 in Concord; woodsman; b. ME; Alvah Pike and Nannie Goodwin
Jennie F., d. 10/6/1953 at 77 in Warren; housewife; married; b. Benton; DeElden Tibbetts and Rose Anna King

Joseph Walter, d. 1/27/1961 at 90 in Warren; farmer; widower; b. Warren; Walter Pike and Sarah Swain
Robert Arthur, d. 5/24/1981 at 60 in Warren; fish culturist; b. NH; Alanson J. Pike and Dorothy I. Morey
Sarah E., d. 9/5/1893 at 59/7 in Warren; apoplexy; housekeeper; Josiah Swain (Sanbornton) and Jane Eaton

PILLSBURY,
Anson M., d. 6/26/1895 at 67/1/26 in Warren; Bright's dis.; blacksmith; b. Warren; Thomas Pillsbury and Sally Clement
Emerson, d. 5/10/1896 at 63/6/19 in Warren; apoplexy; blacksmith; married; b. Warren; Thomas Pillsbury and Sally Pillsbury

PLACE,
Melinda, d. 6/18/1898 at 82/11/27 in Warren; tuberculosis; housewife; widow; b. Benton; David Elliott

PLUMMER,
William H., d. 10/24/1905 at 37/7/26 in Plymouth; typhoid fever; painter; married; b. Plymouth; Henry Plummer (Meredith) and Flora Young (Plymouth)

POLK,
William, d. 12/12/1951 at 80 in Concord; mill worker; b. Canada; Alec Polk

POOLE,
Robert W., d. 8/23/2003 in Warren; Leroy Poole and Margaret Shuman

POTTER,
Wilbur, d. 11/2/2000 in Glencliff; R. Potter and Margaret Gollar

POWELL,
Erika, d. 6/23/1980 at 59 in Hanover

PRESCOTT,
Esther B., d. 1/9/1892 at 73/9/5 in Warren; la grippe; housekeeper; b. Warren; Isaac Merrill (Warren) and Annie Blodgett
Hester A., d. 9/2/1934 at 88/0/13; at home; single; b. Warren; G. W. Prescott (Hill) and Esther Merrill (Warren)

Julia F., d. 10/10/1914 at 82/5/9 in Warren; widow; b. Stratford;
   Abijah French (Maidstone, VT) and Hannah Pratt (Stratford)
Lucian W., d. 8/27/1909 at 77 in Warren; nephritis; clergyman;
   married

PREW,
Fred, d. 8/18/1887 at –; b. Warren; Fred Prew and Mary -----

PROUTY,
Audrey R., d. 7/7/1982 at 55 in Hanover; housewife; b. Medford, MA;
   Augustus Horsch and Nellie Finn

PROVENCHER,
Grace, d. 4/29/1938 at 55/9/11; housewife; married; b. Inverness,
   Canada; James Currier (Inverness, Canada) and Ellen Dexter
   (Bethlehem)

PUSHEE,
Clarence L., d. 3/25/2003 in Warren; Clarence Pushee and Evelyn
   Tattersall

PYKE,
Hartley Lee, d. 2/24/1911 at 20/2 in Warren; pneumonia; carpenter;
   married; b. NS; Edward Pyke (NS) and Helen Moura (NS)

QUIMBY,
Lenna, d. 12/27/1962 at 77 in Meredith; housewife; widow; b.
   Warren; George Gale and Belle Simpton

RAMSDELL,
Agnes, d. 1/24/2000 in Glencliff

RAMSEY,
Sarah E., d. 9/30/1918 at 72 in Concord; retired; widow; b. Warren;
   Jacob Gale (NH) and Mary Heath

RAY,
Doris H. Rowell, d. 6/30/1958 at 53 in Haverhill; housewife; married;
   b. Meredith; Frank C. Rowell and Agnes Hoyt
Floyd R., d. 10/2/1989 at 76 in Lebanon; postmaster; b. Dorchester,
   MA; Edward E. Ray and Sara Stock

RAYMOND,

Gertrude, d. 12/21/1938 at 19/7/29; housework; single; b. Claremont; Joseph Raymond (Canada) and Jennie Palmer (Bradford, VT)

READE,

Amos L., d. 5/5/1957 at 61 in Warren; millwright; married; b. NS; James Reade and Priscilla Ripley

REDMAN,

Howard B., d. 11/4/1985 at 71 in Plymouth; engineer; b. Chelmsford, MA; Walter Redman and Edith Bliss

Phyllis C., d. 12/20/1988 at 57 in Plymouth; nurses aid; b. Tilton; Charles Belyea and Alberta Harriman

REED,

Frank E., d. 7/6/1947 at 77 in Concord; widower

Winifred M., d. 11/10/1932 at 60/0/15; housewife; married; b. Orford; Wallace W. Johnson (N. Stratford) and Jane R. Curtis (N. Stratford)

REILL,

Johann, d. 6/22/1960 at 56 in Haverhill; waiter; b. Nuinech, Bavaria; Hans Reill and Anna -----

RICHARDSON,

Cyrus, d. 1/30/1901 at 74/9/7 in Warren; anaemia; married; b. Monmouth, ME; Jonathan Richardson (Standish, ME) and Ruth Lewis

Martha, d. 12/9/1910 at 84/5/3 in Summit; acute bronchitis; housewife; widow; b. ME; John Richardson and Mary Orcutt

RITTAL,

Mary J., d. 2/13/1929 at 89/9/4; housewife; widow; b. Gloucester, MA; John Morgan (England) and Rebecca Morris (England)

RIOUX,

Dolores A., d. 11/20/2000 in Glencliff; James Bagwell and Margaret King

ROBERT,
Ethel M., d. 9/1/1984 in Plymouth; burial permit

ROBERTS,
Kenneth E., d. 8/15/1982 at 71 in Plymouth; sawmill worker; b.
Warren, AZ; Elmer C. Roberts and Alma St. John

ROBERTSON,
Roberta Lee, d. 12/12/1990 at 75 in Hanover; paper machine
operator; b. Stark; Robert J. Emerson and Zilpha L. Lee

ROBINSON,
Charles Orrin, d. 4/14/1936 at 83 in Belmont, MA; leather bus.;
widower; b. Winsted, CT; Otis S. Robinson and Malissa B.
Walker
Earl J., d. 1/6/1906 at 26/5/21 in Warren; typhoid fever; farmer;
married; b. Dorchester

ROBY,
Hattie Bell, d. 1/14/1942 at 79/6/28; retired; single; b. Concord;
George Baxter Roby (Concord) and Mary Sargent (Concord)
Melia M., d. 3/13/1887 at 0/2; Fred Roby and Mary E. -----

ROGERS,
Emma L., d. 2/12/1940 at 94/4/7; single; b. Haverhill; Charles
Rogers (Orford) and P'lia Hutchins (Campton)
Ronald W., d. 3/24/1964 at 56 in Hanover; storekeeper; married; b.
Roxbury, MA; Otis Rogers and Lena F. Permenter

ROLLINS,
Hiram B., d. 5/28/1919 at 55 in Warren; laborer; married; b. Orford;
Moses J. Rollins (Ellsworth) and Esther Brown (Rumney)
Louise, d. 12/21/1914 at 80/1/24 in Warren; widow; b. Haverhill;
Joseph B. Cutting (Haverhill) and Esther Gould (Haverhill)

ROMON,
Jose A., d. 2/22/1962 at 16 hr., 54 min. in Haverhill; b. Haverhill;
Anthony J. Romon and Marie M. F. Roulx

ROULX,
Mabel L., d. 1/18/2003 in Warren; James Godville and Edna Short

Sandra Mary, d. 11/13/1943 at 0/4/4; b. Warren; Oscar Roulx (PQ) and Mabel Godville (Warren)

ROWELL,
Agnes H., d. 6/16/1953 at 79 in Concord; teacher; widow; b. Meredith; George C. Hoyt and Mary Cornell
Frank C., d. 6/28/1939 at 65/10/3; mechanic; married; b. Alexandria; Weston Rowell (Alexandria) and Nettie Follansbee (Franklin)
Nettie A., d. 6/25/1932 at 86/9/25; retired; widow; b. Hill; Isaac Follansbee and Jane Gale

ROY,
son, d. 7/4/1898 at – in Warren; stillborn; b. Warren; George Roy

RUEL,
Leon A., d. 11/26/1893 at 20/11 in Warren; consumption; laborer; b. Canada; Lawrence Ruel (Canada) and Angel. Poulint

RUELL,
son, d. 10/7/1907 at – in Warren; stillborn; b. Warren; Joseph Ruel (Canada) and Mary M. Vallar (Canada)

RUSSEAU,
Lawrence R., d. 8/8/1993 at 68 in Plymouth; plasterer; b. Ann Arbor, MI; Lawrence Russeau and Edith Filmore

RUSSELL,
Ada, d. 2/8/1933 at 79/2/13; inmate; widow; b. Lowell, MA
William B., d. 5/3/1923 at 64/4/26 in Warren; physician; married; George W. Russell (Sutton) and Sarah J. Bean (Newbury)

SACKETT,
Norman L., d. 1/10/2000 in Plymouth; Charles Sackett and Janice Ball

SAKOVICH,
Esther, d. 10/25/2001 in Benton; John Sakovich and Stephania Seraichik

SANBORN,
Amelia G., d. 3/20/1898 at 20/3 in Warren; tuberculosis; housewife; married; b. Cincinnati, OH; Alonzo Day
Joseph, d. 11/24/1900 at 75/3/18 in Warren; dropsy; merchant; married; Gilford; Joseph Sanborn (Gilford) and Ruth Carter (Kingston)

SARGENT,
Frank V., d. 7/6/1889 at 34/5/12 in Warren; fracture of skull; lumberman; married; b. Franklin; Vit. Sargent and Nancy -----
John, d. 9/12/1913 at 58/0/29 in Wentworth; pneumonia; farmer; married; b. Piermont

SAVAGE,
Thomas, d. 1/1/1903 at 44 in Warren; heart disease; farmer; married; George Savage and Rosanna Merrill

SCHLEICHER,
Michael, d. 2/6/2004 in Plymouth; Emil Schleicher and Catherine Zerby

SCONTSAS,
Andrew, d. 2/10/2000 in Woodsville; George Scontsas and Zaphiro Pappadopoulos

SEARS,
George F., d. 4/4/1986 at 74 in Haverhill; laundry supvr.; b. Plymouth, MA; Fred Sears, Jr. and Della Newhall

SEAVEY,
George Ellet, d. 6/3/1973 at 64 in Franklin; retired funeral dir.; b. NH; Ellet Seavey and Laura B. Keniston

SEELEY,
Nellie L., d. 8/7/1962 at 81 in Keene; homemaker; widow; b. Brockton, MA; Frank Edwards and E. French
William, d. 6/24/1958 at 80 in Keene; caboron bob'n; married; b. Underhill, VT; Reuben Seeley and Florence Story

SEEWALD,
Xavier F., d. 7/4/1957 at 55 in Hanover; waiter; married; b. Austria

SEVERANCE,
Lucy P., d. 7/19/1926 at 76/10/0 in Warren; at home; b. Hebron;
Daniel Hobart (Hebron) and May Frys (Mathews, MA)

SHATTUCK,
Ursula, d. 11/9/1933 at 91/2/25; housework; widow; b. Bethlehem

SHELDON,
Caroline, d. 5/19/1909 at 75 in Medford; accidental burns

SHELLEY,
Aulay Oscar, d. 11/27/1966 at 69 in Warren; merchant; married; b.
Pike; Sidney Shelley and Flora Archer
Glenna Hunt, d. 11/1/1945 at 59/10/16 in Woodsville; housewife;
married; b. Johnson, VT; Bertron A. Hunt (Johnson, VT) and
Nettie Morse (Stowe, VT)
Sidney C., d. 2/20/1949 at 74 in Glencliff; millwright; widower; b. N.
Haverhill; John Shelley and Mina T. Ward

SHELLY,
Nettie Louise, d. 10/22/1991 at 92 in Woodsville; store keeper; b.
Plymouth; James Belyea and Mary Fifield

SHORT,
Albert H., d. 5/29/1928 at 80/3/10; farmer; widower; b. Bl'dford,
England; William Short (Bl'dford, England) and Catherine Wells
(Blandford, England)
Earl E., d. 11/27/1929 at 2/1/13; b. Warren; George Short (Walpole)
and Nellie Wright (Piermont)
William, d. 11/22/1903 at 75/11 in Warren; carcinoma; laborer;
married; b. England; William Short (England) and Katherine
Weeks (England)

SHORTT,
daughter, d. 1/20/1913 at 0/2/2 in Warren; b. Warren; William Shortt
(Newfoundland) and Mabel Gould (Warren)
Charles B., d. 7/20/1952 at 65 in Warren; highway laborer; single; b.
Fairlee, VT; William Shortt and Rose Weymouth
Doris A., d. 7/26/1987 at 67 in Exeter; at home; b. Plymouth; Grover
C. Prescott and Della Hardy

Edward B., d. 8/9/1954 at 69 in Hanover; unemployed; widower; b. Fairlee, VT; Edwin Shortt and Laura Warner

Edwin, d. 8/12/1941 at 86/1/9; mason; widower; b. Manchester, England; William Short (England)

Ellis Everett, d. 7/2/1980 at 69 in Warren; retired IPC; b. NH; William J. Shortt and Mabel M. Gould

Frank Warren, d. 6/15/1949 at 71 in Warren; woodsman; widower; b. Whitefield; Frank C. Shores and Elsie Dexter

George A., d. 12/4/1966 at 84 in Warren; farmer; widower; b. Walpole; William Shortt

Harry E., d. 1/29/1972 at 64 in Hartford, VT; laborer; b. NH; William Shortt and Mabel Gould

Lela L., d. 11/25/1941 at 68/4/21; housewife; married; b. Warren; H. D. Whitcher (Warren) and H. M. Caswell (Haverhill)

Leon, d. 4/11/1977 at 72 in Haverhill; b. NH; William Shortt and Mabel Gould

Mabel Maria, d. 4/1/1958 at 79 in Warren; housewife; widow; b. Warren; Lewis Edwin Gould and Mary Helen Fellows

Marjorie L., d. 1/19/1996 at 60 in Warren; housewife; b. Warren; Almer Libby and Vera Ball

Milton Roy, d. 4/27/1952 at 33 in Warren; beater man; single; b. Warren; Edna Shortt

Nellie May, d. 4/16/1949 at 55 in Plymouth; housewife; married; b. Piermont; Ximenis P. Wright and Emmagene Harris

Rose D., d. 5/14/1926 at 84/3/17 in Warren; at home; b. St. John, NB; William Waymouth and Jane King

Stanley Fay, d. 4/27/1992 at 61 in Lebanon; mechanic; b. Warren; George A. Shortt and Nellie M. Wright

William J., d. 5/4/1942 at 68/5/6; section man; married; b. Newfoundland; William Shortt and D. Weymouth

SIMONDS,
Linda, d. 6/27/2005 in Plymouth; Ernest Holt and Alma Morse

SIMPSON,
Curtis H., d. 10/23/1980 at 61 in Littleton; dist. mgr. NH Elec.; b. NH; Harry C. Simpson and Lydia Brown

Ethel P., d. 9/16/1984 at 81 in Plymouth; homemaker; b. Northampton, MA; Christopher Poppy

Margery S., d. 9/3/1970 at 47 in Lisbon; housewife; b. MA; Robert Dunbar and Lillian Whitcomb

SINCLAIR,
daughter, d. 8/7/1891 at 0/0/1 in Warren; accident of birth; b. Warren; Charles Hodgdon (laborer) and Margery Sinclair (Warren)

SISKE,
Henry E., M.D., d. 11/2/1937 at 60 in Hanover; physician; married; b. Monson, MA; James M. Siske and Elizabeth MacLeod

SMART,
Annabelle E., d. 3/12/1965 at 79 in Ashland; housewife; widow; b. Haverhill; Elroy Hildreth and Ida Flanders
Frank W., d. 3/25/1945 at 69/11/0 in Hanover; foreman; married; b. Plymouth; Willis G. Smart (Subec, ME) and Ada Rossell (Bangor, ME)
Julia A., d. 9/22/1927 at 66/1/19; housewife; married; b. Magog; William Chase (Landaff) and Marg. McGivern (Ireland)
Willis G., d. 3/27/1933 at 78/11/13; lumberman; widower; b. Sebec, ME; James Smart (Sebec, ME) and Mary Chase (Brownville, ME)

SMITH,
Arthur Milton, d. 6/13/1959 at 65 in Haverhill; RR work; married; b. Warren; Walter E. Smith and Nellie Smith
Carrie Maud, b. 9/3/1917 at 42/7/9 in Warren; housewife; married; b. OH; Alonzo L. Day (OH) and Carrie Stevens (OH)
Charles H., d. 9/27/1952 at 68 in Barnet, VT; farmer; widower; b. Norwalk, CT; Samuel Smith and Martha Searles
Edith Haugaad, d. 5/26/1997 at 84 in Haverhill; newspaper; b. Ridgefield Park, NJ; Christian L. Haugaad and Camilla Jensen
Eliza E., d. 1/27/1935 at 72/4/28 in Warren; retired; widow; b. Warren; Sylvester Flanders and Sarah Willey
Emma T., d. 12/8/1949 at 67 in Warren; housewife; married; b. Werum, Sweden; Per Pierson and Hannah Monson
Eveline F., d. 3/2/1901 at 80/6 in Warren; heart disease; housekeeper; widow; b. Bristol; Moses Smith (Bridgewater) and Lucy Grundy (Bristol)
Evelyn May, d. 4/21/1928 at 2/2/15; b. Plymouth; Harry W. Smith (N. Woodstock) and Catherine Whitcher (Warren)

George F., d. 12/30/1901 at 35 in Warren; tuberculosis; farmer;
    widower; b. Belmont; George R. Smith (Tilton) and Elnora Whitcher
Harry W., d. 8/27/1967 at 84 in Meredith; section hand; divorced; b.
    Woodstock; Willie A. Smith and Hattie Sawyer
Harvey N., d. 2/6/1899 at 21/9/23 in Warren; typhoid fever; clerk;
    married; b. Plymouth; Obediah G. Smith
Joshua P., d. 6/29/1891 at – in Warren; general debility; farmer
Livona G., d. 3/27/1962 at 88 in Laconia; prac. nurse; widow; b.
    Gilford; Zebulon Smith and Phoebe Goss
Marie Mabel Floret, d. 6/18/1993 at 48 in Lebanon; sander; b.
    Warren; Oscar Roulx and Mabel Godville
Nellie M., d. 4/23/1941 at 85/2/27; housework; widow; b. Burlington,
    VT; Russell Upton (Lyndeboro) and N. M. Eastman (Warren)
Norman P., d. 11/16/1994 at 90 in Warren; civil engineer; b.
    Newburyport, MA; Arthur G. Smith and Grace A. Page
Sarah Harriet, d. 6/4/1950 at 81 in Warren; single; b. Brooklyn, NY;
    Amos A. Smith and Sarah P. Smith
Victor R., d. 7/16/1939 at 66/5/26; laborer; married; b. Plymouth;
    Frank Smith and Hattie -----
Walter P., d. 5/10/1931 at 76/11/10; farmer; married; b. Grantham;
    Joshua Smith (Enfield) and Eveline Smith (Bridgewater)
William David, d. 12/26/1988 at 61 in Haverhill; railroad; b. Monroe;
    Eben Smith and Mabel MacKay
William E., d. 2/10/1924 at 0/1/5 in Warren; b. Warren; Harry Smith
    (N. Woodstock) and Catherine Whitcher (Warren)
Zebulan, d. 8/12/1919 at 77/1/16 in Warren; ret. blacksmith; married;
    b. Sanbornton; Bernard H. Smith (Sanbornton) and Sally
    Woodman

SMOLIJ,
Hryhorij, d. 7/8/1999 at 90 in Glencliff; disabled; b. Ukraine; Vasil
    Smolij and Irene Voloscak

SORRELL,
daughter, d. 2/15/1904 at – in Warren; premature birth; b. Warren;
    Frank Sorrell (Northfield, VT) and Delia Ruel (Canada)

SPARKS,
Lizzie May, d. 7/28/1895 at 3/5/25 in Warren; inf. bowels; b. Warren;
    Henry A. Sparks (laborer) and Mira Andrews

SPENCER,
Evelyn, d. 11/5/1990 at 62 in Warren; housewife; b. Piermont; Clinton W. Stetson and Edna Robie
Martin L., d. 5/26/1995 at 31 in Boiling Spring, NC; disabled; b. Plymouth; Edward Spencer and Marie White

SPOONER,
Chester, d. 10/19/1896 at 93/9/19 in Warren; heart disease; farmer; married; b. Lisbon; Simeon Spooner and Precilla Priest
Edward, d. 11/4/1918 at 19/11/7 in Warren; board marker; single; b. Warren; Daniel Spooner (Benton) and Nora Burke (Lewiston, ME)
Irene, d. 10/8/1916 at 73/2/21 in Warren; retired; widow; b. Warren; Page Kimball (Warren) and Eugeney Page (Warren)

SPRAGUE,
John R., d. 6/17/1972 at 93 in Haverhill; retired; b. VT
Lizzie, d. 12/7/1923 at 45/8/20 in Warren; housewife; married; b. Keene; George Thayer and Emma Day
Mary R., d. 7/10/2002 in Woodsville; William Kelliher and Mary Murphy

STANLEY,
George, d. 12/9/2005 in Tilton; Leonard Stanley and Bertha Gambell

STARCK,
Eleanor L., d. 1/18/2001 in Lebanon; Russell Starck and Anna Falk

STEARNS,
Sarah B., d. 7/8/1907 at 70/1/8 in Warren; albuminuria; widow; b. Haverhill

STEERE,
Montraville I., d. 8/18/1942 at 79/8; carpenter; single; b. Lyman; Lewis Steere (Littleton) and E. M. Smith (Lowell, MA)

STETSON,
David F., d. 8/11/1903 at 73/1/1 in Warren; cerebral abscess; engineer; married; b. Lyme; Nathan Stetson (Orford) and Sarah Brown (Hanover)

Ella J., d. 6/25/1901 at 50/7/24 in Warren; heart failure;
    housekeeper; married; b. Lowell, MA; Isiah F. Ford (Benton)
    and Harriet N. Chase (Croydon)
Emma B., d. 1/7/1932 at 70/6/25; housekeeper; single; b. Lyme;
    David Stetson (Lyme) and Martha Lund (Warren)
Martha, d. 3/9/1913 at 82/6/13 in Warren; widow; b. Warren
Silas C., d. 8/9/1929 at 87/4/8; retired; widower; b. Dorchester;
    Nathan Stetson and Sarah Brown (Lyme)

STEVENS,
Abbie J., d. 4/5/1908 at 71; heart disease; housekeeper; widow
Althea, d. 6/2/1979 at 66 in Haverhill; NH Home for the Elderly; b.
    Piermont; Leon Gould and Clara Buzzel
Christine, d. 9/10/2003 in Glencliff; Orborne Stevens and Mary
    Lynch
Cora Frances, d. 5/24/1998 at 85 in Plymouth; bookkeeper; b.
    Ryegate, VT; Elmer Chamberlin and Lottie P. Chamberlin
Dorothy P., d. 7/8/1919 at 0/2/26 in Warren; b. Warren; Walter
    Stevens (Covington, VT) and Pearl Whitcher (Warren)
Ernest W., d. 1/12/1937 at 20/10/15; caretaker; single; b. Lowell,
    MA; Walter Stevens (Coventry, VT) and Pearl Whitcher
    (Warren)
Hannah I., d. 6/7/1894 at 58/9 in Warren; heart disease;
    housekeeper; b. Warren; Asa Heath and Polly Ingalls
Harry, d. 10/25/1970 at 79 in Haverhill; retired; b. ME; John Stevens
    and Dora -----
Josiah D., d. 4/18/1890 at 50/3 in Warren; pneumonia; laborer;
    Walter Stevens (Wentworth, deceased)
Lydia A., d. 1/12/1892 at 48/3 in Warren; heart disease; housewife;
    b. Laconia; Joseph Parsley and B. J. Hodgdon
Sandra Jean, d. 10/19/1943 at 8 hrs.; b. Warren; Wallace A.
    Stevens (Warren) and Althea J. Gould (Piermont)
Wallace, d. 12/28/1982 at 71 in Haverhill; mill worker; b. Warren;
    Walter Stevens and Pearl Whitcher
Walter E., d. 9/27/1940 at 56/3/25; carpenter; married; b. Coventry,
    VT; Eben Stevens (Stanstead Pl., Canada) and Evelyn Slippe

STEVENSON,
Willie H., d. 7/10/1888 at 24/11/28 in Warren; brakeman; single; b.
    Concord; William S. Stevenson and Mary L. Pierce

STEWART,
Sally A., d. 10/16/1893 at 72/11 in Warren; heart failure;
    housekeeper; b. Warren; Benjamin Bixby and Mary B. Cleasby

STIMSON,
Delton, d. 9/7/2003 in Glencliff; Elmer Stimson and Lilla Martin
Elmer, d. 4/11/1972 at 76 in Glencliff; RR telegrapher; b. NH; Henry
    Stimson and Etta Thayer
Lilla, d. 9/3/1970 at 80 in Haverhill; retired; b. NH; Henry Martin and
    Ellen Wescott
Raymond, d. 10/12/1959 at 62 in Haverhill; laborer; widower; b.
    Glencliff; Henry Stimson and Etta Thayer
Rita M., d. 9/1/2000 in Glencliff; Forrest Chase and Georgia Knight

STROBRIDGE,
Lydia, d. 12/14/1933 at 74/1/19; housework; single; b. Peacham, VT;
    Lafayette Strobridge (VT) and Elizabeth Clark (VT)

STUBBARD,
Carrie M., d. 7/28/1894 at 52/9/14 in Warren; phthisis pul.;
    housekeeper; b. Gilmanton; Theopolis Stevens (Raymond) and
    Phebe Prescott
Mary J., d. 6/29/1905 at 28 in Warren; tuberculosis; housewife;
    married; b. Newfoundland; William Short (England) and -----
    (Newfoundland)

STUPEY,
Deborah B., d. 2/18/1999 in Bensalem Twp., PA

STURTEVANT,
Maria, d. 11/13/1918 at 80/5/24 in Warren; housekeeper; married; b.
    Warren; Samuel Whitcher (Warren) and Mary Whitcher
    (Warren)
William L., d. 5/5/1926 at 71/7/18 in Warren; farmer; b. Norwich, VT

SULLHAM,
Ralph M., d. 10/6/1918 at 0/3/8 in Warren; b. Warren; Ralph G.
    Sullham (Worcester, VT) and Iva E. Reed (Wentworth)

SULLIVAN,
Francis, d. 10/13/1901 at 4/4/24 (?) in Warren; acute alcoholism; b. Boston

SWAIN,
son, d. 2/18/1911 at 0/0/2 in Warren; infantile cononliuns; b. Warren; Grace Swain (Warren)

Darius O., d. 5/21/1908 at 65; paralayis; farmer; married; b. Warren

Eben O., d. 8/3/1903 at 83/7/3 in Warren; cerebral congestion; farmer; widower; b. Sanbornton; Josiah Swain (Sanbornton) and Jane Eaton (Sanbornton)

Elmer E., d. 4/11/1937 at 73/1/4 in Warren; retired; married; b. Warren; Samuel Swain and Mary Jane Gale

Guy K., d. 2/10/1902 at 32/11/16 in Nashua; suicide by shooting; brakeman; married; b. Warren; William Swain (Hebron) and Sarah Caswell (Haverhill)

Harry W., d. 12/30/1952 at 79 in Piermont; farmer; married; b. Warren; William Swain and Sarah Caswell

Jennie Nancy, d. 2/12/1937 at 78/5/4 in Lowell, MA; at home; single; b. Warren; Eben Swain and Nancy Libbey

Joseph, d. 12/12/1930 at 49/3/25; married; b. Pt. Clyde, NS; Horace Swain (NS) and Sarah Boyd (NS)

Josephine Ada, d. 9/1/1955 at 78 in Concord; housekeeper; single; b. Warren; William Swain and Sarah Caswell

Josiah, d. 3/9/1895 at 79/7/3 in Warren; farmer; b. Sanbornton; Josiah Swain and Jane Eaton

Lottie M., d. 10/7/1896 at 2/8/5 in Warren; scalding; b. W. Thornton; Harry W. Swain and Mattie L. Downing

Mattie Louise, d. 10/11/1961 at 89 in Piermont; housewife; widow; b. Ellsworth; Benjamin Downing and Martha Sherburn

Nancy, d. 6/11/1900 at 75/8/7 in Warren; old age; housekeeper; married; b. Warren; Nathaniel Libby (Landaff) and Nancy Abbott (Warren)

Ruth G., d. 4/25/1897 at 0/4/22 in Warren; strangulation; b. Warren; Charles I. Swain and Grace S. Little

Samuel E., d. 10/14/1894 at 58/4/21 in Warren; cerebral apoplexy; farmer; b. Weare; Josiah Swain (Sanbornton) and Sarah Eaton

Sarah E., d. 3/21/1893 at 81/10 in Warren; old age, dropsy; housekeeper; b. Weare

Sarah L., d. 7/4/1911 at 74/2/23 in Plymouth; paralysis of bowels; married; b. Haverhill; Newell Caswell and Mary Caswell (Haverhill)

William, d. 5/6/1913 at 81/9/19 in Warren; nephritis; farmer; widower; b. Sanbornton; Josiah Swain (Sanbornton) and Jane Eaton (Sanbornton)

SWETT,

Elijah N., d. 1/27/1905 at 62/0/17 in Warren; pneumonia; farmer; married; Aden Swett and Jane Noyes (Groton)

TANGUAY,

Louis, d. 10/11/1910 at 0/4/4 in Warren; acute indigestion; b. Warren; Nobert Tanguay (Canada) and Leona M. Sorrell (W. Thornton)

TAYLOR,

Grace M., d. 6/30/1946 at 79/4/18 in Warren; retired; widow; b. Carlton, NS; Joseph B. Miller (Forks, NS) and Hannah Perry (Chebogue, NS)

TENSEL,

Cathrine, d. 7/18/1999 in Benton; Patrick Manning and Margaret McDonald

TEWKSBURY,

Lydia, d. 3/14/1976 at 82 in Woodsville; housewife; b. NH; Russell Bailey and Mary Wright

THISTLE,

Emma I., d. 10/31/1954 at 68 in Plymouth; housewife; married; b. Haverhill; Onslow Perry and Anna B. Leighton

Olive M., d. 3/21/1962 at 66 in Unity; housewife; married; b. Newport; Henry Jordon and Addie Potter

TIBADEAUX,

Flavian, d. 1/5/1887 at 16/0/11; farming; single; b. Canada

TIBBETTS,

daughter, d. 7/24/1906 at – in Warren; malnutrition; b. Warren; Leon R. Tibbetts (Haverhill) and Carrie R. Fifield (Warren)

Carrie Rosemond, d. 11/7/1943 at 73/5/14; retired; widow; b.
Warren; Edwin L. Fifield (Warren) and Mary Ann Gerald
(Warren)
Clarence M., d. 4/14/1909 at 17/7/25 in Warren; tiannotic meningitis;
laborer; single; b. Warren; Leon R. Tibbetts (Haverhill) and
Carrie Fifield (Warren)
George E., d. 1/1/1911 at 70 in Warren; apoplexy; leather cutter;
single; b. Stoneham
Leon H., d. 3/27/1903 at 19/10/3 in Warren; typhoid fever; RR
section; single; b. Benton; Delden Tibbetts (Haverhill) and Rose
A. King (Canada)
Leon R., d. 6/16/1926 at 60/0/13 in Glencliff; laborer; b. Haverhill;
William Tibbetts (Haverhill) and Urantha Page (Haverhill)
Maryann, d. 10/24/1989 at 85 in Woodsville; homemaker; b.
Glencliff; Leon Tibbetts and Carrie R. Fifield

TILLEY,
Harry Merrill, d. 5/6/1968 at 63 in Warren; farmer; married; b. NH;
William Tilley and Sarah J. Merrill
William, d. 10/2/1933 at 65/10/21; farmer; widower; William Tilley
and Elenor -----

TITUS,
Doris R., d. 1/21/1982 at 65 in Warren; housewife; b. Somerville,
MA; Leonard Rockwell and Katherine Tholander
Frank A., d. 7/23/1962 at 47 in Hartford, VT; carpenter; widower; b.
Boxford, MA; Frank Titus and Ruth Gilliland

TOBIN,
Margery, d. 5/18/1993 at 83 in Woodsville; self employed; b.
Bloomfield, NJ; Richard Tobin and Stella Schiener

TODD,
William Merrill, d. 10/6/1951 at 81 in Warren; phone test man;
married; b. Amesbury, MA; Albert Merrill Todd and Emily
Bradbury

TOMASO,
Joseph, d. 8/5/1902 at 40 in Warren; accident; laborer; b. Italy

TREGANZA,
L. Robert, d. 9/4/1952 at 66 in Moultonboro; minister; married; b. Hazelgreen, WI; James R. Treganza and Eliza Laurie

TRUELOVE,
Margu. J., d. 12/24/1904 at 0/0/2 in Warren; manition; b. Warren; Harry Truelove (Patterson, NJ) and Cora M. Elliott (Warren)

TUCKER,
Hugh B., d. 10/3/1929 at 35; laborer

TUTTLE,
Arthur Eugene, d. 7/12/1949 at 73 in Warren; farmer; married; b. Jefferson; John M. Tuttle and Mary E. Hicks

TWOMBLEY,
William, d. 6/20/1938 at 66/6/18; farming; married; b. Ashland

TYLER,
Jesse, d. 4/15/1903 at – in Warren; paralysis; married
Mary O., d. 9/1/1921 at 82/1/8 in Glencliff; home making; widow; b. Concord; Richard Sargent

TYRRELL,
Amy, d. 5/28/1912 at 59/8/14 in Warren; accidentally killed; housewife; married; b. Warren; Roxanna Willey (Warren)
Charles C., d. 7/9/1919 at 70/0/9 in Hinsdale; farmer; widower; b. Haverhill; Benjamin H. Tyrrell (Antrim) and Louise Cox (Haverhill)
Clara E., d. 2/14/1899 at 16/1 in Warren; pneumonia; student; single; b. Warren Summit; Charles Tyrrell

UPTON,
Charles A., d. 12/27/1933 at 75/7/27; blacksmith; married; b. Warren; Russell Upton and Nancy Eastman
Nancy M., d. 4/3/1915 at 81/9/27 in Warren; retired; widow; b. Benton; Jesse Eastman and Sally Wyman
Russell, d. 6/20/1908 at 80/4/20; heart disease; farmer; married; b. Lyndeboro; Russell Upton and Lydia Upton

Willmetta, d. 1/11/1944 at 81/3/24 in Warren; housewife; widow; b. Lowell or Chelmsford, MA; ----- Philbrook and Luceby O. Libbey (Warren)

VADEBONCOUER,
Ernest, d. 1/24/1978 at 63 in Concord; laborer; b. NH; Deus Vadeboncouer and Olive Hamel

VALLEY,
Clifton, d. 3/19/1969 at 67 in Haverhill; b. NH; Colburn Valley and Emma Ball
Margaret, d. 10/28/1893 at – in Warren; canc. stomach; housekeeper
Velma Mae, d. 1/25/1998 at 85 in Parma Heights Valley, OH; nurse's attendant; b. Akron, OH; Espy Litz and Edna Shirk

VANNAH,
Catherine, d. 5/3/1909 at 84/5/15 in Warren; apoplexy; housewife; widow; b. Jefferson, ME; Robert Cunningham (ME) and Eliza Vannah (ME)

VANNOH,
Emma F., d. 1/6/1926 at 74/2/1 in Concord; housework; b. Warren; Levy Jewell (Warren) and Mary Vopp (Warren)

VEASEY,
Hosea, d. 1/5/1919 at 78 in Warren; farmer; widower; b. New Hampton; Daniel Veasey (New Hampton) and Betsey Smith

VINCELETTE,
Blanche I., d. 12/13/1981 at 51 in Plymouth; homemaker; b. NH; Alma M. Libby and Vera Ball
Brenda Lee, d. 9/19/1993 at 53 in Plymouth; graphic artist; b. Stewartstown; Richard W. Frizzell and Cleona -----

WALLS,
Helen A., d. 12/29/1943 at 41/4/3; without occupation; single; b. Woburn, MA; Arthur W. Walls (NS) and Harriet M. Kinsley (MN)

WARD,
Kathryn, d. 5/30/1981 at 83 in Plymouth; housewife; b. MA;
Alexander Matson and Bridget J. Sample
Ralph Brown, d. 10/8/1989 at 93 at Golden View HCC; engineer; b.
Newton, MA; William W. Ward and Emma A. Brown

WARREN,
Mary L., d. 6/16/1896 at 68/6/8 in Warren; apoplexy; housewife;
married; b. Haverhill; Rufus Stearns and Sarah P. Davis

WASHBURN,
Claude D., d. 5/17/1994 at 68 in Jacksonville, FL; accountant; b.
Wentworth; Claude Washburn and Violet Smith
Donald W., d. 5/25/1946 at 18/10/23 in Kingville, MD; US soldier;
single; b. Wentworth; Claude Washburn (Wytopitlock, ME) and
Violet Smith (Dublin)
Glenna H., d. 9/16/1958 at 33 in Keene; teacher; married; b.
Warren; Harry B. Houghton and Helen R. Chasson
Horace H., d. 5/17/1929 at 67/8/16; blacksmith; married; b. Canaan;
Charles W. Washburn and Hattie Richardson
Lilla Ann, b. 5/4/1931 at 61/2/15; housewife; widow; b. W. Newbury,
VT; George E. Jewell (Newbury, VT) and Elizabeth Brock
(Newbury, VT)
Madeline D., d. 6/8/1973 at 60 in Littleton; waitress; b. VT; Henry F.
Dickey and Marion McAllister
Violet S., d. 4/10/1991 at 84 in Woodsville; domestic; b. Dublin;
Claude Smith and Flora Wilkinson

WEEKS,
daughter, d. 8/28/1915 at – in Warren; b. Warren; Vallie J. Weeks
(Warren) and Lillian M. Dennis (Boscawen)
son, d. 5/30/1923 at 8 hrs. in Warren; b. Warren; Sidney Weeks
(Warren) and Elizabeth Streeter (Franklin)
Albee C., d. 2/21/1896 at 42 in Toledo, OH; ph. pulmon.; b. Warren
Carrie D., d. 6/22/1931 at 71/2/27; retired; single; b. Warren; Alba C.
Weeks (Warren) and Elizabeth Kelly (Wentworth)
Clara Louise, d. 5/26/1928 at –; b. Warren; Henry Edgar Weeks
(Warren) and Jessie May Spencer (Troy, NY)
Eldred, d. 5/14/1906 at 9/6/9 in Warren; pneumonia; b. Warren;
Charles L. Weeks (Warren) and Sarah W. French (Haverhill)

Eliza P., d. 1/5/1955 at 63 in Center Harbor; housewife; married; b. Haverhill; George Pickering and Emma -----

Ella Francis, d. 7/9/1923 at 73/3/4 in Warren; book keeper; single; b. Warren; Alba C. Weeks (Warren) and Elizabeth Kelly

Elvira C., d. 9/30/1914 at – in Warren; b. Warren; Vallie J. Weeks (Warren) and Lillian N. Dennis (Penacook)

Elvira L., d. 7/9/1934 at 70/10/16; at home; widow; b. Brownington, VT; Valentine J. Smith (Brownington, VT) and Julia E. Gray (Brownington, VT)

Fanny Mills, d. 6/9/1971 at 71 in Newbury, MA; housewife; b. ME; Jesse Mills and Carrie Mason

Fred W., d. 12/15/1895 at 0/3/15 in Warren; heart dis.; b. Warren; Henry E. Weeks (painter) and Elvia L. Smith

George H., d. 5/18/1967 at 58 in Meredith; painter; divorced; b. Warren; Ira M. Weeks and Lisa Pickering

Henry, d. 10/2/1970 at 62 in Hanover; b. NH; Henry Weeks and Elvira Smith

Henry E., d. 11/23/1932 at 70/5/27; house painter; married; b. Warren; Ira M. Weeks (Warren) and Laura Merrill (Warren)

Ines E., d. 7/1/1894 at 0/11 in Warren; pneumonia; b. Warren; Charles L. Weeks (Warren) and Sarah W. French

Ira M., Sr., d. 2/16/1976 at 89 in Meredith; retired blacksmith; b. NH; Henry Weeks and Elvira -----

James R., Jr., d. 1/12/1929 at –; b. Warren; James R. Weeks (Warren) and Josephine Currier (Moultonboro)

Kate Cordelia, d. 3/15/1929 at 2/1/4; b. Warren; Sidney Weeks (Warren) and Elizabeth Streeter (Franklin)

Laura A., d. 12/21/1905 at 73/1/4 in Warren; apoplexy; housewife; widow; b. Warren; Nath. Merrill (Warren) and Betsy Bixby (Warren)

Mildred, d. 5/2/1964 at 77 in Haverhill; housewife; widow; b. Boston, MA; William Libby and Susie Morse

Natt Carl, d. 2/13/1940 at 50/10/12; shipping clerk, mica; married; b. Warren; Henry E. Weeks (Warren) and Elvira Smith (Barton, VT)

Roger L., d. 9/9/1904 at 1/8 in Warren; gastro-enteritis; b. Warren; Charles L. Weeks (Warren) and Sarah W. French (Haverhill)

Sarah Elizabeth, d. 11/12/1937 at 47/0/29 in Waltham, MA; housewife; married; b. Franklin; Walter Streeter and Cora Morehouse

WELCH,

Barbara T., d. 7/31/1984 at 63 in Glencliff; engineer; b. Manhattan, NY; Edmund Templin and Berenice Liventritt

Oscar, d. 1/10/2001 in Glencliff; Frank Welch and Mary Boutin

WETHERBEE,

Lois, d. 3/7/2004 in Warren; John Merrill and Hattie Elliott

Walter H., d. 7/26/1983 at 80 in Haverhill; carpenter; b. Haverhill; William G. Wetherbee and Prudence Pelton

WHITCHER,

son, d. 1/30/1888 at 0/0/8 in Warren; b. Warren; Samuel Whitcher (Warren) and Almina Whitcher (Corinth)

Adoniram, d. 3/14/1898 at 61/4/2 in Warren; malarial poisoning; farmer; married; b. Wentworth; John Hooper

Almina P., d. 3/7/1908 at 58/5/1; apoplexy; housekeeper; married; b. Corinth, VT; Joseph Whitcher (Warren) and Eliza Jane Albert (Etonville, Canada)

Annellor, d. 8/12/1935 at 70/0/17 in Concord; housewife; married; b. Danville, VT; Daniel Houghton and Myra Badger

Annie M., d. 12/31/1901 at 18/7/21 in Warren; tuberculosis; school girl; single; b. Wentworth; Ovando Whitcher (Wentworth) and Sarah E. Kimball (Manchester)

Arthur D., d. 6/21/1932 at 70/5/4; farmer; married; b. Warren; Henry Whitcher (Benton) and Hattie Caswell

Bert O., d. 12/19/1905 at 37 in Warren; fall upon head; laborer; single; b. Wentworth; Ovando Whitcher (Wentworth) and Sarah E. Kimball (Manchester)

Bertha, d. 3/1/1981 at 82 in Woodsville; housewife; b. Warren; Elroy Hildreth and Ida Flanders

Betsey, d. 11/17/1894 at 86 in Warren; old age; housekeeper; b. Orford; Stephen Boynton and Betsey Palmer

Charles A., d. 1/22/1925 at 74/3 in Warren; farmer; widower; b. Warren; Joseph Whitcher (Warren) and Jane Albert (Warren)

Charles E., d. 11/18/1920 at 67/2/23 in Nashua; grocery clerk; single; b. Warren; Levi C. Whitcher (VT) and Sarah A. Weeks (Warren)

Charles H., d. 1/17/1973 at 81 in Haverhill; retired - st. hwy. dept.; b. NH; Arthur Whitcher and Eleanor Shortt

Clayton S., d. 10/21/1960 at 62 in Laconia; carpenter; married; b. Warren; George Whitcher and Sarah Stickney

Eleanor S., d. 5/19/1957 at 86 in Warren; housewife; widow; b. Newfoundland; William Shortt and Diana R. Weymouth

Eliza Jane, d. 3/23/1891 at 60/8 in Warren; ascites; b. Canada; Henry Albert (Ashburnham, laborer) and Hannah Albert (Warren)

Elsie, d. 6/12/1959 at 75 in Plymouth; housewife; widow; b. Belmont, NS; Samuel Lindsey and Barbara Reed

Emeline, d. 3/13/1938 at 99/4/1; retired; widow; b. Warren; A. Whitcher (Warren) and Sarah Patch (Warren)

Emily B., d. 4/13/1928 at 69/9/5; housewife; married; b. Wentworth; James Hall (Orford) and Susan M. Davis (Orford)

Ethel M., d. 7/2/1895 at 5/2/23 in Warren; pyeneia; b. Warren; Samuel Whitcher (farmer) and A. P. Whitcher

Etta H., d. 3/12/1906 at 41/3/8 in Warren; uraemia; housewife; married; b. Warren; William Currier and Avilla Pearson

Eugene L., d. 3/31/1974 at 59 in Haverhill; maintenance man; b. NH; Eugene Whitcher and Elsie Lindsy

Eugene Rand, d. 7/24/1946 at 67/11/23 in Hanover; farmer; married; b. Warren; Samuel Whitcher (Warren) and Almina P. Whitcher (Warren)

Frank A., d. 4/19/1917 at 66/5/25 in Warren; retired; married; b. Warren; Adoniram Whitcher (Warren) and Sarah Patch (Warren)

Fred J., d. 2/24/1943 at 74/4/1; carpenter; widower; b. Warren; Samuel Whitcher (Warren) and Almira P. Whitcher (Warren)

George W., d. 5/6/1936 at 74/3/1 in Warren; carpenter; divorced; b. Warren; Joseph Whitcher and Jane Albert

Harry, d. 5/11/1932 at 73/7/26; town clerk; widower; b. Warren

Harry A., d. 12/20/1927 at 55/11/8 in Laconia; farmer; married; b. Warren; Adoniron Whitcher (Warren) and E. Whitcher (Warren)

Hattie M., d. 2/12/1914 at 75/5/25 in Warren; widow; b. Haverhill; Newell Caswell (Centre Harbor) and Mary Hodgsdon (Centre Harbor)

Henry D., d. 7/16/1908 at 72; farmer; married; b. Warren; Samuel Whitcher (Warren) and Mary Richardson (Warren)

Ivan, d. 8/17/1910 at 21/3/15 in Warren; typhoid fever; clerk; single; b. Wentworth; Ovando Whitcher (Wentworth) and Sarah Kimball (Manchester)

Jerome C., d. 4/8/1893 at 42/5 in Warren; unknown; farmer; b. Warren; John Whitcher (Warren) and Betsey Boynton

John, d. 7/4/1888 at 83/11 in Warren; farmer; married

Joseph, d. 12/26/1893 at 84/10 in Warren; la grippe; farmer; b. Warren; Dearborn Whitcher and Ruth Cook

Joseph L., d. 7/13/1914 at 4/2/11 in Warren; b. Warren; Eugene R. Whitcher (Warren) and Elsie Lindsay (Belmont, NS)

Kenneth Everett, d. 2/12/1988 at 70 in Warren; sawmill operator; b. Warren; Harry A. Whitcher and Mildred Libby

Laura E., d. 1/17/1935 at 80/1/24 in Warren; housewife; widow; b. Warren; Amos L. Clement and Mary C. Merrill

Lucasta A., d. 4/28/1915 at 74/10/18 in Warren; housewife; married; b. Warren; Hazen Libbey (Landaff) and Mehitable Clifford (Wentworth)

Margaret C., d. 5/18/1916 at 0/5/18 in Warren; b. Warren; Clifton L. Whitcher (Warren) and Bertha Tibbetts (Warren)

Marion Cotton, d. 4/9/1993 at 79 in Warren; teacher; b. Warren; Ralph Pillsbury Cotton and Mary E. Moran

Mary, d. 3/4/1898 at 79/2/11 in Warren; heart disease; housewife; married; b. Danville, VT; Levi Whitcher

Mary L., d. 3/13/1906 at 65/7/22 in E. Tilton; cancer; housewife; married; b. Warren; Enoch Noyes and Mary Homans (Warren)

Mary S., d. 1/3/1892 at 74/6 in Warren; pneumonia; b. Bath; Richard Rollins

Maurice, d. 12/25/1977 at 69 in Franconia; NH State Highway Dept.; b. NH; Harry Whitcher and Mildred Libby

Ovando, d. 3/21/1906 at 60/9/28 in Warren; chronic nephritis; farmer; married; b. Warren; John Whitcher (Wentworth) and Ann Ellsworth (Wentworth)

Rinaldo, d. 8/29/1911 at 76/8/12 in Tilton; bronchial pneumonia; farmer; widower; b. Warren; John Whitcher (Warren) and Betsy Boynton (Orford)

Ruth D., d. 11/30/1922 at 82/11/8 in Warren; widow; b. Warren; Nathan. Merrill (Warren) and Betsey Bixby (Warren)

Samuel, d. 12/30/1918 at 75 in Warren; farmer; widower; Samuel Whitcher (Warren) and Mary Richardson (Warren)

Samuel A., d. 4/8/1925 at 24/8/3 in Benton; chauffeur; single; b. Warren; Fred J. Whitcher (Warren) and Nellie Houghton (VT)

Sarah Nellie, d. 3/30/1947 at 82/6/1 in Warren; housewife; divorced; b. Campton; Samuel Stickney (Campton) and A. Smith

William Harry, d. 11/24/1974 at 67 in Warren; woodworking; b. NH; Harry Whitcher and Mildred Libbey

WHITE,

Lawrence R., Sr., d. 8/15/1985 at 44 in Haverhill; construction; b. Wilmington, MA; Lawrence White and Gertrude Melanson

Lottie B., d. 10/16/1998 at 87 in Haverhill; health care; b. Haverhill; Herbert Beamis and Mary Flanders

Robert F., d. 5/5/1984 in Benton; burial permit

Stanley, d. 9/22/1995 at 75 in Haverhill; never worked; b. Henniker; Warren White and Inez Robbins

WHITEMAN,

Hattie, d. 7/3/1892 at 24 in Warren; blood poison; housewife; b. Ellsworth; William Kelley

John, d. 3/12/1897 at 74/11 in Warren; interstitial nephritis; laborer; married; b. Johnsville, PQ

Mabel A., d. 3/7/1939 at 67/5/1; retired; widow; Louis E. Brown and Lydia -----

Nancy, d. 1/21/1900 at 70/1/5 in Warren; cancer; married; Olcott Colby and Abigail Barker

Sarah S., d. 9/12/1908 at 95/1/12; old age; housewife; widow; b. Warren

Willie E., d. 12/8/1936 at 74/1/1 in Middlesex, VT; farmer; married; b. Warren; John Whiteman and Nancy Colby

WHITNEY,

Benjamin F., d. 2/4/1940 at 77/3/23; laborer; married; b. Northumberland; J. T. W. Whitney (on boat from France) and Elizabeth Morse (Whitefield or vic.)

Edith A., d. 3/8/1951 at 85 in Warren; housework; widow; b. Groveton; Harras Remich and Amy Bartell

Evelyn L., d. 11/7/1960 at 35 in Laconia; housewife; widow; b. Warren; Joseph Hilliard and Leona Short

Percy L., d. 6/11/1955 at 55 in Hartford, VT; marble cutter; married; b. Lincoln; Benjamin Whitney and Edith Remick

WILKINS,

son, d. 8/25/1924 at 0/0/0 in Warren; b. Warren; Tracy Wilkins (Craftsbury, VT) and Lula Fellows (Rumney)

Richard, d. 12/12/2005 in Plymouth; Roger Wilkins and Violet Johnson

WILLEY,
John F., d. 7/27/1902 at 69/9/23 in Warren; Bright's disease; physician; married; b. Warren; Nathan Willey (Warren) and Mary French

Philla E., d. 2/2/1901 at 63/8/13 in Warren; gastric abscess; housewife; married; b. Castleton, VT

Roxanna A., d. 5/19/1891 at 68 in Warren; tuberculosis; b. Warren Summit; Nathan Willey (farmer) and Polly French

WILLIAMS,
Edward N., d. 2/–/1902 at 28 in Warren; exposure; physician

Elmon H., d. 5/9/1905 at 64 in Warren; hanging; merchant; married

George M., d. 6/4/1942 at 82/4/22; wood-coal dealer; married; b. Warren; J. M. Williams (Warren) and Mary Clough (Warren)

James H., d. 10/12/1933 at 83/11/2; retired; b. Warren; James M. Williams (Warren) and Mary Clough (Warren)

James M., d. 10/28/1888 at 67/10 in Warren; insurance agent; married; b. Warren; James Williams (Humstead) and Anna Hom'ns (Warren)

Jennie C., d. 11/3/1889 at 41/10 in Warren; typhoid fever; housekeeping; b. Bath; William P. Carbee and Euseba Smith

Mary, d. 4/22/1891 at 68/11/11 in Warren; pneumonia; housekeeper; b. Warren; Jno. Clough (farmer) and Sally Pillsbury (Warren)

WILLIAMSON,
Dennis L., d. 10/31/1948 at 4/11/7 in Colebrook; b. St. Albans, VT; James D. Williamson (Ashland, KY) and Mary Parrish (Warren, VT)

WILLIS,
Isaac T., d. 3/6/1911 at 81/4/18 in Warren; acute bronchitis; farmer; married; b. Foxboro, MA

Job, d. 6/28/1891 at 88/8/10 in Warren; old age; farmer; b. Foxborough, MA; Job Willis (Foxborough, MA, farmer) and Sela Bramand (Newton, MA)

WILLOUGHBY,
Katherine Louise, d. 1/10/1949 at 70 in Warren; housework; widow; b. Waban, MA; Philip Riley and Bridget McGobb

WILSON,
Mary, d. 5/13/1910 at 0/0/13 in Warren; hemorrhage; b. Warren;
Mary Eva Wilson (Lakeport)

WISTNER,
Catherine, d. 5/12/1953 at 71 in Hanover; none; widow; b.
Newfoundland; William B. Shortt and Rose Weymouth

WOLCOTT,
Electa, d. 9/2/1890 at 73 in Warren; heart failure
George S., d. 8/30/1906 at 89/0/10 in Warren; old age; carpenter;
married; b. Barnet, VT; Solomon Wolcott and Keziah Cady

WOOD,
Amy, d. 8/21/1981 at 91 in Haverhill; b. NH; Walter Smith and Nellie
Upton
John R., d. 6/15/1924 at 76/3/12 in Warren; grocer; widower; b.
Kerby, VT; Roger Wood (VT) and ----- Fisher (VT)
William D., d. 2/12/2001 in Plymouth; William Wood and Amy Smith
William L., d. 8/25/1960 at 75 in Plymouth; painter; married; b. E. St.
Johnsbury, VT; George Wood and Eva Young

WRIGHT,
Althea, d. 6/15/1992 at 77 in Woodsville; cooks helper; b.
Wentworth; Cuthbert Dow and Ethel E. Downing
Arthur Gilbert, d. 11/8/1968 at 85 in Plymouth; laborer; married; b.
NH; Exminus P. Wright and Imogene G. Harrison
Clarence P., d. 12/17/1926 at 25/11/26 in Laconia; farmer; b.
Warren; Frank N. Wright (Piermont) and Sarah Smith (Gilford)
Emmagene, d. 2/12/1940 at 86/6/28; housewife; widow; b. Warren;
Moses E. Harris and Abigail Eaton
Ethel E., d. 7/21/1970 at 77 in Haverhill; housewife; b. NH; Eugene
Downing and Luny M. Poor
Fay, d. 10/30/1984 in White River Jct., VT; burial permit
Frank N., d. 9/19/1966 at 88 in Plymouth; carpenter; widower; b.
Piermont; Xinnenus Wright and Emogene Harris
Fred, d. 5/23/1936 at 61/5/1 in Haverhill; laborer; divorced; b.
Wentworth; X. Wright and Emma Harris
Freda D., d. 4/25/1991 at 89 in Boscawen
George, d. 3/27/1974 at 68 in Warren; lumberman; b. NH; Tilden
Wright and Mary Page

Glenn G., d. 7/11/1986 at 42 in Warren; paving; b. Warren; George
    Wright and Martha Foote
Harry, d. 3/28/1936 at 50/6/5 in Haverhill; railroad work; divorced; b.
    Piermont; X. Wright and Emma Harris
Isabell, d. 1/15/1994 at 71 in Hartford, CT; millworker; b. Ireland;
    William Dunleavy and Mary Mcaugherty
Louise G., d. 12/30/1905 at 0/6/20 in Wentworth; pneumonia; b.
    Haverhill
Madelyn L., d. 2/1/1929 at 1/9/0; b. Warren; Arthur G. Wright
    (Piermont) and Nancy Flanders (Warren)
Mamie L., d. 5/25/1908 at 34/10/15; peritonitis; married; Procter E.
    Harris (Warren) and Lucy M. Taylor (Bristol)
Philb'k X., d. 1/14/1920 at 20/4/7 in Warren; single; b. Wentworth; Z.
    P. Wright (Groton, MA) and ----- Harris (Warren)
Sarah P., d. 6/13/1956 at 74 in Plymouth; housewife; married; b.
    Gilford; Zebulon Smith and Eliza Flanders
Wallace F., d. 9/19/1995 at 72 in Concord; boiler fireman; b.
    Warren; Clarence Wright and Freda Dame
Ximenes P., d. 6/30/1933 at 83/3/4; farmer; married; b. Groton, MA;
    Joel A. Wright and Martha Bartlett

WUJCIK,
Walter E., d. 10/4/1989 at 81 at Scenic View; highway dept.
    foreman; b. Warren, RI; Kostanty Wujcik and Bronislawa Tetka

YOUNG,
Annie R., d. 2/21/1958 at 71 in Plymouth; housewife; married; b.
    Blackburn, England; George Rostron and Elizabeth Aspin
Grover A., d. 12/25/1998 at 76 in Hanover; b. Lisbon

ZEBLEY,
Nellie, d. 6/24/1920 at 75/0/4 in Warren; artist; widow; b. Campton;
    Loami Bean

Other books by the author:

Alton, New Hampshire Vital Records, 1890-1997

Barnstead, New Hampshire Vital Records, 1887-2000

Barrington, New Hampshire Vital Records

Dover, New Hampshire Death Records, 1887-1937

Gilmanton, New Hampshire Vital Records, 1887-2001

Marriage Records of Dover, New Hampshire, 1835-1909

Marriage Records of Dover, New Hampshire, 1910-1937

Milton, New Hampshire Vital Records, 1888-1999

Moultonborough, New Hampshire Vital Records

New Castle, New Hampshire Vital Records, 1891-1997

New Hampshire Name Changes, 1768-1923

New Hampshire Name Changes, 1923-1947

Ossipee, New Hampshire Vital Records, 1887-2001

Rochester, New Hampshire Death Records, 1887-1951

Vital Records of Durham, New Hampshire, 1887-2002

Vital Records of Effingham and Freedom, New Hampshire, 1888-2001

Vital Records of Farmington, New Hampshire, 1887-1938

Vital Records of Lyme and Dorchester, New Hampshire, 1887-2004

Vital Records of New Durham and Middleton, New Hampshire, 1887-1998

Vital Records of North Berwick, Maine, 1892-2002

Vital Records of Orford and Piermont, New Hampshire, 1887-2004

Vital Records of Tamworth and Albany, New Hampshire, 1887-2003

Vital Records of Wakefield, New Hampshire, 1887-1998

Wolfeboro, New Hampshire Vital Records, 1887-1999

www.ingramcontent.com/pod-product-compliance
Lightning Source LLC
Chambersburg PA
CBHW070553270326
41926CB00013B/2302